THE POLITICS OF THREAT

The Politics of Threat

Minuteman Vulnerability in American National Security Policy

David H. Dunn
Lecturer in International Studies
Department of Political Science and International Studies
University of Birmingham

Foreword by Lawrence Freedman

First published in Great Britain 1997 by
MACMILLAN PRESS LTD
Houndmills, Basingstoke, Hampshire RG21 6XS and London
Companies and representatives throughout the world

A catalogue record for this book is available from the British Library.

ISBN 0–333–67816–8

First published in the United States of America 1997 by
ST. MARTIN'S PRESS, INC.,
Scholarly and Reference Division,
175 Fifth Avenue, New York, N.Y. 10010

ISBN 0–312–17611–2

Library of Congress Cataloging-in-Publication Data
Dunn, David H.
The politics of threat : Minuteman vulnerability in American
national security policy / David H. Dunn.
p. cm.
Includes bibliographical references (p.   ) and index.
ISBN 0–312–17611–2 (cloth)
1. Ballistic missile defenses—United States—Combat
survivability—History.   2. Soviet Union—Military policy.   3. First
strike (Nuclear strategy)   4. Minuteman (Missile)   I. Title.
UG743.D86 1997
358.1'7'0973—dc21   97–13669
                                                         CIP

This book is printed on paper suitable for recycling and made from fully managed and
sustained forest sources.

10   9   8   7   6   5   4   3   2   1
06   05   04   03   02   01   00   99   98   97

Printed in Great Britain by
The Ipswich Book Company Ltd
Ipswich, Suffolk

To my mother, Marian
and the memory of my father, Ronnie

Contents

Acknowledgements

Some books take longer to write than others. This one started life as a PhD thesis and was written during two years' full-time research at Kings College, London between 1987 and 1989 and thereafter while I lectured at the Royal Military Academy Sandhurst and at the University of Birmingham. During that time I have been supported and encouraged by many people academically and personally whom it is not possible to thank individually here. I would like to express my gratitude to them collectively. My supervisor, Lawrence Freedman, deserves special mention for his invaluable comments in helping me develop and express my ideas, and his constant encouragement to complete the task. I would also like to thank Stuart Croft, Phil Sabin, Terry Terriff and Phil Williams for commenting on various drafts of this work throughout its gestation.

Most of the interviewing took place in the summer of 1989 in Washington. This trip, as was my full-time study, was made possible by an Economic and Social Research Council Student Scholarship. The willingness of those I wished to interview in Washington and elsewhere to give so freely of their time and knowledge was invaluable to this study. I also benefited while in Washington from the provision of office facilities at the Council for a Livable World and special thanks are due to John Isaacs for this and for his helpful advice and comments.

I have used many libraries as part of this study and would like especially to thank those who helped me at the British Library, IISS, the Jimmy Carter Presidential Library in Atlanta, and the Liddell Hart Centre and Military Archives. I would also like to thank dePixion studies Inc for permission to reproduce Mike Keefe's cartoon 'Watch Carefully ...' from the *Denver Post*. Finally, I would like to thank my wife Jayne for her support and encouragement throughout this project and my daughter Harriet for inspiring me to finish it.

Foreword

As the cold war fades from memory it is going to be increasingly difficult to explain the issues of threat and vulnerability that dominated so much of the political debate in the United States over this period. The assumptions and analyses upon which so many policy demands were based now appear highly dubious, even preposterous, in retrospect, yet they were taken seriously by serious people.

Could any one *really* have believed that Leonid Brezhnev, whose failing health mirrored the Soviet system over which he presided, would have dared at any point to have unleashed a pre-emptive nuclear strike when he could have no confidence that it would not be followed by a massive American retaliation? Yet this is what those who focused on the problem of Minuteman vulnerability would have had us believe. The idea was that the elimination of the ICBM element of the deterrent in a surprise attack would leave a President only with less accurate submarine-based missiles available as a response. This meant that the only response would have been disproportionate, an attack on Soviet cities rather than missile silos. The implication was that faced with this prospect, which would have invited Soviet retaliation in kind, the President of the United States was likely to back down.

This scenario could be taken apart at each stage, and as David H. Dunn demonstrates it was largely being used to symbolise more general anxieties about a series of foreign policy reverses in the third world. During the last years of the 1970s an urgency was attached to this issue which suggested that without emergency, and invariably expensive action the United States could find itself at a decisive disadvantage during the course of some steadily escalating foreign crisis. Their fear was essentially that given the deterioration of the strategic balance since 1962, a re-run of the Cuban Missile Crisis would this time produce a much less satisfactory result.

So formidable was this argument that President Jimmy Carter lacked the nerve to stand up to its implications and authorised a new basing mode for the MX ICBM based on multiple protective shelters unparalleled in its complexity and cost. Ironically when many of those who had raised the issue of Minuteman vulnerability arrived in government, with the administration of President Ronald Reagan in 1981, they discovered that they had created a problem for which there was no obvious, practical solution. It took a panel led by General Brent Scowcroft in 1983 to put the issue back into perspective and point out that there were other means of stabilising the strategic balance.

The great virtue of David H. Dunn's lucid and readable study of the development of this issue lies in his ability to explain why it was taken so seriously at the time. He addresses the political dramas surrounding the issue and the quality of strategic arguments deployed. In particular he explains how it came to be entangled in a series of wider political debates over the introduction of anti-ballistic missiles (ABMs) and strategic arms control, over the direction of American foreign policy, and over the role to be played by nuclear weapons in crisis management. American nuclear policy over this period cannot be explained solely by reference to Soviet policy, but must take account of domestic political developments. This is a fine contribution to the history of the cold war.

Lawrence Freedman
Department of War Studies
King's College, London

here is that the ICBM vulnerability issue has been used for various political and strategic purposes throughout the nuclear age, which did not necessarily reflect a genuine concern for the issue in its own right. This was the case primarily because the issue was inextricably entangled with the question of the role of ICBMs within US strategy and the challenges to the orthodoxy of Assured Destruction which occurred during this period. As one analyst observed, the ICBM vulnerability debate 'is operating as a catalyst to open, or reopen, discussion of a wide-ranging set of strategic and political issues'.[8]

The issue also operated at another level in its politicised form as the window of vulnerability. Cast in this way the issue was more a symbol of US political insecurity and a reflection of perceptions of military vulnerability following the Vietnam war, the Soviet attainment of nuclear parity and the failure of detente to deal with Soviet adventurism in the third world, rather than the plausibility of the ICBM vulnerability scenario itself.

For the period of the Carter administration the issue represented the political manifestation of a fear of vulnerability which had haunted the American political psyche since the attack on Pearl Harbor in 1941. Although this feeling of vulnerability was articulated through a debate at the elite level which focused on the gradually diminishing survivability of the US force of land-based Minuteman ballistic missiles, the issue developed a resonance which indicated a much more widespread sense of alarm and vulnerability. It was a feeling heightened in the 1970s by a fear that the world was out of control, or more precisely events were beyond the control of US foreign policy. The oil shocks, the loss of Iran and the subsequent hostage crisis, together with Soviet activity in Africa and the invasion of Afghanistan led to a heightened sense of unease. It was in this context that the threat to the ICBM force was presented as a symbol of weakness of the United States itself, not just in terms of this specific vulnerability, but of its deterrent posture, its military establishment and its moral stature in the face of what was considered to be a Soviet policy of rampant adventurism fuelled by a desire for world domination in pursuit of an ideological goal. As such this issue has an importance beyond the more technical strategic environment in which it was first expressed.

The issue is also important in that it provides an interesting case study of the relationship between popular threat perception and the effects of government actions on that fear. The study demonstrates the way in which the strategic debate often develops as a side effect of policies advanced for short term, expedient purposes. Once propelled with authority into the public arena these arguments often have consequences far beyond that which was intended in shaping the strategic debate. The ICBM vulnerability issue achieved the importance that it did because at significant junctures it suited government and opposition alike to advance the argument that this problem mattered. The work therefore is also a commentary on the political process. It also shows the difficulty of addressing such politically constructed problems and the need for them to be recast in order to be solved. This is illustrated by the different approaches adopted by Carter and Reagan. The Carter administration failed to redress the concern over ICBM vulnerability despite tackling the issue head on in a serious and thoughtful manner. By contrast the Reagan administration was able to defuse the issue without solving it in the way it had been presented by recasting it.

The study is both a history of ideas and a commentary on the way that strategic ideas are handled within a political process. It is an analysis of the political and strategic debates which surrounded the argument that the US Minuteman ICBM force was vulnerable to a pre-emptive counterforce attack by the Soviet Union's strategic rocket forces and that the threat of this had serious political consequences for American security. As such it demonstrates that while the construction of strategic reality may be prompted for a short-term, expedient purpose, and represent only one of a series of alternative realities available at any time, once propelled with authority into the public arena, particular constructions can shape the terms of the subsequent debate, long after the particular issue which prompted it has passed.

For much of its history the issue was conducted almost exclusively at an elite level. It was too arcane and technical to register as an issue in public opinion surveys. When it did become a public concern it did so as part of other debates, notably those over SALT or the benefits of detente. Where such opinion polls have had something to offer this analysis they have been cited, but the study is primarily concerned with the intellectual and political interaction of the ideas surrounding the development of this debate.

The study begins by looking at the development of the issue of ICBM vulnerability in the 1960s and early 1970s in Part One. Chapter 1 examines the early studies on the potential threats to the ICBM force and the plans for reducing these. Chapter 2 analyses the relationship between SALT and the vulnerability issue, while Chapter 3 studies the way in which this subject was presented in the debates surrounding the promulgation of the 'Schlesinger Doctrine'. Chapter 4 deals with the issue in the early debates on the Vladivostok accords and contains a detailed analysis of the ICBM vulnerability scenario. Part Two is concerned with the issue during the Carter administration. This section deals with the substantive questions of the political debates surrounding the vulnerability issue. Chapter 5 explains the politicisation of the issue at this time and the assumptions of the vulnerability alarmists. Chapter 6 explains the political and tactical reasons why the Carter administration accepted the vulnerability agenda of its strategic critics in support of SALT. Part Three concerns the vulnerability issue in the first Reagan administration. Its first chapter examines how the ICBM vulnerability question, together with the political promises Reagan had made concerning the issue, complicated and delayed his strategic modernisation plans for the MX. The deliberations of, and reactions to, the two Townes Committees are analysed in Chapters 7 and 8 while Chapters 9 and 10 concern the politics of the Scowcroft Commission.

Part One

A Threat Established

At what point shall we expect the approach of danger? By what means shall we fortify against it? Shall we expect some transatlantic military giant to step the Ocean and crush us at a blow? Never! All the armies of Europe, Asia and Africa combined, with all the treasure of the earth (our own excepted) in their military chest, with a Bonaparte for a commander, could not by force take a drink from the Ohio, or make a track on the Blue Ridge, in a trial of a thousand years.

Abraham Lincoln,
address before the Young Men's Lyceum of Springfield,
Illinois on 27 January 1838.

1 ICBM Vulnerability: The Development of an Issue

This chapter sets out to explain the development of the issue of the vulnerability of America's land-based intercontinental ballistic missiles. It traces the idea of the need for an invulnerable deterrent from the first studies on the basing of the US strategic deterrent through to the development of the theoretical vulnerability of the ICBMs to accurate counterforce attack.

Strategic Vulnerability

With the dawn of the nuclear age, the American population was now vulnerable to atomic attack. The detonation of the Soviet hydrogen bomb in 1953 led President Eisenhower to acknowledge that 'our former unique physical security has almost totally disappeared before the long range-bomber and the destructive power of a single bomb'.[1]

As the 1950s progressed, however, the assumption that no defensive action could be taken to lessen the vulnerability to strategic offensive forces began to be questioned. With the growth of the Soviet intercontinental bomber force the vulnerability of US air bases, and therefore US bombers, began to be re-examined. Studies conducted by Albert Wohlstetter and his colleagues at the RAND Corporation on the basing of the US bomber force concluded that the vulnerability of these systems on the ground compromised the credibility of the American deterrent. Wohlstetter argued that it was not enough just to have forces capable of destroying large amounts of Soviet society if those same forces were vulnerable to attack themselves. Wohlstetter began to argue that for American deterrence to be assured, the US needed strategic forces capable of surviving a counterforce strike by the USSR and then having the ability to 'retaliate in kind'.[2]

In demonstrating the need for an invulnerable deterrent, Wohlstetter described the balance of terror which the deterrent relationship between the superpowers represented as a 'delicate' one. This was so because the capability to execute a second strike after absorbing a Soviet first strike could never be guaranteed. If deterrence was to be maintained in these circumstances, he argued, it would only be the result of 'sustained intelligent effort and hard choices, responsibly made'.[3] It was the absence of this diligence and the reluctance to make those choices which Wohlstetter sought to warn against. His 1959 article in *Foreign Affairs* was a direct result of several rounds of briefings in Washington in 1956 and his testimony before the Gaither Committee in 1957.[4]

Wohlstetter's concern with surprise attack was partly motivated by the events of 1941. The study of the Japanese attack on Pearl Harbor conducted by Wohlstetter's wife, Roberta, demonstrated the inadequacy of strategic warning and the importance of force vulnerability. This study's conclusions, that '... since we cannot rely on strategic warning, our defenses, if we are to have confidence in them, must be designed to function without it', were not lost on Albert Wohlstetter.[5] He argued that the failure of the United States to appreciate its strategic vulnerability and to act accordingly presented the same threat to the US in the 1950s as it had done in 1941. Wohlstetter's highlighting of this concern about the vulnerability of US strategic forces, the 'Pearl Harbor Syndrome', was responsible for establishing the issue at the centre of US strategic discourse.[6]

For Wohlstetter and others, a strategic force which was vulnerable to attack was not only an inadequate deterrent, it was an invitation and an incentive for an aggressor to strike first. Schelling made this point in the introduction to *Pearl Harbor: Warning and Decision,* observing that, 'Had we not provided the target... the attack would have been called off'[7]. The formulation of these concepts of strategic vulnerability and their promulgation throughout the policy-making framework in Washington established the need for an invulnerable second strike capability as the basis of US deterrence theory.

The most immediate impact of Wohlstetter's analysis, however, was its implications for the vulnerability of US strategic forces in the 1950s and 1960s. While primarily focused on the threat presented by bombers against bombers, Wohlstetter's consideration of the development of the ICBM did much to fuel the debate over the 'missile gap'.[8] Wohlstetter warned that the Soviet acquisition of a critical number of ICBMs before the USA would render the American retaliatory forces vulnerable. Indeed, as early as 1954 Wohlstetter, in a RAND study conducted with Fred Hoffman, was forecasting that it was only a matter of time before ICBMs themselves would be vulnerable to attack.[9] Thus even before ICBMs were developed, their vulnerability to attack was being considered by US strategists.

Despite Wohlstetter's efforts to alert the Strategic Air Command (SAC) to the danger which their vulnerability represented, the Air Force was slow to embrace the recommendations of the RAND studies. Indeed, in 1956 in a follow-up study to his initial report, Wohlstetter complained that 'national defense programs do not give adequate consideration to the problem of protecting the strategic force as distinct from the problem of force size and targets'.[10] This concern with the adequacy of retaliatory capabilities in response or in preference to the implications of vulnerability *per se*, was to characterise the debate which followed the launch of Sputnik the next year.[11] Despite the fact that the Soviet capability to launch missiles represented a threat to US strategic forces, the debate was conducted almost entirely in terms of the alleged inequality or 'gap' which existed in the offensive capabilities of the two countries involved. This feature of the 'missile gap' episode, responding to a perceived vulnerability with a desire to match the offensive capability of the Soviet Union, was to become an enduring component of the vulnerability question. It found its ultimate expression in the MX programme and the window of vulnerability. While the MX deployment was initially designed to address the vulnerability question directly, as with the 'missile gap', notions of strength and equality overtook the primary strategic concern in the political debate.

As the RAND Corporation continued to produce studies demonstrating the vulnerability of the US strategic bomber force to Soviet ICBMs, programmes were initiated to alleviate the problem. The number of SAC bombers on alert was increased and measures were undertaken to improve and protect the strategic command and control system which the studies had identified as being vulnerable. Ballistic missile warning systems were also introduced in an attempt to ease this anxiety.[12] The most significant response to the vulnerability problem, however, involved missiles. The vulnerability of the first generation of US ICBMs meant that they were lucrative targets for a pre-emptive strike. The Atlas and Titan missiles relied on the cumbersome technology of liquid fuels and were based above ground in small clusters. This basing method and the small numbers in which they were initially deployed, a mere nine in 1961, made the destruction of the entire force by a determined aggressor an easy prospect. The recognition of this led to the acceleration of the second-generation solid-fuelled missiles, and the initiation of a number of basing studies to determine the most appropriate method of deployment.

Invulnerability Through Mobility: The Early Studies

Embracing the need for an invulnerable deterrent, SAC Commander General Thomas S. Power argued the case for the new Minuteman ICBM force to be made mobile. The value of mobility as a method of achieving invulnerability had already been adopted in the new force of Polaris missile firing submarines, and SAC was keen to establish the same degree of protection for its system. Indeed, President Kennedy proclaimed his faith in mobility shortly after his inauguration, stating that 'we must provide funds to step up our Polaris, Minuteman and air-to-ground missile development program, in order to hasten the day when a full mobile missile force becomes our chief deterrent and closes any gap between ourselves and the Russians'.[13]

SAC presented plans in June 1960 for five mobile squadrons of ten railroad trains each, with five missiles aboard each train, 250 missiles in total.[14] This mobile portion of the Minuteman force was to be fired through the roofs of its specially constructed cars. One report suggested that they were to be 'camouflaged as ordinary freight trains'.[15] An evaluation exercise, Operation Big Star, was conducted in the summer of 1960 to establish the feasibility of this basing plan. With SAC pleased with the results the Boeing Corporation began work immediately designing the missile trains.[16] The cost of the mobile Minuteman force, however, at up to ten times as much per missile as the proposed fixed site force, was one of the major factors that persuaded Defense Secretary McNamara to cancel the programme at the end of 1961.[17] While cost was perhaps the most decisive argument against the deployment of mobiles, a number of other considerations were taken into account. These included a concern for the vulnerability of the launchers to terrorist attack and for the opposition mobile deployment would generate from the environmental lobby; concern that the movement of the missiles would lead to vibrational damage; and concern over the 'civilian interface' between the military and the rail unions.[18] McNamara was also unconvinced of the need for a mobile missile force, expressing publicly his scepticism with the missile gap. Furthermore he was against anything which might have seemed to be turning the United States into a 'garrison state'.[19] His appointment as Secretary for Defense in December 1960 effectively sealed the fate of the mobile. Citing his fears of insufficient command and control: collision, fuel explosion and nuclear spillage, he announced to the Air Force his plans to 'defer' the development of the missile train.[20] Another reason why Minuteman was concentrated in silos was that 'greater accuracies can be achieved with fixed missiles'.[21]

The basing of the Minuteman force in widely dispersed hardened underground silos represented such a considerable improvement on the vulnerability of the Atlas and Titan force, that the benefits of mobility were not considered to be worth the additional cost. The silo basing of Minuteman, which began in 1962, was considered adequate protection for the twenty-year projected lifetime of the force. The large numbers in which it was to be deployed, initially to be 1250, together with the degree of protection afforded by the silos, 'hardened' to withstand 300 psi of blast overpressure, created a great deal of confidence in the Minuteman force. It was calculated in 1962 that in order for the Russians to destroy the new ICBMs in a first strike they would have to target four missiles against each silo, and in order to do that they would need to out-pace US missile production by the same ratio.[22]

Viewing the dynamics of vulnerability in terms of industrial production potential could not fail to inspire confidence in Minuteman. While not indestructible individually, the Minuteman force seemed invulnerable as a whole. Taken together with the new Polaris fleet, the survivability of a redundant deterrent force seemed assured.

Minuteman Vulnerability

In order to preserve the survivability of the Minuteman force all potential threats to the ICBMs needed to be considered by SAC as they arose. As early as 1961–2 Soviet atmospheric testing of a number of high-yield large-megatonne warheads presented intelligence information suggesting a threat to the Minuteman force from the Electro-Magnetic Pulse (EMP) effects of these weapons. The detonation of one high-yield SS-8 ICBM on a Minuteman field, while destroying one missile with its blast effects, could disable a great many more by crippling their electronic systems with its EMP. This early threat to the credibility of Minuteman was resolved in two ways. First, the threat presented by the SS-8, a missile believed to be 'seeded' to enhance its 'gamma effects' – its EMP – did not materialise.[23] The Soviet Union failed to develop the large rocket technology necessary and in 1965 deployment of the SS-8 was curtailed.[24] Second, SAC took defensive measures: the wiring in the silos and the circuits in the missiles were reworked in order to be protected from EMP. This work 'involved considerable design changes in the second model of the Minuteman, then under development' and demonstrated the seriousness with which SAC regarded the threat of EMP to Minuteman.[25]

In addition the shadow of doubt cast over the survivability of Minuteman by the prospect of high-yield Soviet rockets was dispelled once more by reference to the inferior size of the Soviet force. It was assumed that any threat to US ICBMs could simply be resolved by interpreting Soviet intentions and acting accordingly. As McNamara informed the Senate Foreign Relations Committee in 1963, 'If they were to undertake the construction and deployment of a large number of high yield missiles, we would probably have knowledge of this and would have ample time to expand our Minuteman force, or to disperse it more widely.'[26]

The slow rate at which the Soviet Union deployed its first ICBMs in the early 1960s did nothing to challenge this view. In both its size and accuracy the Soviet ICBM force did not possess the capability to destroy a significant number of American ICBMs in a first strike. With the deployment of the Polaris and Minuteman systems, the ratio of American to Soviet ICBMs and SLBMs increased significantly, reaching almost 4 to 1 in 1964.[27] The Soviet

Union seemed to have little prospect of, and less incentive to match the capabilities of the US force, a trend seemingly confirmed by US satellite reconnaissance. In the US view, therefore, the Soviet Union seemed content with the capability for an assured second strike force, even though this level was considerably inferior to the American force.[28]

These assessments of the Soviet ICBM deployment programme presented no great concern for the survivability of Minuteman. The invulnerability of America's deterrent seemed assured. This assessment remained valid when the production of a new Soviet ICBM was announced in July 1964, despite the enormous dimensions of the missiles. At twice the length of the Minuteman and with a single warhead in the 12–25 megatonne range, the SS-9 was by far the largest ICBM built to date. With the appearance of a second though much smaller ICBM the following year, the SS-11, it was assumed that the SS-9 would not form the bulk of the Soviet arsenal. Instead it was estimated that the Soviet Union would deploy a relatively small number of SS-9s targeted against industrial and civil centres on the East coast of America.[29] The identification of approximately a hundred silos for the SS-9, together with an assessment of its potential targets, led the CIA to conclude that this figure represented the complete complement of the SS-9 force. There seemed little need for a larger number of such heavy missiles and accordingly it was assumed that by 1970 'the bulk of the force will consist of the smaller payload SS-11'.[30]

This interpretation of the Soviet strategic force structure, however, was not shared by all the intelligence agencies, especially at the Pentagon.[31] While a force comprised mainly of SS-11s offered no advantages over the American force, the sheer size of the SS-9 presented several possibilities for a large force of such missiles. The magnitude of the SS-9 rocket booster presented an opportunity to match, if not exceed, the total megatonnage of the US Minuteman force with a much smaller number of missiles.[32] While the validity of megatonnage as a militarily significant index is questionable, the importance of the Soviet Union gaining an advantage in any measure of strategic nuclear armaments was not lost on the Pentagon. Besides this psychological consideration, a large force of SS-9s also had military implications. While neither the SS-9 nor the SS-11 were particularly accurate, the former's size gave it a capability against hard targets which the latter did not possess. Even with a CEP of 1.0 n.m. the SS-9's huge 25 MT warhead had a capability to destroy a Minuteman in its silo.[33] The use of the SS-9 against single Minuteman silos was not the Pentagon's main concern however, as such an employment would not be an economical use of the SS-9's megatonnage. Rather, the Pentagon was concerned with the potential counterforce capability of the SS-9 booster, whose throw-weight made it the ideal rocket for MIRVed warheads. For these reasons the place within the Soviet strategic buildup of the SS-9 was closely scrutinised by the Department of Defense.[34]

The modest pace at which the Soviets were acquiring their ICBM force was rapidly accelerated in 1965–6. This followed a change in policy within the Kremlin which involved a number of considerations including domestic political debate and internal disagreement over resource allocation within the Soviet leadership.[35] The Kremlin's decision to proceed more hastily with the ICBM force was also influenced, however, by its internal analysis of the Cuban Missile Crisis and its perception that the US was engaging in a more active foreign policy in Vietnam and the Dominican Republic under the shadow of its nuclear superiority.[36] The Soviet Union considered this conduct unacceptable and set about narrowing the gap between the strategic forces of the two countries in order to 'sober the imperialists'.[37] The precise nature of the relationship between an active foreign policy and the central strategic nuclear balance is one of the central themes in the strategy and politics of this period. Indeed candidate Kennedy made an early reference to the consequences of the loss of US nuclear superiority in 1960, stating

> Their missile power will be the shield from behind which they will slowly, but surely, advance – through Sputnik diplomacy, limited brush-fire wars, indirect non-overt aggression, intimidation and subversion, internal revolution, increased prestige or influence, and the vicious blackmail of our allies. The periphery of the Free World will be nibbled away ... Each such Soviet move will weaken the West; but none will seem sufficiently significant by itself to justify our initiating a nuclear war which might destroy us.[38]

Indeed, it was the realisation that the growth of the Soviet nuclear arsenal was neutralising the American nuclear advantage which led Secretary of Defense Robert McNamara to propose the need to build up conventional forces and to adopt Flexible Response. The perception of the gradual erosion of US nuclear superiority played a major role in the politics of the vulnerability question.[39]

The rate at which the Soviet strategic buildup progressed was not McNamara's prime concern. The number of missiles that the Soviets deployed was viewed as secondary to their role. In the logic of assured destruction, if the addition of more ICBMs to the Soviet arsenal resulted in a more secure second strike capability, then the stability which this provided would be mutually beneficial. If, however, the Soviet force was being configured to present a first strike capability against the American deterrent, then such a move would be inherently destabilising. Therefore, the precise role of the

ICBMs in the Soviet buildup was crucial in assessing the threat which these developments represented.

Up until 1968 the concentration within the Soviet buildup on the SS-11 convinced both the administration and the military that the main purpose of the missile programme was to achieve an assured second strike capability. The SS-11 was considered too small and inaccurate to be used against the US ICBM force, while the counterforce role of the SS-9 was not considered credible in the absence of a multiple warhead.

Nevertheless, a number of studies were conducted at this time on the question of strategic vulnerability. The first analysis to seriously address the question was the Air Force's 'Golden Arrow' study of 1964–5.[40] This report argued that the Minuteman force would become increasingly vulnerable to Soviet attack and suggested several ways in which this threat could be diminished. These included simply increasing the number of Minutemen or adding further hardening to the missile silos. However the favoured option of the Golden Arrow report, and the one which the Air Force began to advocate, was the development of a new ICBM.[41] In response to increased Soviet construction throughout 1966, the threat of a counterforce attack began to be considered more seriously within the administration. This concern led to the initiation of a major Pentagon study on force requirements known as Strat-X (Strategic Exercise). This was set up in the autumn of 1966 by McNamara to examine 'future ballistic basing concepts and missile performance characteristics required to counter potential Soviet strategic forces and anti-ballistic missile proliferation'.[42] The aim of the study was 'to evaluate offensive missile and warhead designs in terms of different sea and land-based options, and weigh the resulting force 'mixes' against various levels of threat from the Soviet Union and Red China'.[43] Strat-X was competitive in nature and exhaustive in its analysis of the long-term strategic threats to the Triad. The need for a secure second-strike capability led to a thorough examination of the alternative basing modes available to secure the survivability of the US deterrent. Strat-X considered a number of different basing schemes involving a mixture of concepts, including hardening of the launch site, mobile launchers, concealment, deception and active defence. This analysis, which included the consideration of a new ICBM and SLBM, formed the basis of many of the discussions which were to take place in the 1970s and 80s on basing mode. The technical options of how to reduce the vulnerability of land based missiles were easy to deduce. The difficulty surrounding the issue was political in nature, deciding what was necessary and what was expedient and whether priority should be given to the vulnerability question or some other related issue.

While the specific question of the survivability of the land-based strategic force was addressed in this study, no special or necessary qualities of the ICBM force as such were identified. Rather, the Strat-X recommended the development of the Underwater Long-range Missile System (ULMS), renamed Trident in 1971, and the Ship Launched Missile System (SLMS) as probable follow-ons to the Polaris and Poseidon SLBMs in preference to USAF's proposal for a new large ICBM.[44] This heavy land-based system, later developed as the MX, was rejected by the study on the strategic grounds that a deterrent based on this system 'would involve larger payloads with fewer launchers and so would present a limited number of concentrated targets for the Russians'.[45] The Strat-X study also rejected the Air Force's proposed basing scheme for its new missile. This concept sought to overcome McNamara's objections to the rail mobile scheme by limiting the movement of the missiles between a large number of silos strengthened to withstand nuclear explosion. This in essence was the 'shell game' basing scheme which would later be resuscitated for MX. The drafters of the Strat-X study were unconvinced by this proposal, however, concluding that the Soviet Union could conceivably develop sensors to detect which silos actually contained missiles.[46] Strat-X was a secret technical study of the issue conducted in a context devoid of the political sensitivities which would later develop over the ICBM vulnerability issue. For that reason it is interesting to note its conclusions, as many of the solutions to the problem which it rejected would later find existence for political, rather than technical reasons.

As Edwards observes, 'Strat-X looked at the problem of ICBM vulnerability, and agreed it was a long way off because of the accuracies the Soviet Union would need to develop in their missiles.'[47] This sentiment was expressed by John Foster, Director of Defense Research and Engineering, citing Strat-X in Congressional Hearings in 1968. Foster described the vulnerability of the Minuteman force as a 'potential problem' that could 'reduce seriously our strategic strength' and warned of the need to 'provide a timely response to such a possibility, as well as long term solutions'.[48] In searching for such a response, the impact of MIRV technology was seen as a benefit in the short term in that the amount of warheads surviving an attack would be increased, assuming that the number of launchers destroyed in the attack scenario remained constant.

In a sense, MIRVing was viewed as the long envisaged production of new systems in response to the developing Soviet threat. The long-term implications of this technology, however, making ICBMs both more capable as hard target killers and more valuable as targets, does not appear to have been seriously applied to the survivability of the land-based force. This is the case despite the study's conclusions that Minuteman vulnerability was a 'potential problem' for the future, and one which was not amenable to solution in the long term by presently available technologies. Hardening the missile silos would offer valuable protection against early improvements in Soviet missile accuracy, but once Soviet accuracy improved to the point at which Minuteman became more seriously threatened, the protection afforded by the additional concrete and steel would no longer be adequate. In a similar way, actively defending the Minuteman force with ABMs, while effective against large warheads such as that on the SS-9, could not offer the same degree of protection against multiple re-entry vehicles, especially MIRVs. Thus, in evidence to the committee, Foster concluded that while 'either is an acceptable hedge against the early threat, neither necessarily is an adequate long-term solution'.[49]

Despite these findings Foster did not rule out the deployment of both these measures to protect Minuteman in the long term in a 'new basing concept of hardened and defended complexes'.[50] Indeed the issue of 'hardpoint' defence of Minuteman sites was one of three deployment plans under active consideration at the time, the other two being a comprehensive, 'thick', population defence and a 'thin' area defence for other contingencies such as accidental launch or attack by China.

Invulnerability Through Defence

Pressure for some form of ABM deployment at this time was considerable, yet none of the services supported hardpoint defence in preference to population defence. The Army and Navy both had elaborate plans and ambitions for their own population defence systems, while the Air Force did not consider the defence of Minuteman to be either the most appropriate use of ABMs or the best way of securing ICBM survivability. As Halperin notes, 'The Air Force clearly preferred that the funds for missile defence be used by the Air Force to develop new hard rock silos or mobile missiles.'[51]

The pressure on the President to deploy some form of ABM defence was considerable as ABM was already an issue in the forthcoming presidential election campaign. So as far as the administration was concerned, if some form of ABM deployment was inevitable as a consequence of domestic politics, then the most logical strategic rationale and the one least threatening to a Soviet assured strike capability, was that of hardpoint defence.[52] This form of Anti Ballistic Missile defence also had the advantage over area defence that it required a less rigorous technical capability as a near perfect system would not be essential. Despite these advantages and the advice and re-commendations of the Arms Control and Disarmament Agency (ACDA) and the Pentagon unit for International Security Affairs (ISA), McNamara chose to justify the deployment of a light area defence system by reference to the Chinese threat. In September 1967 McNamara announced the new Sentinel ABM system explaining that it had as 'a concurrent benefit: a further defence of our Minuteman sites against Soviet attack'.[53] In elaborating these proposals, however, McNamara seemed to ascribe Sentinel's point defence rationale a much greater prominence than had initially been indicated. In doing this the Secretary of Defense antagonised and alarmed the NATO allies who felt that they ought to have been consulted on the deployment of an ABM system aimed at Soviet ICBMs. As a result McNamara refrained from emphasising this element of the Sentinel programme in order to avoid further complicating the ABM debate.[54] The justification for the ABM system of defending Minuteman silos pulled precisely in the opposite direction to that for which the China rationale had been chosen – that Sentinel was not aimed, and must not be seen to be aimed, at the Russians' assured strike capability. The distinction between Sentinel's ability to defend population centres against Chinese missiles and Minutemen sites against Soviet missiles was one which did not convince the allies and could not be expected to convince Moscow. Sentinel's ability against Soviet ICBMs in defence of Minuteman was accordingly dropped from the official presentation of the system. No action was taken by the Air Force or the Joint Chiefs of Staff to save this role, as they did not consider defending Minuteman to be a serious concern. They preferred to push instead for a full-scale anti-Soviet population defence. The defence of Minuteman silos was discreetly dropped as a publicly stated role of the Sentinel system. Instead it was described as an option available in the future if it was considered necessary by the development of the threat.[55]

Thus the rationale for defending Minuteman silos was abandoned as an immediate policy in favour of a possible future. The administration was able to do this without creating major controversy because no one saw Minuteman vulnerability as a serious or impending problem.[56] It was not seen as an issue in its own right but as a sub-issue of the ABM debate. It was an area of concern but not sufficiently important to avoid being subordinated to the larger goal of ensuring that the administration's ABM programme succeeded. When defending Minuteman seemed like an added bonus of the Sentinel system, at marginal cost, the administration was content to use this rationale in support of the programme. Once this proved problematic, however, this rationale was not considered to be a benefit worth fighting for. It was also a benefit which was not persuasive in terms of ICBM vulnerability itself. The conclusions of Strat-X, noted earlier, which took the survivability of US strategic forces as its main focus of study, indicated the unsuitability of active defence of ICBMs in the long term. While such a system offered some capability against the present array of large warheads, it was not able to deal with small re-entry vehicles such as those dispersed from a MIRVed missile. This consideration was overlooked by the advocates of the Sentinel ABM system because the vulnerability of Minuteman was seen by them as unimportant and certainly secondary to the issue in hand.[57]

The entirely expedient use of the ICBM vulnerability issue in the Sentinel ABM debate was indicative of much of the history of the strategic debate in general and the vulnerability issue in particular. As Freedman observes, the policy debate,

> tends to get organised around the vices or virtues of particular weapons systems rather than around particular roles or missions. Ostensibly weapons are supposed to provide solutions to recognised strategic problems. But rather than think in terms of abstract concepts it is easier to think in terms of weapons systems which are tangible in their immediate consequences, economic, political and military.[58]

It is also interesting to note that the coalition behind the decision to deploy the Sentinel ABM system consisted of constituencies drawn together for disparate and conflicting motivations. The decision to deploy Sentinel against the Chinese threat was supported by various constituencies for reasons different to and at odds with the official rationale. Johnson felt he needed the deployment politically; the military saw it as an embryonic thick area defence against the Soviets; McNamara saw it as the deployment least damaging to strategic stability when some deployment was politically essential. Thus the case for the Sentinel ABM defence system and the first public debate of the threat to the survivability of the ICBM force, were advanced for reasons other than the ostensible strategic case presented. Such political actions setting in train unforeseen strategic consequences were to characterise the entire history of the ICBM vulnerability issue.

The Nixon Administration and the Rise of the Issue

The relationship between the ABM debate and ICBM vulnerability, while remaining constant in one important respect, was to change substantially during the Nixon administration. The element of continuity in the relationship was that the vulnerability of the Minuteman force was consistently used to justify the survival of the ABM programme rather than the survivability of the ICBM force actually requiring an ABM defence. The difference, however, was that it was used as a complete reversal of that employed by the Johnson administration in defence of Sentinel. Instead of the defence of Minuteman being played down in favour of the threat from China, it was embraced as the main rationale of the ABM.

In 1969 the Nixon administration inherited an ABM programme which was deeply unpopular with many sections of the American polity. Opposition on strategic and technical grounds was bolstered by popular anxiety about the deployment of nuclear-tipped ABM interceptors near population centres. Concern about 'bombs in the back yard' severely undermined the case for population defence.[59]

In order to accommodate these concerns, in February 1969, Nixon ordered a review of the ABM programme and halted work on Sentinel while this was carried out. The new President was reluctant to cancel the system entirely as one of his first acts of office. In addition, Henry Kissinger wanted to proceed with the ABM for military and diplomatic reasons. He saw ABM deployment as a hedge against the failure of the proposed arms control negotiations with the Soviet Union, and the prospect of Congress banning MIRV deployment. While recognising the bargaining potential of the ABM with Moscow, he also felt that the US needed defences against third country nuclear forces and accidental launches.[60] Once more the advantages of 'thick' and 'thin' area defence together with point defence were analysed in light of new developments. This time, however, the technical and political arguments in favour of hardpoint defence of Minuteman were considered most persuasive. The administration's study recommended the defence of the deterrent whilst pointing out that the new deployment would also offer a limited population defence.[61] Under this two stage deployment plan the ABM interceptors were to be based away from population centres. It was hoped that the rationale for the new 'Safeguard' system of defending the US ICBM force from missile attack would disarm the ABM critics, some of whom, such as Hans Bethe, had testified that an ABM designed to defend ICBM might be acceptable.[62] It was argued in support of Safeguard that point defence was technically more feasible than population defence and that this deployment would be less provocative to Moscow in that it would be supporting assured destruction rather than challenging it. In addition, the deployment plan, with its provision for a limited city defence, satisfied advocates of population defence while assuaging the fears of those concerned by the proximity of nuclear weapons. The administration justified the threat to the Minuteman force by reference to the continued Soviet buildup of strategic forces.

In its attempt to appease several constituencies at once, however, the administration's rationale for ABM failed to gain the outright support of any. As Freedman notes, 'The [Safeguard] decision was geared solely to the needs of the administration; it was not based on the expressed wishes of any other interested party. The political reasoning behind the decision was to neutralise several such parties rather than to satisfy them.'[63] In this respect it failed. Once it was appreciated that the 'new' Safeguard system relied on the same technology as Sentinel the entire ABM debate was thrown open again. The change in rationale only seemed to give credence to those, like Herbert York, who chided that the 'ABM appeared to have all the characteristics of a solution in search of a problem'.[64] The scientific community was also effective in expressing its doubts over the hardware's ability to perform the missions stated.[65] The military could only manage to give token support for the system. It remained unconvinced of both the need to defend ICBMs and the wisdom of not using ABM for thick population defence. The new rationale for Nixon's ABM system brought the first real public debate on whether the US ICBM force was vulnerable to attack, whether this was important in the context of the strategic Triad, and whether defending Minuteman with ABMs (and Safeguard in particular) was an adequate or appropriate response if this threat was serious. While it was the third of these questions by which the case for Safeguard would stand or fall, the administration sought to bolster its case for its ABM system by establishing the threat to the Minuteman force.

The outgoing Secretary of Defense, Clark Clifford, had mentioned the growing Soviet threat to the Minuteman force in his last posture statement in January 1969, stating that 'It is quite evident that if the Soviets achieve greater accuracy with their ICBMs, together with a MIRV capability, our land based strategic missiles will become increasingly vulnerable to a first strike.' He concluded however, that 'it is also apparent that they are still well behind us in advanced missile technology-accuracy, MIRVs and penetration aids'.[66] In short, while noting this trend in the Soviet arsenal, Clifford was prepared to accept that though there was a threat to the Minuteman force, it was not a cause for immediate concern.

The attitude of the new administration to this issue was much less sanguine. In March 1969, in the first of many disputes with the intelligence community, the new Secretary of Defense Melvin Laird claimed that new evidence showed an accelerated Soviet buildup which meant that by the mid-1970s the US land-based deterrent could be threatened by an expanded force of MIRVed SS-9s. He stated further that 'With the large tonnage the Soviets have they are going for a first strike capability. There is no question about that.'[67] This view was not shared by the intelligence agencies who found the administration's use of the available information highly questionable. The CIA, in particular, was at odds with the Pentagon's interpretation of the Soviet buildup, Secretary Laird's inference of intentions based on capabilities. Laird saw nothing but sinister implications in the large payload of the SS-9, stating that, 'If they were going to go for our cities and not try and knock out our retaliatory capability ... they would not require weapons that have such a large megatonnage.'[68]

This explanation of the SS-9 as a 'first strike weapon', rather than as a weapon which may have had a first strike capability, was not necessarily a logical function of the missile's size. There are a number of reasons which could adequately explain why the Soviet Union built large missiles, as Talbott explains;

> Scarp's [the SS-9] mammoth size could be seen as a function of Soviet technological inferiority, rather than a harbinger of Soviet strategic superiority. Arguably, the USSR was impelled towards a reliance on heavy missiles by the backwardness of its propulsion and guidance systems. The less accurate a warhead, or cluster of warheads, the bigger it has to be to destroy its target.[69]

Other reasons why the Soviets chose to build large ICBMs were also debated, including the propaganda advantage which the possession of the ultimate 'terror' weapon might bring, the desire to maximise the residual city busting capability of their ICBM force following a US counterforce attack, and the Soviet affinity for a deterrent which was large and therefore solid and dependable.[70] Such arguments were of little interest to Laird, who seemed content to use material from the intelligence reports in a selective and unsubtle manner for his own political purposes. Specifically, he seemed intent on promoting the idea that the Minuteman force would be vulnerable to a Soviet attack with SS-9s unless the US deployed the Safeguard ABM system. There was neither a consensus on the identification of the threat presented by the Secretary of Defense, nor agreement in support of the corrective action of the ABM which he proposed.[71]

Laird's refusal either to accept or to challenge directly his critics' argument concerning the mutually supportive nature of the US Triad did little to generate support for his position and further served to widen the gap between the intelligence community and the Secretary of Defense. His response to the argument that vulnerability in one leg of the Triad, such as the ICBM force, was offset by the assured destruction capabilities of the bomber and submarine legs, was as unsophisticated as it was unconvincing. In a letter to Senator Fulbright, Laird stated that by the mid-1970s it was 'entirely possible' that a Soviet strike on the US could leave 'strategic offensive forces below the minimum level required for "assured destruction".' Elsewhere Laird warned that, 'should they also greatly improve the accuracy of their small ICBM's, which the intelligence community considers possible, the survivability of our Minuteman force as presently deployed would be virtually nil by the mid to late 1970's'.[72] The developments necessary for these threats to materialise were considerable and varied yet the evidence presented was insubstantial and incomplete. Technological developments in three separate areas – anti-submarine warfare against Polaris, depressed trajectory SLBMs against US bombers, and ABMs against the surviving US force – would all be necessary to achieve Laird's scenario, one which also assumed no corresponding improvements in the US strategic arsenal during this time.[73]

While Laird's case for the vulnerability of the US ICBM force was explicit in detailing the requirements of the Soviet force, this was not the case with the other elements of his scenario, especially the threat to the US strategic submarines. Laird's letter stated that the capability to destroy 'virtually all of our Minuteman missiles' would require a force of at least 420 long-range, accurate, retargetable SS-9 missiles with three MIRVed warheads of 5 megatons each. In contrast, the threat to the US Polaris fleet was attributed to a hypothetical 'possibility that the Soviet Union in the next few years may devise some weapon, technique or tactic which could critically increase the vulnerability of those submarines'.[74] Laird was unwilling to provide any evidence in support of his assertion because there was none.

Laird's alarm about the survivability of the land-based leg of the Triad derived from intelligence concerning the construction of new SS-9 ICBM silos in new fields and the testing of a new multiple warhead for this missile. He testified that: 'According to the latest intelligence estimates they are expected to have somewhere around 400 SS-9 types operational by the mid-1970s.'[75] The increased deployment of the SS-9 was also accompanied by improvements in the capability of the missile. In test flights the Mod-2 version demonstrated that it had the range to cover a wide set of targets in the continental US. More significant than this was the SS-9's new multiple warhead which contained three warheads of five megatons each. This combination of missiles and warheads, it was argued, presented the prospect of a potentially disarming first strike against the Minuteman force. The multiplication of the projected number of SS-9s, 420, by the number of warheads, three, resulted in a figure of 1260; substantially larger than the number of US ICBMs which stood at 1052. The number of Soviet warheads alone, however, was an insufficient basis on which to conclude that the Minuteman force was vulnerable. In order for this threat to be established it was necessary to demonstrate that the Soviet rocket force was both reliable and flexible enough to be retargeted to account for failure and that it was sufficiently accurate to pose a counterforce threat to Minuteman.

On both these matters, intense and highly technical debates developed between the supporters and opponents of Safeguard, who focused their attentions on these esoteric arguments surrounding this alleged threat to the Minuteman force. The ability of the SS-9 to be retargeted was the subject of a battle royal in Congressional hearings between anti-ABM witness

George Rathjens and Safeguard supporter Albert Wohlstetter. So technical did the issue become that the broader political context of the debate became lost in the detail of the operational research methods involved.[76] The absence of this broader view, so characteristic of the entire development of the ICBM vulnerability issue, gave credence to the promulgation of strategic concerns which failed to take account of relatively simple arguments which were no less germane because of their simplicity. In focusing on precisely what percentage of ICBMs could be expected to fail to launch and exactly how that calculation ought to be made, Rathjens's less controversial points concerning the mutually reinforcing and redundant nature of the US Triad, and the unsuitability of Safeguard for Minuteman defence, were lost.

The other main question at the forefront of the controversy over accuracy was whether the SS-9's 'Triplet' warhead was a MRV or a MIRV. In essence this distinction was essentially irrelevant and a distraction from the main question: whether the individual warheads were sufficiently accurate to destroy Minuteman silos. Nevertheless, this distinction became the focus of a major disagreement within the intelligence community and between the CIA and the White House. The controversy surrounded differing interpretations of the same intelligence material and centred on whether the 'footprint' left by the SS-9 triplets in tests demonstrated a capability to accurately target three separate Minuteman silos.

The intelligence material at the centre of the debate had also been available to the Johnson administration, at which time Secretary Clifford had concluded that the SS-9's triplet was similar in nature to the Polaris A-3 'Claw' warhead and was intended to be a more efficient counter city weapon able to foil ABM defences rather than a counterforce weapon.[77] Air Force telemetry analysis of the 'Triplet' tests conducted since 1968, however, introduced a dissenting interpretation of this programme, arguing that this warhead had primitive MIRV characteristics.[78] It was left to the White House to adjudicate and the administration decided in favour of the interpretation that the triplet was a MIRV. It was this view which prevailed despite the CIA remaining entirely unconvinced of this position.[79]

The evidence on which the administration based its conclusions about the triplet being a MIRV was not particularly convincing. The variation in the spread of warheads released from the SS-9 triplet in tests was insufficient to cover all the deployment patterns of Minutemen silos.[80] In addition to this, the calculations that the administration employed to show the accuracy of the triplet were not based on a capability that the Soviets had actually demonstrated; rather, they were based on a projection of Soviet capabilities for 1974–5 which was in turn based on the accuracy of the latest American missile, the Minuteman III, still being tested.[81]

Secretary Laird, however, continued to argue that the Soviets were on the brink of developing accurate MIRV technology which could be deployed in the next two years. In August 1969 he announced that a deployment of Soviet MIRVs by 1972 looked like 'a very realistic projection'.[82] As further tests of the SS-9's multiple warhead were observed throughout 1969 and 1970 it became clear that the triplet could not target Minuteman silos individually. Not until 24 February 1972, however, did Laird concede that the Russians 'probably have not flight tested MIRVed missiles thus far'.[83] Only at this point, as the SALT negotiations neared completion, was it in his interest politically to relent in his portrayal of the Soviet threat to the Minuteman force.

The Nixon administration's presentation of the threat to the survivability of the Minuteman force then, while grounded in the realm of possibility, represented a construction based more on worst case thinking than on what was probable. The assumptions made concerning the Soviet Union's ability to retarget for failure and on the accuracy of their missiles to target individual silos were based on best case technical developments, extrapolated from American technological developments, in combination with worst case intentions. Focusing on the payload, yield, and deployment rate of the SS-9 it was identified as a possible counterforce weapon as soon as it entered the Soviet arsenal. The SS-9's potential to be MIRVed, together with the observation of the triplet warhead tests and the construction of new silos in 1969, seemed to confirm the worst suspicions of the new administration that the SS-9 was designed to pose a counterforce threat to the Minuteman force. This was the case despite the fact that 'only the minimum pre-conditions for such a judgement had been fulfilled'.[84]

Indeed, the Nixon administration's estimates with regard to the threat presented by the SS-9 demonstrated a willingness to draw the most sinister and threatening conclusions from the evidence available and a reluctance to re-evaluate this information more favourably in light of new intelligence. Indeed it is clear that the administration was ideologically predisposed to believe the worst of Soviet intentions as indicated through capabilities and was more willing to favour intelligence analysis which reflected this mindset. Furthermore, the administration was politically predisposed to use the emerging concern surrounding the threat to the Minuteman force to promote the need for the Safeguard ABM system. As Freedman observes the case on which the administration based its arguments for Safeguard

> involved shaky estimates based on facile extrapolations, hasty judgement on limited evidence, and stretched assumptions about those crucial Soviet capabilities about which little was known. The threat of 420 MIRVed SS-9s

with warheads of 5 MT and 0.25 n.mi. CEP was a contrivance, involving a permutation of figures from a range of possible numbers of incoming warheads, yields, accuracies, reliabilities and retargeting capabilities ... designed to provide a suitable 'problem' for an available 'solution' [ABM].[85]

For the Nixon White House the ICBM vulnerability issue provided a very convenient problem for an existing solution which neatly tied together a number of domestic and strategic loose ends. Unfortunately for the administration, the neatness with which the problem and solution corresponded at the conceptual level was not matched at the interface of the specific technologies earmarked for the programme. The component parts of the Safeguard system were actually designed for the Sentinel area defence programme and as such were not suited to the role of point defence. This did not become apparent to the administration until after the decision to deploy the system had been announced. Kissinger solicited advice as to the feasibility of ABM defence of ICBM sites and was assured of some measure of support from the scientific community. This, however, was given to the concept, not to the specific technologies which the administration had in mind.[86] As a consequence, once the nature of the administration's plans became public there was very little expert support for the programme.[87] The deployment decision brought to the fore once again the recently rehearsed arguments against the effectiveness of Safeguard in this deployment mode, such as the vulnerability of its radars and its ability to offer only limited defence against a narrow band of threats.[88] The administration's response was again to turn to the threat to the Minuteman force for its justification for its ABM deployment. The limited capabilities of Safeguard presented the Nixon White House with a difficult task in this regard, however, and one which rendered the motivation for their actions all the more transparent in consequence. In presenting the case that a threat to Minuteman could develop by the mid-1970s, the administration was faced with the task of making the threat real enough to justify Safeguard, yet insufficiently threatening to render the ABM system incapable of defending against it. Accordingly, Laird's 1970 posture statement set out three alternative sets of Soviet force structures and what these forces implied for the administration's Safeguard deployment plans. The first two alternatives projected relatively minor improvements in Soviet capability: the first suggesting hardly any change to the existing capability and the second only those changes which could still conceivably be dealt with by Safeguard. Specifically it postulated an end to ICBM construction and no MIRV deployment for the SS-9, requiring 'a combination of activity and restraint' by the Soviet Union which would threaten the US ICBM force just enough to justify the Safeguard system but not enough to render it useless.[89] Specifically, the Safeguard decision was based on the assumption, 'that the Soviets stop building ICBMs beyond those now operational or started; they do not develop a MIRV for the SS-9; but they do improve the accuracy of their entire ICBM force. Under these circumstances, the force could constitute a threat to the Minuteman force and Safeguard would be quite effective against that threat.'[90] By contrast the third alternative was essentially Laird's 1969 threat construction. On this occasion, however, the picture painted by Laird of unrestrained Soviet deployment was intended to be fantastic to illustrate the circumstances in which Safeguard would be unable to defend the Minuteman force. Having used this projection to inflate the threat to Minuteman the previous year in its efforts to sell Safeguard, the administration was now open to criticism from those who pointed to the inability of the ABM system to deal with this threat. Rathjens for instance, calculated that the interceptor missiles defending Minuteman sites could be overwhelmed with additional SS-9s equivalent to only a few additional months of Soviet production. Such a defence he observed, 'would be effective only if the Soviet Union were to tailor its threat to match Safeguard's limited capabilities'.[91]

The administration's failure to garner support from the scientific and technical community for Safeguard's defence of Minuteman was compounded by the DOD's own internal analysis of this subject. Under the chairmanship of Lawrence O'Neil the Pentagon's Ad Hoc Group on Safeguard reported to Laird on 27 January 1970 that

> If the only purpose of Safeguard is defined to be to protect Minuteman, Phase IIa as defined in March 1969, it should not proceed. Instead a dedicated system for active defence of Minuteman should replace or, if need for the MSR [radar] is proved, augment Phase IIa.[92]

The administration's initial inclination in the face of this reversal was to revert to the 'thin' area defence against China rationale. The defence of Minuteman so recently presented as the long-term rationale for Safeguard was to be downgraded to that of a short-term stop-gap role as a by-product of area defence.[93] This option however was effectively closed to the administration for a number of reasons, not least of which was the lack of enthusiasm for such a move from the Pentagon where the departments responsible for the programme had convinced themselves of the case for Minuteman defence.

For entirely opposite reasons the anti-ABM lobby in Congress had come to the same conclusions about the desirability of promoting the defence of the ICBM force. Seizing the opportunity to limit the ABM programme in both its scope and its geographic deployment, while at the same time eager to avoid being accused of undermining the President's hand diplomatically, the Congressional critics sought to limit Safeguard to the defence of Minuteman. Their rationale can be gleaned from a memorandum circulated by Senator Brooke in July 1970 in which he argued, 'I still see no proposal other than the option for defense in depth at Phase I sites which meets our objective of limiting the system and yet is not vulnerable to the charge of completely undercutting the President's diplomacy.'[94] In this way for purely tactical reasons the defence of Minuteman, and by implication the idea that Minuteman needed to be defended, was advanced by the anti-ABM lobby in their efforts to limit and curtail the administration's Safeguard programme. It was this reasoning, together with the acceptance of ABM supporters such as Senator Henry Jackson that Minuteman defence was the most convincing of the two strategic rationales, which persuaded the administration to stick with the only viable rationale for Safeguard at its disposal. This in turn led the Senate Armed Services Committee to accept an amendment from Senator Cannon which 'expressly defined the mission of Safeguard as defence of the deterrent'.[95] While some Congressmen had undoubtedly become convinced of the need for Safeguard to defend Minuteman, the administration was only able to muster a Congressional majority in the 1970 vote in support of its ABM system on the grounds that a unilateral abandonment of the programme would have undermined its bargaining position in SALT. Thus from both pro- and anti-ABM lobbies came purely tactical support for the defence of Minuteman silos with Safeguard interceptors.

In attempting to counter the inflated threat projections to the Minuteman force and the exaggerated predictions of Safeguard capability presented by Secretary Laird, the anti-ABM lobby had three possible avenues of approach. Firstly, it could challenge the validity of the threat by showing how misleading the administration had been in presenting the threat to Minuteman and by demonstrating the robustness of both the ICBM force in isolation and the deterrent as a whole.[96] This approach was unattractive as it was prone to the accusation that the ABM opponents were not qualified to judge this question because they were ignorant of the relevant secret intelligence information.

The second option was to present alternative ways to deal with ICBM vulnerability other than ABM. While silo hardening, MIRVing, and launch on warning were all discussed, none of these approaches was seriously advocated as being preferable to Safeguard. This approach was also unappealing as it illustrated how attractive a solution an ABM defence was by comparison to other solutions to ICBM vulnerability.

The third alternative, to challenge the effectiveness of the proposed solution to the vulnerability question, was considered the most appropriate since it could be conducted on the administration's own terms, namely as an esoteric technical discussion apparently devoid of the need for political judgement. In addition the opponents could attack Safeguard from two sides as being unnecessary for a small range of threats but inadequate if these threats were expanded. This allowed the anti-ABM lobby to attack the administration from the safer political ground of the right. Thus in overstating its case in support of Safeguard the administration had undermined its argument for its ABM system. The administration's willingness to cry wolf when the wolf was not actually at the door had the effect of heightening the fear of wolves. The anti-ABM lobby's attempt to silence the administration's 'cry wolf' policy by implying that nothing could be done was also responsible for contributing to the fear of wolves, or rather the concern for the survivability of the US ICBM force. Freedman sums up the irony which resulted, observing, 'The problem of Minuteman vulnerability had been dramatically introduced – by an administration which believed it had the solution. When that solution was found to be wanting it was the unresolved problem that remained.'[97] Nor was there an active and informed lobby ready to challenge the administration's case for Minuteman vulnerability as Nixon's strategic critics were also supporting this threat construction in order to oppose ABM defence. As a consequence, for reasons which were entirely tactical and politically expedient the issue of ICBM vulnerability was established on the political strategic agenda. It was a situation which was to be repeated throughout the life of the ICBM vulnerability issue, most notably in regard to the plan to deploy the MX missile in the 1970s. With the MX the Air Force was happy to accept the need to base its new ICBM survivably, even though it did not see this as a pressing problem, because it thought it had a solution. When various solutions failed, however, the problem remained and the programme's viability was damaged.

2 SALT I and Minuteman Vulnerability: An Issue Established

The establishment of a threat to the Minuteman force as a consequence of the debate over Safeguard presented the Nixon administration with the problem of how to address this issue. While the threat was not considered urgent there was a general acceptance that, as the size and quality of the Soviet arsenal developed, this problem would grow in strategic importance and political salience. With the technical and indeed strategic limitations of Safeguard being well demonstrated, the administration had no long-term solution readily at hand to deal with this problem. The Nixon White House had deliberately understated the potential role of MIRV as a force multiplier for the Minuteman force during the ABM debate in order to protect Safeguard.[1] It was also understandable that the administration would wish to avoid the advocacy of MIRV on this rationale at this particular time in order not to be embroiled in a controversial debate on counterforce. The administration was once again guided more by short-term political considerations than by long-term strategic concerns.

The Underwater Long Range Missile System (ULMS), the long-standing programme designed to offset the potential vulnerability of the ICBM force, on the other hand, was being developed at an accelerated rate. Even this policy, however, was now being justified in relation to the Soviet naval buildup which was, 'even more alarming for Washington' because 'far more than any accumulation of ICBMs, [it] lent substantive credence to the Soviet quest for global power status'.[2] ULMS was also being justified because of its range and therefore wide geographic area of operation as a valuable addition to the SLBM force in the face of a potential Soviet breakthrough in anti-submarine warfare (ASW) capability. This rationale for ULMS suited the Air Force who were anxious lest a sea-based system be seen as a logical and necessary replacement of the ICBM force. SAC was also keen to stress that the strength of the US deterrent lay in the intrinsic value of the Triad and therefore by implication required the perpetuation of the land-based leg. The USAF argued strongly that the threat to Minuteman was greatly exaggerated and that the Minuteman force could survive well into the 1980s.[3] Despite its desire to retain the land-based leg of the Triad, the Air Force was unenthusiastic about the Office of the Secretary of Defense's suggestion that a mobile deployment mode for the ICBM force be investigated once again. The Air Force preferred a fixed site ICBM as this configuration provided better accuracy, tighter command and control, and was cheaper and less complicated to operate. The Pentagon, State Department and ACDA were also concerned with the potential problems which mobile basing would pose for the verification procedures necessary for a SALT agreement.[4]

Undeterred by the political travails of the Safeguard ABM system, the means of securing the survivability of the ICBM force in the long term most favoured by the Air Force, Joint Chiefs of Staff and the Pentagon civilians was a dedicated hard point ABM defence of the Minuteman sites.[5] The Air Force proposal envisaged an initial silo hardening programme for the ICBM force followed by a new purpose-built ABM interceptor system known as Hard-Site. This, they argued, was the most logical way to address the threat to the survivability of the land-based deterrent. Though attractive conceptually this proposal was at odds with the implications of the Soviet ABM programme and the administration's efforts to curtail it through SALT. Specifically, while the USAF ABM programme would have strengthened strategic stability by protecting Minuteman, the decision to deploy Hard-Site would most likely have prevented an agreement on ABM with the Soviets through SALT, curtailing their much more destabilising area defence deployments. As a consequence, the administration decided that it was a higher priority to seek an agreement limiting ABM deployments in order to ensure the vulnerability of Soviet society to US attack, rather than remedy the vulnerability of the Minuteman force through this means. The administration was also persuaded on this course of action by their recent bruising experience with Safeguard and by the fact that the technologies proposed for the Hard-Site ABM were as yet underdeveloped.[6]

SALT Accords, Vulnerability Discord: Threat Reduction Through Arms Control

Having denied the Air Force and the Pentagon their favoured method of securing the survivability of the Minuteman force, the administration was eager to demonstrate that it could negotiate a SALT regime which could stave off the threat to Minuteman. Accordingly, from April 1970 the US delegation pursued a negotiating strategy aimed at both restricting ABMs and limiting the growth of the Soviet ICBM force. Specifically, four formulations were developed, and 'All four options were shaped by an abiding concern with the potential threat to Minuteman of an SS-9 force equipped with MIRV's.'[7] All the options were concerned with the various possible interplays between ABM and MIRV, ranging from Option A which permitted both technologies, to Option D which proposed a ban on MIRV and a ban on ABM or else its limitation to the defence of the National Command Authority (NCA). Option D also proposed that both sides would reduce their forces to 1000 ballistic missiles by 1978. In an attempt to persuade the Soviets to move away from their reliance on heavy ICBMs, and also to pursue the construction of a more balanced Triad, each option proposed 'a one way freedom to mix' among the launcher totals which would permit the substitution of ICBMs with SLBMs. This provision, together with several 'collateral constraints' such as restrictions on the modification or enlargement of existing missile silos, was designed to inhibit the growth of the SS-9 force.[8] The Soviet response to these proposals, however, was far from enthusiastic, accusing the Americans of one-sided proposals which lacked seriousness.[9] What for the Americans was a proposal to encourage the Soviets away from a destabilising reliance on ICBMs which were a threat to Minuteman, was to the Soviets an attempt to limit their one area of strategic advantage in the face of much superior US bombers and submarines.

This negative Soviet reaction, however, generated a new proposal from the White House. Dated 4 July 1970, National Security Decision Memorandum 69 outlined the new composition of Option E.[10] Much more modest in its aims, this proposal offered neither a ban on MIRV nor a reduction in ICBMs, suggesting instead a total of 1900 strategic bombers and missiles. Option E did retain the sublimit of 250 SS-9s, the prohibition on modifying silos and the one-way freedom to mix. It also offered Moscow the option of either a total ban on ABM or the defence of the NCA only. In its attempt to produce an agreement more negotiable with the Soviets the administration gave up on its more substantive efforts to protect the Minuteman force. As Newhouse observes,

> Whereas Options C and D would have done something about [protecting ICBMs] – the one by banning MIRV tests, the other by reducing Soviet missile strength – Option E would have deprived the United States of the right to defend Minuteman without necessarily removing the alleged threat of a first strike.[11]

Those most concerned with the survivability of Minuteman, such as Senator Henry Jackson and Wohlstetter from the scientific community, protested to the White House about the implications of this proposal. The administration's response was to task the Defense Programme Review Committee (DPRC), a subcommittee of the NSC, to investigate. So the DPRC commissioned a study on the survivability of all US strategic systems, conducted by the Systems Analysis staff at the Pentagon. Confirming the worst fears of the critics, this study suggested that the threat to Minuteman could be imminent and that if attacked in the 1973/4 period the ICBM force could be down to 200, while a year after that a Soviet first strike could be possible.[12] Embarrassed by the conclusions of this study from his own bureaucracy, Kissinger immediately set another study in motion in order to avoid the DPRC study damaging the administration's Option E proposal. This analysis of survivability, eschewing the worst case analysis of the previous study where unlimited resources and the best available US technical level were assumed, came to less dramatic conclusions. The NSC study suggested that not until 1976 at the earliest would the Soviet Union be in a position to destroy as many as 700 Minuteman silos.[13] This episode shows the entirely contrived manner in which the administration approached the vulnerability issue. When it suited its purposes to play up the threat to Minuteman to promote Safeguard it did so. When it was necessary to down-play the issue for SALT it made sure that supporting evidence was at hand.

Far from providing a clarion call to the defence of the endangered Minuteman force the DPRC study and the NSC report which it generated had the effect of defusing the ICBM vulnerability issue. Having stated such an extreme case for the threat to the deterrent, the subsequent strategic and bureaucratic debate left the proponents of the vulnerability issue isolated and discredited. The Joint Chiefs of Staff were reportedly so outraged by the DPRC report that they conducted their own study on the issue, eager to avoid the dangers they saw in stressing the weakness of the deterrent. The response of the Air Force to these two studies was to challenge the whole basis of the narrow technical analysis of accuracies and yields used by those worried about ICBM vulnerability, developing instead an analysis of its own which took a more rounded approach, stressing the organisational problems that would be involved in planning and conducting such an attack.[14]

Undeterred by this setback and the opposition of Kissinger within the bureaucracy which it had engendered, the Pentagon, and the Office of the Secretary of Defense in particular, persisted in its efforts to protest about the vulnerability of the Minuteman force. Specifically, Secretary Laird, who had taken a leading role in this campaign, was urging both the President and Congress to reconsider the deployment of a Hard-Site defence of the Minuteman fields. Far from wishing to see ABM abandoned or severely constrained by the arms control process, the Pentagon was eager that SALT contain the provision to deploy a Hard-Site defence system in three years time.[15] Such counsel to the President from his Secretary of Defense at this stage of the SALT process was unlikely to be met with a positive response. Undeterred and only a month after this approach, the supporters of Minuteman defence received what they must have considered as a boost to their cause when the CIA produced intelligence information detailing evidence of new Soviet ICBM construction. Not only did this revelation end an apparent period of inactivity on the part of the Soviet Union, but the new silo construction was characterised by the digging of much larger holes than those which were previously excavated for the deployment of SS-9s. After receiving this information from Laird, Senator Jackson wasted no time in making it public in a television appearance in early March 1972. Jackson spoke of 'a new generation, an advance generation ...[of] huge new missiles ... [as] big or bigger than SS-9's'. He went on to speculate about the significance of these 'new missiles', stating 'that I am sure, or reasonably sure, that the Russian use of this huge buildup will come not in the form of a first strike on the United States, but to use this growing power to take greater and greater international political risks in the 1970s ...'[16] Interestingly, Jackson's statement demonstrates as much of a concern with the impact of parity on Soviet diplomacy as it does with the threat to the Minuteman force as such. Yet it was the issue of Minuteman vulnerability which was pursued as the central concern. It was as if the purported vulnerability of the Minuteman force had become a symbol of the attainment by the Soviet Union of parity and the implications for superpower diplomacy which this implied.

While Jackson and Laird might have hoped that this new information would force the administration to reconsider the case for limitations on ABM, in practice the opposite was true. While the new construction turned out to be no more than a novel way of building hardened silos, it did present an increase of 25 new SS-9s and 66 new SS-11s. More importantly, this renewed deployment demonstrated Soviet willingness to keep up the momentum of its ICBM programme in the absence of any agreement limiting such a development. The pace of these deployments throughout the SALT process and the absence of any comparable US ICBM production programme, or even facility, had forced the administration to temper its proposals throughout the negotiations. The 'equal aggregate' component of Option E which demanded equality in numbers of offensive systems was eventually abandoned in the face of the Soviet deployment programme. As Newhouse observes,

> the Nixon White House, which began life leery even of parity, was conceding the Soviet Union a three-to-two edge in ICBM's ... [and, into the] bargain, it was implicitly conceding that little, if anything could be done to hedge against a potential threat to Minuteman posed by big Soviet missiles.[17]

The White House could now only try to limit the growth rather than contract the size of the Soviet ICBM force through SALT. It did this with added urgency following a further CIA report of Soviet activity in April 1972, this time detailing the preparation for a test of a new ICBM 'larger than any other'.[18]

To the surprise and indeed consternation of the official SALT negotiating teams in Vienna, the basis of an agreement was reached through the expedient of the 'back channel' between Soviet Ambassador Dobrynin and Kissinger, in mid-May 1971.[19] Eventually signed a year later at the May 1972 Moscow summit, the Interim Agreement on the Limitation of Strategic Arms was intended to be just that; a 'short term hold to permit negotiations for a treaty to continue while aggregate Soviet missile launcher levels were not increasing very much'.[20] While the more substantive ABM Treaty was of unlimited duration, the Interim Agreement was given a five-year term with the expectation that a more far reaching deal would be achieved long before it expired. The thinking behind the Interim Agreement was that an effective freeze on Soviet ICBM construction at this level, limiting the Russians to 1618 launchers, with a sub limit of 313 SS-9 type heavies, would put off the threat to the US ICBM force until the 1980s. While not an ideal protection of Minuteman, this arrangement did stem the growth of the threat to the ICBM force and hold out the prospect of deeper cuts in Soviet offensive forces in the future. At the same time, however, the ABM treaty, while providing for the protection of one ICBM site and the National Command Authority, effectively curtailed the prospect of any substantive active defence of ICBMs in the future as a hedge against a heightened threat. Furthermore, the provisions on SLBMs allowing for substantial growth in the Soviet ballistic missile submarine force contributed to the imbalance in offensive missile throw-weight, a characteristic of particular concern to those exercised by the threat to Minuteman.[21]

A Ban on MIRV?

By not seeking to ban MIRVs in SALT the administration excluded one avenue of policy which would have significantly reduced the threat to the Minuteman force. The approach which the administration took was to focus on the short-term advantage of MIRV for the US force posture rather than the long-term threat which Soviet MIRVing would eventually present. The administration presented MIRVing as a way of increasing the post-attack number of US ICBM warheads and also of increasing the deterrent capability of the Poseidon fleet. More relevant to the absence from the negotiations of a serious MIRV ban proposal, however, were three other factors. First, Laird and the Pentagon argued strongly that there was no way that a ban on MIRV could be verified and therefore a breakout guarded against in a SALT agreement.[22] Second, the White House became convinced of its inability to persuade both the senior military and the political right to accept a ban on both ABM and MIRV. Accordingly, and primarily for good strategic reasons, a decision was taken to pursue a ban on ABM. Since a ban on MIRVs would have strengthened the case for the defence in the strategic debate this was another reason not to ban the new offensive technology.[23] Third, was the deployment by the US of MIRVs substantially before the Soviet Union also had advantages of its own.[24] Specifically, Kissinger calculated that MIRVing would extend US superiority in nuclear warheads until late into the decade and possibly into the next. By maintaining a clear advantage in warheads, Kissinger felt, the US could offset the growth in the number of launchers deployed by the Soviets and any perception of superiority which might be deduced from that. While ultimately a transitory advantage, it was calculated that this expedient would provide America with an opportunity to fully absorb the strategic implications that parity and mutual vulnerability posed and possibly delay the need for more substantial remedial action until such a time when Congress and the country would be more predisposed to such an agenda.[25]

The Congressional scrutiny which followed the signing of the SALT I accords paid particular attention to the survivability of the Minuteman force. This situation was exacerbated by the decision of Nixon and Kissinger to change the way in which the agreement was presented to Congress from the NSC staffers' original formulation. Whereas the NSC had initially presented the agreement in terms of warheads, where the US had a clear advantage by virtue of its ongoing MIRVing programme, the White House preferred a presentation based on launchers, which ignored both MIRVing and the US advantage in bombers. Whilst the NSC was concerned to sell the agreement on Capitol Hill, the prime motivation of the White House was to present the deal so that it highlighted the areas of Soviet advantage in order to ease the passage of its defence budget.[26] The effect of this was to raise Congressional concern about the pace and implications of the buildup of Soviet strategic forces, particularly their potential impact on Minuteman vulnerability, in the absence of both continued defence spending and the SALT process. Drawing attention to the threat, however, increased the critical scrutiny of the agreements. The superiority in numbers of offensive missile launchers which the agreement gave to the Soviets was the key factor picked up on by those Senators eager to question the prudence of the accords. The theoretical vulnerability of the Minuteman force was the strategic issue of concern around which the apparent inequality of the treaty could be focused and the advisability of the agreement questioned. Once again the politicisation of the threat to the Minuteman force had a major bearing on the way the issue was evaluated.

The Arms Control Process and the Threat to Minuteman

Critics of SALT complained that far from removing the counterforce threat to Minuteman, the Interim Agreement gave the Soviet Union 50 per cent more ballistic missiles and a four-to-one superiority in overall throw-weight.[27] Such concern over Soviet 'gains' was at heart a consequence of the debate within SALT over the definition and meaning of parity. While the administration was convinced that it had negotiated an agreement which codified strategic parity, the nature of the agreement, like any arms control agreement, was one in which critics could point to specific parts of the bargain and cry foul. The very nature of arms control encourages this focus on the specific technicalities of an agreement. Symbolising those militarily relevant aspects of the strategic relationship which are necessarily excluded to make negotiation possible, the actual counters of bargaining, such as the amount of throw-weight and the number of ballistic missile launchers, take on more significance than they would otherwise merit as a consequence of their intrinsic value. As Freedman observes, 'the consequence of high level negotiations on matters that touch on each side's most vital security interests is to ensure that the subject-matter increases, not decreases, in salience'.[28]

Since the currency of negotiations was weapons and not targets, the SALT process also radically altered the way in which the superpower arsenals were evaluated, with the ability to destroy so much population and economy being replaced by a focus on objects which were at once both more easy to count and more difficult to evaluate.[29] Such a clear focus on treaty limited materials also played to the advantage of SALT's critics, for many areas of American advantage, such as its technological lead and bomber and MIRV superiority were excluded from the substance or the language of the accords. More important, though, was the tendency to define parity as equal numbers and rough symmetry in the major measures of strategic power. While such a simplification helped to promote an acceptable definition of parity, it also perpetuated the notion that parity depended on the addition and subtraction of the relative merits of various weapons systems. Such an approach promoted the establishment of the view that equal numerical levels in the key weapons systems were central to the strategic relationship; that there was a basic symmetry in both the numbers and capabilities of the arsenals of the US and the USSR, and that this parity could be easily and meaningfully upset by significant developments away from this symmetry by one side's unilateral action. This view of parity allowed critics of the Interim Agreement to focus with such alarm on throw-weight and launcher levels and to see these indices as militarily and politically significant as a consequence of the theoretical vulnerability of the Minuteman force. Thus the attempts by the administration to redress the perception of ICBM vulnerability by arms control actually contributed to the concerns by the very process itself and the debates which it generated.

SALT, Parity And ICBM Vulnerability

The codification of parity in SALT I was in itself a cause for alarm within the United States for those who feared the consequences of the growth in Soviet strategic forces. This was because the issue of ICBM vulnerability was presented by SALT critics and strategic alarmists as evidence of Soviet superiority in a significant category of strategic systems. Such a view was made possible by the conceptual confusion over the meaning of parity which prevailed during the period.

The view which the Nixon administration took of the concept of parity did not contribute to a clear understanding of this issue. According to Betts, the Nixon White House refrained from a tight definition of parity as this provided it with flexibility in presenting different interpretations of US strength when competing official purposes demanded it. This looseness of definition, however, encouraged both the premature acknowledgement by the administration that parity had been reached and the suggestion by critics, especially towards the end of the 1970s, that parity had been replaced by Soviet superiority. Betts differentiates between four different levels or meanings of parity, explaining that whether one assumed that parity had given way to superiority depended on what sort of parity one had in mind, stating

If it meant mutual vulnerability to unacceptable damage, parity came in the mid-1950s; if it meant nearly equal levels of civil damage, it arrived by the early 1970s; if equality in missiles or delivery vehicles, by the mid-1970s; if the measure is the balance of forces as a whole or of counterforce capacity, by the late 1970s.[30]

He goes on to explain that while Nixon relied primarily on parity defined as mutual urban-industrial vulnerability, it suited him not to over-state that the US retained the strategic advantage in the overall balance of forces in the early 1970s.[31] The consequence of this policy, however, was that subsequent developments in the Soviet force posture were presented by the critics as evidence of a transition from parity to superiority rather than a move from one kind of parity to another.[32]

Thus Senator Jackson, reacting to the loss of clear US superiority and responding to a view of parity which was as narrow and technical as it was vulnerable to Soviet developments, expressed just such a concern for the future, stating,

no one has been able to spell out to me what kind of credible deterrent posture we are going to be left with by 1977 ... In the pasts (sic), we always insisted on strategic superiority. Then we said we would settle for parity. Now we are going to move from parity to what I call subparity.[33]

The Nixon administration took a more relaxed view of the political effects of incremental increases in the numbers of nuclear forces, believing in the merits of a force posture with high quality weapons systems rather than the weight of numbers alone. This was evident in Nixon's 1971 address to Congress on foreign policy when the President observed that,

> The United States and the Soviet Union have now reached a point where small numerical advantages in strategic forces have little military relevance. The attempt to obtain large advantages would spark an arms race which would, in the end prove pointless.[34]

Indeed, in marked contrast to the Soviet Union, the US actively withdrew from service over 300 B-52 bombers and almost 1000 ICBMs between the early 1960s and the mid-1970s. Furthermore, this policy continued even after the beginning of the SALT process when it was clear that the overall numbers were going to be seen as relevant. As Freedman, notes, 'If they had remained operational, a quite different image to the one that actually prevailed could have been presented.'[35] Instead the US concentrated on the Minuteman force in a conscious effort to prioritise penetration over throw-weight. Accordingly, between 1964 and 1981 the US reduced the equivalent megatonnage of its second strike force whilst significantly increasing the number of warheads in this component of the deterrent.[36] While Nixon remained relaxed about the US second-strike capability those with other concerns became highly critical of the recent trends in strategic developments.

This was particularly true for those concerned with the loss of US superiority. Implicit in this argument was a critique of assured destruction and the assumption that not only were nuclear strikes below the level of a central strategic exchange possible but they were the only way to keep Soviet military risk-taking in check. From this it followed that in the absence of such a US capability, with the advent of parity not only would this role be denied to the US but it would now be open to an adventurist Soviet Union who could use it for diplomatic advantage. For advocates of this argument it was a zero sum game, there was no parity of interests, only superiority or loss of superiority. For them the way in which the loss of superiority would be realised was over its impact on the vulnerability of the Minuteman force and the consequent effect which this would have on Soviet diplomacy. The scenario repeated in the SALT hearings during Senator ̲son's questioning of William Van Cleave and elsewhere was one in which et improvements in accuracy and MIRVing would render their advantage in throw-weight a strategic threat to the pre-launch survivability of the Minuteman force. This would be the case because such a Soviet ICBM force would be theoretically capable of destroying Minuteman by a disarming first strike with only a fraction of its offensive systems while leaving a numerical superiority in assured destruction forces in reserve. Under such a scenario, it was argued, the credibility of the US deterrent posture could be questioned. Van Cleave asked rhetorically,

> whether it is credible that the United States would so respond with the reduced force and only call down on itself retaliatory destruction ... would we use our surviving force [against] Soviet industrial urban complexes when we would be faced at the same time with a Soviet residual assured destruction force far greater than our own? ... the spectre of that type of scenario cannot help but have the most profound political implications for our Government, our foreign relations, and Soviet behaviour.[37]

As a consequence of these concerns, Minuteman vulnerability became the fulcrum about which anxiety over Soviet strategic advances turned. That is not to say that those such as Van Cleave were unconcerned about the specific vulnerability of the Minuteman force within the American strategic posture. Rather, their concern went further than this and was primarily motivated by the loss of US superiority and its resulting influence on the superpower relationship. This point is best illustrated by Edward Teller's testimony where he set out another scenario of foreboding consequences resulting from the Soviet strategic buildup. In his scenario, rather than focusing on the potential inequality of survivable land-based missiles, Teller was concerned with the civil defence gap, describing the extensive Soviet network and warning,

> We have no civil defense, practically none ... if the Russians execute this evacuation plan, and then give us an ultimatum, and if they attack us and we retaliate. If our retaliation is successful ... then our retaliation against the Russians will give rise to a casualty rate of 3 to 4 percent of the Russian population; while [with] the same exchange much more than 50 percent of our people will die.
>
> The Russian cities may be in ruins but Russia will then have a way to tell everybody what to do, and their recovery will be fast and their domination of the world complete.[38]

While as incredible as it is rambling, this scenario illustrates that the concerns being expressed arose from the advances in Soviet strategic forces first and foremost. The concern was a result of the consequences of parity but was expressed in different ways. The scenario concerning Minuteman vulnerability was the most popular, but not the only way of expressing that anxiety. The Minuteman vulnerability issue provided those concerned with the Soviet buildup and the failure of SALT to halt that advance in every category of comparison, with a mechanism to link the fear generated by the end of superiority with a clearly identifiable threat to US interests. What is more, the Minuteman vulnerability problem pointed to the precise piece of hardware which needed a technical fix for the problem. Such a technical problem with a hardware solution also appealed to the American liberal rationalist psyche in a way which other more intractable political problems did not.

It was partly because the Minuteman issue had such a political resonance that the Defense Department was unwilling to dismiss out of hand the ICBM vulnerability scenario. Instead the DOD supplied supporting evidence to Congress in hearings, such as the written answer to Senator Saxbe's question in which the Pentagon stated that, 'the SS-9 force could be a severe threat to the pre-launch survivability of our land-based force. Or, other Soviet land-based missiles exist in sufficient numbers so that, with accuracy improvements, they could threaten our land based force, *leaving the SS-9 for other things such as threatening cities.*'[39] The willingness of the Pentagon to tacitly endorse this scenario stemmed from its continuing desire to see the Minuteman force protected by a dedicated ABM system. Not only did Laird pledge 'to continue the site defence programme, making modifications to accelerate its development and testing' because 'we need this important hedge for insuring the survivability of our land-based ICBMs', but he also testified that the abrogation of the ABM Treaty 'would be the only option available' if further limitations in offensive forces were not achieved in SALT.[40] Laird supported SALT only conditionally. For the Pentagon the ability of SALT to limit the growth of the Soviet arsenal and to reduce the potential threat to the land-based deterrent had yet to be proved. While this remained the case Laird was eager to retain both the technological base and the perception of threat necessary to support unilateral action.[41]

Overselling the Threat in Support of SALT

By the logic of its own approach to strategic arms policy the administration presented the case for the SALT agreement to Congress on the basis that, without it, the threat would get much worse. In hearings Laird spelled out the pace of the Soviet buildup and projected this momentum forward over the five-year life of the agreement in order to show that the accords provided a limit on this momentum, despite intelligence reports which indicated that this growth rate was already subsiding. Laird warned of the Soviet ICBMs that had there 'been no stop in Soviet momentum you could get yourself in the position where they could have up to 400 or 500 of these large missile systems. That particular momentum is stopped by this agreement.'[42] He painted a similar picture of the Soviet SSBN building programme.[43] Nixon lent his support to these dire projections of Soviet forces in the absence of the agreements, predicting the construction of both 1000 new ABMs and 1000 new ICBMs over the treaty's five-year duration.[44] In the absence of the accords, Nixon warned, the US would need to commit $15 billion dollars a year for five years in additional defence spending to offset the growth he projected in the Soviet arsenal. Such expenditure would be needed for additional Minuteman III, ten more Trident/ULMS submarines and additional ABM defence of Minuteman fields.[45]

One of the results of this approach was to raise still further the anxiety which resulted from the Soviet buildup, an anxiety which threatened to undermine Congressional support for the SALT agreement. Rather like the administration's presentation of the threat to Minuteman used to promote Safeguard, the White House was in danger of losing support for its available solution, SALT, by its over-dramatic presentation of the threat. This was especially ironic since the Interim Agreement had substantially failed to redress the concerns over Minuteman vulnerability which the ABM debate had generated. In further inflating the threat to secure the passage of SALT I it was thus undermining the prospect of further support for the arms control process.

This was especially true for the threat to Minuteman where the administration found itself arguing against Laird's 1969 threat construction which was being represented by Senator Jackson.[46] As Jackson repeated the assumptions underlying the threat to Minuteman in the Safeguard hearings, the uniformed military questioned the validity of those assumptions asserting that the ICBM was a survivable, credible deterrent. General John D. Ryan, Air Force Chief of Staff, General Royal B. Allison, military representative on the SALT negotiating team and General W. P. Leber, Safeguard system manager, each set out their objections to the administration's case. General Allison, for example, after outlining the argument that ICBM vulnerability needed to be seen in the context of the synergistic effect of the Triad, offered this evaluation of the analysis conducted on the SS-9 threat to Minuteman; 'these studies' he argued,

> are sensitive to the number, accuracy, and yield of the attacking missiles, to the hardness of the Minuteman silo; to projected reliability factors of the SS-9's themselves; to very complex factors such as a projected retargeting capability, and to the degree of effectiveness of an ABM defence. In each of these studies and analysis with which I have been

concerned the threats in the analysis were illustrative of possible Soviet forces or projected Soviet forces and the number of surviving Minuteman was substantial.[47]

Such illustrative testimony infuriated Senator Jackson who was moved to remark, 'I think the military is going to lose its credibility, to be very candid about it. It is now throwing away the arguments that it has made for the last three years in a row.'[48] In further frustration at the use by the administration of different variables manipulated to give different answers when required, Jackson complained

> You can't come up here when you are demanding a weapon system with one line and then when you are trying to justify a treaty take an opposite line ... I am fed up getting one set of answers under one set of circumstances and exactly the reverse under another.[49]

This was precisely what the administration intended to do, however. As Senator Jackson's statement of further exasperation indicates, the military were indeed trying to have it both ways.

> If it is the view of the Joint Chiefs that there is no threat to the survivability of Minuteman, it is going to be hard for you to argue that the other elements in the Triad have to be upgraded to compensate for a threat to Minuteman. But, if your position is that Minuteman is threatened, it's going to be hard to defend a SALT agreement that scraps the ABM defence of Minuteman. So which is it?[50]

The response of the military was that while Minuteman was potentially vulnerable it was not as vulnerable as predicted in the Safeguard debates, partly because of the assumptions used and partly because of an ongoing hardening programme against the effects of electromagnetic pulse (EMP) in the silo and in flight.[51] The administration was guilty of wanting to have its cake and eat it, with the result that Congress was unwilling to digest either SALT or the systems the administration wanted to compensate for the threat to Minuteman. This was to manifest itself in the continued refusal by Congress to grant the Pentagon funds for accuracy improvements for its Poseidon and Minuteman III MIRV programmes and the passage by the Senate of Public Law 92-448, the Jackson Amendment to the SALT I Accords, demanding that future arms control negotiations proceed on the basis of 'equality'.[52]

The Nixon administration, with its cavalier manipulation of ICBM vulnerability to suit its other strategic purposes succeeded only in entrenching even further the concern that the threat to Minuteman was real, significant and unsolved as a security threat to the United States. Both in presenting its case for Safeguard and in its efforts to sell SALT to Congress the administration cynically used the ICBM vulnerability issue to suit its short-term political purposes. In doing so it created a strategic concern with its own constituency of supporters. The administration's failure to cap the vulnerability issue through SALT ensured that the subject remained an issue.

3 Strategic Innovation and ICBM Vulnerability: Evaluating the Threat to Minuteman

With improvements in the quantity of Soviet strategic developments accounted for by the SALT I agreement, the focus of the administration's concern about the Soviet arsenal turned to issues of qualitative advance. Specifically, the American defence community concentrated on several questions: the foremost of these was when and how developments in Soviet missile accuracy and multiple independently targeted warhead technology would affect US force posture. The impact on Soviet capability of cold launch technology with its innate reload potential was also of concern to the Pentagon, as were the measures which could be undertaken to redress these advances.

The Soviet MIRV

Various projections of Soviet MIRV testing and deployment were made along with the reports of incremental progress in different aspects of this arcane technology.[1] Secretary of Defense James Schlesinger announced the first Soviet test of a MIRV in August 1973, together with the fact that US intelligence had discovered four new types of ICBM capable of fielding this new technology. The USSR was also well advanced with the development of a new submarine and SLBM and a new bomber of uncertain range (Backfire).[2]

Of the new generation of ICBMs, the SS-16, SS-17, SS-18, and SS-19, the latter two models seemed to offer the most potential as counterforce weapons. A missile of the size of the SS-18 had been expected as a follow on to the SS-9 and the provision of a limit on Soviet 'heavies' to 313 in the Interim Agreement was intended to minimise the threat of this new force to Minuteman. What had not been expected, however, was a new missile the size of the SS-19, some forty per cent larger than the SS-11, which it was due to replace. Indeed, the Kremlin had agreed not to convert 'light' into 'heavy' missiles and not to increase the size of their missile silos by more than fifteen per cent. Now it seemed that they had a different interpretation of 'Agreed Interpretation J' and 'Common Understanding A', which were attached to, rather than formally a part of, the Interim Agreement. Rather than seeing the 15 per cent expansion applying to either diameter or depth as the Americans understood it, the Soviets had applied the expansion criteria

46

to both dimensions. The result of this was that the American intention to limit the counterforce potential of the SS-11's replacements was substantially negated. Whereas the US had intended the restriction to limit any replacement 'light' ICBM to 2000 pounds of throw-weight, two of the new missiles destined for the SS-11 silos had payloads much larger than this, with 4000 pounds for the SS-17 and 7000 for the SS-19. The sloppy language used in the agreement did not precisely define the terms 'light' and 'heavy' and was partly responsible for this loophole.[3]

The technology which made these substantial increases in volume possible, the 'cold launch' of the missiles from silos, presented additional concerns to the US.[4] The technique of ejecting a missile from its silo using hot gases, perfected by the US for its SLBM force, allowed the space previously needed to vent the hot engine ignition gases to be taken up by a larger missile. Equally worrying, this new technique left the vacated silo intact after launch, allowing it to be reloaded in a relatively short period of time. This reload facility, together with the fact that the old SS-11 silos could soon contain missiles with MIRVed warheads, each with a hard-target kill capability, represented a serious advance in the Soviet Union's counterforce potential.

With the prospect of the Soviet Union ready to deploy large numbers of MIRVed missiles, improvements in guidance technology together with the projected deployment rate of the new missiles became matters of prime importance to the US. While the SS-17 was believed to have sufficient accuracy for hard-target kills only in its single warhead form, the SS-19 and the SS-18 presented more cause for concern. Despite improvements in SS-19 accuracy to a CEP of 0.25 n. m., however, Schlesinger still regarded its hard-target lethality against hardened Minuteman silos to be some years off. In September 1974 he forecast that the SS-19 threat to Minuteman would not materialise until the 1980s.[5] Intelligence on the accuracy of the SS-18 suggested a similar delay in the onset of its capability. The deployment rate of the new generation of Soviet ICBMs failed to meet earlier American estimates. The expectation at the time of the Interim Agreement was that the Soviets would MIRV their 313 'heavy' missiles in short order and then from 1975 onwards deploy 200 MIRVed ICBMs a year.[6] In practice, however, the rate of deployment was much slower than Schlesinger predicted. Even when these estimates were revised in 1974, with Schlesinger predicting the retrofitting of SS-9 silos with SS-18s at a rate of 40–50 a year, the Soviets managed only to deploy at half this rate with 20 or so new missiles per annum. At this rate the SS-18 deployment would not be completed until the late 1980s. More important for Minuteman vulnerability, this initial SS-18 deployment was entirely comprised of the non-MIRVed version of the missile.[7] A similar situation applied to the SS-17, where the deployment rate was slower than expected and was comprised of non-MIRVed types. Another surprising development was Moscow's decision to deploy numerous SS-11 Mode 3 ICBMs which, while MIRVed, had no hard-target kill capability. Only the SS-19 missile was deployed at anything like the rate projected with 100 in place by September 1976. These developments were the subject of much speculation in the US.[8]

Whatever the reason, the ability of the Soviet Union to translate its ICBM development programme into a fully operational large MIRVed rocket force at this time proved elusive. Nevertheless, the idea of a threat to the US Minuteman force from heavily MIRVed Soviet missiles was one which had become firmly established as an important strategic issue. Indeed, the 1974/5 time period when the first Soviet MIRVs were becoming operational was the date given by Laird in his 1969 threat projection for a fully functioning and highly accurate threat to Minuteman.[9] So successful was he at spelling out the potential counterforce threat of MIRVs that Congress acted to limit US testing of this technology in order not to destabilise the strategic balance. A coalition led by Senator Brooke effectively blocked funds for Minuteman accuracy improvements for five years from 1969 in an attempt to prevent the Pentagon developing what these Senators perceived to be a first strike capability.[10] Forced to respond to this criticism, the administration issued declaratory statements to the effect that the US had 'not developed, and are not seeking to develop, a weapon system having, or which could reasonably be construed as having, a first-strike potential'.[11]

The failure of the Soviet MIRV threat to materialise in quite the way that Laird had predicted, however, together with the constraints on strategic developments imposed by SALT, generated a degree of reflective scepticism towards the idea of ICBM vulnerability. This was particularly true of the Air Force, which had scrutinised the threat to its ICBM force with considerable care and a great deal more technical and political sophistication than those who persisted in proclaiming the imminent demise of Minuteman as a viable system. In a series of articles in the *Air Force Magazine* in the early 1970s the vulnerability of the ICBM force was critically questioned. In 1971 the head of Air Force R and D complained that Minuteman had a 'wide-open susceptibility to calculations of vulnerability by anybody with a slide-rule and a fundamental knowledge of structural engineering.'[12] In March 1973 an article was published describing the technical difficulties that an attack on the ICBM force would need to overcome as 'staggering'.[13]

The Air Force was not alone in expressing its scepticism towards the idea that an attack on Minuteman was an attractive proposition. At the end of 1974 Kissinger was reported to view the idea of an attack on the US ICBM force as 'plain crazy'.[14] Schlesinger had been convinced by his time at RAND that the technical requirements of such an attack meant it could not be contemplated as a rational option.[15] He expressed similar reservations in testimony, stating that 'neither side can acquire a high-confidence first strike capability' and that there 'will never be a powerful incentive for a strike against land-based strategic forces taken by themselves'.[16] Schlesinger was not, however, willing to dismiss the threat to Minuteman as unimportant. Speaking of the transitory advantage of US warhead numbers in SALT compared to Soviet launcher totals, for example, he noted that 'the potentiality for a perceived major first-strike capability against our ICBMs is built into the weapons that they have under test at the present time, plus the throw-weight and numbers they have as a result of SALT I'.[17] While not endorsing the fear of a 'splendid' disarming first strike on the US deterrent as a whole, Schlesinger clearly did consider the vulnerability of the Minuteman force as a source of strategic concern. That concern was rooted not in Minuteman's continued ability to contribute to the deterrence of general nuclear war, but in situations short of such an eventuality, involving limited nuclear exchanges.

ICBM Vulnerability and Limited Nuclear Options

When in 1969 Secretary Laird prophesied dire consequences resulting from the vulnerability of the Minuteman force, he did so on the basis that it was folly to allow any one element of the Triad to be compromised. For him ICBM vulnerability mattered because having made Minuteman vulnerable the Soviet Union might go on to threaten the other two legs of the Triad. For Schlesinger, however, Minuteman vulnerability mattered more for the particular qualities of the ICBMs themselves. This was because of the roles and missions of the ICBM force within the strategy of assured destruction but beyond the assured destruction mission. These roles and missions and thus the concern with Minuteman vulnerability were to become even more important as a consequence of the innovations in strategic doctrine developed by the Nixon White House.

Within some quarters of the defence community concern with the credibility of assured destruction grew proportionately with the development of the Soviet strategic arsenal. The ABM debate brought tirades against assured destruction from former Pentagon officials such as Donald Brennan, who added the word 'mutual' to McNamara's formulation to create the acronym MAD, and Henry Rowen, who criticised the doctrine as 'a policy of genocide'.[18] In a 1973 article in *Foreign Affairs*, Fred Ikle criticised a strategy which made 'survival depend on the rationality of all future leaders in all major nuclear powers' and which was far too narrow in its focus in selecting 'for nearly exclusive emphasis a very special type of intended attack'.[19]

The re-evaluation of US strategy was not confined to those outside the administration, however. The implications of parity and the growing theoretical vulnerability of the ICBM force were not lost on the White House.[20] While these developments did not seriously affect the central strategic relationship directly, the same could not be said for America's other national security interests. This was the case because parity, while strengthening assured destruction at the declaratory level, eroded America's ability to offer nuclear security guarantees to its allies in the form of extended deterrence. This was because the Soviet buildup had caused a far more marked deterioration in the American first-strike capability than it had on its second strike forces.[21] It was to this that Van Cleave pointed in his critique of SALT. This provision for the use of strategic nuclear forces, although eschewed in public discourse, had been an element of assured destruction since its inception, made possible by the large number of targetable warheads deployed primarily for the purposes of redundancy. With the advent of parity and the nuclear stalemate in central strategic systems which this portended, the reality of assured destruction moved much closer to the version of the strategy enunciated at the declaratory level.

While ultimately assured destruction had always been a cities doctrine, in practice the US had up until the 1970s also had the provision, at the operational level, for attacks in support of extended deterrence while holding the countervalue strikes in reserve. While these contingencies did not aspire to the disarming counterforce role which McNamara intended in 1962, they did offer the prospect of damage limiting counterforce attacks through controlled escalation on targets relevant to the European theatre. Such target lists included Soviet IRBM and MRBMs aimed at Europe, SSBNs in port, medium-range bomber bases, command posts and concentrations of conventional forces.[22] The advent of parity, however, threatened to neutralise the American arsenal's redundant capacity for such provisions. This was the case for two reasons. First and foremost of these was the strengthening of the Soviet Union's second strike capability as a result of its strategic buildup. This made the prospect of using nuclear weapons for anything other than the assured destruction mission an altogether more risky proposition. As Van Cleave made clear in his testimony on SALT 'I would say that we had a difficult enough time checking the Soviet Union and extending strategic deterrence to allies when we had a 5 to 1 superiority. I can't imagine what it is going to be like with the situation that these agreements seem to freeze.'[23]

Secondly, the deployment by the Soviet Union of a large MIRVed ICBM force posing a threat to the survivability of Minuteman was a development which threatened the very instrument of this counterforce capability. Far more serious than the prospect of Minuteman vulnerability precipitating an attack on American central strategic systems, as far as the administration was concerned, was the effect which this development had on the credibility of extended deterrence, and thus the entire edifice of assured destruction. An essential element of assured destruction was the counterforce role which US ICBMs played. Unique among other nuclear delivery systems ICBMs offered the qualities of a prompt kill capability, constant and immediate availability, high accuracy, and secure and reliable communications with the National Command Authority, allowing them to be tightly though flexibly controlled. Up until the advent of Soviet MIRV and accuracy improvements the Minuteman force was also regarded as invulnerable. The erosion of confidence in this capability which was considered indispensable to the assured destruction employment policy mortally weakened the doctrine's credibility as far as extended deterrence was concerned.[24]

Hence, the concern which the creeping vulnerability of Minuteman now engendered within the administration had a new focus. The threat to the ICBM force related less to the credibility of America's central strategic systems to deter attack on the continental United States and more to the ability of the US to extend that deterrent to allies, particularly to NATO. As Gregory Treverton observed, 'American (ICBM) vulnerability is essentially a problem for deterrence in Europe.'[25] This loss of capability was one which the US was unwilling to accept and it was for this reason, among others, that the Nixon administration set out in search of greater strategic options.[26]

The loss of credibility for the extended deterrent mission within assured destruction was something which the Nixon White House and Kissinger in particular viewed with great concern. Hence the administration's first public statement of disquiet with the consequences of the prevailing trends in the strategic balance. In his first Foreign Policy Message to the Congress in February 1970, in a line written into his speech by Kissinger, President Nixon asked rhetorically,

> Should a President, in the event of a nuclear attack, be left with the single option of ordering the mass destruction of civilians, in the face of a certainty that it would be followed by the mass slaughter of Americans? Should the concept of assured destruction be narrowly defined and should it be the only measure of our ability to deter the variety of threats we may face?[27]

While overstating the case with regard to the starkness of his choice in order to make the point, the administration was clearly unhappy that, 'The caricature of Assured Destruction as no more than the threat to employ nuclear weapons against cities and people was becoming a grotesque reality.'[28] While the President already had a variety of options short of the suicide or surrender

choice spelled out before Congress, these were all considered too massive
to offer any real degree of choice or flexibility. The preparation of Congress
and the public for a strategy with more flexibility was developed in the
President's two subsequent annual addresses, with Nixon telling Congress
in February 1971 that the US 'must insure that we have the forces and
procedures that provide us with alternatives appropriate to the nature and
level of the provocation'.[29] At the policy level, one of Kissinger's first acts
as National Security Advisor was to have the President order a review of
'our military posture and the balance of power'.[30] Despite resistance and
disquiet from several quarters of the bureaucracy to Kissinger's search for
flexibility in force planning, he remained eager to explore these options.[31]
Accordingly, authorisation was given in the form of National Security Study
Memorandum (NSSM) No. 3 for a study which presented its findings on 8
May 1969. This report roundly questioned the continued utility of assured
destruction in US strategic policy. The NSSM-3 inspired study stated that
nuclear war might not consist of a series of 'spasm reactions', suggesting
instead that it 'may develop as a series of steps in an escalating crisis in which
both sides want to avoid attacking cities, neither side can afford unilaterally
to stop the exchange, and the situation is dominated by uncertainty'.[32] The
study went on to say that in circumstances where the Soviet Union considered
itself likely to be attacked by US nuclear weapons it '... might consider using
a portion of its strategic forces to strike US forces in order to improve its
relative military position'.[33] In short, it might launch a preventive counterforce
attack. The study did caution, however, that such attacks 'have no precedence
in Soviet military doctrine or tradition' thus making it 'highly unlikely that
such a situation would develop'.[34] This Soviet capability for counterforce
attacks, while retaining forces for the assured destruction countervalue
mission, was pointed to as a development which denied America's ability
to credibly threaten such strikes. NSSM-3 generated the desire for a more
comprehensive study and in April 1971 a 'Strategic Objectives' review was
initiated in the NSC.[35] Shortly after this an independent study was undertaken
within the Pentagon investigating the same subject led by John Foster,
Director of Defense Research and Engineering. Eventually both studies
were brought together by Kissinger in February 1973 when he initiated a
full interagency review to examine a series of limited-war options involving
small-scale nuclear strikes, demonstration shots of nuclear weapons, together
with those problems associated with the loss of the US counterforce option
as a result of the destruction of the Minuteman force by Soviet attack.[36] The
resultant report, National Security Study Memorandum 169 (NSSM-169),
was a product of a group chosen for their sympathies towards a radical
revision of US nuclear employment options. It did not take long, therefore,

for the report preparation of an official response to NSSM 169. A draft of the memorandum was initialled by President Nixon in the Autumn of 1973 indicating his approval in principle of the conclusions of the review.[37] National Security Decision Memorandum (NSDM) 242 as the policy document was known, or more formally *Planning the Employment of Nuclear Weapons*, was not afforded a high priority for immediate implementation within the NSC, however. This was due to a degree of ambivalence towards the proposed revisions from within the NSC by senior staff members such as David Aaron and Jan Lodal.[38] It was not until the appointment of a new Secretary of Defense in July 1973 that the new strategy gained the support of an energetic and enthusiastic exponent of these reforms in the bureaucracy. Schlesinger had a professional background in strategic studies from his time at the RAND Corporation in the 1960s and made no secret of his criticisms of assured destruction, criticisms which he repeated during his appointment hearings before Congress.[39] Perhaps not unsurprisingly then, it was Schlesinger who made the decision to announce the revision of American nuclear strategy which the bureaucracy had formulated but hesitated to implement. In doing this the new strategy became known as the 'Schlesinger Doctrine' even though its political genesis had preceded his appointment.

It was at a meeting of the Overseas Writers Association on 10 January 1974 that Schlesinger announced 'a change in the strategies of the United States with regard to the hypothetical employment of central strategic forces. A change of targeting strategy as it were.'[40] He went on to explain the details of the new doctrine in subsequent interviews, lectures and public statements.

The objective of the new targeting policy was to try to impose some order and flexibility into the Presidential decision-making process should deterrence fail. In order to avoid an uncontrollable escalation of nuclear strikes, Schlesinger explained, what was needed was 'a series of measured responses to aggression which bear some relation to the provocation, have prospects of terminating hostilities before general nuclear war breaks out, and leave some possibility for restoring deterrence'.[41] These measures were also necessary, he explained, to deter 'Threats against allies', a mission which demanded 'both more limited responses than destroying cities and advanced planning tailored to such lessor responses'.[42] Schlesinger did not limit his defence of his limited nuclear options policy to strengthening the credibility of the US commitment to extended deterrence, however. Instead, he was careful to present his controversial new policies in a way which had direct relevance to the US Congress and public. Thus in explaining his new doctrine before American audiences he was insistent upon linking the need for options to threats to the continental United States rather than the need to secure the option of nuclear first use in defence of Europe. The US commitment to the latter was not widely known and the Pentagon was not eager to change this situation. This was especially so given the criticism from Congress that the new options would make the use of nuclear weapons easier to contemplate. This, of course, was precisely the point of the doctrinal shift: nuclear use would have more utility, would be easier to contemplate and would therefore be a more credible deterrent. To explain this in those terms, however, would have been politically unwise, especially since the controversial nuclear first use option was planned and necessary in the defence of allies. Thus when asked by Senator Edmund Muskie whether 'the principal stimulus for developing this strategy arises out of the European problem', Schlesinger replied:

> No, Sir, I think it is much broader than Europe. It is external at this time to the United States because the Soviet capabilities have not come along so rapidly as we expected some years ago.
>   The timing of this relates less to the United States than to the external obligations, but in the longer run it relates to the United States as well.[43]

The threat to which Schlesinger made reference here and elsewhere was the need to deter prospective limited strikes by the Soviet Union against the continental United States. His efforts to raise the spectre of Minuteman vulnerability again were prompted by a desire to link the call for limited nuclear options directly to the core security interests of the US. It was a scenario which envisaged a disarming first-strike and virtually the complete destruction of the US ICBM force as a viable component of the Triad. Schlesinger reintroduced it for political purposes. It was also a threat which the strategic right, such as Van Cleave, had warned of as part of their fear over the Soviet threat. In order to deflect attention away from the more unpalatable aspects of limited nuclear options for the American audience, particularly nuclear first use, 'The age-old red flag of SAC vulnerability could be waved with new vigour.'[44]

Thus in his FY 75 Defense Department Report to Congress, Schlesinger argued that 'nuclear threats to our strategic forces, whether limited or large-scale, might well call for an option to respond in kind against the attacker's military forces'.[45] He went on to repeat the suicide or surrender scenario described by Nixon four years previously, using the growing threat to the Minuteman force to justify his strategic innovations. Alluding to the deployment of MIRVed ICBMs and warning of the 'Soviet weapons momentum', Schlesinger explained that: 'We do not propose to let an opponent threaten a major component of our forces without our being able to pose a comparable threat. We do not propose to let an enemy put us in a position where we are left with no more than a capability to hold his cities

hostage after the first phase of a nuclear conflict.'[46] Although he was willing
to use this argument to satisfy those Congressional hawks concerned about
a 'bolt from the blue' attack on Minuteman, Schlesinger was never convinced
by this rationale. Indeed, he considered 'the possibility of such an attack as
close to zero under existing circumstances', regarding the outbreak of nuclear
hostilities as much more likely to result from the escalation of conventional
conflict in Europe.[47] While calling for the forces necessary for a 'comparable
threat' to the threat to Minuteman, Schlesinger was not at all convinced of
the case for a comprehensive counterforce capability for large-scale nuclear
exchanges. Instead, Schlesinger believed in genuinely limited nuclear options
which he saw as relevant for the European theatre. Yet in explaining the case
for the capabilities necessary to implement his new doctrine Schlesinger was
meticulous in crafting every sentence to the sensibilities of his two audiences,
domestic American and concerned allies. Thus in explaining the need for
counterforce systems he reasoned that the US needed

> a more efficient hard target-kill capability than we now possess: both to
> threaten specialised sets of targets (possibly of concern to allies) with a
> greater economy of force, and to make it clear to a potential enemy that
> he cannot proceed with impunity to jeopardize our own system of
> hard targets.[48]

Even in their effort to demonstrate the limited nature of the options
proposed by the new administration, Pentagon officials chose as their example
the relatively small amount of collateral damage that an attack by the Soviet
Union on the US Minuteman force would produce. The intention of the
scenario was to show that such attacks had military utility and were limited
in their consequences. The choice of example was probably intended to limit
the concerns of those domestic critics who opposed the US acquisition of a
counterforce capability against Soviet ICBM, while at the same time indicating
that such an attack was within Moscow's capability if not its intention. Thus
Terrence King from the Office of the Secretary of Defense testified that a
Soviet strike against every Minuteman silo using a one-megaton air burst
on each would result in a 'mere' 800 000 casualties.[49] In doing this, however,
the Pentagon was inadvertently contributing both to the perception that the
US ICBM was vulnerable and that such an attack could be contemplated as
a limited strike with low-level collateral damage. Such a consequence was
ironic given the other efforts which Schlesinger made to justify the adoption
of limited nuclear options, most notably his elucidation of the requirements
of 'essential equivalence'.

Essential Equivalence

The concept of essential equivalence was introduced by the Nixon administration, conscious of the need to demonstrate the maintenance of some measure of equivalence between the strategic forces of the United States and the Soviet Union in their overall characteristics, such as numbers of deployed nuclear delivery systems, throw-weight and overall capabilities. This was particularly important, Nixon felt, in the context of SALT. The concept was in part influenced by the Jackson Amendment which sought an equal and balanced force posture as a requirement of the SALT process. In order to maintain such a balance and so maintain deterrence, Schlesinger explained, four requirements had to be met. The first was the need for an invulnerable second-strike force, the basis of an assured destruction capability. It was in the subsequent criteria where the essential equivalence concept manifested itself, with the requirement for a basic symmetry in all 'factors which contribute to the effectiveness of strategic weapons and to the perception of non-super-power nations'. In order to achieve this the third requirement demanded a 'force that, in response to Soviet actions, could implement a variety of limited pre-planned options and react rapidly to retargeting orders so as to deter any range of further attacks'. The final requirement brought the previous two together in the need for 'a range and magnitude of capabilities such that everyone – friend, foe, and domestic audiences alike – will perceive that we are the equal of our strongest competitors'.[50]

This need to be perceived as equal by all and sundry, although laudable in aim, was essentially equivalent to a strategic blank cheque and could virtually be used to justify the need for any and all capabilities. This opportunity was not lost on the Secretary of Defense. While protesting that limited nuclear options did not require additional strategic forces, Schlesinger was willing to use these new criteria to argue that even though the US ICBM force was not vulnerable to a pre-emptive strike, the perception by some that it might be was sufficient reason to mount a 'comparable threat' to the equivalent Soviet systems. Schlesinger argued, accordingly, that US forces must be capable not only of threatening urban-industrial targets, but must also have the forces and command and control for a limited number of other options and 'sufficient and dynamic countervailing power so that no potential opponent or combination of opponents can labour under any illusion about the feasibility of gaining diplomatic or military advantage over the United States'.[51] Such forces were necessary, he argued, against the possibility that the Soviets might proceed with the 'deployment of large numbers of heavy and possibly very accurate MIRVs'. This capability was necessary according to this logic, not only because 'this kind of development could in time come to threaten both our bombers and our ICBMs' but because 'future Soviet leaders might be misled into believing that such apparently favourable asymmetries could, at the very least, be exploited for diplomatic advantage'.[52] In the absence of such an advantage it was also argued that the Soviets would be more willing to negotiate limits in SALT II.

In this way the administration used the potential threat from Soviet counterforce systems to justify the requirement for a 'comparative' or 'countervailing' US counterforce capability. The Schlesinger Doctrine had not only demonstrated the prized qualities of ICBMs as the instruments of limited options, its advocates had also argued that this new strategy was necessary as a response to the Soviet threat to the US ICBM force. Without the essential equivalence criteria, however, the threat to Minuteman which the administration outlined did not stand up. Thus when Schlesinger argued that Minuteman vulnerability was a development which 'could bring into question our ability to respond to attacks in a controlled, selective and deliberate fashion' his argument had more political than intellectual force.[53] For while survivable ICBMs were necessary as the instruments of the limited options which the Secretary of Defense proposed, the availability of the relatively small number of Minutemen necessary for this role was not in question. If the Soviet Union destroyed only a percentage of the US ICBM force then sufficient Minutemen would survive for limited options. If, on the other hand, all the Minuteman force was destroyed then the ability to effect a limited response would not matter as this would no longer be an appropriate option.[54] With Schlesinger's requirement for essential equivalence, however, not only was there a need to remove asymmetrical vulnerabilities such as the threat to Minuteman, it was also considered necessary to pose an offsetting counterforce threat to the Soviet Union's hardened targets. While in practice this had more to do with the perceived need for political purposes to balance the deployment by the Soviet Union of its new generation of ICBMs, the administration chose to justify it, as the quotation above shows, by linking it to Schlesinger's limited options. By pointing to the SS-17, SS-18 and SS-19 ICBMs, each of which had been tested with a MIRVed warhead and which taken together represented a three-fold increase in Soviet throw-weight, the administration could use the threat to Minuteman to justify the acquisition of a counterforce capability much as they had tried to do in 1969 with Safeguard.

In order to provide for a capability to use ICBMs flexibly and for limited strikes, the Nixon administration had exalted the status of the ICBM as an instrument of counterforce with a value greater than its contribution as an independent leg of the strategic Triad. In doing this they had also rekindled the issue of the potential vulnerability of the Minuteman force, providing it with both a legitimacy as a serious issue which it did not warrant and a justification in essential equivalence which was difficult to challenge. The decision to allow perception a role in the determination of a deterrent posture, in effect meant that 'all aspects of military power became of potential importance and nothing could be discounted'.[55] This observation is particularly germane with regard to ICBM vulnerability.

As Terriff points out, the spur to this issue was given for political reasons rather than a genuine concern for the implications of the growing theoretical vulnerability of the ICBM force;

> Schlesinger propagated the possible threat of limited Soviet strategic attacks, which he ... believed to be exceedingly remote, to set the right political tone to facilitate Congressional acceptance of the change in strategy ... In doing so, however, Schlesinger's worst case threat analysis of theoretical limited Soviet counterforce attacks provided an inadvertent impetus to the controversial question of Minuteman vulnerability, which was to plague US politics in the years ahead.[56]

Although he himself would come to regret the way in which his hypothesising about possible threats to the Minuteman force were later used in criticism of SALT, Schlesinger's role in re-energising this issue is clear.[57] As the vulnerability of the Minuteman force had earlier become embroiled in the ABM debate, so too was the reaction of the different constituencies in the defence community conditioned in their response to this issue by the prevailing strategic context; in this case the Schlesinger Doctrine.

For those who opposed the case which the administration put for a counterforce capability to offset the threat to Minuteman, the answer to the vulnerability of the US ICBM force was obvious; if this leg of the Triad was vulnerable then it ought to be abandoned. The strategic vulnerability would then be removed and so too would any destabilising counterforce threat to the Soviet deterrent. In support of their argument the critics pointed to the progression of the Navy's ULMS project which had originally been initiated as a way of ensuring the long-term survivability of the strategic deterrent.

Not surprisingly this argument was unpersuasive to the military and the administration. For the military the abandonment of one component of the deterrent as it became vulnerable was an invitation to the Soviets to redouble their efforts in an attempt to compromise the credibility of the remaining forces. As a whole the military remained convinced of the importance of a Triad of strategic nuclear forces and the Air Force was already investigating ways in which the ICBM force's survivability could be enhanced. Two such measures were the installation of the Command Data Buffer system allowing the target set of each Minuteman III to be remotely reprogrammed in 36 minutes, and a plan begun in 1970 for a major improvement in the accuracy of the ICBM force to provide it with the 'capability of striking targets at ICBM ranges with a circular error probability of 600 feet'.[58] Both these measures had the advantage of improving two of the qualities for which ICBMs were most highly prized: flexible command and control, and the accuracy which is essential to hard-target kill capability. The debate over ICBM vulnerability and whether the US Minuteman force should be retained, however, provided an opportunity for such improvements to be discussed in those terms rather than as improvements which allow the ICBM force to better fulfil its requirements in its counterforce role. In this way the ICBM vulnerability issue provided a level of debate which distracted attention away from a topic of greater substance. For this reason there was a greater willingness on the part of those who favoured a counterforce role for US ICBMs to engage in a debate on the 'problem' of Minuteman vulnerability than might otherwise have been the case.

Weapons Procurement and ICBM Vulnerability: Missile Experimental

The concern raised with the vulnerability of the Minuteman force also presented the Air Force with an opportunity to combine the need for its improved counterforce capability with the chance to build a more survivable ICBM. Thus even the Air Force in its eagerness for a new ICBM was willing to sustain the argument that Minuteman vulnerability was a serious and pressing problem. Indeed the Air Force had already begun to evaluate the alternative basing modes available for a new advanced generation ICBM in order to ensure the long-term survivability of the land-based deterrent. Its concern was motivated more by the fear that the Navy's ULMS/Trident submarines would rob it of a role rather than the threat posed by the Soviet Rocket Forces. The impressive invulnerability of the Navy's SSBN force led the Air Force to investigate a number of schemes including the 'flying submarine' proposal. This scheme consisted of a plan to place 10–12 ICBMs on-board a Lockheed C-5A cargo plane from which the missiles could be fired during flight.[59] This 'air mobile' concept was later to be revised in subsequent attempts to find a satisfactory basing mode for the MX. Its suggestion here, however, owed more to a desire to show that the Air Force could react to the survivability agenda set by the Navy than it did to any inherent logic in the project or enthusiasm for it from SAC.

Other ICBM deployment schemes followed from the Air Force's unsuccessful submissions to the Strat-X study, including a further examination of silo deployment. The Minuteman III silo construction programme was designed 'not only for existing missiles but for larger missiles as well, so that each new system will have potential for growth'.[60] Five other deployment concepts were also under investigation by the Air Force in 1969. Three proposals firmly addressed the question of survivability; 'Ranger' – a road or rail mobile ICBM; 'Nemesis' – a deep underwater deployment mode; and 'Vulcan' – an underground deployment in superhardened silos in old brimstone mines. The other two suggestions were WS-180, an advanced Minuteman, and 'Janus', a dual-purpose missile for an ICBM and an ABM interceptor.[61]

These studies into the basing mode were conducted alongside research programmes into other aspects of missile design and performance. USAF had begun work on a warhead development programme at a much earlier stage than studies on missile basing which reflected SAC's priorities. Initiated in 1963 this much larger warhead, designated Weapons System (WS) 120, was designed for an 'Improved Capability Missile'.[62] The Air Force wanted WS-120 to replace the existing force of Minuteman IIIs with their Mark 12 warheads with a hard-target kill capability of altogether greater proportions. Only when this was eventually cancelled in 1971 did the Air Force make an official Required Operational Capability (ROC) request to Congress to develop a new generation, large, accurate, MIRVed successor to Minuteman.[63]

It was this request which brought together the various technological research programmes on ICBMs into one programme.[64] As early as 1967 the Air Force had set out to define its requirements for a new missile. Not only would it be larger than the Minuteman III with a greater throw-weight and more warheads, each missile would be individually equipped with a guidance system capable of adjusting itself to the position from which the missile was fired. This was considered necessary not only in the context of the ICBM's overall accuracy but in order that it could be deployed in a mobile mode.[65] Thus the Air Force was able to bring together, in its 1971 ROC for the new missile, requirements for a hard-target counterforce capability and the provision for a more survivable basing mode three years before the Soviet development of its SS-18 and SS-19s which Schlesinger would point to in 1974 as justification for this capability. As General Cross observed at the time, the new missile, known at this stage as ICBM-X or Missile Experimental (MX), was not a direct reaction to external events. Instead 'the ROC as it was submitted from the SAC was in anticipation of what any potential enemy might do'.[66] Thus the Air Force's initial interest in MX resulted more from a desire for counterforce capability than a concern for the missile's survivability.

Though viewed as controversial because of its counterforce capability by Congressional critics, especially in the Senate, the MX received the backing of the administration as part of a larger programme of strategic modernisation.[67] 1973 was also the year in which large-scale funding was allocated to the Trident programme and the Air Force received the go-ahead for two new systems, the new B-1 strategic bomber and the cruise missile programme. All these systems were justified partly by reference to the need to fortify the strategic nuclear Triad in the face of the potential vulnerability of the ICBM force.

By the end of 1973 the Ballistic Missile Office had established many of the characteristics of the new missile. With the ability to employ cold launch technology, the MX would be able to have twice the launch-weight of Minuteman III while still being fired from the same silo. With this extra weight the missile booster would be able to carry twelve warheads, each a hard-target killer with a CEP of 100 feet.[68] Within the executive branch Schlesinger had proven himself a powerful patron and providing the momentum necessary to ensure the development of MX in order to secure its counterforce capabilities. What was much less clear at this stage was the precise way in which the MX would be deployed.

The MX was designed for deployment in Minuteman III silos. In 1971 it was thought that if the vulnerability of the force proved problematic, then an ABM defence would be the most appropriate response. With the advent of the ABM Treaty in 1972, mobility and concealment were once again considered. By 1973 the two schemes incorporating the survivability features which the Air Force most favoured were the air mobile concept and the buried trench plan. While the air-mobile scheme offered the advantages of a large degree of invulnerability and a high state of readiness for launch, the costs of the programme together with its command and control difficulties rendered it problematic. The buried trench idea was an extension of the road and rail mobility proposals which had earlier been rejected for security and political reasons. If the public disliked the idea of missiles on the open roads, it was felt, then why not cover the roads in, hence the trench. The Ballistic Missile Office accordingly set about investigating the feasibility of building a 4000-mile covered trench across the Great Basin of Utah and Nevada and possibly as far as Arizona and New Mexico.[69] This too, however, had technical problems and financial implications which made it less simple than it first appeared.[70] Nevertheless, the prospect of the new ICBM being based in a secure manner was enough for some traditional critics of counterforce to be supportive of the MX.

Senators Edward Brooke and Tom McIntyre had made reputations in the Senate as two of the most implacable opponents of ABM deployments and missile accuracy improvements in Congress. As Chairman of the Research and Development Subcommittee of the Senate Armed Services Committee,

McIntyre was well placed to exert great influence over the crucial development stages of military technology and frequently did so in conjunction with Brooke. Together they rallied support in the Senate against those technological developments which they considered would threaten the Soviet second strike capability and thus strategic stability. These included the ABM programme, MIRV, Trident and any improvement in missile accuracy which would improve the US counterforce capability. While opposing the Mark 12A warhead and the development of an inertial guidance system for the Minuteman III, however, these Senators argued the case for a new missile on the grounds that such a deployment would alleviate the problem of ICBM vulnerability. Thus in a June 1974 vote in which they led a call against the Mark 12A warhead (a system which would eventually be modified to fit the MX) they also voted for the new generation missile. Brooke justified this by arguing that improvements in the Minuteman force were not necessary because of the development by the Air Force of 'the advanced ICBM, which could provide a new missile, less vulnerable than Minuteman, in time to counter the hypothetical threat'.[71] A year later this pattern was repeated when in June McIntyre voted against funding for the Mk 12A, on terminally guided warheads, and on an advanced re-entry vehicle, but at the same time stated his support for 'continued R and D on mobile systems'.[72] Brooke justified similar actions by stating that, 'one can identify programmes in the Defense Department budget request that conform to the defensive criterion. The MX programme emphasizing land mobility for our ICBM is one such programme.'[73] What this evidence suggests is that the potential vulnerability of the Minuteman force led traditional opponents of any and all counterforce systems to embrace a large new counterforce weapons system on the basis that its mobile deployment mode would reduce the risk of a pre-emptive strike on the US deterrent.

In practice, however, the motivation of these two senators was more complex. While both were persuaded of the merits of reducing the vulnerability of the ICBM force as part of a general move towards a more stable strategic posture in which such missiles were less inviting targets, neither was particularly convinced that the Minuteman vulnerability scenario was anything other than hypothetical. Furthermore, their support for the MX was both tactical and conditional. It was tactical in that it made political sense to be seen to support some major weapons programmes, hence Brooke's comment above. It is also much easier and less risky to support a yet-to-be developed system and to oppose those which are much more real and ready to deploy. Their support was conditional in the sense that they supported a new missile which could be deployed invulnerably, but would oppose the counterforce capabilities of that system if and when that need arose. The net result of these positions, however, was that the MX programme was given Congressional funding by an odd combination of supporters. As Edwards notes, 'The doves were attracted by its mobility. The hawks were attracted by its counterforce capability.'[74] Perhaps more interestingly, both groups had used the vulnerability of the Minuteman force to support the case they made, while neither lobby was particularly convinced that this threat was real or urgent. Thus the pattern was repeated in which, for a variety of different reasons in different circumstances, the vulnerability of the US ICBM force was advanced as a justification for a position while the motivation for that position lay elsewhere. This was as true for the development of selective nuclear options in the Nixon administration as part of the Schlesinger doctrine as it was for the procurement rationales advanced in support of a new ICBM, the MX.

4   Vladivostok, Nitze and the Vulnerability Scenario

Vladivostok and ICBM Vulnerability

In November 1972, six months after the signing of the SALT I accords, negotiations began on the next round of strategic arms limitation talks. Both sides began with the intention of building on the foundations of the Interim Agreement a more comprehensive arms control regime of indefinite duration. From the American perspective the new set of negotiations was seen as a fresh opportunity to shape the development of the still growing Soviet Strategic Rocket Forces. Specifically, it was hoped that the Soviet arsenal could be reduced both in its overall size and in the categories of its heavy missiles and overall throw-weight. The inequality in launcher numbers and throw-weight totals which SALT I had codified was the issue most heavily criticised by opponents of the accord. In addition to these indices of advantage being seen as intrinsically undesirable in themselves, they were the key determinants of the potential threat which Soviet forces presented to the survivability of the Minuteman force. As such the nature of the agreement reached by this new stage of the SALT process would be judged as to its adequacy on the basis of how it reduced the threat to Minuteman.

It was largely for this reason that, in 1972, the Senate passed the Jackson Amendment instructing the Nixon administration to negotiate an agreement on the basis of 'equal levels' of weaponry which must 'not limit the US to levels of intercontinental strategic forces inferior to the limits provided for the Soviet Union'.[1] Although sufficiently ambiguous to allow for a certain degree of flexibility, Jackson himself made it clear that he interpreted the amendment as including both the number of heavy missiles and the overall throw-weight of the respective ICBM forces.[2] Intended to force the administration to take seriously the threat posed by the Soviet heavy missiles to the US ICBM force, certain members of the SALT team viewed this measure as a cumbersome constraint which merely limited their ability to prioritise the limitations of certain systems within an overall agreement. As Hyland observes, 'a greater opportunity was missed, the chance to bargain for limits on those Soviet weapons that concerned us most, even if the trading resulted in an outcome that was not strictly equal'.[3] In practice, however, Jackson's strictures were loosely interpreted by Kissinger in his early efforts to negotiate 'offsetting asymmetries' which would address American concerns with a MIRVed force of Soviet heavy missiles. Kissinger put forward a series of proposals in 1973 and early 1974 which addressed these concerns, his goal being a cut in the number of Soviet heavy missiles and a reduction or halt in their MIRV programme. To this end he proposed a low ceiling on MIRVed ICBMs, a ban on MIRVed heavy missiles, and an equality in missile throw-weight rather than in overall launcher numbers.[4] None of these proposals was attractive to Moscow, however, and the framework agreement which finally resulted from the Vladivostok summit in 1974 did not include specific limitations on throw-weight. Instead the Vladivostok framework was reached on the basis of equal aggregates with a ceiling of 2400 for total offensive strategic nuclear delivery vehicles (SNDVs) together with a sub-ceiling of 1320 MIRVed ballistic missile launchers (land- and sea-based). While this met the criteria demanded by the Jackson Amendment in one sense, the agreement incorporated too many elements in common with the Interim Agreement for the critics to be satisfied. It was, however, this agreement which was eventually to form the basis of the SALT II Treaty signed in 1979. For this reason it is necessary to analyse the terms of the accord and to outline the objections which its critics raised.

A good deal of the argument over SALT both between and within the superpowers was over an acceptable definition of parity, a task complicated by the different compositions of the strategic arsenals. As a consequence, implicit in the conclusion of the Interim Agreement was the need for a tradeoff between Soviet heavy missiles and America's areas of advantage: strategic bomber and submarine numbers and its technological lead, particularly in warheads. Even this conceptually simple agreement was only made possible by the Soviet Union postponing its claim for the inclusion of third country nuclear forces and US nuclear systems based in Europe and the Americans suspending their concern over the threat which the large Soviet ICBMs presented to the Minuteman force.

Despite a desire to move beyond this framework in an attempt to assuage concern over the threat to Minuteman, when negotiations recommenced for SALT II this structure was an obvious starting point. Furthermore, new developments made progress of any sort slow and laboured even without the American attempt to restructure the basis of equality between the two arsenals. Such complications included the development in 1974 of Soviet MIRV technology ahead of US expectations and the development of cruise missiles by the United States. Further complicating factors included the Soviet Backfire bomber and a new Soviet missile, the 'medium-heavy' SS-19, both of which caused alarm and disagreement over their definition within SALT and over their military significance. As a result the deal finally reached was structurally similar to the Interim Agreement. At its most basic it was an attempt to freeze the arsenals at or slightly above existing levels of missile launchers while allowing some growth in warhead numbers. Moscow would give up its insistence on the inclusion of forward-based nuclear systems in Europe in return for an American commitment to forgo its attempt to limit Soviet heavy missiles. It was a compromise based on the continued acceptance of missile launchers rather than missile throw-weight as the basic unit of account and it was an agreement which, by its own admission, did little to limit the growing Soviet ICBM threat to the pre-launch survivability of the US ICBM force. As a consequence of its terms, the protracted and tortuous nature of the negotiating process, and the political climate in which the agreement was reached, SALT II was destined to be highly controversial.

Its failure to redress the growing threat to the US ICBM force was one of the most persistent and damaging criticisms of both SALT II and indeed the entire SALT process. This was in part a consequence of the way in which successive administrations presented the relationship between SALT and ICBM vulnerability. SALT was portrayed by Nixon as a means of achieving strategic stability and predictability, and, as part of detente, a relaxation of tensions in superpower relations. The first two of these objectives were substantially achieved with the ratification of the ABM Treaty which foreclosed a threat to assured destruction. Where SALT I was unsuccessful, however, was in its attempt to limit the long-term threat to the US ICBM force presented by Soviet heavy missiles. Though less important militarily than the ABM Treaty, the Nixon administration decided to play up the threat to Minuteman in order to ensure Congressional acceptance of SALT I. Similarly, while the Nixon and Ford administrations used SALT in order to manage and structure the superpower competition in strategic armaments while the Soviets built an arsenal to match that of the United States, this was not the way it was presented to the American people.

As far as US public opinion was concerned SALT had created an expectation of restraint in both armaments competition and, as part of detente, in superpower global rivalry. The public was consequently alarmed at both the size and pace of the Soviet strategic buildup and the continued exploitation of regional crises for political gain by Soviet proxies.[5] The concern that the SALT process had, in Raymond Aron's words, 'accompanied and concealed' a significant Soviet military buildup was widespread.[6] Indeed it was increasingly believed, that 'Far from stabilizing world politics, the Interim Agreement has been an important structural feature of the most turbulent and dangerous period of the cold war.'[7] The gap between the expectations raised by SALT and the political reality of the late 1970s was bridged by the critics in their focus on the Soviet threat to the US ICBM force and the consequences of this for US diplomacy. SALT, they argued, had allowed the Soviet Union to develop unhindered a real threat to American security. Even under the conditions of SALT II, Rostow testified,

> the Soviet Union will have significant nuclear superiority in the early 1980s, [for] a pre-emptive first strike by destroying our ICBM's, our planes on the ground and our submarines in port with a fraction of their nuclear force, holding enough accurate missiles in reserve to neutralise the whole of our own nuclear arsenal ... Under these circumstances, we should be vulnerable to nuclear war or nuclear blackmail. We should face a condition of diplomatic impotence and be totally unable to use our conventional forces. That is the linkage between the nuclear balance and the whole of our foreign policy, which can never be escaped.[8]

SALT and the Minuteman Vulnerability Scenario

One of the most vocal and influential critics of the strategic arms limitation process as it progressed from Vladivostok to the SALT II treaty was Paul H. Nitze. He had resigned as the Pentagon's representative on the SALT delegation in Geneva in 1974 in protest at the way in which the negotiations were proceeding.[9] He did so because he 'felt that the throw-weight loophole in the Vladivostok accord was in fact a serious deficiency that promised to create future strategic instability'.[10] For Nitze and for other critics, the ceilings in both categories which had made the agreement possible at Vladivostok, were so high as to be worthless. In a speech in Los Alamos in 1975 Nitze warned that the US would soon have only half or a third as much throw-weight in its ICBM force as the Soviets and that 'It is difficult to see how the [Vladivostok] accord reduces, in a meaningful way, the US strategic defense problem posed by the new family of Soviet missiles and bombers which are now completing test and evaluation and whose large-scale deployment is now beginning.'[11] Nitze's most noted critique of the embryonic SALT agreement took the form of two articles published in 1976.[12] In the first, 'Assuring Strategic Stability in the Era of Detente', Nitze proclaimed the prospect that, under SALT

> the Soviet Union will continue to pursue a nuclear superiority that is not merely quantitative but designed to produce a theoretical war-winning capability. Further, there is a major risk that, if such a condition were achieved, the Soviet Union would adjust its policies and actions in ways that would undermine the present detente situation, with results that could only resurrect the danger of nuclear confrontation or, alternatively, increase the prospect of Soviet expansion through other means of pressure.[13]

For Nitze the SALT agreement codified the Soviet advantage in overall throw-weight in such a way that, taken together with Soviet strategic doctrine and civil defence preparation, the Soviets were accorded a theoretical military advantage which could be exploited either directly or indirectly for political advantage. Nitze cited the Cuban Missile Crisis as an example of an occasion where nuclear superiority at the strategic level had been decisive at the conventional level.

Of particular concern to Nitze was the Soviet advantage in MIRVed heavy ICBMs. While under the putative SALT agreement, he explained, 'both sides are permitted equal numbers of MIRVed missiles, the new Soviet SS-19s have three times the throw-weight of the Minuteman III, and the new SS-18, seven times'.[14] Nitze saw the exploitation of this advantage by the further fractionation of the Soviet heavy boosters as increasingly destabilising. This was the case, he argued, because the Soviet Union was not merely interested in attaining an assured destruction capability but was building a war fighting posture in line with its strategic doctrine and ideological goals.

Furthermore, Soviet civil defence preparations provided additional evidence of their determination to achieve a strategic posture which they could exploit for political gain. In support of this argument, Nitze pointed to the Soviet Civil Defence Manual which detailed their 'massive and meticulously planned civil defence effort', their planned relocation of key industries away from major population centres and their evacuation procedures designed to 'limit civilian casualties to five to eight percent of the urban population or three to four percent of the total population – even after a direct US attack on Soviet cities'.[15] In making this particular argument Nitze drew on the expertise of T.K. Jones who, since working for him on the SALT delegation, had spent some time studying Soviet civil defence at the Boeing Corporation. The conclusion Nitze drew from Jones's research together with Soviet publications was stark: 'the ability of US nuclear power to destroy without question the bulk of Soviet industry and a large proportion of the Soviet population is by no means as clear as it once was, even if one assumes most of US striking power to be available and directed to this end'.[16]

Nitze saw the throw-weight advantage, Soviet strategic doctrine and their extensive civil defence capability as the means to exploit diplomatic advantage if not political extortion from the United States. Specifically, this article warned against the possibility that the Soviets could 'profitably attack US forces with a fraction of their forces and still maintain reserves adequate for other contingencies'.[17] His concern, although never actually spelled out as such in this article, was that if the Soviets simultaneously evacuated their cities and destroyed the US ICBM force with its accurate warheads, the US would be left with a stark choice indeed. The alternatives would be to retaliate with its remaining force of less accurate submarine-launched missiles against Soviet urban areas emptied of population, thus inviting its own societal destruction, or to do nothing.

It was for this reason that Nitze placed such strong emphasis on the indices of throw-weight. For him it was a 'crucial test ... to consider the possible results of a largescale nuclear exchange in which one side sought to destroy as much of the other side's striking power as possible, in order to leave itself in the strongest possible position after the exchange'.[18] Moreover, this was not the full extent of the former SALT negotiator's concern with throw-weight. Nitze was animated not only by the political effect on the superpower relationship of the asymmetrical amounts of throw-weight which might result from the SALT II agreement, he was also concerned with how these calculations could be affected after the first round of a strategic nuclear exchange. As Nitze explained, 'It is the situation *after* attack, of course, that is most important ... since the targets remaining after the exchange would almost all be soft ones, missile accuracy and other refinements in the original postures no longer have the same significance. Surviving throw-weight thus becomes an appropriate *total* measure of the residual capability on both sides.'[19] In support of this argument Nitze supplied two tables of US Soviet throw-weight ratios and differentials which showed 1976 (the year of publication) as the year at which the advantage in total amount of throw-weight 'after' an exchange crossed the curve depicting the amount 'before' an exchange, 'signifying that the Soviets could, by initiating such an exchange, increase the ratio of advantage they held at the start of the exchange'.[20] This example is typical of the character of this article: arcane, fantastic, mathematical and technical. Above all, however, these concerns ostensibly about Soviet advantage, were in reality a lament for the loss of US superiority.

It fell to his second article to spell out in more stark political terms the implications of his analysis. This article, 'Deterring Our Deterrent', which appeared in *Foreign Policy*, in Winter 1976–7, while still technical in subject matter – replete with charts and tables – was much more direct in its message.[21] Nitze repeated his concerns with Soviet military doctrine, civil defence and relative throw-weight advantage both before and after an initial Soviet counterforce attack. Once again drawing on the calculations of T.K. Jones, he added to the latter a further set of computations concerning the residual throw-weight levels remaining to 'each side after a two sided counterforce exchange in which all useful counterforce targets have been addressed'.[22] From this and other calculations Nitze concluded that 'Today, after a strategic nuclear counterforce exchange under normal US alert conditions, the Soviet Union would hold superiority in all indices of capability except numbers of warheads, and even that sole remaining advantage would be gone within two or three years.'[23] Accordingly, he concluded that the strategic nuclear 'relationship is becoming unstable; [and] the Soviets in coming years will be able to increase their ratio of advantage by attacking US forces'.[24] Nitze further warned that US 'megatonnage is now so low that it is possible for the Soviet Union to plan a civil defence programme which would make a far smaller percentage of their population hostage to a US countervalue attack, particularly after it has been reduced in capability by an initial Soviet counterforce attack, than our population is to a Soviet countervalue response'.[25] The importance of these calculations, short of an actual nuclear exchange, Nitze explained, was the impact that these inequalities would have on the ability of the US to contain the expansion of the Soviet Union by projecting its power overseas. For years, he explained 'US strategic nuclear preponderance has made it possible to offset Soviet military superiority at the periphery and to deter its offensive employment.'[26] What Nitze now saw as an imbalance favouring the Soviet Union in these crucial indices heralded the reversal of this trend and the growth in influence of an adversary ever more confident in its own power projection policies.

Nitze did not consider this situation and these trends to be irreversible, however. On the contrary, as in the first article, he was eager to set out criteria as well as policy prescriptions which could remedy these strategic developments. For Nitze, the first criterion was 'to assure the relationship of the yield, accuracy, survivability and reliability of the two sides' forces such that the Soviet side could not hope by initiating a counterforce exchange to improve either the absolute excess *in pounds* of its throw-weight over ours, or the ratio of its throw-weight to ours'.[27] Bizarre, technically arcane and mechanistic as this criteria might have appeared to some, Nitze felt it sufficiently important to justify a vast and immediate increase in the strategic forces of the United States. Specifically, Nitze recommended the speedy deployment of large numbers of Trident II missiles, B1 bombers with strategic cruise missiles, and 550 MX missiles in a multiple aim point basing mode. In the gap, the window between the growing Soviet preponderance and these systems coming into service in the mid-1980s, Nitze recommended certain 'temporary fixes' in order to be able to deal with 'the problem as it is apt to emerge in the late 1970s and early 1980s'. For this Nitze recommended the deployment of a mobile transporter-erector-launcher and hardened capsule for the Minuteman II, a variety of point defences, increased alert states for bombers and ballistic missile firing submarines, and the provision for launch under attack for the Minuteman force as a whole.[28]

As Kaplan rightly observes, these two articles 'hit new heights of abstraction in strategic thought' reflecting as they did 'an absolute faith in the power and significance of theoretical calculations' completely devoid of political and human considerations.[29] Nevertheless, and more remarkable as a consequence, these ideas developed a constituency both in and outside of government which took these concerns seriously on their own terms in such a way as to shape an entire strategic and political debate. Furthermore, as the main author of these concerns and as one respected for his political and diplomatic status, Nitze was to prove a key player in that debate for the remainder of the 1970s. Given the rather technical and obscure nature of some of the arguments advanced by Nitze, it is necessary to ask why his ideas were given so much credence. Such an explanation can not be understood outside the political and psychological climate of the time.

The Predisposition of the American Public Mood

Part of the explanation as to why considerations such as those advanced by Nitze were given so much credence can be found in the nature of the subject matter itself. Because it is so esoteric it is very difficult to refute on an *a priori* basis. For this reason, there tends to be a reliance on the evidence and analysis of experts to a much greater degree than in any other area of public policy. It was for this reason that the case which Nitze made in his two articles had an impact as much for who he was as for what he said. As Newhouse observes, 'Owing to the author's experience and standing, it had unusual resonance.'[30] Rather like the children's story of the Emperor's new clothes, once the assumption is made that the Emperor (or 'expert') cannot be mistaken because of who he is, then the willingness to believe the existence of his invisible robes follows despite what might seem to be evidence available to the contrary. The fact that the ICBM vulnerability issue had been introduced into the public realm by the government gave further credence.

Another contributory factor to the credulity of both the American body politic as a whole and the politically engaged elite, was the degree of certainty with which these views were presented. Jones and Nitze took an engineering approach which presented these ideas as rationally deduced 'facts' rather than opinions based on questionable assumptions.[31] This approach was made easier to accept by both the very literally-minded and rationality-based American political culture and the fact that most observers were too ignorant of the subject matter to challenge the authenticity of the views presented. Citing Jones's 'silly assertion about Soviet civil defence' as an example of this, Newhouse reflects that

> Reality in the nuclear age is the stuff of trendy perceptions and often their victim. Gifted scientists and competent technicians are available to promote

even the most farfetched argument. They may be vulnerable to ridicule but not to being deflated by facts; these are obscured by abstractions and unprovable assumptions.[32]

Looking at the problem in purely engineering terms it is easy to see how someone unfamiliar with the subject could be impressed with the apparent thoroughness with which the analysis had been conducted. This quotation from Nitze demonstrates the point. 'In working out what would actually happen in the assumed exchange, full account has been taken of all relevant factors – in particular the number, yield, accuracy and reliability of the re-entry vehicles associated with that throw-weight, and the hardness of the targets against which they are assumed to have been targeted.'[33] While this passage might prove persuasive to those unfamiliar with the subject, to others what is striking is the absence of any consideration of any political component in his 'working out of what would actually happen'. After all he does claim that 'full account has been taken of all relevant factors'. For Nitze, human decision-making considerations are obviously not 'relevant factors' in such calculations where the rational actor model is taken to the extreme of technical determinism. The Soviet Union would have a throw-weight advantage after an attack of 'X'lb, therefore it would be in its interest to attack. For the argument to work, however, the audience must both share the assumptions of these analysts and be unaware (like these analysts) that these assumptions are colouring their judgement. For this to be the case did not require a similarity of strategic view between the analysts and those they sought to influence, however, since the most important assumption concerned the shared acceptance of an enemy image of the Soviet Union.

Nitze's willingness to dismiss any criticisms of underlying assumptions as irrelevant to the superpower struggle was another feature of his approach which allowed him to pursue his 'number crunching' calculations of danger, taking his followers along without ever engaging the critics. This was the case because Nitze and Jones would only talk about their calculations. This left the critics responding to the agenda which Nitze and Jones had set and unable to challenge them on the fundamental assumptions on which these calculations were based. The following two quotations illustrate this phenomenon. For George Kennan, Nitze

felt comfortable with something only if it could be statistically expressed. He loved anything that could be reduced to numbers. He was mesmerised by them. He was not content until he could reduce a problem to numbers ... Of course, the numbers were predicated on a total theoretical hostility that had to be assumed to give these figures meaning. He had no feeling for the intangibles – values, intentions. When there was talk of intentions, as opposed to capabilities, he would say, 'How can you measure intentions? We can't be bothered to get into psychology; we have to face the Russians as competitors, militarily. That's where I come in; that's where I'm in my element.'[34]

No less revealing is Nitze himself talking about his analysis in the two articles above. 'It makes a difference whether you look at the facts and try to look at them with open eyes. If you're just looking at the *words* you get into trouble. You're much better off looking at the *facts*.'[35] One of the appealing aspects of this engineering approach to the strategic balance for its target audience was that it reduced the superpower competition to a rather simplified technical level. Furthermore, those who were pointing to the problem were also advocating an available solution. For Jones this was an American crash programme of civil defence, while for Nitze it was civil defence, greater strategic offensive capability and a remedy for the imminent vulnerability of the US Minuteman force.

This analysis, indeed this whole approach to the strategic nuclear balance between the Superpowers and from this the fear of nuclear war which followed, could not have occurred, however, had it not been for the state of the American national psyche at this particular moment in time. The apparent failure of detente during the Presidency of Gerald Ford predisposed the American defence establishment to take notice of critics of the strategic balance, especially those who drew a link between these two events. The authority of the Presidency was weak following the Watergate affair. This was especially true for the area of national security where the Vietnam debacle had robbed many Americans, both in the defence community and in the country as a whole, of their confidence in the Government's handling of this subject. For liberals there was an unwillingness to believe a government who had so consistently lied to them over its various policies in Vietnam. For conservatives, on the other hand, the government had failed in its efforts to prevent the fall of Indo-China to the Communists and could therefore not be trusted in its judgement on national security concerns. The authority of the executive branch was weakened with the Commander-in-Chief forced out in disgrace, Kissinger under attack over Watergate, and a rapid turnover of Secretaries of Defense at the Pentagon. The result was that many arguments were given by forfeit rather than being lost in debate.[36]

It was against this background that critics of the established foreign and defence policies of detente were able to make their mark. Opposition to detente, and SALT in particular, was not limited to defence intellectuals like Nitze. Attacks on the Ford administration were also led from within Congress, primarily by leading Democrat and Presidential hopeful Senator Henry

Jackson supported by his assistant Richard Perle. Another source of criticism of the administration resulted from the fact that 1976 was an election year and candidates from both the left and right were seeking to establish themselves by taking positions critical to Ford on policies such as SALT and detente. Most notable of these candidates were two state governors, Ronald Reagan from California and Jimmy Carter from Georgia. Reagan ran against Ford for the Republican party nomination from a position on the right of fierce anti-communism. Amongst his castigations of Ford, Nixon and Kissinger over detente, he was highly critical of the Vladivostok agreement on the lines that Nitze and others had delineated. Carter was also critical of Ford over SALT II; his main complaint was the limited scope of the agreement rather than the fear that the treaty was one-sided.

The reaction of the Ford administration to these critics was to give ground by moving to the right. In March 1976 Ford himself prohibited the use of the word 'detente' by his staff in official statements and publications. On SALT, Ford also accepted the advice of Rumsfeld at the Pentagon and Ikle and Lehman at ACDA in vetoing the tentative deal which Kissinger had negotiated with the Soviets in early 1976 to bring SALT II to a swift conclusion.[37] Of more importance with regard to ICBM vulnerability, however, was the reaction of the administration to pressure over the CIA's estimates of the development of Soviet strategic nuclear forces. For it was the actions of the administration over these criticism which propelled the ICBM vulnerability issue with authority to the heart of the government process.

The Team 'B' Exercise

Criticisms of the CIA's National Intelligence Estimates were forthcoming from those who disliked the fact that their views of the strategic balance were not supported at an official level. Most influential of these critics was Wohlstetter, who wrote a series of articles in 1974 and 1975 lambasting the CIA for what he claimed was a record of inaccurate forecasting. This 'failure', he alleged, substantially and seriously underestimated the likely future development of the Soviet Union's strategic nuclear forces.[38] The critics of the CIA were spurred on in their efforts in early 1976 when the agency was persuaded to revise upwards its estimates of Soviet defence spending. This revision of the amount of Soviet GNP spent on the military from 6–8 per cent to 11–13 per cent was the result of a change in methodology brought about as a consequence of criticism from the DIA, and newly gained access to secret Soviet documentation.[39] Despite the fact that this development showed that Soviet industry was nearly twice as inefficient as previously thought and that there was no actual increase in the amount that the Soviets were actually spending, the hawks seized upon it as further grist to their mill.

It was in this political climate that the President's Foreign Intelligence Advisory Board (PFIAB) decided to use its influence to question the accuracy of the CIA with regard to these matters. The PFIAB had been receiving dissenting voices from within the intelligence community on the validity of the CIA's Soviet estimates since at least 1974. This was particularly true of the Air Force where dissent was emanating from General Daniel Graham and, more importantly, General George J. Keegan.[40] Chief of Air Force Intelligence, Keegan was most outspoken in his views that Soviet civil defence preparations together with their progress in new guided missiles meant that the US 'had lost the strategic balance' in 1972.[41] Keegan reportedly persuaded the PFIAB to approach the President.[42] He did this with the idea of letting a panel of outsiders conduct a 'competitive analysis' using the same raw material on the Soviet Union in parallel to the regular analysts.[43] After CIA Director William Colby put up resistance to the idea he was replaced in November 1975 by George Bush. A politician with no background in intelligence, Bush knew the importance of being accommodating in order to fend off the challenge from the right wing of his party. Accordingly, Bush gave the go ahead and in June 1976 two 'teams' of individuals set about analysing the raw intelligence data on the Soviet Union. 'Team A' consisted of the regular CIA analysts chaired by Howard Stoertz, while 'Team B' had a very different makeup. Chosen by Bush and deputy National Security Advisor William Hyland, Team B was stacked with hard-liners who had a pessimistic view of the Soviet Union and the prevailing strategic balance. This was justified on the grounds that such a composition was necessary to offset the alleged arms control bias of the CIA team. As panel member General Graham observed, 'The evidence didn't speak for itself, assumptions were very important. A much more sombre view of the evidence got a very different answer.'[44] More succinctly, Graham also observed that, 'There's the "peace through trust guys" and the "peace through strength guys".'[45] A similar if slightly less colourful sentiment was expressed by Team B chairman, Sovietologist Richard Pipes, who explained that,

> There is no point in another, what you might call, optimistic view. In general there has been a disposition in Washington to underestimate the Soviet drive. The moderately optimistic line has prevailed ...[46]

The task which Team B set itself was to reverse this trend. It consisted of individuals who were all outsiders as far as the CIA estimating process was concerned, though some of them were 'insiders' in that they were still in government service in some official capacity.[47] The members brought to the panel a welter of experience, and more significantly, they shared a particular view about the strategic balance and Soviet intentions and were eager to shape the intelligence community's views accordingly.

As the process of analysing the estimates began, the members of Team B accused the CIA of dealing in 'faulty assumptions, faulty analysis, faulty use of intelligence, and faulty exploitation of available intelligence' in discussions which one CIA insider described as 'absolutely bloody'.[48] The Team B members intended the process not only to show up the differences between the two sets of estimates, they also set out by dint of peer pressure to make the exercise an 'education' process for the regular CIA analysts. They were not disappointed with the impact they had on Team A, producing the CIA's own estimates. The CIA's NIE was the most conservative and sombre estimate that the agency had produced for more than a decade. Indeed, a senior military intelligence officer was reported at the time as saying that 'It was more than sombre – it was very grim. It flatly states the judgement that the Soviet Union is seeking superiority over the United States forces.'[49] The CIA's estimate was cautious, however, compared to that produced by Team B itself. Going well beyond its mandate the panel made sweeping statements challenging well established views. It even recommended a crash programme for an American military buildup. Its main conclusion was that the Soviet Union did not share 'Western' conceptions of deterrence theory and indeed was well advanced in its plans to deploy a war-fighting capability. The scenario it described was that which Jackson, Nitze and Jones had outlined earlier, a first strike on the land-based deterrent in conjunction with a civil defence evacuation plan designed to blunt the impact of a US retaliatory strike.

Team B also challenged the CIA assumption that the US had a technological lead in things such as missile accuracy and disputed the agency's dismissal of Soviet claims to have an effective civil defence establishment. Where any uncertainty existed the outsiders insisted that caution rather than judgement be the order of the day. For this reason they concluded that since the accuracy of Soviet missiles could not be determined with any certainty, they must be assumed to be more accurate than their American counterparts. From this they concluded that the US ICBM force could therefore be vulnerable to a pre-emptive Soviet attack in the near future.[50]

These views were not new nor were they based on any new intelligence information which the panel had been privy to as part of this exercise. Rather the panel began its analysis with its conclusions already decided. As Nitze concedes in his memoirs, Team B's analysis was not confined to the material presented by the CIA; rather, 'we relied on material that was already in the public domain'.[51] What was new was that views which had previously been considered to be heresy were elevated to a position of respectability. This was done as a political act by an administration eager to placate the right. Ironically for Ford this move backfired, and 'The exercise turned out to be a license for an attack on Ford's own administration – a case of self-inflicted damage.'[52]

Team B's conclusions, which were widely leaked to the press, were not based on any indisputable evidence. Rather, they were a matter of political judgement. As one intelligence officer observed at the time, 'There was disagreement beyond the facts.'[53] The differences lay in the imponderable and the unprovable realm of Soviet intentions. Given the opportunity to review the intelligence data, Team B proved that it was possible to put another interpretation on these facts. It is significant, however, that no Team C was constituted to see whether a less threatening and more liberal interpretation of the data was possible. This was the case because the Team B exercise was an attempt to pacify the administration's critics on the right. It was both a response to a changed political agenda in US politics and at the same time a furthering of the cause of that new agenda. Team B did this by establishing its views of the Soviet Union as a new orthodoxy while simultaneously damaging the credibility of those individuals and institutions who questioned these views. One result of the exercise was to diminish the influence of the CIA in the estimating process for years to come, with the DIA and Air Force gaining at its expense and the NIEs becoming more conservative as a consequence. As Lebow observes, 'In the opinion of many observers of this process, the NIEs reveal much more about the changing balance of power in Washington than they do about changing Soviet strategic capabilities.'[54] As Stephen Rosenfeld observed, 'Intellectually, that argument was not resolved. Politically, it was. Team B won.'[55]

Reaction to both the existence and the conclusions of Team B, after it reported to the PFIAB in December 1976, was mixed. Given that the exercise constituted an attack on the existing orthodoxy, a great deal of the reaction was hostile. Former Deputy Director of Intelligence Ray Cline described the exercise as a 'kangaroo court', while for Senator Gary Hart 'The correspondence about the exercise shows that the President's Foreign Intelligence Advisory Board (PFIAB) included members more interested in altering the conclusions of the national estimate than in improving its quality.'[56] Kissinger was also dismissive of the implications of the Team B report which its members were loudly trumpeting in the press. In his departing press conference on 10 January 1977, he repeated a remark which had been a central foundation of detente but which was now being challenged, 'I do not believe the Soviet Union is achieving military superiority over the United States' and furthermore 'Military superiority has no practical significance ... under circumstances in which both sides have the capability to annihilate one another.'[57] In a similar vein a *New York Times* editorial remarked that 'policy debates that are won by debasing the intelligence currency in which we all must trade will not long count for much or be worth winning'.[58] This conclusion, however, missed the important point, that the Team B exercise represented a turning point in the currency of ideas in American national security policy. Team B was an attempt to shape the policies of the new administration, of whatever hue, by changing the intellectual and political climate. While its efforts were unsuccessful with regard to Kissinger, at least in the short term, it was not necessary to convince every actor of their case for their goals to be achieved.[59] What the Team B exercise did do, however, was to place these views onto the agenda and into the news from an apparently authoritative source.

Nor was every member of the Ford administration hostile to these views. Secretary of Defense Donald Rumsfeld agreed with the outsiders, warning against the shifting 'correlation of forces' which could give the Soviets leverage over the United States, and observing that while 'absolute proof eludes us about the intentions of Soviet leaders ... no doubt exists about the capabilities of the Soviet armed forces' which 'indicate a tendency toward war-fighting ... rather than the more modish Western models of deterrence through mutual vulnerability'.[60] Rumsfeld's views, like those of critics from the right, represented a loss of confidence with detente as a means of containing the growth of Soviet influence. This in turn resulted in a loss of trust in MAD since the assurance part of deterrence theory was no longer accepted by those who believed that the Soviet Union was pursuing a war-fighting capability. An extreme worst case prescription was the end result of this thought process. Once it was assumed that the Soviets were trying to escape from the MAD condition, many felt that the United States should seek some sort of advantage in what was seen as a new zero sum competition. These views were no longer the exclusive preserve of outside critics on the fringe of the debate. The fact that Rumsfeld shared these views lent further credibility to the opinions being expressed by the members of Team B, even though his tenure at the Pentagon was coming to an end following the election of a new Democratic President, Jimmy Carter, in November 1976.

It quickly became apparent that the new administration did not share the sense of danger which the Team B members had promulgated. Both Carter's new Secretary of State, Cyrus Vance and Defense Secretary Harold Brown were quick to dismiss the notion that the Soviets possessed or were about to possess superiority over the US. The new administration neither accepted the crude technical reductionism of the critics nor did it believe that the US was behind in the overall strategic nuclear balance. Instead it believed, as Carter himself proclaimed in January 1977, that 'we're still by far stronger than they are in most means of measuring strength'.[61] This was a view, however, which was no longer universally shared either in the defence community or indeed the wider public as a whole. Furthermore, the Team B exercise had established this voice of dissent at the heart of government. As Marder wrote in The *Washington Post*, 'Even if the Carter Administration disagrees with the new National Intelligence Estimates on Soviet strategy it cannot be readily rewritten. It will appear in two or three volumes that serve as a reference for policy-makers across the top echelon of the government.'[62] The critics of the prevailing orthodoxy who had been so galvanised by the publicity surrounding the leaked finding of the Team B report were not content to trust in the judgement of the new administration, however. Instead two approaches were adopted to promote the acceptance of their analysis and its attendant policy prescriptions. First, the critics sought to gain access to positions of influence in the new administration or to influence the appointment of candidates favourable to their views. Second, they sought to influence the formulation of national security policy by indirect means, most notably through the establishment of political interest groups, principally the Committee on the Present Danger.

Part Two

ICBM Vulnerability in
The Carter Administration

Mankind has a pressing psychological need to explain the world; it has no such need to see it explained correctly.

Patrick M. Morgan [1]

I'm not sure that our country has ever been willing, or ever will be willing, to accept genuine equality. What we define as equality almost inevitably is going to be superiority.

President Carter [2]

There is an enormous gulf between what political leaders really think about nuclear weapons and what is assumed in complex calculations of relative 'advantage' in simulated strategic warfare. Think tank analysts can set levels of 'acceptable' damage well up in the tens of millions of lives. They can assume that the loss of dozens of great cities is somehow a real choice for sane men. They are in an unreal world. In the real world of political leaders – whether here or in the Soviet Union – a decision that would bring even one hydrogen bomb on one city of one's own country would be recognised in advance as a catastrophic blunder; ten bombs on ten cities would be a disaster beyond history; and a hundred bombs on a hundred cities are unthinkable.

McGeorge Bundy [3]

5   Carter, His Critics and the Politicisation of the Issue

Introduction

The initial attempts by the right to gain influence in the Carter administration took place simultaneously with the formation of the CPD and the Team B exercise in the latter half of 1976. The origins of the Committee on The Present Danger (CPD), however, went back to 1972 and were rooted in the 'Henry Jackson wing' of the Democratic Party.[1] As founding member of the CPD Eugene Rostow explains, 'We had formed a committee within the Democratic party to try to rally the faithful to the traditional policy of the party ... [but] It didn't gain much headway, and therefore we decided to form a bipartisan committee ...'[2] This was to be the CPD, the purpose of which Rostow explained 'was to say to the American people: well, Vietnam was a failure, but *there is no other policy*, and we must rally public opinion to realise that we've lost a battle and not the war ...'[3] Its initial aims were a general reaction against what it perceived to be a weakness in national security policy following Vietnam, and a rejection of detente in favour of a more traditional containment policy. As part of the process of doing this, however, the CPD's role developed in a way which became much more narrowly focused on the debate surrounding SALT and the strategic nuclear balance.

Although many discussions took place throughout 1975 in preparation for the launch of the CPD, the organisation did not actually 'go public' until 11 November 1976 so as not to influence the Presidential election.[4] Once it did so, however, it became very clear that the efforts of the critics had been unsuccessful in influencing the composition and views of the new administration. This was the case even though Nitze and others had supported Carter from an early stage and had been presented with several opportunities to persuade him of their case.

At the outset Carter, a graduate of Annapolis Naval Academy who served eleven years in the navy, looked a promising candidate for the right. Carter also gave the speech nominating Henry Jackson at the 1972 Democratic Convention and had sought advice on defence policy early on in his 1976 campaign from both Jackson and Nitze.[5] In practice, however, Carter had sought the advice and support of both wings of the Democratic party on foreign and defence policy matters. In July 1976 Carter held one of a series of seminars on these subjects at his home in Plains, Georgia, to which he invited a group of experts with varying approaches to the subject.[6] Those present ranged in view from Paul Warnke on the left to Paul Nitze on the right. Also present were Warnke's former colleagues from the McNamara Pentagon, Cyrus Vance and Harold Brown, together with four younger analysts, academics Barry Blechman and Lynn Davis and lawyers Walter Slocombe and James Woolsey. The idea was to discuss the major issues and for Carter to get to know those who might serve him in a new administration. Instead of a seminar led by the Democratic party nominee, however, Nitze proceeded to lecture Carter on the imminent threat to the US ICBM force and the portent of danger which this implied. Using the charts and graphs which Jones had compiled, Nitze spelled out the now familiar scenario, warning Carter of the need to cut social spending in order to finance a crash rearmament programme. With the exception of Woolsey, the remainder of the group were awkwardly silent. Like Carter they were unimpressed either with the message or the way in which it had been presented. Nitze himself later recalled that 'It didn't go over very well' and that 'He didn't want to listen.'[7] Carter's own reflections were more candid, 'Nitze was typically know-it-all ... He was arrogant and inflexible. His own ideas were sacred to him. He didn't seem to listen to others, and he had a doomsday approach.'[8] The result of the meeting was that all those present that day received positions in the new administration with the exception of Nitze. The new administration was to be staffed by individuals who did not accept the analysis of the right-wing critics that America was inferior and vulnerable. Indeed at several points when Nitze's name was put forward for possible positions within the administration, Carter himself would intervene to block the appointment. On one occasion Carter rejected Nitze's appointment, commenting to Vance that 'I don't think that man has the breadth or balance we need.'[9]

Attempts by Nitze and other critics to secure positions in the administration for individuals who shared their views were unsuccessful. Nitze failed to find positions in the Pentagon for Jones and chairman of the SALT negotiating team Ralph Earle. The Jackson wing of the party was also upset not to have either Nitze or Schlesinger appointed to the top Pentagon job.[10] As it was, Warnke's nomination for the position of Director of the Arms Control and Disarmament Agency and Chief negotiator at SALT ran into considerable opposition, most notably from Nitze.[11] Carter's nomination of Theodore Sorensen as Director of the CIA also met with strong opposition and had to be withdrawn. In both cases the opposition made much of the liberal credentials of the candidates who were seen as representative of the ideological colour of the new administration.[12] The exclusion from the new national security policy team of representatives of the Jackson wing of the Democratic party was in one respect a significant tactical error in that it exposed the administration to 'constant criticism and powerful opposition'.[13] Yet it also

reflected a different philosophical approach adopted by Carter to foreign policy
from that represented by the Jackson democrats and the CPD. While the latter
were eager to return to the foreign policies of the Cold War, the Carter
administration was eager to establish an entirely new agenda which
transcended containment. Instead of focusing on the minute details of the
East–West struggle, Carter sought to down-grade the importance of US
Soviet relations in its relationship with the rest of the world. As Williams
and Bowker observe, in its argument with its critics on the right, its differences

> went well beyond different threat assessments. In essence the administration
> and the Committee formulated two competing paradigms about the
> contemporary international system and the nature of power within it ...
> Whereas the administration believed that military power was increasingly
> irrelevant to the problems of the late twentieth century, the CPD argued
> that it still retained a crucial role in contemporary international politics.
> The historical references for these conclusions were very different. The
> administration was influenced by the Vietnam war, which had revealed
> very clearly the limits of military force; the members of the CPD were
> much more impressed by the Cuban Missile Crisis – which had shown
> the effectiveness of coercive diplomacy.[14]

The implications of these views manifested themselves in very different
attitudes towards the nature of the superpower competition and the utility
of nuclear weapons within that. On the whole, those in the administration
had a sanguine view of nuclear weapons, viewing them as having little
utility beyond deterring general nuclear war. For the critics, on the other hand,
such views were reckless, naive and completely inappropriate for the
approaching period of imminent danger and vulnerability. It was against this
background that the battlelines were drawn and the CPD began to organise
and agitate.

The Committee on the Present Danger: The Critics Coalesce

While the nominations to the Carter administration had provided an impetus
to the work of the CPD, '[t]he intellectual basis for the Committee grew out
of the work of the now-famous Team B'.[15] Following preliminary discussions
between Eugene Rostow, David Packard, Charles Walker, Joe Fowler and
Paul Nitze throughout 1976, the Committee was launched three days after
Carter's election victory. Drawing on the membership, analysis and general
approach of the Team B exercise, the CPD was to become a caucus for the
critics of the foreign and defence policies of the new administration. The
Committee's 141-member board was, according to Nitze, 'distinguished by

its expertise in foreign affairs and military matters'.[16] Although diverse in geographical spread and professional background and bipartisan in nature, the Committee was united in its view of the Soviet Union and the threat which they believed it presented. In its first policy statement, *Common Sense and Common Danger*, issued in November 1976, it pronounced that

> The principle threat to our nation, to world peace, and to the cause of human freedom is the Soviet drive for dominance based upon an unparalled military buildup. The Soviet Union has not altered its long-held goal of a world dominated from a single centre – Moscow ... If we continue to drift, we shall become second best to the Soviet Union in overall military strength...[therefore] Our national survival itself would be in peril, and we should face, one after another, *bitter choices between war and acquiescence under pressure.*[17]

The CPD's philosophy was both simplistic and a reversion to the cold war containment policies of the 1950s. Its rhetoric and content were reminiscent of the call to arms of both NSC-68 and the Gaither committee report, two documents which Nitze had also been instrumental in formulating.[18] Despite this apocalyptic approach, however, the CPD was to prove a highly successful opponent to the policies of the Carter administration and one which brought to the public's attention its concern over the vulnerability of the Minuteman force. As with the Team B exercise, the CPD was instrumental in affecting the debate without any new evidence. Nor was their influence derived from the inherent logic of the case they presented. The power of their argument was that it had a resonance with a particular audience. This was in spite of the fact that two of its central unifying ideas, the offensiveness of Moscow's strategic doctrine and the assumption of Soviet malice were roundly criticised at the time. It is worth analysing these elements of the CPD's platform in order to show that its appeal was not self-evidently rooted in the strategic arguments which it presented.

Soviet Strategic Doctrine

Concern over Soviet strategic doctrine was fuelled by what was perceived as alarming evidence in openly available Soviet military publications. These ideas had been seized upon by Keegan, Jones, Nitze and Van Cleave as unmistakable evidence of Soviet intentions and these publications had been widely drawn upon in the Team B exercise. This was particularly true for the Team B chairman, Richard Pipes, who developed his ideas at length in an article in *Commentary*, in July 1977.[19] This article, 'Why the Soviet

Union Thinks it Could Fight and Win a Nuclear War' was one of many to stress the importance of Soviet pronouncements on nuclear war.[20] The article was in many respects 'the Team B report edited for public consumption'.[21]

Pipes's main premise was that US strategic doctrine was based on 'mutual deterrence' eschewing any deployment options short of this in favour of a 'counter*value* targeting policy' threatening to retaliate and 'lay waste Soviet cities' while 'Soviet doctrine, by contrast, emphatically asserts that while an all-out nuclear war would indeed prove extremely destructive to both parties, its outcome would not be mutual suicide: the country better prepared for it and in possession of a superior strategy could win and emerge a viable society.'[22] He then asserted that this 'fundamental doctrinal discrepancy' was in part the result of the feelings of guilt on the part of the scientific community who invented the bomb and the concept of deterrence which accompanied it. As with the highly questionable nature of much of his supporting evidence Pipes's article demonstrates that he had very little understanding of US strategic doctrine which has always included counterforce options.[23] As Brown made clear in his FY 1981 Posture Statement,

> The notion that, somehow, our only available response to enemy attacks on allied targets would be to strike at enemy cities is incorrect. We have had, and will continue to improve, the options necessary to protect our interests ... [and furthermore] To recognise that strong war winning views are held in some Soviet circles ... is not necessarily to cast any accusation of special malevolence, for these are traditional military perspectives by no means unreflected even in current Western discussion of these matters.[24]

Such inaccuracies were deeply frustrating to those more intimately acquainted with US policy because of the misleading impression they gave. As Richard Garwin testified, 'Although he had been the leader of Team B and had access to all the information we had on the Soviet Union, he didn't have the least understanding of US Forces ... He was just wrong.'[25] In a similar way Pipes's application of the thought of Clausewitz is also selective and consequently misleading.[26] It was through his expertise on the Soviet Union, however, that his pronouncements on their strategic doctrine were regarded as so persuasive. His judgement here too, however, can be seriously questioned.

The work of Pipes and others can be criticised for both the sources used and the way in which they were used. Part of the attraction of focusing on Soviet military doctrine at this time resulted from the release by the CIA in 1976 of English translations of the Soviet journal *Military Thought*. These publications provided rich pickings for those who sought evidence of Soviet hostile intent. The first batch to be translated were those written between

1963–9 with the 1971–3 period being released in 1979. It was the first batch, however, which was widely drawn upon in this initial debate, particularly by analysts such as Joseph Douglas. This was the case even though a great deal of the material was no longer valid due to changes in Soviet doctrine in the late 1960s and early 1970s.[27] Indeed, the publication in 1979 of Joseph D. Douglas Jr and Amoretta M. Hoeber's *Soviet Strategy For Nuclear War* contained 84 references, all before 1969.[28] The fact that this material was no longer reflective of current thinking, however, did not prevent it from fuelling the debate.

The second major criticism of the use of Soviet sources to argue that Moscow possessed a theory of victory was that the use of the available material was extremely selective and lacking in conceptual rigour. Certainly, while the pages of *Military Power* were largely given over to views which saw war as a continuation of policy, there were also substantive and frequent dissensions from this perspective.[29] Furthermore, most pronouncements by the Soviet military were in the context of seeing war as undesirable and extremely destructive, yet nevertheless viewing the job of the soldier to prosecute a war as best as possible if required. In this sense there was little difference between the Soviet and American military in their planning for damage-limiting strategies, a point which Pipes failed to grasp. While such views should not be entirely unexpected from the military, the evidence suggests that Soviet civilian analysts were much more sober in their view of the destructive and futile nature of nuclear war. Statements by the Soviet leadership in the early 1970s seem to further compound the ambiguity. While Brezhnev could be found declaring in 1975 that 'the starting of a nuclear missile war would spell inevitable annihilation for the aggressor himself, to say nothing of the vast losses of many other countries not even formally involved in the war', other public statements can be found supporting the opposite position in front of a different audience.[30] Such contradictory signals ought to have induced caution in those analysts who sought to interpret the meaning of these statements, but instead they were plundered in an ideological manner. As one analyst observed, it was an

> approach to Soviet military writing from the standpoint of not learning how the Soviets actually thought and saw these matters but just seeing these writings as ammunition, selecting writings out of context and often unfairly ... It was an attention to the literature that buttressed a point of view rather than trying to get an understanding of the subject. Other evidence was ignored or dismissed as propaganda.[31]

Even if the authenticity of the claims which the right-wing critics made was accepted, the case they presented was a long way short of proving that the Soviet Union had an aggressive intent. If the professional debate among military strategists was to be taken as such evidence, then the Soviets could be equally forgiven for attributing aggressive intentions to the US.

The Assumption of Soviet Malice/Intentions

The claims of the right did not stop with a focus on Soviet doctrinal advantages, throw-weight and civil defence, however. Instead Moscow was attributed a ruthlessness which would allow it to act in a way which might seem reckless to western minds. Jones testified to Congress that 'I firmly believe that the present Soviet leadership would have no qualms in risking the loss of 20 million or so of its population.'[32] Pipes, using the Soviet defeat of Nazi Germany as evidence of an approach to war in which 'inured to casualties running into tens of millions, the Soviet generals tackled the job with relish', claimed that 'as of today the USSR could absorb the loss of 30 million of its people and be no worse off, in terms of human casualties, than it had been at the conclusion of World War II'.[33] For Pipes there was no distinction between the devastating losses suffered over several years by an invaded country fighting for its survival and the prospect of its leadership considering such action as a means to attain some unspecified advantage from the west. Instead, Pipes argued that a country which had lost so many of its citizens to wars, famine and purges 'must define "unacceptable damage" differently from the United States' and concluded from this that 'Such a country tends to assess the rewards of defence in much more realistic terms.'[34] Pipes's assumptions concerning the willingness of the Soviet Union to accept hugely disproportionate losses in pursuit of its foreign policy, however, does not explain Soviet caution in past crises such as that over Cuba. Nor does Pipes's correlation between war dead and attitudes towards present conflict stand up. Those Europeans who suffered considerably more war destruction than America were not less concerned about the prospect of nuclear war than the US despite their experiences.[35] For Pipes, however, the blend of Russian historical barbarism together with its modern layer of Godless communism was pointed to as further evidence of Soviet willingness to fight to win. While Pipes pointed to these characteristics as Soviet strengths in its competition with the West, still other right wingers warned of the dangers of its weakness.

Colin Gray, for one, wrote that '"the Soviet threat" in the 1980s flows from the dynamics of empire, from geopolitics – and fundamentally from weakness' with the result that 'the temptation to restructure the terms of this unequal competition, before it places the Soviet Union in an enduring position of inferiority, has to be substantial'.[36] Other observers, however, saw the weak legitimacy of the Soviet state over its multinational empire as a source of restraint rather than recklessness. For if, as Pipes argued, the continuation of the communist system was a higher concern than the survival of its people, then a destructive nuclear war killing proportionately vastly more Great Russians than ethnic Slavs and exposing the country to possible Chinese aggressive opportunism, Eastern European and Baltic secessionist and Pan-Moslem revivalism would not be a wise policy.[37]

The argument that Soviet official publications showed there was a 'doctrine gap' between a naive US and a ruthless Soviet Union willing to use nuclear war as an instrument of policy was based on bad research and shoddy logic. Not only were the Soviet sources selectively used and in many cases outdated, but the debate proceeded from an unforgivable ignorance of US operational strategic planning. It seems that experts on the USSR were wrong-footed by the strategic debate, while analysts of strategy used Soviet sources out of context of their wider political and strategic setting. In addition, assumptions and inferences were made from evidence which was then presented as fact when equally plausible explanations and interpretations were available giving an entirely contradictory view. Nevertheless, these views of what was perceived to be Soviet strategic doctrine gained a common currency in the political debate and were used to support the idea that the US ICBM force was vulnerable and that this vulnerability was of crucial concern for American national security. As Gray explained, the

> Soviet leadership would be most deterred by the credible prospect of a threat to the continuity of central political control in the USSR. Such a threat, in US targeting terms, entails prompt strikes against [the] military ... [and] the political-command structure of the Soviet state. This targeting design could be implemented, with confidence, only by a US ICBM force – the very leg of the strategic Triad proclaimed by Harold Brown to be under sentence of Soviet first-strike counterforce death.[38]

Thus Gray makes another linkage between the perceived adverse trends in the superpower strategic nuclear balance and the vulnerability of the US land-based missile force. It was this theoretical vulnerability which was to become the central metaphor for criticising the strategic policies of the US in the 1970s.

From the outset the philosophical divisions between the Carter administration and its critics in the CPD were clear. Nor was any concession given in the form of even junior appointments in the administration. As a result the critics were allowed to coalesce around individuals and issues critical of the administration and its influence on the Carter administration can only be understood from that perspective.

6 Carter, the MX and the Window of Vulnerability: The Political Context

Selling the Idea of ICBM Vulnerability

With the establishment of the Committee on the Present Danger immediately after Carter's election victory in November 1976 it was clear that the fate of these two different policy actors would be inextricably intertwined. On matters of foreign policy the CPD acted almost as an official opposition to the Carter White House in what was to be a fundamental debate on the very basis of Soviet–American relations. The CPD's role in this process was carefully considered. Incorporated as a nonprofit research and educational organisation, the Committee did not seek to reach a vast audience directly through TV and radio advertising, direct mail or a mass membership.[1] Instead, Rostow explained 'Seeing our special function in quite another light, we firmly rejected that advice.'[2] The Committee, as former staff member Charles Kupperman observed, 'is not a grassroots organisation. To the contrary ... [it] deliberately focused on the upper echelon of American public opinion leaders.'[3]

Nor was the CPD alone in this role, with a number of neo-conservative think-tanks such as the Heritage Foundation, the American Enterprise Institute and the Institute of Foreign Policy Analysis being formed in the 1970s.[4] While supportive of the activities and perspective of the CPD, however, none was as influential as the Committee itself. This was the case because the CPD was much more narrowly focused in its approach to security issues, much more explicitly political in its operations and much more distinguished in the expertise and experience of its members. Furthermore, in focusing on the SALT II Treaty the CPD had an issue at the heart of the administration's foreign policy which could be got at by the legislative process. Acting as a fount of information critical to the policies of the Carter administration, the Committee 'could be called the brains behind the opposition. While it does not lobby, it kindles the fire of those who do with its detailed analyses of strategic issues.'[5] Much of the actual leg work was left to other groups.

Working most closely with the Committee in its opposition to SALT II were the American Security Council (ASC), the American Conservative Union (ACU) and the Coalition for Peace Through Strength (CPTS). The ACU, for example, had a mass membership of 325 000 and produced and distributed an anti-SALT film. More influential still in Washington was the

ASC which in 1979 had a membership of 200000 and a budget of $4 million. As a lobbying organisation the ASC was not tax exempt or non-profit but it had built up a good working relationship with Congress since its establishment in 1955.

Thus this experience was able to complement that of the CPD whose members were veterans of the executive branch.[6] The relationship of the CPD to groups like the ASC was a useful division of labour. As a Committee staffer explained, 'We provide the intellectual underpinnings for the other groups who lobby Congress. The American Security Council take out full page ads, we hold press conferences, we have good access to the media because of the expertise we have on our board of directors.'[7] It was the ASC through its 'Operation Alert' campaign which pioneered the close monitoring of the voting records of Congressmen on national security issues in order to score their performance on a rating of 1–100. This information was gathered to use against liberal Congressmen in order to either modify their voting behaviour or campaign against their re-election.[8] Perhaps more influential in the campaign against SALT II, however, was the series of short films which the ASC produced, warning against what it considered were the trends in the strategic balance. The first of these, *Only the Strong,* which was shown on TV more than 800 times, was followed in 1978 by *The Price of Peace and Freedom* and then in 1979 by *The SALT Syndrome.* The latter was shown on television more than 600 times in 1979 alone and had a substantial influence on public attitudes toward the SALT II treaty.[9] Indeed, the Carter administration was so incensed by both the misrepresentations contained within this film and its widespread viewing, that it produced its own line-by-line rebuttal.[10] The impact of the images and message of this twenty-five-minute film, however, made available for showing to local church groups, veterans, fraternal associations and schools, was not countered by an official publication despite the convincing counter arguments.[11]

The other organisation which worked closely with the CPD in opposition to SALT was the Coalition For Peace Through Strength (CPTS) which originated in the ASC. Founded in 1978 the Coalition was an ad hoc umbrella group which brought together 177 organisations in the fight against the national security policies of the Carter administrations and claimed the support of over 200 Congressmen.[12] It worked very closely with the ASC and was itself a product of the lessons learned by the conservative opposition to the Carter administrations in their fight over the Warnke nomination and the ratification of the Panama Canal Treaties.[13] The most influential lesson of the Panama campaign was the use of computerised mailing lists as a fundraising and lobbying device which added between 250000 and 400000 new names to the conservative cause.[14] As Howard Philips of the Conservative

Caucus realised at the time, however, 'raw numbers alone won't do the job when you're up against something like the American foreign policy establishment. People look to experts for answers not to a group of outsiders.'[15] This was precisely where the CPD's expertise and standing came into its own and how the fusion of these different talents made such a formidable force.

Without spreading itself too thinly and by targeting the groups to which it spoke, the CPD was able both to focus its efforts and maintain its status as a high-level group of experts. Thus Nitze and others were able to concentrate their energies on press conferences to small numbers of specialist journalists who would then syndicate the CPD's analysis of the SALT process in a manner which served their purpose. Similarly, the CPD's executive committee and board members participated in several hundred TV and radio programmes, public debates, lectures and public forums, and during the Senate hearings on the SALT II Treaty testified on 17 different occasions. It was able to address these audiences with authority not only because of the expertise of its members, however. The CPD was also persuasive as a result of being privy to current, sensitive information from the Pentagon and the negotiations in Geneva on SALT and the strategic balance. 'The old channel between Rowney, who remained the Joint Chiefs' representative for SALT, and Richard Perle remained very much intact, and Nitze was sometimes cut in on the flow of information.'[16] Vance was caustic in his recollection of the critics' use of sensitive information, noting that many critics of SALT 'Felt no compunction about confidentiality. They released classified materials; they made false charges about US "concessions"; they published unsubstantiated allegations about Soviet cheating on the SALT I agreement.'[17] Not only did the CPD command the attention of the media and Congress, however. Aware of the attention which the Committee's ideas were attracting, the administration granted CPD officials access at the highest levels in order both to engage them in debate and to be seen to be taking their criticisms seriously. Accordingly, meetings were held with Brown, Brzezinski, Vance and Carter himself. At a meeting in the White House on 4 August 1977 Carter met the Committee hierarchy and engaged it in debate on its criticisms of SALT, only to be met by Nitze quietly murmuring 'No, no, no ...', to which Carter is reported to have replied, 'Paul, would you please let me finish?'[18] The meeting did not go well and served to illustrate the fact that while both parties were eager to influence the perspective of the other, they were effectively talking past each other and no return to a consensus on the national security debate was in prospect. The encounter probably damaged the administration more. Meeting with the executive branch at once strengthened the CPD's standing and legitimacy without exacting any concession. Furthermore, it presented a spectacle of a bipartisan consensus on national security policy being rejected by an administration increasingly seen as both partisan and outside the US foreign policy tradition.[19] Rather than an accommodation being reached as a result of the meeting, it ended with the realisation that the debate between the two was destined to be conducted before a wider audience and in the public rather than the private realm. For the CPD, the negotiation and subsequent attempt at ratification of the SALT II Treaty provided an ideal issue around which to conduct such a debate.

This conclusion was also reached by other groups critical of the policies of the Carter White House and concerned about the vulnerability of the US ICBM force. Amongst these was the Strategic Alternatives Team (SAT), an organisation chaired by CPD member William Van Cleave and containing many of the policy analysts who had done much to promote the idea of the growing urgency of the Soviet strategic threat. While the CPD and its allied groups campaigned for a general reversal in the security policy of the United States using the threat to the ICBM force as an example of the military threat that the US faced, SAT was much more narrowly focused on the precise danger which the Minuteman vulnerability question posed and how it could be remedied. As Van Cleave wrote at the time

> The group's concern was with a Soviet strategic threat that now seems very likely to peak relative to US capabilities in the early 1980s, well before the US could respond, given ordinary programme procedures and lead times.[20]

Group member Frank Barnett described their concern and purpose in more dramatic language,

> very shortly now, the Politburo in Moscow will have an 'open window' of military opportunity as a result of cumulative Soviet gains over the past fifteen years ... American ingenuity can help to 'close the window' with a series of quick improvisations that may afford us time to address the adverse balance.[21]

Nor was SAT interested in lobbying to promote its concern. Instead it saw its role as identifying the issues and the options and leaving the rest to other groups whose concerns and memberships overlapped. Nevertheless it produced an edited volume, *Strategic Options for the Early Eighties: What Can Be Done?* which provides a valuable insight into their views. Not only are the familiar vulnerability scenario arguments rehearsed but they are also extended and elaborated on. Contributors speculated about the prospect of Soviet missile-firing submarines sailing unchallenged through the undefended St Lawrence Seaway and into Hudson Bay, or Soviet tactical bombers being redeployed to Cuba after an initial attack on the US.[22] Although setting out to warn against the 'danger of embracing despondency and even defeatism' as the US passed through 'a "time valley" of maximum military peril', some of the contributions sounded as if the effects of 'Finlandisation' were already apparent. This is particularly true of Jones, who seemed to embrace appeasement when he argued that it was 'just unreasonable to expect that US leaders would avenge the death of that many Americans [10–12 million] by risking another 180 million ... with our present posture ... if we are threatened, we ought to give them what they ask for; if we are attacked we ought not to shoot back'.[23]

SAT's plans to remedy the deficiencies it perceived were equally radical in their view. In a crash programme lasting a thousand days SAT estimated that America could be made secure by massive new deployments of strategic armaments including more Minuteman IIIs, a new ICBM, an operational ABM system and a civil defence programme. The incompatibility of these programmes with the outline SALT II agreement was obvious. While Nitze argued that the administration should be persuaded to incorporate these plans into SALT, warning that 'no SALT' would 'at least in the short term, be an increase in the risk' and that 'The necessary actions are not going to be taken unless the Executive Branch is supportive', others disagreed.[24] Perle argued that 'The only way that I can see to move the Executive Branch to seriously entertain the kinds of proposals we have been discussing here is if SALT fails and is not ratified.' Van Cleave agreed, stating that 'If it is defeated, it is the strongest possible call to action.'[25] This debate among the strategic right was born of their frustration at having enough support to block the SALT II Treaty yet not enough to fund new programmes. This was a result of Senate votes in which a two-thirds vote was necessary for ratification while a simple majority was necessary to authorise or block new systems. Despite these disagreements in tactics among the strategic right, the group was united in its opposition to the Carter administration's security policies and in particular to SALT II.

Why Were the Critics Successful?

The success which the CPD and its associated groups achieved in their opposition to Carter's national security policy can be attributed to the fact that they were better organised, better resourced and more united than their opponents. Despite the numerous attempts by defence experts, both serving and retired, to counter the vulnerability argument advanced by the CPD, this perspective did not gain as much exposure or convince as many citizens as the message of vulnerability. Nor was there as large a network of organisations devoted to countering these messages as there was for their promotion. Not until efforts were made in preparation for the ratification of SALT II was a serious effort made to counter the arguments advanced by the Committee. 'Americans For SALT', for instance, was not formed until the summer of 1978, only a year before SALT II was signed. Thus the CPD, founded in November 1976, had a crucial time advantage during the long gestation period of the agreement in which to make their case against the Carter administration's efforts to modify Soviet strategic developments. As arms control lobbyist John Isaacs of the Council for a Livable World observed, 'By the time they got around to SALT and attempted to sell it, the debate had been won. They [the right wing] had too much time out there on their own to make their case.'[26]

While a core level of support remained for SALT II within the public, the CPD did much to erode this and delay the passage of the treaty. Thus when external events such as the 'discovery' of a Soviet Brigade in Cuba and then the invasion of Afghanistan occurred, the public and Congress were already predisposed to reject the treaty on the grounds that the Soviets could not be trusted. The critics were also helped in their cause by their use of leaked information, safe in the knowledge that the administration would not confirm the authenticity of this material by engaging in open debate. Indeed, not only were the teams from ACDA and the State department not allowed to acknowledge the authenticity of the opposition's material, they were also under strict guidelines as to what they could and could not say.[27] The result of this policy, as one Congressional staffer observed, was that

> The administration was too intellectual. It didn't scare people into saying this is the only way to avoid nuclear war. They didn't want to talk about dead babies so they talked instead about sublimits.[28]

This approach in turn was a result of the fact that the administration did not decide upon a clear strategy to deal with its critics early on. As one participant noted, 'They didn't know whether to sell the treaty on national security grounds or on disarmament grounds when they started out and instead they tried a mixed approach which just didn't work.'[29]

A further disadvantage was that there were no nongovernmental groups of equivalent status or performing the same role as the CPD. Americans For SALT, for instance, was an organisation aimed at influencing grass-roots opinion rather than elite opinion formers. Indeed, the pro-treaty organisations failed to develop a consensus of liberal opinion behind SALT II, with many critics on the left, such as Senators Hatfield and McGovern, remaining dissatisfied with the agreement for not being radical enough. As William Kincade (of the Arms Control Association) pointed out,

> The pro-treaty groups were not effective because they were not united. Nobody on the left is satisfied with half a loaf, and consequently they usually get nothing. That's what happened with SALT II.[30]

Lack of resources was also a severe handicap for the pro-treaty groups who spent as much of their time raising funds as they did promoting their cause. In all, the *Christian Science Monitor* estimated that SALT's foes spent 15 times more than its supporters in the battle for public support over the treaty.[31]

Even when groups supportive of the administration were formed, this was done largely in the context of SALT II which itself was presented as being useful to American security even though it did not directly address the vulnerability of the ICBM force. Thus one of the main pillars of the CPD's case was conceded by the supporters of SALT II who sought to defend the benefits of the treaty for what it did rather than for what it did not try to do. Such ground rules were not observed by the CPD who criticised both the failure of the treaty to address the question of throw-weight and the wider implications of the agreement. Even before the treaty was agreed, its prospect was welcomed by its critics as providing an opportunity for a much wider debate. Robert Ellsworth even argued that an agreement would further the cause of the critics in that:

> with a SALT Treaty, the public would become interested in the issue. You are going to have issues of *Newsweek* and *Time* devoted to the strategic balance ... For the first time since the ABM debate, the ordinary person who is halfway interested in these issues is going to start looking at what has been happening ... you could have the beginning of a ground swell in the opposite direction.[32]

This was certainly the way in which the CPD used the SALT debate, especially the Congressional hearings in which Committee members testified more times than all other expert witnesses combined.

Furthermore, and much to the annoyance of the Carter administration, the CPD did not limit its comments on these occasions to the terms of the treaty itself.[33] The CPD's testimony was skilfully handled to follow its own agenda, 'Time and again the hearings were turned away from the Treaty's alleged shortcomings to the larger accusation of the long-term decline in US defence posture.'[34] This policy was no accident, as Rostow himself explained, 'Now that SALT II has been signed ... the critical debate on the adequacy of our defence programme, indeed US foreign policy itself, has already begun to overshadow considerations by the US Senate of the Treaty terms.'[35] Such comments convinced the administration that these attacks were politically motivated rather than indicating specific concerns. As Vance indicated,

> There is no doubt that the Committee on the Present Danger had a great deal to do with undermining SALT. No question. And to hear people talk about a hopelessly flawed agreement ... they cannot tell you what is wrong with it. It leads you to believe that it is ideological rather than based on fact or hard thought.[36]

This point illustrates the fact that the SALT II treaty was not itself the main focus for attention. What it presented instead was an opportunity to voice its wider concerns about the more general state of the strategic balance.

Given the nature of this frontal assault it was even more remarkable that the administration did not do more to present its case and that it was slow to join battle directly with its critics.[37] In an internal White House document discussing meeting the CPD, a proposal to meet and brief 'progressive' (that is, supportive) groups was met with the hand-written response 'doubt need'.[38] Others remained unconvinced that the administration had done enough to face the critics. In June 1979 a *Wall Street Journal* opinion leader declared that if ratification failed, 'I think it will be possible to look back and say it is because the administration didn't start early enough to counteract Paul Nitze and others.'[39]

The CPD was also helped by factors linked to the American political process. Conservatives tend to lobby their representatives more than liberals and opponents more than supporters. Furthermore, in a system with multiple points of decision it is much easier to block than to advance a position.[40] The CPD also benefited from the simplicity of its message. Not only was the scenario easy to explain in short order but it was extremely difficult to refute without a long and detailed elaboration. To the general public it seemed a plausible scenario being advanced by experts. Even when the ACDA and the State Department finally made a concerted effort to sell the SALT II agreement by taking their case to middle America, the complexity and technical nature of the subject meant that the issue remained impenetrable. In reply to a simple and stark scenario of vulnerability and political defeat the administration was only able to offer qualifications on the threat to the Minuteman force and technical explanations as to the synergistic effect of the strategic Triad. As one congressional staffer observed, 'For the most part the issues were so arcane and technical that people didn't latch on. The right wing talked with such certainty while the administration said maybe this or that.'[41]

This was even the case in explaining the crucial point that the vulnerability of the ICBM force did not constitute the vulnerability of the deterrent as a whole. As one journalist, complaining of the difficulty in covering the story, explained, 'there is just no way that 50 000 words of talk about how to avoid a nuclear war with Russia can be reported conventionally ... the reporting challenge to both friend and foes of any sort of nuclear arms constraint treaties with Moscow can overwhelm you with "expert" testimony.'[42]

One of the strengths of the CPD, however, was its ability to engage in a technical debate with experts as experts and yet at the same time to present a case to the country at large which was persuasive in its simplicity. The Committee evoked nostalgic images of earlier episodes of strategic danger, warning that, 'The Soviet military buildup of all its armed forces over the past quarter century is, in part, reminiscent of Nazi Germany's rearmament in the 1930s.'[43] Rostow similarly declared that 'We are now living in a pre-war not a post-war world.'[44] While crude, the message was also direct in linking the growth of Soviet adventurism to the strategic nuclear balance. This linkage offered both explanation and solution. For the Committee America's declining influence was due not to a loss of economic leverage or an unwillingness to use or threaten the use of force in the aftermath of Vietnam, but simply to the strategic nuclear balance. It was able to reduce the multi-faceted domestic and international constraints on American power in the 1970s to a narrow technical strategic problem. As Johnson explained, in searching for a basis of international politics this is an easy way out: problems are defined in technical ways in order to be solved in a technical way.[45] Furthermore, it was a technical problem for which it had a solution readily at hand in the form of a strategic modernisation programme.

Once again ICBM vulnerability was being used instrumentally for other, in this case broader, political purposes. As Bowker and Williams point out, 'the CPD offered a counsel of hope rather than despair' in their argument that

> by an act of will the United States could regain its status as the dominant power in the international system. This contrasted starkly with President Carter's rhetoric, which increasingly emphasised not American leadership and strength of purpose – as it had done at the outset – but the need to cope with complexity and come to terms with the limits of power. Carter played into the hands of the critics as he seemed to offer pessimism and defeat rather than the regeneration he had initially promised.[46]

This tactic of the critics was perhaps most clearly visible in their assertion that there had been a 'decade of neglect' in US defence policy, particularly in procurement of strategic nuclear systems. While conveniently ignoring the American MIRV programme and the decisions to procure the MX and

Trident D5, this argument offered explanation and hope.[47] By blaming the failures of the past decade on the shortcomings of the American leadership rather than insurmountable world events, the critics were able to argue that this trend could be easily reversed with new, stronger leadership. This was a theme which Reagan was to make his own,

> the Soviet Union had been engaged in the most massive military buildup in history. Clearly, their goal was not to catch us up but to surpass us. Yet, the United States remained a virtual spectator in the 1970s, a decade of neglect that took a severe toll on our defense capabilities ... in the last half of the 1970s we were not deterring, as events from Angola to Afghanistan made clear. Today we are ... Gone are the days when the United States was perceived as a rudderless superpower, a helpless hostage to world events. American leadership is back. Peace through strength is not a slogan, it's a fact of life.[48]

The perception of weakness in the Carter administration was certainly a factor in the ability of its critics to drive home their message with as much success as they did. The activities of the Soviet Union and Cuba in the Horn of Africa, the fall of the Shah in Iran and the invasion of Afghanistan were international events with profound consequences on the way the Carter administration was viewed at home. Yet these events alone were not entirely responsible for the domestic mood which proved so receptive to the ideas of the critics. The change in the American mood can be traced back to the period between Carter's narrow electoral defeat of Ford and his inauguration. As Gaddis Smith has observed, Carter 'had the good fortune to ride into office on the waning hour of a vaguely anti-military tide of public and congressional opinions and the bad luck to take office just as that tide turned'.[49] This change in view toward foreign and defence policy was also recorded by the opinion polls. A Gallup Poll conducted in 1976, for example, concluded that 'public support for defense spending has increased to the highest point recorded over the last seven years'.[50] Indeed, in an early indication of some of the arguments which he would repeat as a member of the CPD, Rostow outlined his perception of the public mood to the Platform Committee of the Democratic Party Convention in May 1976 indicating that the views were present on the campaign trail;

> After a period of drift and uncertainty, the American spirit is recovering from the self-inflicted wound of the last decade. In this regard the lessons of opinion polls and primaries throughout the country is clear: A strong and angry tide of concern about the safety of the nation is running through the country ... On the chief issues of our foreign policy, our people are

ahead of our leaders, far more realistic, and far more aware of the true dimensions of the problems we face.[51]

Neither external events nor the changing internal political mood was entirely responsible for creating a climate receptive to the CPD's criticisms, however. Rather, the views and activities of the Carter administration in foreign and defence policy generally and over the threat to Minuteman in particular were also responsible for the rise of the vulnerability issue.

The Carter Administration and Defence Policy

Not least of these were the initial statements by Carter immediately after his election victory in 1976. Meeting with the Joint Chiefs of Staff at Blair House before his inauguration, Carter astonished the military by suggesting that the US could make do with a minimum deterrent capability of 200 nuclear weapons.[52] In his inaugural address Carter pledged that 'We will move this year toward our ultimate goal – the elimination of all nuclear weapons from this earth.'[53] Such ideas, which constituted a radical departure from the mainstream of the US foreign and defence policy tradition, did much to create an image of naivete in defence policy. These perceptions were accentuated by Carter's campaign rhetoric and his initial defence policy decisions. During the election Carter had promised to cut defence spending by between $5–$7 billion, a commitment which coloured the public's view of the administration even though defence spending actually increased beyond the level of the Ford administration. Clearly then the perception of the situation was more important than the reality.

What helped shape this public view was a series of high-profile decisions early in the term. Most notable of these was the announcement on 30 June 1977 of the cancellation of the B-1 bomber. This single act, which Vance described as Carter's most 'politically costly defence decision of his presidency', played straight into the hands of the critics. In presenting it as a cost-cutting exercise the administration handled the decision very badly. As Vance later conceded, 'given the ... concerns about the long-term strategic trends, more attention should have been given to finding ways to soften the impact of this decision on congressional and public attitudes about the administration's commitment to a strong defense'.[54] A similar impression of unilateral restraint was given by the decision to defer production of the Enhanced Radiation Weapon or neutron bomb in April 1978, a move which also lost Carter support among America's allies in Europe. Carter also slowed down the development of the MX and D5 missiles and in his fiscal year 1979 defence budget announced that the Navy's shipbuilding programme would suffer a 20 per cent cut in funding below that of the previous year.[55] Congressional feeling was so strong on this issue that they added funds to the defence budget for a fifth nuclear-powered aircraft carrier. This move was in turn met with a Presidential veto, an action which showed how out of step with opinion Carter was on such issues.

Carter's standing among right-wing opinion in Congress was also damaged as a consequence of his agreement of the Panama Canal Treaties in September 1977. Their ratification convinced many critics that Carter was unable or unwilling to stand up for America's interests abroad. At the same time the fierce debate which accompanied these decisions used up a great deal of Carter's political capital in the Senate.[56] This in turn created a hostile political climate for Carter's most controversial national security policy, the negotiation and agreement of the SALT II Treaty.

SALT: The Comprehensive Proposal

Carter's decision not to move immediately and exclusively to ratify the already agreed framework of the SALT II treaty negotiated at Vladivostok was a controversial decision motivated by a number of considerations. As former NSC aide William Hyland explained, one of these was that, 'Completing the Vladivostok accords seemed to Carter to be an admission of failure. Critics were arguing that it was not "real" arms control', and it was seen to be finishing off the old Republican administration's business.[57] Knowing that whatever agreement he signed would have to be negotiated through the Senate, Carter was very keen that it represented substantial progress rather than some of the earlier agreements which he regarded as 'cosmetic'. Carter later confided that 'I wanted to go much further than they had gone ... I wanted to have a much more dramatic reduction in nuclear arsenals.'[58] What this meant in terms of substance was a focus on the threat presented to US ICBMs by the Soviet force of heavy missiles, principally the SS-18. Specifically, the proposals called for a limitation on the number of missile test flights (to curtail accuracy improvements) and a plan to halve the number of Soviet large missiles, cutting the SS-18 force from 308 to 150, in exchange for the cancellation of MX.[59] If achieved, such a cut would indeed have been substantive but this was not the only reason for the form of Carter's 'Comprehensive Proposal' (CP) of March 1977. As deputy National Security Advisor David Aaron observed early in 1977, 'The whole issue of Minuteman vulnerability [was] coming up fast on the horizon' and Carter's Comprehensive Proposal was an attempt to 'stave off th[is] strategic problem'.[60] Moreover the Comprehensive Proposal was seen by Carter as a way to prevent the need for a new generation of ICBMs, and the reciprocation of a threat to the other's ICBM force which this implied. As Powers observes, Carter realised that, 'If SALT failed, unbelievable pressure would build for a big American land-based missile with enough accurate warheads to threaten Soviet silos.'[61] For Carter this meant an opportunity to swap the MX for a substantial reduction in the Soviet threat to Minuteman.

If he was to secure Congressional approval for an agreement which gave up the right to deploy this new American missile, however, Carter realised that the Treaty would also have to satisfy the demands of the defence policy hawks in the Senate. This, he knew, would be no easy task,

> I recognised that members of the Senate would be a much more difficult challenge because a substantial number of the senators will never support any agreement with the Soviet Union; ... nor one that puts any constraints on our ability to build our military arsenal ... my restraints were just as much with the Senate as they were at the bargaining table with the Soviets.[62]

Accordingly, Carter sought the advice of the Senate's recognised expert in these matters, Henry Jackson, in the formulation of his ideas for the Comprehensive Proposal. Not surprisingly, Jackson's long-standing concern with Minuteman vulnerability was much in evidence in the memo on SALT, drafted with his aide Richard Perle, which the Senator delivered to Carter in February, 1977.[63] Taken together it was these influences which shaped the formulation of the Comprehensive Proposal.

The Proposal was an attempt to take account of the concerns of the Pentagon and the Senate over ICBM vulnerability and fuse them with a plan for radical reductions. It was not, however, something which had been brokered with the Soviets who responded to both the substance and the form of the proposals with surprise and disbelief, rejecting it out of hand as not serious.[64] As one critic observes, 'In its eagerness to placate both sides of the domestic conflict, Soviet interests were overlooked, leaving the Russians feeling that they were being asked to bear the brunt of the administration's bargain with its critics at home.'[65] Not only did the CP set back the SALT process with the Soviet Union, however, its terms gave a hostage to fortune to the administration's critics. As Vance notes,

> The comprehensive proposal gave a weapon to anti-SALT and anti-detente hard-liners, who held up the deep-cuts proposal as the only standard against which to measure the success of the ultimate agreement. A SALT Treaty that contained limitations less stringent than the comprehensive proposal would be attacked as falling short of 'real arms control'.[66]

As such it was also used as evidence that the administration wanted to reduce the threat to Minuteman by arms control but was prevented from doing so by Soviet intransigence. The implication of this was that Carter accepted the analysis and warnings of the critics yet favoured an arms control agreement, any arms control agreement, with the Soviets to unilateral actions to redress the imbalance. The CP would be pointed to in the ratification debate over SALT II to illustrate the lack of provisions in the latter which addressed the threat to Minuteman.[67] The administration was constantly asked to justify its arms control and strategic programmes with reference to the objectives it outlined in the Comprehensive Proposals on reducing the threat to the Minuteman. The CP had set an impossible standard for the administration while at the same time giving ground to its critics in its apparent acceptance that the threat to Minuteman was something which it was vital for SALT to address. The real position, namely that Carter saw the need to address ICBM vulnerability as a domestic political issue rather than an external strategic problem, was a subtlety lost in the debate.

Criticisms of SALT II

Forced to abandon the CP in the face of Soviet intransigence, Carter eventually signed a SALT II Treaty on the basis of the Vladivostok accords. Having taken seven years to conclude, however, the critics' case against the agreement was well established by the time the public debate began. As a consequence of the activities of the CPD and others, particularly over SALT II, considerable damage was done to the reputation of the administration's national security policy. Furthermore, it was the failure of the treaty to redress the threat to the ICBM force which generated most opposition to the agreement.

The continued reliance in the Treaty on missile launchers as the primary unit of account rather than of throw-weight was particularly alarming for the critics. Nitze, for example, derided the limits on launchers as 'almost meaningless', 'counterproductive' and 'the wrong currency' on the grounds that the 'number of RVs is a secondary consideration' to throw-weight.[68] To critics, throw-weight mattered because of its potential for fractionation, that is, putting greater numbers of smaller warheads on large missiles. Reliance on launchers as the unit of account, it was thus argued, was an inadequate measure for limiting the number of actual warheads on each side. Thus Kissinger testified that 'The danger to our security derives from warheads, not from launchers, and the Soviet total of ICBM warheads will increase from 3200 at the time of the signing of SALT to over 6000.'[69] This argument was made despite the fact that SALT II put ceilings on the throw-weight and launch-weight of light and heavy ICBMs and froze the number of re-entry vehicles on specific types of ICBMs and SLBMs.[70] The development of cold launch technology facilitating silo reload, the critics argued, also allowed for the stockpiling of missiles and thus the potential for treaty breakout. This argument was also used against the idea that the treaty would actually reduce the Soviet arsenal in that the missiles removed from redundant silos could be stockpiled in readiness for use elsewhere.[71] The absence of any provision in the treaty for counting missiles in warehouses or of any possibility of verifying such an agreement was also cited against SALT II.[72] Furthermore, the failure of the Interim Agreement to prevent the deployment of the SS-19 as a replacement for the much smaller SS-11 by placing limits on the dimensions of missile silos was cited as evidence of the futility of an indirect approach to reducing throw-weight. The fact that the Soviet Union had ignored the American unilateral statement appended to the Interim Agreement in order to do this was taken as evidence both of Soviet duplicity and the importance with which they regarded such a gain in throw-weight.

Of equal concern to those who saw throw-weight as a measure of the threat to Minuteman was the provision in the Treaty which allowed the Soviet Union alone to deploy its pre-existing force of 308 'heavy' ICBMs.[73] This was especially so in the light of Secretary of Defense Schlesinger's testimony in 1975 that the Soviet SS-18 could carry as many as 45 MIRVed warheads of the size carried by the US Poseidon missile while the SS-19 could carry 25.[74] Thus the SS-18 force alone could deploy 13 875 MIRVed warheads. Although SALT II limited MIRV warhead numbers on the SS-19 to 6 and the SS-18 to 10, the critics argued that adherence to those limits would be difficult to verify. Similar concern with regard to a Soviet breakout from the treaty was expressed with regard to the SS-20, which as a theatre nuclear system was excluded from the treaty, but which the critics argued could be easily converted into an SS-16 by the addition of a third-stage rocket.[75] The Backfire bomber could also be made strategic, it was claimed, by the addition of a refuelling probe.

A related concern was the implications of the limited duration of the treaty. Five years was seen as an insufficient time-frame in which to place meaningful limits on new weapons systems given the long lead times necessary to develop and deploy strategic forces. Soviet and American defence planners, it was explained, would need to make assumptions about the other's strategic programmes after 1985, and SALT II would offer little help in this planning process.[76] In an extension of this argument it was also pointed out that SALT II's limits reducing the number of warheads which could be targeted against the MX in its Multiple Protective Shelter (MPS) provided no benefit. Due to delays in MX development and the difficulty in deciding a basing mode, the MX/MPS would not have been operational until the period between 1986 and 1990, after the treaty had expired in 1985.[77] This argument in turn gave rise to the suspicion that the administration was working under the assumption that the agreement would be extended beyond the initial time-frame in much the same way as the Interim Agreement had been. This, the critics argued, could be used as a justification for inaction in strategic modernisation without any guarantee of Soviet compliance. As part of this concern, the fear was expressed that limitations agreed to in the three-year protocol would be extended beyond this time period. Thus the deployment of cruise missiles and mobile ICBM schemes such as the MX/MPS would be delayed or cancelled as a result of the precedent set by the protocol. Kissinger warned,

> the Soviets know the history of moratoria and protocols very well; they are aware that such 'provisional' agreements almost never end on their expiration date, especially if a negotiation is then taking place. At a minimum the Protocol's terms will be the point of departure for the next round of negotiations.[78]

Thus, not only were the supposed benefits of the treaty criticised for being illusory but the agreement was castigated for actually and potentially inhibiting the United States from taking unilateral action which could better improve its security. This argument was made with particular reference to the threat to the ICBM force, though it was also applied to the European balance. Typical of the arguments is Kissinger's statement that,

> The Treaty does not reduce the Soviet first-strike capability against our land-based forces, or improve our ability to survive a first strike. It does not diminish the Soviet residual capability to destroy civilian targets in the United States. And it does not enhance – indeed it may slightly inhibit – the possibility for the United States to catch up in the capability of our strategic forces to attack military targets.[79]

The substance of these criticisms was based on the premise that SALT did not sufficiently compensate the US for the Soviet advantage in throw-weight and, additionally, that alternative ways to mitigate the threat to Minuteman were prevented by the agreement. Specifically, Rostow and Nitze wanted a 'quick fix' to the ICBM vulnerability problem by the immediate construction of 'a great many Minuteman IIIs; and to deploy them in multiple vertical protected shelters'.[80] Such action it was argued, prohibited by the treaty, would be a better safeguard against the consequences of ICBM vulnerability than SALT. Similarly, the prohibition of cruise missiles under the protocol was criticised for putting the requirements of arms control above security. Because cruise missiles were difficult to verify, it was argued, the United States was being denied this opportunity to offset the threat to the Minuteman force through a new offensive capability. As Burt argues, 'The irony, of course, is that although cruise missiles posed a threat to SALT, their deployment in large numbers would be more likely to strengthen than to weaken deterrence.'[81]

A similar argument was made over the plans to deploy the MX in an invulnerable basing mode. It seemed that all the options which would increase its survivability were in some way limited by SALT. Multiplying the number of both missiles and launchers was limited by the new agreement, while defending the MX with an active ABM system was severely constrained by the 1972 ABM Treaty.[82] Furthermore, the ability to deploy the MX using concealment and mobility was hampered both by the need for verification by remote 'national technical means' and by the provision in the protocol limiting mobile systems for three years. A further complication to the MPS deployment plan was the Soviet complaint that each of the individual missile shelters should be counted as a launcher.[83] It was partly for this reason that the Carter administration had decided to deploy the MX in a horizontal rather than a vertical MPS scheme. This decision was much criticised for its additional cost, $7 billion, and for being less hardened.[84] The capability of the horizontal MPS deployment to allow the MX a 'dash' capability between shelters was dismissed by the critics as unnecessarily expensive, making it cost effective for the Soviets to build more warheads to overcome it.

In short, for the critics, the failure of SALT II to reduce those areas of Soviet advantage which presented a threat to Minuteman or prevented it from being reduced was a shortcoming of the treaty. Even outlandish provisions which could possibly offset the threat to Minuteman, such as a ban on ICBM deployment on surface ships, were seized upon as having given unnecessary concessions to Moscow.[85] The testimony of the critics was uniform in its warning of the impending vulnerability of the US ICBM force and the peril which this presented for US security and diplomatic freedom of action.

While initially unpersuaded that the growing theoretical threat to the US ICBM vulnerability force was a cause for serious concern, the administration was forced to reassess this position for a mixture of strategic and political reasons.

The Carter Administration and the Window of Vulnerability

For the most part, on coming to office, Carter's national security team was highly dubious about the threat implied by the growing theoretical

vulnerability of the US ICBM force. This was certainly the case with Carter
and his two principal advisors Cyrus Vance and Harold Brown.[86] In November
1976 on the campaign trail, Carter, the former nuclear submariner,
declared that

> There would be no possibility under the sun that a first strike capability
> could be adequate in preventing mass destruction of the country that
> initiated the strike ... There is no way to prevent a massive retaliatory strike
> because, for all practical purposes, atomic submarines are invulnerable.[87]

Defense Secretary Harold Brown made a similar point in testimony, explaining
that the vulnerability scenario 'has never seemed realistic to me', because
of the capability of the submarine force to retaliate against unhardened
military targets. Adding 'The only thing missing from this scenario is the
capability to hit their strategic ICBM's within half an hour instead of ten hours.
I submit that it is not a central issue in the midst of thermonuclear war.'[88]
This assessment was also shared by the Deputy Secretary of Defense for
Research and Engineering, William Perry, in his analysis of the development
of the MX.[89] Perry was also unimpressed by the vulnerability scenario on
the basis of his calculations that, even with increased accuracy, the Soviets
would have needed to target two or three warheads against every Minuteman
silo in order to have even reasonable confidence of destroying them. Perry
drew further comfort from the consideration that even if this capability were
achieved it was most likely that a number of missiles would miss or
malfunction and that the warheads would still have to overcome the problem
of fratricide.[90]

This assessment of the implications of the state of the Minuteman force
was reinforced by two studies conducted in the early months of the new
administration. The first of these was Presidential Review Memorandum
(PRM) 10, *Comprehensive Net Assessment and Military Force Posture
Review*, which was an interagency review of the overall relationship between
the superpowers. Initiated on 18 February 1977 it lasted five months and was
presided over by Sam Huntington of the NSC. The section of the review which
looked at the 'details of the military balance' was Annex C, entitled *Military
Strategy and Force Posture Review*. It was conducted by the Office of the
Assistant Secretary of Defense for International Security Affairs.[91] The
Review's conclusions were both sanguine and optimistic about the central
deterrent relationship in general and the prospects of withstanding a surprise
attack in particular. If a central nuclear exchange did take place, it concluded
that 'neither side could conceivably be described as a winner'. Nor, it went
on, would there be any advantage to either side in launching a limited nuclear
attack against the other's land-based ICBM forces, because 'whichever side

initiates a limited nuclear attack against the ICBM forces of the other side will find itself significantly worse off' in terms of surviving numbers of missiles and missile warheads.[92]

These findings were reinforced by a second, parallel study conducted by the President's science advisor, Frank Press. Also initiated in early 1977 this analysis was conducted by the Office of Science and Technology Policy and looked at both the need for a new ICBM and the proposed basing mode for the MX, the buried trench scheme. It too concluded that while the Minuteman would one day be vulnerable this would probably not be until the mid-eighties at the earliest, and, as Edwards reports, 'even when it was vulnerable, there would be so many uncertainties associated with an attack on it that it was not a serious military option'.[93]

It was on the basis of these findings that Carter reversed the Ford administration's decision for 'full-scale development' of the MX and opted for 'advanced development'. Cutting the Air Force's request by $100 million in the September 1977 annual budget review, Carter was responding in part to these studies which sought to play down the timing and the implications of the threat to Minuteman. Funding for the MX was also slowed in order to prevent the missile getting out of synchronisation with a survivable basing mode following analysis by the Press study which cast doubt on the technical feasibility of the buried trench scheme.[94] Concerned to use the deployment of MX as an opportunity to alleviate the vulnerability of the US ICBM force, Carter and Brown trimmed the pace of the new missile in order to ensure that its arrival in service coincided with a survivable mode in which to base it. This decision reflected the general view of the administration at the time, that while neither urgent nor menacing, the growing threat to the Minuteman force was a problem which it would be prudent to take measures to rectify in the longer term. This position, however, was to be reversed during the remainder of Carter's single term in office.

The Carter administration gradually accepted the agenda of its critics in strategic policy for a number of interrelated reasons. The most obvious of these was a result of the central foreign policy tension of the administration created by the very different attitudes towards the Soviet Union held by Secretary of State Cyrus Vance and National Security Advisor, Zbigniew Brzezinski. This tension also extended to the different views which both men held with regard to the purpose and state of the American strategic deterrent. For Vance the nuclear deterrent was to deter a central attack on the US, and provided that this condition of mutual vulnerability was maintained then deterrence was stable. As part of this view he also believed that the prospect of such a conflict created stability which prevented lower level conflicts. Thus

Vance shared Carter and Brown's relaxed views as to the implications of
the growing vulnerability of the US ICBM force.

For Brzezinski, however, nuclear weapons were required to do more than
act as passive deterrents of central war. Instead, he viewed the potential utility
of nuclear weapons, and indeed their perceived utility, in situations short of
central war as vital to the interest of the US. Accordingly, for Brzezinski the
prospect of ICBM vulnerability mattered because of the adverse way in which
it might be perceived. Indeed Carter's National Security Advisor was to prove
central in promoting the idea within the administration that the American
deterrent was inadequate in the face of the threat to the ICBM force.

Soviet Missile Tests and the Window of Vulnerability

The biggest cause of readjustment in the Carter administration's view of the
threat to the Minuteman force resulted from events outside the US.
Specifically, in late October and early November 1977, US satellite
intelligence recorded a series of six Soviet missile tests which had alarming
implications. To the CIA it was immediately obvious that the Soviets had
made a major breakthrough in their missile accuracy. What was even more
alarming was the fact that they were testing this on modified versions of their
existing heavy missiles, the SS-18 and SS-19s.[95] They had built an entirely
new front end for the heavy missiles. Powers cites a CIA analyst explaining
that,

> They built a whole new post-boost vehicle – new accelerometers, better
> timings of RV releases, with more aerodynamic stability for RVs, they
> began to spin their RVs on re-entry the way we do. They were really
> cranking it down. We reported, 'Oh shit! the modification is going
> to work!'[96]

These tests suggested that the Soviets were going to retrofit their existing
missiles with a better guidance system rather than wait until the next
generation of missile to improve their accuracy. While this was precisely
what the US was already doing by fitting the Mark 12A warhead to its
Minuteman III force it had not expected the Kremlin to be in a position to
do likewise. US calculations that the threat to the Minuteman force was
unlikely to emerge until between five to eight years time were based on this
assumption. Accordingly, in reporting this development to Brown in
November 1977, Perry warned

> I think we have a problem. The preliminary information we have indicates
> that the Soviets have tested a new guidance system and placed it on their

current systems. It will advance the threat to our land based force. We are going to have to watch this very closely.[97]

The implications of these missile tests became increasingly apparent throughout the remainder of 1977 and into 1978 as more tests confirmed that Moscow had perfected this capability and was engaged in its deployment. Rather than the threat to Minuteman coinciding with the deployment of its follow-on system, there would now be a time period during which the US ICBM force would become increasingly threatened before this gap could be plugged by deployment of the MX in an invulnerable basing mode. The Soviets would now be able to achieve an 80 to 90 per cent probability of kill on Minuteman by targeting two warheads to a silo in 1981 or 1982 rather than 1985 as originally envisaged.[98] As Pentagon officials, such as James Wade, plotted Minuteman survival rates after a hypothetical Soviet attack, the ICBM force looked disproportionately vulnerable in this time-frame compared to the period before and after it. As Powers explains,

> The graph line swerved way down as fewer and fewer American land-based missiles could be expected to survive. It would not swerve up again until the late 1980s, when new American missiles – the MX ... would begin to be deployed. Wade described this dip in the graph line as the 'bucket of vulnerability'.[99]

As news leaked out of these developments the critics of the administrations' strategic policies seized on these new revelations as further evidence of their case. In particular the period of heightened ICBM vulnerability was portrayed as a likely time period in which the CPD's scenario would be put into effect to intimidate the US. This period of time would present the Soviets with an opening, a window, in which to take an opportunity. This developed in the critics' writings into the shorthand phrase a 'window of opportunity'. Later this expression was more specifically melded together with the vulnerability of the ICBM force to become the 'window of vulnerability'.[100] This phrase gave the vulnerability scenario a name, a label which was both technical and scientific-sounding and yet also was very menacing. It was to become a metaphor not only for the specific threat to the Minuteman force but for the feeling of decline and insecurity which Americans felt as a whole in the late 1970s. In linking these two levels together, however, it presented an opportunity for critics to point to a technical issue on which the Carter administration was allegedly deficient and to promote a catchy slogan which people could identify as symbolic of the way they viewed their country's position in the world. It was also a slogan and an issue which took off in a substantial way in the campaign against SALT

II in 1979 and which was popularised widely by candidate Reagan in the 1980 Presidential race.

The discovery of the Soviet accuracy improvements advanced the issue of Minuteman vulnerability to political prominence in 1978 in an unprecedented way. Indeed, Richard Thornton argues that for Carter this 'sudden, unexpected, and disadvantageous turn in the strategic weapons balance ... was undoubtedly the single most significant development affecting – no, dominating – his Presidency'.[101] This interpretation exaggerated, for while these developments forced the administration to address this subject more seriously than it had done previously, its impact on the Carter White House was gradual and complementary rather than immediate and decisive. There was some concern, not least because the MX missile scheduled to relieve the vulnerability problem in the mid-1980s had been slowed in its development as a result of the buried trench deployment mode being technically inadequate. There was also genuine surprise within the administration that this breakthrough could have occurred.[102] For the critics, and especially the members of the Team B exercise who had warned of this possibility, the fact that the administration was surprised was used as evidence of its naivety and unsuitability to govern.

Under the influence of such criticism the administration looked once again at the issue and implications of ICBM vulnerability. Carter's instinctive reaction was to push ahead with the SALT process as a way of structuring the evolution of the superpower arsenals in a controlled way and of containing the threat to Minuteman. Of particular concern in this regard was the development of the MX. The progress of the MX was not only worrisome because of the impact of its delay on Soviet–American relations but because this would give succour to the administration's critics who were demanding large-scale strategic deployment programmes as a response to these developments. Perry in particular was very keen to advance the progress of the missile in the light of the Soviet tests. As an insider remarked, 'Perry was so unnerved that he pulled the emergency whistle on the MX and so that's what got things going in the winter of '78/'79 ... it was just lolling along before that.'[103] Despite this desire to see the MX deployed, however, Perry, like Brown, was reluctant to advance the missile without a basing mode and testified to Senator McIntyre's sub-committee in early 1978 that

> we think there are very significant technical difficulties in the programme
> as now conceived. As a result of this, we are not today in a position to
> recommend going into full scale development on this programme, nor do
> we have any confidence that we will be in that position by October, which

is the date that the full scale development decision was originally scheduled to be made.[104]

This conclusion, however, was tempered by the news of the Soviet missile tests and a number of studies were conducted as to how the problem could be addressed. Brown asked the MX Program Office at Norton Air Force Base to look at the alternative basing modes available for the missile and convened a Defense Science Board panel under Michael May of the Lawrence Livermore Laboratory to conduct a parallel analysis of the options.[105] The Air Force Systems Command also began a study of its own on the question. After exhaustive study all three investigations concluded that the threat to the Minuteman force needed to be taken account of, that the MX was indeed necessary but that the trench idea was technically flawed. The May panel in particular had gone over a variety of air- and sea-based deployment schemes before coming back to favour a mobile land-based deployment. It recommended a system with many more hard points than there were missiles, thus employing concealment, deception and mobility.[106] After various internal wrangles the Air Force also came down in favour of this scheme for a vertical shelter Multiple Aim Point (MAP) system. However, two problems dogged the proposed system. First, the missiles would take 24 hours to move between shelters, meaning that they would be vulnerable if their Preservation of Location Uncertainty (PLU) was compromised. Second, it was unclear whether the shelters proposed would be designated as 'launchers' under SALT counting rules, creating problems for an arms control agreement. Accordingly, a decision on the MX basing mode was put off until August 1978. If the administration was to go ahead with MX as a way of addressing the vulnerability issue it wanted to do so in the context of SALT.

Thus, while acting as a spur to decide on an invulnerable basing mode for the MX, the growing concern with the threat to the Minuteman force was not decisive in itself in persuading the administration to embrace the arguments of its critics. This is evident from Secretary Brown's Annual Report for Fiscal Year 1979, delivered on 2 February 1978.

In recognising that the MINUTEMAN vulnerability problem is a serious concern for us, we also realize that the Soviets would face great uncertainties in assessing whether they would have the capability we fear – and still greater uncertainties as to its military or political utility. On all the technical judgements – how accurate the missiles are, how reliable, how well the system would work in actual practice, whether they could explode two re-entry vehicles on each silo without excessive fratricide, or only one – we, quite properly, are conservative, from our point of view. Similarly, the Soviets must make cautious assumptions from their perspective. In particular, they must recognise the formidable task of actually executing (as planned) a highly complex massive attack in a single cosmic throw of the dice.

[and further]

vulnerability of MINUTEMAN is a problem, but even if we did nothing about it, it would not be synonymous with the vulnerability of the United States, or even of the strategic deterrent. *It would not mean that we could not satisfy our strategic objectives.* It would not by itself even mean that the United States would lack a survivable hard target capability or that we would necessarily be in a worse post-exchange position in terms of numbers of weapons, payload, or destructiveness.[107]

Clearly then, despite the improvements in Soviet accuracy Brown in early 1978 did not regard the threat to Minuteman as anything other than an unfortunate development affecting one part of the strategic Triad. This view, however, was to change over the remainder of Carter's term. Critical to that change of view was the influence which Brzezinski and his NSC staff had on Carter and Brown in altering their view of nuclear war. The impact of the improvements in Soviet accuracy had raised the issue of ICBM vulnerability to prominence and this in turn had helped focus Carter on the arcane subject of nuclear strategy.

The President was unusually diligent in the attention which he gave to this subject.[108] As Powers observes, 'Carter was the first President ever to study seriously what his role in fighting a nuclear war would be like.'[109] This interest was heightened as a consequence of a series of Command Post Exercises conducted by the NSC which showed the provisions for actually executing a nuclear war to be shambolic. A participant, General Rosenberg, described one such exercise as 'a nightmare, just a complete disaster'.[110] Carter's typical thirst for detail in policy matters meant that he became absorbed in the subject. As NSC aide General Bill Odom explains,

he really got into the procedures, ran through numerous scenarios, and became very comfortable with it ... He wanted to be able to be awakened at three o'clock in the morning and not be confused, and understand what he was going to have to see, or what he was about to hear; what the voice would sound like on the other end of the line, and that sort of thing.[111]

Carter's detailed involvement in the mechanics of this process went a long way in persuading him to move away from his original positions on nuclear weapons. This was precisely what Brzezinski had intended by initiating a series of studies on strategic warfare early in the administration. 'My hope' he wrote 'was that these memoranda would spur within the Defense Department a broader review of our strategic doctrine and also interest the President himself in this difficult and complicated issue'.[112]

The Conversion of the Carter White House

Brzezinski did not share the predominant view of the administration on deterrence. For him 'nuclear weapons have a very rightful place in a global conflict, not just in a spasm tit-for-tat'.[113] This view was reflected in the staff he appointed and the conclusions which their studies reached.[114] Following on from PRM-10 the first of these studies was Presidential Directive (PD) 18, issued in August 1977. This document reaffirmed the retention of NSDM 242 pending further review and set in motion a series of studies. There were three main reviews together with numerous other supporting studies. The main studies were a Nuclear Targeting Policy Review (NTPR), a study on the modernisation of the ICBM force, and a review of the secure reserve force (particularly C^3I required to support it).[115] These studies, begun early in the administration, started to come to fruition in mid-1978. It was this time that Brzezinski identified as the 'takeoff phase' for many of his efforts for 'doctrinal innovation'.[116] Working inside the White House and with the Pentagon, Brzezinski's NSC brought some of the views and arguments of the strategic right to bear on the formulation of Carter's defence policy. As Brzezinski notes,

> Their impact on their colleagues in DOD was significant, and Harold Brown's associates worked closely with them. There thus developed a fruitful and constructive interchange, with Harold Brown gradually becoming himself more involved in the effort to generate strategic renewal.[117]

The result of this Trojan Horse-like operation was the gradual persuasion of key figures in the Carter administration to an acceptance of the need for more strategic options and capabilities for the execution of nuclear war. Starting in September 1978 Carter gave his approval to these recommendations by signing a series of Presidential Directives, PDs 41 to 59, which gave sanction to these changes. PD 41, for example, accepted the idea 'that civil defence, like strategic defence, is part of the overall balance'.[118] Similarly, other studies were premised on the idea, popularised by the CPD and the Team B exercise and now apparently accepted in the Carter administration, that Soviet strategic doctrine was inherently war-fighting. As Sloss and Millet explain,

Policy makers came to share more widely conclusions that had long been advanced by a number of expert observes of the Soviet Union: namely that Soviet decision makers considered victory to be possible in a nuclear war and that they were actively prepared to achieve such a victory, should a nuclear war occur.[119]

The most substantial review undertaken as part of this series, however, was the Nuclear Targeting Policy Review (NTPR) conducted by Leon Sloss at the Pentagon and presented to Harold Brown in December 1978. It was this study which provided the basis for the most far-reaching revision in US strategic doctrine and which was eventfully signed by President Carter in July 1980 as PD 59. This study, which was in part an update of NSDM 242, set out a revision in the US target list and also spelled out the need for a C^3I capability able to survive and able to execute a protracted nuclear exchange. Soviet targets, it explained, were growing both more numerous and increasingly hardened and were able to withstand blast overpressures of 4500 pounds per square inch. By comparison, the study found an alarming degree of vulnerability in the US infrastructure for nuclear war. This was not, however, the vulnerability of the ICBM force but rather the weakness of the communications system, what Powers describes as 'the wiring for an extended nuclear war, the C^3I, which would allow the nation to negotiate while it fought in the hope that a war might be ended'.[120]

This conclusion is particularly interesting with regard to the ICBM vulnerability issue in that it shows that, at the policy level, it was not the survivability of weapons systems which caused most concern. Indeed, Powers cites an analyst who worked on the study as saying that 'We could live with the current inventory [of weapons] as long as we got the C^3.'[121] Nor was this situation a revelation when in 1980 a special Presidential Directive on telecommunication policy, PD 53, was published. Steinbruner and Garwin made the point in 1976 that 'hardened fixed site missiles' are less vulnerable than 'the command channels and the communications and information processing systems which service the command structure'.[122] This was also the conclusion of Strat-X in 1968. The concern with the original threat to the Minuteman force from the SS-9 was based in part on the belief that this force of 300 missiles was most likely targeted at the 100 Launch Control Centers (LCC) which would have fired Minuteman rather than the ICBM silos themselves.[123] This point only reinforces the idea that the concern with ICBM vulnerability was as much about the fact that the missiles were highly visible political symbols of a presumed military weakness as it was for an actual concern with the forces themselves. It also shows that the ICBM vulnerability issue became a political issue not because this vulnerability was a pressing political problem in its own right, but as a by-product of other concerns. The fact the C^{3}I vulnerability did not become a political issue, while the less critical threat to the Minuteman force did, shows the primarily political construction of this issue.

The Carter administration Presidential Directives do not in themselves explain the shift in attitudes within the Executive branch with regard to ICBM vulnerability, except in a general sense of the hardening in attitudes towards the Soviet Union and to nuclear weapons. While the acceptance as part of the NTPR of a decision to abandon the conceptional distinction between theatre and strategic nuclear weapons enhanced the importance of the use of ICBMs for selective limited strikes, this would have no relevance to the latter's vulnerability since it would be inappropriate to respond to an attack on the Minuteman force in such a fashion. The NTPR did make a case for the MX, however, as a source of additional hard-target kill capability in order to deal with more numerous and harder targets. Such a case would have been difficult to make on its own merits given past Congressional opposition to these developments. The need for the MX to forestall the threat of ICBM vulnerability, however, would have been a much less difficult political hurdle to overcome. It was partly for this reason that Harold Brown delayed the NTPR for 15 months, refusing Brzezinski and Odom's suggestion that it be completed as a Presidential Directive, in order to establish the force of their arguments within the bureaucracy. As Edwards reports,

> Brown did not want the draft to go forward because he saw that, by raising again the question of countersilo strikes and limited nuclear war, the decision to deploy MX would be complicated. He believed that MX should be presented as a means of stabilising the arms race, of making US missiles less vulnerable, and that the countersilo, damage limitation, first strike implications of a system that would be able to take out the entire Soviet missile force in one thirty-minute attack, should be hidden.[124]

The way to hide this most effectively was for Brown to accept the ICBM vulnerability argument in a more persuasive way than he had hitherto done. He already accepted that the ICBM force was becoming vulnerable and that it needed to be replaced. Throughout 1979 and 1980 Brown's statements began to indicate that he had embraced the idea that the perception of ICBM vulnerability was indeed an important consideration in strategic policy. This argument was of course supportive of the idea that ICBM vulnerability mattered in a political sense and thus supportive of the MX as the adminis-tration's answer to that problem. The familiar pattern in which ICBM vulnerability was embraced to serve other political purposes was once again being repeated. Accordingly, Brown, in June 1979, two months before a crucial NSC meeting on the future of the MX, told an audience at the Council On Foreign Relations that 'the growing vulnerability of our land-based missile forces could, if not corrected, contribute to a perception of US strategic inferiority that would have severely adverse political – and could have potentially destabilising military – consequences'.[125] This statement was in marked contrast to his FY 1979 Annual Report which stated that 'the vulnerability of MINUTEMAN is a problem, but even if we did nothing about it ... *It would not mean that we could not satisfy our strategic objectives.*'[126] The evolution of Brown's thinking is evident elsewhere. In his FY 1980 Annual Report he explained that,

> it can be argued that a decision not to modernize the ICBM force would be perceived by the Soviets, and perhaps by others, as demonstrating US willingness to accept inferiority ... Others could argue, however, that such a decision could be viewed as playing to US strengths in SLBMs and cruise missiles rather than investing in an inherently less survivable element of our strategic forces. My own judgment lies between these alternatives, but closer to the former view.[127]

By the time of his FY 1981 Report his judgement had clearly swung to this view, with the announcement that essential equivalence required that

> We need forces of such a size and character that every nation perceives that the United States cannot be coerced or intimidated by Soviet forces. Otherwise the Soviets could gain in the world, and we lose, not from war, but from changes in perception about the balance of nuclear power. In particular we must insure that Soviet leads and advantages in particular areas are offset by US leads or advantages ... we must also insure that the Soviet Union does not have a monopoly of any major military capability.[128]

The latter point was a clear reference to MX. Indeed, Brown's FY81 Report reiterated many of the points which he made in his August 1980 Newport Address in which he took the idea of perception within essential equivalence to new heights in outlining the countervailing strategy. In this speech, not only did Brown embrace the importance of perception in defence policy, he also seemed to accept the criticism of the right that the 1970s was indeed a decade of neglect, stating that

> our investment in strategic programs in that decade was less than one-third of what the Soviets spent on their strategic programs. If we had let that trend continue, we would have faced, by the mid-1980s, at best a perception of inferiority, at worst a real possibility of nuclear coercion.[129]

This level of abstraction, whereby US value for money in comparative defence spending could lead to it being coerced with nuclear weapons, was almost matched by the contorted way in which the MX was justified. Eager to present the MX as a stabilising development, despite its highly accurate ten warheads with their unparalleled hard-target kill capability, Brown declared that 'MX survivability is evidence that we plan our strategic forces in a retaliatory role. A survivable system is *less* threatening than the vulnerable one it replaces.'[130] While less easy to attack and therefore less of an invitation for a counterforce strike, the MX would, however, be a more attractive prize were such an attack successful. Moreover, its own counterforce capability together with its invulnerability would make it highly threatening as far as the Soviet Union was concerned. These arguments were not intended to convince the Soviets, however. Instead they were meant to persuade Congress to accept both the MX and the Carter administration's SALT II Treaty, the futures of which had become inextricably intertwined by the middle of 1979.

SALT, MX and ICBM Vulnerability

Having failed to pre-emptively disarm those concerned with the vulnerability issue through its Comprehensive Proposal, the Carter administration was now using the threat to Minuteman in support of SALT II by arguing the case for an invulnerable MX deployment. That this was what Brown was doing in the Newport Address was confirmed by him some years later. When asked whether these arguments were an endorsement of the line taken by the Committee on the Present Danger, Brown replied that

> when I made that speech there was, in place, a US programme to remove this element of vulnerability, and a SALT II agreement whose ratification would have assured a limitation on the number of Soviet warheads. *So I posed a threat, and I said what we were doing to respond to it.*[131]

The threat he posed to justify MX was the threat to the ICBM force which in turn was seen as necessary to support SALT II. Thus while Brzezinski and the CPD felt they needed MX to offset ICBM vulnerability in Soviet perceptions, Brown felt he needed ICBM vulnerability to offset the vulnerability of MX and SALT II in Congressional perceptions. This was certainly the view of one policy analyst who worked with Brown at the Pentagon, who remarked that 'Brown didn't see the problem as acute ... [he] believed there was a problem and there was a solution. If he had not seen a solution he wouldn't have stated the problem.'[132] Other commentators were more direct. Spurgeon Keeney, of the Arms Control Association, for one believed that 'Brown embraced the vulnerability argument to get the MX.'[133] Brown himself admitted that the MX decision was in part 'motivated by the need to show the hawks in the Senate that SALT was not a sign of administration weakness'.[134] Thus SALT and MX in its MPS deployment, along with arms control, were seen by the Carter administration as ways to deal with the vulnerability problem. Indeed, the interrelatedness of the invulnerable MX deployment and the fractionation limits and warhead ceilings of SALT II meant that the threat to Minuteman could be harnessed in support of the Treaty.

Nor was Brown the only one to embrace the MX missile as a necessary requirement for SALT. At a key meeting on MX at Camp David in August 1978 at which a decision to go ahead with the missile in a survivable and verifiable deployment mode was taken, the relationship between MX and SALT was a clear factor in the decision-making process. Carter was prevailed upon to accept this judgement by a disparate coalition, from Brzezinski who considered the missile essential to offset the implications of perceptions of vulnerability, to Vance and Mondale who saw the political wisdom of supporting the missile to safeguard SALT II.[135] These considerations were also present at the NSC meeting which approved the Multiple Protective Shelter (MPS) deceptive basing scheme for MX in June 1979, eleven days before SALT II was signed in Vienna.[136] Thus even those such as Vance who rejected out of hand the notion that MX was necessary to counter negative perceptions of ICBM vulnerability were affected by the latter issue in their support for MX/MPS and SALT II. This was the case because of the insistence of the Senate Armed Services Research and Development Sub Committee under Senator McIntyre that the MX be deployed in a basing mode which was invulnerable to a Soviet counterforce attack, and Carter's insistence on both invulnerability and verification of the scheme under SALT. The SALT II regime itself was also an ingredient in ensuring the invulnerability of the MX in its 4600 shelters, in that the warhead limits were necessary to stop the system being overwhelmed. Similarly, part of the logic of the countervailing rationale for the MX, supported by Brown, Brzezinski and Perry, was that the 'MX was a vehicle to drive the Soviets away from their reliance on heavy missiles such as the SS-18s and SS-19s that would be vulnerable to MX.'[137] Thus from whatever perspective the Carter administration officials supported the MX, it was in some way influenced by the ICBM vulnerability debate. Indeed, not only was the ICBM vulnerability argument presented in its own right in this debate, Perry was apparently instrumental in persuading Carter that ICBM modernisation was necessary in order to hedge against Soviet breakthroughs in the other legs of the Triad by suggesting that the SLBM force was a good deal more vulnerable than it actually was. In May 1980 Perry repeated such views to the Senate Appropriations Subcommittee on Military Construction, stating that 'We have designed techniques for submarine detection that, if deployed, could detect their submarines in ten years time', and, to an audience of citizens in Utah, where he added 'I have no reason to believe that the Soviets will not be able to do a similar thing.'[138] Thus Perry was willing to go even further than Brown in utilising not only the prospect of ICBM vulnerability but also that of SLBM vulnerability in his efforts to make the case for MX.

The calculations of the Carter White House, that embracing the arguments of its critics in various forms over the ICBM vulnerability question would allow the problem to be solved as part of the SALT regime, were to prove over-optimistic. The Soviet invasion of Afghanistan in December 1979 was to kill what chance the SALT II Treaty had of being ratified and the administration withdrew it from consideration by the Senate. Without the guarantee of SALT limiting the number of Soviet warheads, the basing scheme for MX once again became subject to criticism for not ensuring ICBM invulnerability. Again, however, amongst those making this argument were individuals less concerned with ICBM vulnerability as such than they were about other concerns. This was most obvious in the opposition from the states of Utah and Nevada where the mammoth construction project for the MX/MPS site was planned to be built. The situation was extremely ironic since those protesting against the scheme had previously been amongst the most hawkish members of the Senate in demanding that the window of vulnerability be closed. Nevada Senator Paul Laxalt had made a reputation on Capitol Hill by banging the drum for defence spending, for opposition to SALT II, and warning of the growing threat to the US ICBM force. Similarly, Utah Senator Jake Garn, who had earlier demanded an early administration decision on a base for MX, now declared that the people of his state were 'patriotic, determined, loyal,' but they 'should not be asked to bear an unreasonable share of the burden of national defence'.[139] It was a classic case of Not In My Back Yard (NIMBY) politics. It was also only the most recent instance of the ICBM vulnerability argument being used for other political purposes. Furthermore, despite the fact that the objections of the Western Senators were primarily concerned with its local environmental impact, the ICBM vulnerability argument was used, and used against itself, in the suggestion that in the absence of SALT the scheme would be an inadequate safeguard of ICBM survivability. It was on these arguments that the next administration under Ronald Reagan would have to address the issue of ICBM vulnerability.

Presidential Directive 59

For the Carter administration, however, its efforts to build support both for its strategic policies and more generally for its credibility in the area of defence and foreign policy did not stop with its pronouncements on SALT II and the MX/MPS. Instead, the administration once again addressed the arguments of its critics with regard to the ICBM vulnerability question. This strategy was considered necessary in response to the way in which the issue was being used in the 1980 presidential race. Ronald Reagan, the Republican Party presidential candidate, who was being advised on defence issues by CPD members such as William Van Cleave, made much in his campaign rhetoric of the window of vulnerability as evidence of Carter's weakness on matters of national security. It was for this reason that more attention was paid by the Carter administration to the image which its strategic innovations projected. As indicated above, Brown's pronouncement of the countervailing doctrine and his acceptance of the implications of Minuteman vulnerability were partly intended to rebut suggestions that the administration was weak on national security policy. In July 1980 this approach was taken a stage further when, shortly before the Democratic Party Convention, the NTPR study was finally presented to Carter and signed as Presidential Directive 59. These two events, the signing and subsequent leaking of the directive to the press and the political fortunes of the Carter administration were not unrelated. According to Warnke, 'Had he [Carter] been a shoo-in in 1980, there would have been no PD-59.'[140] William Baugh agreed that 'the entire debate was heated up primarily in response to election campaign attacks on President Carter's defence policies as inadequate to meet the Soviet challenge'.[141] Certainly, the refinement in US strategic doctrine which PD 59 encapsulated was intended to give a very clear message in response to the suggestion that the US could be coerced by Soviet nuclear threats. As Brown explained to the Naval War College, on 20 August 1980, PD 59's aim was to convince the Soviets, that 'no ... use of nuclear weapons – on any scale of attack and at any stage of conflict – could lead to victory, however they may define victory'.[142] The target audience for this presentation as with PD 59 more generally, however, was not just the Soviet Union. This modification to US strategic doctrine was intended to address the arguments of the CPD and the administration's other critics, particularly over the window of vulnerability argument. As one of its authors observed, 'part of the rationale for PD 59 was to make the point explicit that survival or surrender was a fallacy and to make it more credible that the Soviets would believe it too'.[143]

Despite these efforts to placate, embrace and to out-tough its critics on the right, the Carter administration failed to shake the image instilled by its critics that the White House had allowed a window of vulnerability to appear in American defences as a consequence of the threat to the US ICBM force. Despite shifting ground quite markedly during its tenure of office, addressing the ICBM vulnerability question more thoroughly and systematically than at any previous period, and devising a solution to the problem in the form of the MX/MPS scheme which demonstrated the support of Congress, the administration could not shake off the image of failure against the test of the window of vulnerability scenario.

That this situation had less to do with the specifics of ICBM vulnerability and more to do with the more general perception of the Carter administration in foreign and security policy is evident in the way that much less rigorous criteria were applied to solving this issue in the administration which followed.

Part Three

ICBM Vulnerability in the Reagan Administration

If a man is distressed because he is convinced that he has an elephant in his hotel room, it is much easier to walk the elephant out of the room than it is to convince him that it does not exist.

Senator Carl Levin, 1987.

We have not, as many have suggested, reversed or closed the window of vulnerability. Whatever one thinks about the vulnerability of those silos, they are likely to become more vulnerable in the future ... But we feel that survivability at the moment is not so crucial an element of our overall problem as to require further immediate steps.

Lt. Gen. Brent Scowcroft, May 1983.

7   The Window of Vulnerability, Strategic Modernisation and the Townes Committee

Introduction

The election of Ronald Reagan in 1980 brought to the White House a man who had campaigned on a platform of cold war rhetoric and strong defence. Specifically he opposed the SALT II Treaty and called for the restoration of American strategic nuclear superiority over the Soviet Union. A central theme of his campaign rhetoric was the notion of the window of vulnerability which was opening up over the land-based strategic forces of the United States.

Candidate Reagan had committed himself to the MX in the 1980 Presidential election yet had opposed the Multiple Protective Shelter (MPS) basing mode that had been developed for its deployment. Reagan's opposition to the MPS was based on a number of factors. That the MPS was the Carter administration's preferred deployment plan was one such consideration. Reagan was eager to differentiate himself from Carter whom he wished to portray as weak and ineffectual on matters of national security. The Reagan camp, however, was also genuinely suspicious of the motives behind the Carter administration's endorsement of the MPS scheme. There was a belief, shared by some senior Democrats, that Carter's commitment to the MX in MPS was motivated primarily by a desire to secure the passage of the SALT II Treaty and to improve his image in defence matters.[1] The MX in MPS, it was suggested, would be abandoned after the election as unacceptable and unworkable.[2] As Reagan defence adviser William Van Cleave observed at the time, 'one must suspect that the [Carter] administration expects the plan to self-destruct after the fate of SALT II has been determined'.[3]

There was also the belief that the MPS was unnecessarily complicated in order to be acceptable as part of the SALT regime, and frustration that the ABM Treaty prohibited active defence of the missile silos on any scale. Van Cleave was also instrumental in persuading Reagan that it was wasteful to spend billions of dollars on multiple protective shelters in order to hide US missiles and then to tell the Soviets where they were located for verification purposes.[4] The non-ratification of SALT II gave further credence to this argument in that part of the rationale of the MPS had now been undercut. In a strategic environment of unconstrained offensive forces the survivability of each silo could not be assured. It was this reason that Weinberger cites for his opposition to the MPS, stating that 'it would not give us any real additional survivability for our missiles: the Soviets would be perfectly aware of the exact location of each of the 4600 shelters having observed their construction'.[5] There was also a concern that the existing land-based missiles would become vulnerable to Soviet attack before they could be replaced by building the MPS system.

It was these reasons that Senators Cannon, Garn, Hatch, and Laxalt cited in opposition to the MPS in a letter to President Carter in February 1980.

> The racetrack is clearly a product of an era of presumed U.S. – Soviet cooperation which, if it ever existed, is clearly no longer with us. As we see it, the time has now come to recognise that the changed security environment also provides us with a chance to build a new generation ICBM, and to base it in a mode which would be cheaper, more effective, and come on line quicker than would be possible with racetrack.[6]

Although it encapsulated many of the arguments against the MPS, the motivation for the Senators' letter stemmed from an entirely different concern, the environmental impact of the MPS on their respective states, Utah and Nevada, the planned deployment area of the MX. The major disruption to the economic, social and environmental life of these states which the MPS would have involved was very considerable and generated a great deal of local opposition to the deployment.[7] This factor was given further salience by the fact that the senators involved in opposing the deployment were close political friends and allies of the new President. This was particularly true of Senators Paul Laxalt and Jake Garn.[8] Indeed a number of observers have noted that it seemed apparent that Reagan had made a political commitment to these senators not to proceed with the MX in the MPS deployment scheme in order to extricate them from the political problems that this would involve. As one who worked closely on the MX observed,

> I am satisfied that the two of them [Laxalt and Garn] went to the President at an early point and got a commitment from him to do away with it [the MPS] and there's no matter what happened after that; we were playing a game after that.[9]

Despite this opposition to the MPS deployment scheme it was not until October 1981 that the Reagan administration announced a change in the country's strategic modernisation programme. Until then the MPS remained the Pentagon's official deployment policy. During those ten months, however, there was much heated debate as to what scheme should replace the MPS and what criteria that deployment plan must meet. This delay may in part be explained by the composition of the defence department team and the priorities which that team established.

In December 1980 Caspar Weinberger was appointed Secretary of Defense and immediately took over at the Pentagon. One of his first acts was to dismiss William Van Cleave who was the head of the Republicans' Defense Department transition team. Out also went Van Cleave's assistants and aides and many of the ideas which he had hoped to implement in power. Van Cleave had hoped to be Reagan's defence secretary but Weinberger refused even to give him the deputy's job.[10] The loss of Van Cleave from the Pentagon, however, also had a significant impact on the administration's strategic modernisation programme. While Weinberger came to the Pentagon with no background in defence matters and a reputation as a fiscal conservative, Van Cleave had a considerable background and reputation in national security policy.[11] As a professor in international relations at the University of Southern California and a long-serving campaign adviser to Reagan, Van Cleave had been instrumental in promoting the idea that American forces were inferior and strategically vulnerable in a number of ways. His contact with Reagan provided one of the main conduits to the future President for promoting the idea of the window of vulnerability. Through his efforts with the Strategic Alternatives Team, Van Cleave did much to publicise the idea that the United States faced impending danger.[12] He even wanted Reagan to call an emergency joint session of Congress on the day of the inauguration in order to push through a package of quick fixes.[13] Part of Van Cleave's opposition to the MPS deployment plan was that it would not address the immediate short-term problem of ICBM vulnerability. Instead, like Nitze, he advocated reopening Minuteman production lines, deploying these missiles in multiple vertical shelters and equipping the remaining Minuteman force with the more accurate MK 12A warhead.[14] Such action would address what he considered to be the pressing problem of Minuteman survivability and allow for the basing of 'strategic deterrence more on selective military targeting, damage limiting, escalation control, and defence than on massive destruction'.[15]

Such elaborate action as Van Cleave proposed, however, which would have effect within 1000 days of its implementation, was not supported by Weinberger. Indeed, as Weinberger's memoirs indicate, disagreement over the urgency of the threat and scale of the response were part of the explanation for Van Cleave's early departure from the Pentagon. The new Defense Secretary noted that 'the transition team had an agenda of its own. It was not useful to me in developing the President's programme; it was, in fact, the source of a number of problems.'[16]

While Weinberger acknowledged the existence of the Minuteman vulnerability issue as a problem, he did not at this stage see the investment of resources in crash programmes to solve a gap of limited duration as justified.[17] Unlike Van Cleave, Weinberger rejected the idea that urgent action was necessary and saw the answer to the ICBM vulnerability problem as the deployment of MX. Quite how this was to be achieved, however, remained undecided, since Weinberger, like Reagan, had not progressed beyond criticising the attempts by others to solve the problem. The President was uninterested in such questions and concerned himself with domestic issues during this period, primarily the economy. Weinberger, on the other hand, directed the intellectual efforts of his new Pentagon team on strategic matters in other directions while he himself concentrated on administration.[18]

Three studies were initiated on strategic matters at the Pentagon. The new Under Secretary of Defense for Policy, Fred Ikle, was given the task of preparing a report on US targeting plans in order to revise US nuclear equipment plans and the Single Integrated Operational Plan to bring them into line with the developments in strategic thinking initiated under Carter.[19] The other two studies were conducted for the Defense Science Board; one, by former Air Force Secretary Thomas Reed, evaluated the utility of deploying ballistic missile defences, while the other under Principal Under Secretary of Defense, James Wade, looked at C^3 during nuclear war.[20] While all three studies were in some way concerned with strategic modernisation, none of them addressed the question of Minuteman vulnerability directly. In his nomination hearings before Congress in January 1981, however, Weinberger was forced to concern himself with this issue. He used the opportunity to reject silo deployment of MX on grounds of vulnerability, noting

> I would feel that simply putting it [MX] into existing silos would not answer two or three of the concerns that I have, namely, that these are well known and not hardened sufficiently, nor could they be, to be of sufficient strategic value to count as an improvement of our strategic forces.[21]

The new Secretary was much less forthcoming as to what sort of deployment plans were acceptable.

Well aware of the importance of the decision that he would have to make on the deployment of the MX, Weinberger was equally determined in his opposition to the deployment of the new missile in any type of MPS system. In his first few weeks in office he talked loosely and with the zeal of one who was ignorant of the history of the MX, stating that he could see no reason why the missile couldn't be put on ships.[22] He was also dismissive of the attempts by the Department of Defense to brief him on the MX/MPS basing scheme. When Pentagon holdover Seymour Zeiberg, who remained as Deputy Under Secretary of Defense for Research and Engineering, did get to brief Weinberger and Carlucci in February 1981 he was appalled by the technical ignorance which the Defense Secretary displayed by the questions he asked on the basing scheme.[23] Weinberger was apparently uninterested in the details of the MPS and refused to avail himself of the remainder of the briefings which Zeiberg had prepared on the MX/MPS for the new secretary and his appointed officials.[24] This clearly suggests that Reagan and Weinberger were at one in their objections to the scheme. The Air Force encountered precisely the same reaction from the Secretary in its attempts to explain the merits of the MPS. As General Kelly Burke observed

> the last conversation I had with Weinberger, David Jones called me down to talk with him, and we were trying to describe the [MPS] system and Weinberger was saying that he didn't like the rail-road cars and then we'd say 'but that's not what's proposed' and he would say 'It doesn't matter, the boss doesn't want it anyway'. I think that we were really going through a charade after Reagan took office because he had made a political commitment to his best friend Paul Laxalt and Jake Garn.[25]

Ironically, the Pentagon had managed to convince Van Cleave of the merits of the MPS as the long-term basing mode for the MX during his time at the Defense Department as head of the Republican Defense Transition team.[26] Van Cleave was genuinely concerned for the survival of the ICBM force and accepted Burke's technical arguments that the MPS was the best solution available. Because Weinberger's objections to the MX/MPS were primarily political, however, he was unwilling to become embroiled in a technical debate on the subject in the Pentagon. By rejecting the preferred deployment option of the Joint Chiefs of Staff and the Air Force without first having a readily available and credible alternative, Weinberger had placed himself at a bureaucratic disadvantage on this issue. In order both to extricate himself from this situation and at the same time to effectively postpone a decision on ICBM modernisation, Weinberger instituted his own study on this subject.

The Townes Committee

Turning outside the body of expertise which had developed over the years on the MX basing question, Weinberger appointed Professor Charles Townes, a Nobel Prize winning physicist from Berkeley, to chair a committee charged with the task of finding a solution to the ICBM modernisation problem. On 16 March 1981, Weinberger announced its composition. From a list of 40 names, Townes and Weinberger selected 15, all of whom were retired senior military officers or distinguished defence scientists.[27] This composition did not make a solution to the problem easy to arrive at however. Although all were disposed towards MX, agreement on how to deploy the missile was not at all forthcoming and the deliberations of the committee were reportedly 'very acrimonious'.[28] As Woolsey more delicately puts it, 'From the beginning the Townes Committee saw that the problem that it had been handed was an extremely difficult one and not at all susceptible to quick solution.'[29] The formulation of a deployment plan for a missile weighing 100 tons, which was at the same time to be consistent with an arms control policy, was no easy task. As Woolsey observes, in this respect the Carter administration 'had done its work reasonably well. The MX, based in MPS, and SALT II were not an ideal package, but the Reagan administration was soon to learn how difficult it was to produce an alternative.'[30] The task of the Townes Committee was made even more difficult by the various constraints within which it was asked to operate. Zeiberg, for example, in setting out tasks and procedures, limited the role of the panel to an examination of the existing data assembled by the Pentagon over the previous 11 years. This provision was included in order to avoid unnecessary repetition of scientific evaluations. In the absence of being allowed to collect their own technical data, Zeiberg recommended parallel briefings for Weinberger and the panel by Carter holdovers in the Pentagon.[31] Weinberger rejected the briefings but the limitations remained. As a consequence 'the administration left itself vulnerable to proposals and ideas floated by the committee and others in and out of the executive branch that had been thoroughly reviewed and rejected during the previous eleven years'.[32] The absence of the DOD briefings also denied the panel the benefit of the institutional knowledge of why these schemes had been rejected. As a result the committee was not well placed to find a definitive and acceptable solution to the ICBM modernisation problem and a salvation for the MX missile.

The committee's difficulties were further compounded by the informal constraints under which the chairman was operating. It seemed apparent to many involved in the deliberations of the panel, from both inside and out, that Townes was operating under certain instructions from Weinberger which had not been made known to the rest of the panel. Specifically, it was felt that the prime purpose for the panel's creation was to find a technical way to discredit the MPS system, which was so troublesome to the President politically, and that Townes had 'signed a dollar contract with Weinberger' to that end.[33] A major political problem which Weinberger had reportedly stressed to Townes was the delays to any MPS deployment which were likely to follow from lawsuits over the environmental impact of the programme. Accordingly, the importance of scuttling the MPS was stressed to the panel's chairman. As Townes commented at the time, 'The one thing that the secretary was insistent on was his view of the environmental law. As he foresaw it, it would be a very long time getting [the MX] in place in view of the environmental problems.'[34]

A further constraint on the panel's operation was Weinberger's insistence on directing the panel's attention towards his own preferred solutions to the vulnerability problem. Initially this took the form of his desire to place the MX on naval surface platforms, an idea which the panel successfully rejected in an interim report to the Defense Secretary in April.[35] Ships offer no advantages over submarines as a platform for strategic weapons and are in fact more vulnerable because of their visibility, limitations immediately apparent to the committee. The same was not true of the Defense Secretary's next idea, however, which Weinberger suggested at their 30 June meeting. When Townes informed him that the panel was moving towards some form of Multiple Protective Shelter deployment scheme, Weinberger suggested that they examine the feasibility of continuous airborne patrol as a basing mode.[36] Townes agreed to this idea, which eventually ended up as part of the committee's recommendations, despite the fact that continuous airborne patrol had been studied in detail and rejected by both the Ford and Carter administrations.

For four months the committee heard evidence on a variety of schemes which purported to solve the ICBM survivability problem. While the panel's main focus was directed towards finding a technically sound basing mode for the MX, Townes had insisted that the terms of his study be broader than this in order to set the issue within the context of the other strategic modernisation programmes.[37] Although the panel did not concern itself with the bomber leg, leaving this to an ongoing study in the Pentagon, it did look at command and control, sea-based systems as well as the future of land-based forces. More agreement was achieved in these broader strategic areas than on the specific question of an MX deployment plan. Looking at the problem as a whole, the panel argued that given the problematic nature of ICBM modernisation together with the need for a prompt hard-target kill capability, the most prudent way in which sufficient survivable warheads could be assured in the long term was through an acceleration in the deployment of the Trident D5 missile. Interestingly this was precisely the same technical conclusion which had been reached by the Strat-X study on strategic modernisation in 1968 and implemented as the ULMS/Trident D5. The panel was also able to agree 'with little dissent that improvements in command and control, not improvements in weapons, were the quickest and cheapest way of improving America's nuclear deterrent'.[38] The vulnerability of C^3 was not a political issue in the way that the survivability of the nation's missile force was, however, and, as a consequence, this element of the panel's conclusions received little attention. It was the conclusions of the Townes Committee with regard to the deployment of the MX which were most eagerly awaited and so politically dependent. In this area, however, while the panel was able to reach some agreement, no unanimity was achieved. Instead, the committee presented its insoluble disagreements as options for further deliberation.[39]

One of the most crucial, if not the most surprising, conclusions of the Townes Committee concerned the existing deployment scheme for the MX. Looking at the problem in purely technical terms the committee came to the conclusion that, given the trends in Soviet warhead numbers and missile accuracy, it would be possible to overwhelm the Multiple Protected Shelter scheme. In the opening section of the report presented to Weinberger in July the committee stated that any land-based system was not survivable if the other side committed sufficient missiles to destroy it.[40] There was nothing new in this conclusion as testimony before the Carter administration on this subject had made clear. It was quite possible to overwhelm the 4600 shelters by proliferating Soviet launchers.[41] It was for this reason that SALT II, which constrained Soviet offensive proliferation, and MX/MPS were presented as a package. In the new climate of superpower politics in which reliance on Soviet restraint and the acceptance of SALT II were abandoned, however, the worst case technical evaluation which the committee produced sealed the fate of this basing scheme. Unless the MPS could be preferentially defended, they concluded, the Soviet Union would be able to build more warheads than there were shelters. Furthermore, it would be possible for the Soviets to go on building warheads more easily and more cheaply than the US could build further shelters. Even the committee's conclusions on ballistic missile defence, for which it recommended more research, stated that the prospects for a feasible defence of the MX in the MPS scheme were not sufficiently high to redeem this basing scheme. This critique of MPS was as technically demanding as it was absolute. There was no comparison of the relative vulnerability of MPS to the existing situation with Minuteman or with any other proposed deployment plan. Accordingly the committee recommended against the MPS as the long-term basing mode for the MX.

Given the broader mandate which Townes had insisted on, the committee actively considered abandoning the MX altogether. This was in part due to the frustration which the committee felt in trying to find a survivable deployment scheme for the big missile and in part due to the realisation that, despite the problems with this particular system, land-based systems have peculiar qualities which are valuable in themselves. If the main impediment to the country's new ICBM being based on land was that it was too big to be based deceptively and therefore survivably, the committee was asked, then why not build a new, smaller, mobile missile? This was the line argued by many to the Townes Committee, with Senator Glenn proposing that small missiles be carried in trucks on the nation's highways, achieving deception by being disguised as ordinary freight.[42] While the idea of a small missile was attractive to the committee in that it combined de-MIRVing and mobility with strategic flexibility, a suitable basing mode remained elusive.[43] At this stage the idea of a hardened mobile launcher for the small ICBM had not been thought of and most of the panel considered Senator Glenn's proposal to be politically unacceptable.[44] As a consequence of these deliberations the committee concluded that given the technical vulnerability of the US ICBM force there was 'no practical basing mode for the missiles deployed on the land's surface available at this time that assures an adequate number of surviving intercontinental ballistic missile warheads'.[45] As stated, the technical problem of land-based ICBM vulnerability could not be solved. The committee applied the logic of the window of vulnerability scenario to the problem of ICBM vulnerability in a technical manner devoid of political considerations and found all land-basing options wanting in terms of their long-term survivability. This, of course, was the conclusion of the Strat-X study in 1968, hence Trident.

The Townes Committee Recommendations

Despite this gloomy assessment of the future of land-based ICBMs, the Townes Committee reported that there were several possible ways to base the MX that might adequately ensure its survival in the long run.

An Airborne Deterrent

Of these, the panel agreed, the most promising technical solution to the problem was to base the MX in a missile-carrying aircraft. This idea was presented to the committee in two forms; one involved converted C5A aircraft which could either be on strip alert or on continuous airborne patrol, and the other envisaged the creation of an entirely new aircraft constructed of new lightweight materials and with a large wing for long endurance and new turboprop engines for great fuel efficiency.

Of the two it was the latter which the committee considered to be the most promising basing mode for the MX. Keeping a large portion of these 'Big Bird' aircraft on continuous airborne patrol, it was felt, would present a different set of considerations to a potential attacker from those necessary in order to attack the other legs of the Triad. The committee was cautious, however, in suggesting that the vulnerability of this deployment plan to Soviet countermeasures be thoroughly examined. Some panel members were concerned that the aircraft could be easily tracked by Soviet satellites and, as a consequence, were vulnerable to barrage attacks. Accordingly, in addition to further research into the technologies and vulnerabilities of the Big Bird, the Townes Committee recommended the investigation of other long-term solutions to the basing problem.

Land-Based ICBMs
Deep Underground Missile Basing (DUMB). Among these basing plans were two land-based deployment options for the MX which had been rejected but which the committee felt were nevertheless worthy of further investigation. One of these, which attracted the unfortunate acronym 'DUMB', for Deep Underground Missile Basing scheme, was primarily designed as a deep silo reserve force. This system was unattractive to SAC in that it removed the option of employing the MX as a prompt hard-target weapon. Technical uncertainty also surrounded the ability of the missile to burrow out from its 'citadel' in the aftermath of a nuclear explosion.

Dense Pack. The other option suggested for further evaluation was that of the 'Closely Spaced Basing' plan or 'Dense Pack' and hardened silos. This scheme sought to make a virtue out of vulnerability by using the 'fratricidal' effect of incoming warheads to either destroy or disrupt the trajectory of the others which followed. It was an idea which had been developed by using advanced computers to extrapolate data derived from atmospheric tests of nuclear weapons. To have complete confidence in this system, however, would have meant an abrogation of the Partial Test Ban Treaty to test the actual effect of nuclear explosions on missile launch. It was partly for this reason that the scheme had not gained more support as a basing scheme before now.

The final form in which these two land-basing schemes for the MX were presented to Congress, however, was as one of three areas for further research to be investigated for the long term. James Wade explained the proposals in testimony in the following way;

> we will pursue R&D on three promising programs which would give us survivable MX basing for a much longer period: (a) Continuous airborne patrol aircraft – development of a long endurance aircraft which could carry and launch an MX missile. (b) Ballistic missile defence of land-based missiles, the development of an ABM system to provide protective coverage and survivability of land-based ICBMs. (c) Deep underground basing and placement on the south side of mesas, the hardening of MX silos to survive all but a direct hit, and placement of silos in a manner designed to protect them against existing Soviet targeting.[46]

The Interim Solution

In addition to these recommendations for the long term, the committee decided by a 'significant majority' to recommend the immediate deployment of a small number of MX missiles in shelters designed so that they could be expanded if the need arose. This action, the committee argued, was necessary in order to prevent any unilateral delay in the deployment of the MX in the face of Soviet strategic deployments, and, more ominously, as a hedge against the failures of the panel's long-term recommendations.

The desire for an early deployment of the MX was something which the panel all agreed upon in order to get the additional hard-target kill capability that the MX could deliver. The expert opinion of the panel was that it would be better to have the MX deployed even if it was vulnerable. Reflecting the strategic concerns of the Air Force and a technical rather than political calculation of the MX deployment, this decision flew in the face of the window of vulnerability idea. Indeed the idea of deploying the missiles in existing missile silos, which was the Air Force's original recommendation and was now also being strongly advocated by Senators Laxalt and Garn, was considered by the committee before being rejected as entirely unsatisfactory. While the panel was agreed that a vulnerable deployment was better than no deployment, a majority remained convinced that the priorities of an early deployment and a survivable basing mode could be combined. This determination was reflected in the committee's interim deployment recommendation for the MX. This solution was essentially a compromise worked out by Townes to appease the majority of the committee, which wanted to stay with some generic form of multiple shelter scheme as the long-term deployment plan for the MX. While realising that 4600 shelters in the Western deserts was no longer possible, over half of the committee, led by Glenn Kent, Brent Scowcroft and Jim Woolsey, did not believe that multiple redundant shelters ought to be discarded as an idea for MX basing.[47] This approach was firmly supportive of the line that the Air Force still adhered to. Informal contact between the Air Force and the committee had indicated that SAC was lukewarm about the Big Bird but delighted with the MX limited deployment recommendation which they regarded as a 'Starter Set' for an MPS-type scheme.[48] One of the committee explained that the difficulty they faced was that Reagan was against the shell game or 'anything that looked like it might be deceptive'. But,

> The problem was the only thing that could make as big a missile as MX
> survivable that anybody knew anything about then was in fact deception.
> So what we tried to do on the Townes Committee was to say, well you

don't have to make it look like deception right away but the system by which you deploy the MX in vertical shelters ought to be expandable and hence vertical shelters rather than silos.[49]

Indeed, the Townes Committee was only able to achieve a consensus behind its package of recommendations because of the inclusion of the plan to deploy 100 MX in 100 light vertical shelters, as opposed to silos, with the option to expand at a later date. The integrity of the package agreed by the committee, however, was not to last beyond the period of the panel's deliberations.

Presented with the report in late July 1981, Weinberger was enthusiastic about the committee's technical critique of the MPS, its endorsement of the Big Bird deployment plan and its recommendation for improvements in command and control facilities. He was not supportive, however, of the panel's short-term deployment plan for the MX in light shelters. The political imperatives which made the full MPS unacceptable to Weinberger and Reagan remained an effective block on this embryonic deceptive shelter scheme. Furthermore, the Defense Secretary was insistent that the report itself and its findings, particularly over the degree of support for the short-term deployment, be kept secret.[50] Weinberger did not want the Air Force's hand to be strengthened in the ongoing debate by this information and instructed Townes not to discuss it with the military.[51]

The committee had furnished Weinberger with the technical support he needed to further the political position which he had already adopted on the MX. The Townes panel had not made any definite recommendations on how the MX could be based survivably. Instead it had restated the problems which faced the MPS scheme. It had not stated how much the various alternatives would cost, whether they would work, how many planes, missiles and submarines would be necessary and how quickly they could be deployed. Instead it effectively restated that there was a problem over ICBM vulnerability and pushed the problem off into the future to be solved by further technical evaluations. In short, the window of vulnerability scenario of technical vulnerability was still being employed as it had been in opposition, as an essentially negative critique of existing systems with an overlay of political assumptions, and the prospect of resolution at some later date.

8   Reaction to the Townes Committee Report

The presentation of the Report to Weinberger in late July had the effect of renewing the debate on MX deployment at the policy level which had been dormant for the duration of the study. Weinberger let it be known that he favoured the Committee's long-term solution of a continuous patrol aircraft, while the Air Force let it be known that it was highly sceptical about this idea. The USAF expressed public concern about the need for counter-measures to protect this new system from Soviet attack, and private anxiety about the budgetary implications for their service of developing a fourth major aircraft (the others being the B1-B, B-2 and the new long-range transport plane) and of a high annual operating cost for the MX missile. The Air Force was also deeply resentful that Weinberger had been pushing for this deployment system without the knowledge of the service and without consulting the regular engineering structure.[1] Weinberger dealt directly with 'two little guys from nowhere' especially Ira F. Kuhn Jr, a Maryland physicist.[2] Not only did the service resent the fact that their institutional and professional expertise and experience was being ignored on this question but it felt frustrated at being unable to make its case to the commander in chief: Weinberger effectively denied the Air Force access to the President on this matter.

The effect of the Townes Committee's deliberations in Washington was effectively to put a 'hold' on the future of the MX basing question. This was not the case in the states of Nevada and Utah, however, where the MPS remained the official deployment plan. Indeed the Air Force, keen to see the scheme deployed on time, continued to press ahead with the environmental and construction studies necessary for the plan's implementation. The effect of this action was to further galvanise local opposition to the MX/MPS deployment. It was during this period, while the Townes Committee was deliberating, that the influential Mormon Church came out in opposition to the scheme, declaring it 'a denial of the very essence' of the church's gospel of 'peace to the peoples of the earth' – not to mention the peace of the Mormon Church being disturbed by the construction project.[3] Senator Laxalt was also using his position as chairman of the Military Construction Subcommittee to promote opposition to the MPS scheme. After holding hearings during June, Laxalt's subcommittee issued a report stating that the MPS was vulnerable and that the MX would be better deployed in Minuteman silos (none of which are in Utah or Nevada) defended by ballistic missile defences.[4] The result of these activities was two-fold; they provoked interest in the issue in Congress amongst legislators formerly agnostic on the issue and they confirmed Reagan's opposition to the MPS deployment.[5]

The MPS Cancellation Decision

The formal presentation of the Townes Committee findings to the President took place at a meeting of the National Security Council in Los Angeles on 17 August 1981. In attendance were Caspar Weinberger, Secretary of State Al Haig, UN Ambassador Jeane Kirkpatrick, Arms Control Director Eugene Rostow, National Security Advisor Richard Allen, Presidential Counsellors Jim Baker and Ed Meese, and Chairman of the Chiefs of Staff, General David Jones. This meeting was scheduled to resolve the strategic modernisation question for the Reagan presidency, particularly the future of the MX, and those present heard Townes with interest. The Berkeley physicist laid out his objections to the MPS scheme and set out the alternative long-term basing plans which the committee had devised. He advocated further research into ballistic missile defence and pointed to the opportunities presented by deploying the MX in an air mobile mode. His ideas were not universally embraced by those present. Kirkpatrick and Haig were concerned that the US should deploy the MX on land for both strategic and political reasons. All too aware of the political opposition which the European allies were experiencing over the plan to deploy INF missiles, Haig argued that the US could not be seen to abandon its own land-based deployment scheme.[6] The main critic of the Townes proposals was Air Force Chief of Staff Lew Allen. In his first and only opportunity to present the Air Force's case to the President, Allen did his utmost to defend the MPS basing scheme and to express his profound reservations about the continuous airborne patrol aircraft being advocated by Weinberger. In the limited time made available to him, however, he realised that he had failed to convince the President.[7]

The effort to save the MPS scheme did not end there. Five days after the NSC meeting Senator John Tower and Representative William Dickenson flew to California in order to try to persuade the President against the air mobile missile and in favour of a land-based deceptive shelter scheme. As chairman of the Senate Armed Services Committee and minority leader on the House Armed Services Committee respectively, they argued with authority that the President had been badly advised. Aware of the strategic concerns, they argued that no other deployment plan could offer better protection and more surviving warheads in so short a time. Aware of Reagan's political considerations, they argued that the deployment could be limited to 100 missiles in 1000 or even 500 shelters built on an existing air force base or military land.[8] This compromise position, which they presented with the backing of the Air Force, was pushed hard by these congressional defence experts. Tower even suggested siting the MPS scheme in the Trans-Pecos region of his home state of Texas in order to extricate Reagan from his political objections to deployment in the Western States.[9] As Dickenson later remarked, however, they left the meeting with '... the distinct impression that one or both [Weinberger and Reagan] were against MPS and were studying to look for alternatives. Reagan had a deep-seated bias, and Weinberger was affected by Reagan's feelings.'[10] Tower and Dickenson did feel, however, that they had damaged the chances of the Air Mobile deployment scheme by their visit and resolved to continue the fight over the missile's future in Congress if necessary.

Throughout the remainder of August and early September 1981 the prospects for the Big Bird deployment plan began to recede. The strategic wisdom of such a deployment became widely criticised and it also became apparent that the propulsion and construction technology needed for such a plane was a long way off.[11] While Weinberger toyed with the idea of abandoning the MX in favour of the 'Common missile' scheme rejected by Carter, (essentially the land deployment of the Trident D5), support was growing in Washington for some form of limited MPS deployment. This had currency in three forms; 100 missiles in 1000 shelters advocated by the Air Force, 100 in 500 proposed by Townes Committee member Brent Scowcroft and a new idea emanating from a RAND study which envisaged 100 in 600 in 'superstrong' upright silos based at the Nellis Air Force Base in Nevada.[12] These deployment plans combined the strategic advantages of a reasonably quick deployment of MX warheads and an improvement in survivability on the existing ICBM force. As such, while they would not close the window of vulnerability in the way that the full MPS deployment could have claimed to do, they did recognise and attempt to redress the problem. They did not, however, address the new political criteria which motivated the Reagan White House – they did not avoid the political controversy which the MPS had generated, particularly in Utah and Nevada.

Concerned that the idea of a less ambitious MPS scheme was gaining support in Washington, Laxalt and Garn exercised their privileged position as friends of the President to request an audience. Meeting in the Oval Office on 14 September with Reagan, Weinberger and Meese, the two men argued that if 200 missiles were vulnerable in 4600 shelters then 100 in 1000 shelters were even more vulnerable. More crucially they explained that the deployment of a 'foot in the door' type system at Nellis Air Force base and indeed any deployment of MX missiles in Utah and Nevada was unacceptable. Although presented primarily in military terms, the weight of their argument was more political than strategic. Thus Reagan was presented with a dilemma; it was not possible for the President to weigh the merits of the competing arguments against each other in their own terms. As Frye observes, on this unfamiliar issue Reagan was caught in the crossfire between 'Tower and Dickinson versus Laxalt and Garn, his military professionals versus his secretary of defense, strategic requirements versus political feasibility'.[13] The outcome was perfectly in character. The President reacted on this issue the way he had acted consistently on strategic matters as the entire window of vulnerability episode demonstrates – he followed his political intuition rather than the dictates of strategic logic.

The actual decision which cancelled Carter's MPS scheme and changed the direction of the US strategic force modernisation programme was taken in the White House with Reagan's closest political advisors in attendance on 28 September 1981. Present at the meeting with the President were Edwin Meese, James Baker, Michael Deaver, Richard Allen and Caspar Weinberger. They were gathered together not because of their expertise in defence matters but because of their close relationship to the President. On most of the substance of the meeting those present deferred to the position proposed by Weinberger as Defense Secretary. This was not surprising given the fact that not one of those in attendance had worked on strategic questions before taking up office nine months earlier.[14] The meeting took place at the end of the day after the President's return from a speaking trip to New Orleans. It was very informally organised and lasted only for an hour. 'There was no lengthy presentation of options, no audio visual presentation, no detailed calculation of the costs and benefits of alternative strategies.'[15] Instead, Weinberger argued his case using the findings of the Townes Committee against itself. The panel, he explained, had stated that no land-based deployment was invulnerable. From this he made the jump that if this was the case, then the administration might as well base the MX in existing silos in the short term rather than building a new and expensive deceptive shelter scheme. The fact that the MX would be much less vulnerable in an MPS deployment than in missile silos was a subtlety which was lost to the occasion. It was also the least costly solution to the problem both financially and politically.

The case which Weinberger made for his deployment plan was not without props, however. Demonstrating his knowledge of the President, the Defense Secretary substituted image for argument and produced a cartoon from the *Denver Post* which showed Uncle Sam playing the shell game, used as a metaphor for the MPS scheme, with Brezhnev. The Soviet leader in the cartoon responds by destroying all the shells with a hammer. Reagan reportedly chuckled at this and went on to approve Weinberger's plan.[16] The Defense Secretary had a prepared order for a National Security Decision Directive (NSDD 12), which the President signed, ordering the cancellation of the MPS deployment and its substitution with a strategic modernisation programme to be announced a week later.[17]

   This meeting and the incident with the cartoon illustrate several things about the Reagan administration's approach to strategic nuclear issues. The willingness of the President to allow an issue of such importance to be settled without the involvement of the experts, and without an investigation of the strategic rationales involved, demonstrated that Reagan saw this as a political rather than a technical question. In part due to his unwillingness to engage in the technical strategic arguments, Reagan only saw the political dimension which so underpinned this entire question. The window of vulnerability itself, the opposition to MX deployment in the Mid-West and Reagan's own commitment not to deploy the MPS, were all political issues and as such were not amenable to technical solutions. Even the cartoon which at one level can be seen as playing to Reagan's prejudices and providing a simplistic form of technical argument to support Weinberger's case, at another level can be seen as providing Reagan with political evidence that the MPS was genuinely unpopular in the Mid-West.

The Strategic Modernisation Programme

The strategic modernisation plan which the President had agreed to was more coherent in its political than in its strategic logic. Having singularly failed to find a basing mode which could satisfy all of the constituencies involved, and having abandoned the only scheme to have developed sufficient if reluctant support in Congress, the Defense Secretary proposed to delay making a long-term basing decision for the MX until 1984. While the other elements of the Strategic Modernisation Package went ahead at an accelerated rate, the troubled question of how to deploy the 100-ton missile survivably would be further investigated in line with the recommendations of the Townes Committee. The interim deployment of the MX in a limited deceptive shelter scheme recommended by the Committee was not to be pursued, however. Weinberger and Reagan were determined to have that option scotched once and for all, despite the fact that such a deployment plan for the MX was the only one which the record showed could generate Congressional support. Instead, Weinberger returned to the basing plan which President Ford had proposed and Congress had rejected back in 1976 – fixed silo deployment of the MX. Weinberger recommended this deployment plan because it combined several strategic and political attractions. It was not without its failings in both areas. Strategically, it accomplished the administration's desire to deploy the MX as a hard-target killer considered necessary to implement the Pentagon's damage limitation strategy. It failed, however, to assure the survivability of the ICBM force. Politically, while the scheme combined the benefits of low cost with assuaging the western senators, the Mormon Church, Haig and the European Allies committed to INF, it failed to meet Congress's concerns and criteria on survivability as laid down by Senator McIntyre in 1976. On both counts, strategic and political, the administration subordinated the survivability of the ICBM force to other considerations, despite the fact that this had been the very issue from which so much political capital had been gained through the window of vulnerability idea. Weinberger's calculation that this strategic and political combination would be sufficient to push his package through was very optimistic given the record of the MX in Washington. His assumption that while the Joint Chiefs of Staff might complain, they would rather support the MX in this form than not at all and that this would be enough to carry Congress, was to prove cavalier. What Weinberger had not accounted for was that the military's political judgment was based on its institutional familiarity with Congress. It knew what Congress would accept. As Air Force Chief of Staff Gen. Lew Allen observed, 'The deepest concern, of course, that the Air Force had, was that in the absence of a basing mode we felt that the Congress, well, or any, many thinking people, would simply not be in favour of the MX system at all.'[18]

More familiar and more concerned with the politics of the Western United States than the operation of Congress or the history of the MX, the Reagan Administration had let these considerations play an inordinately large part in the MX proposals. Although Weinberger was later to try to minimise the importance of 'the alleged environmental objections of some Western Republican Senators' in the MX deployment it is clear that this factor was highly significant.[19]

Despite the fact that this short-term deployment plan for the MX clearly subordinated concern with survivability to other political and strategic goals, the decision was portrayed as one which closed the window of vulnerability. This fact and the way that the decision was portrayed more than anything else demonstrates that the administration saw the window of vulnerability idea as a general, unspecific and indeed amorphous construct. Certainly, as far as the President was concerned, it did not just apply to ICBMs and their purported vulnerability. This is evident by the way in which Reagan talked about it at the press conference to launch the programme.

By way of introduction to the details of the modernisation programme, Reagan once more conjured up the first-strike scenario which he had used so successfully during his election campaign. This prepared part of his statement set the vulnerability question in its narrow strategic context while also referring to the broader sense of decline and weakness. Reagan stated

> I have repeatedly pledged to halt the decline in America's military strength
> and to restore that margin of safety needed for the protection of the
> American people and the maintenance of peace. During the last several
> years, a weakening in our security posture has been particularly noticeable
> in our strategic nuclear forces – the very foundation of our strategy for
> deterring foreign attacks. A window of vulnerability is opening, one that
> would jeopardize not just our hopes for serious arms reductions, but our
> hopes for peace and freedom.[20]

When he went on to announce his plan to solve this problem by placing
between 36 and 100 MXs in hardened Titan and Minuteman silos, however,
he attracted the attention of the Washington press corps who had become
familiar with this subject. 'Mr President,' asked Helen Thomas of United
Press International, 'when exactly is the "window of vulnerability"? We heard
the suggestion that it exists now. Earlier this morning a defense official
indicated that it was not until '84 or '87. Are we facing it right now?' This
very specific and detailed question caught the President somewhat off guard.
He replied by stating, 'I think in some areas, we are yes. I think the imbalance
of forces, for example, on the Western front, in the NATO line – we are vastly
outdistanced there,' adding further, 'I think right now they have a superiority
at sea.'[21]

More significant than the inaccuracy of the President's statement suggesting
a Soviet naval advantage is the fact that these force levels clearly have
nothing to do with the purported vulnerability of the US ICBM force. Several
possible conclusions could be drawn from this. The most obvious of these,
which is supported by Reagan's statement on the naval balance, is that the
President was not well informed and did not understand the specific threat
which the window of vulnerability idea had come to represent. This is the
line adopted by Scheer, who cites Gerard Smith to make the point that such
utterances 'raise questions about the administration's common sense and,
worse, its credibility'.[22] Another interpretation on this performance, however,
is that the President saw the window of vulnerability as a much broader idea
than the specific question of ICBM vulnerability. For Reagan, under this
interpretation, the window of vulnerability idea was a metaphor for the
perceived military and political decline which the United States had gone
through in the 1970s. Unlike Carter and Brown, who had accepted the idea
of Minuteman vulnerability but who also recognised that rough parity existed,
Reagan had taken the specific vulnerability of the Minuteman force and
generalised it into an allegation of widespread inferiority through the window
of vulnerability idea. A third interpretation, and one which seems to fit
better with the evidence, is that both of the above have some validity in that

Reagan was both ignorant of the details of the specific idea and yet also saw it as a much broader political construct. This is evident in the President's responses to further questioning by the Washington press corps.

In response to Reagan's initial comments, reporter Bill Plante entered into the following dialogue with the President. 'Mr President, if there is, or will be a window of vulnerability, why is the MX any less vulnerable if it's in silos, the location of which the Soviets presumably already know, unless we are going to launch on their attack?' Surprised by the detail of the question the President tried to sidestep it saying 'I don't know but, what, maybe you haven't gotten into the area that I'm going to turn over to the, to the Secretary of Defense. Weinberger, who was standing behind the President, came to his aid stating that 'The silos will be hardened', a theme which Reagan immediately took up saying

> Yes, I could say this, the plan also includes the hardening of silos so that they are protected against nuclear attack. Now we know that is not permanent. We know that they can then improve their accuracy, their power and their ability. But it will take them some time to do that, and they will have to devote an effort, a decided effort to doing that.

Plante rejoined asking 'So this is a way of buying time, Sir?' To which Reagan replied 'In a way of narrowing the window of vulnerability.'[23]

As well as probing the President on the technical inconsistencies in the administration's policies, the press also used this opportunity to demonstrate its understanding of the political context of the basing decision. 'Mr President', asked Sam Donaldson of ABC News,

> some people are already saying that your decisions are based to a large extent on politics, domestic politics, so let me ask you about two points: One that you never considered the racetrack system because it was proposed by Jimmy Carter, and you didn't want to have anything to do with something that he had proposed; and, two, that you're not basing the MX missile in Utah and Nevada because of opposition from the Mormon Church and your good friend, Senator Paul Laxalt.

Becoming tongue-tied in his reply, Reagan refers the questioner to the Townes Committee report as evidence of the technical nature of the decision, conveniently overlooking its secrecy and the political constraints under which that study was conducted, stating:

> Sam, I can tell you now, no, the entire study of the basis for basing – I got tangled up there with two words that sounded so much alike – the MX missile was a very thorough study of all those proposals that had been made.

And actually, I could refer you to the Townes Commission (sic), their study and their report that we would not have an invulnerable missile basing by doing that; that all they would have to do is increase the number of targeted warheads on that particular area and take out the whole area; and while it would force them to build additional missiles, we would be just as vulnerable as we are in the present Minuteman.

Apparently unconvinced by this answer, the questioner rejoined by asking, 'Laxalt didn't persuade you sir?' to which the President replied, 'No, no.'[24] Clearly the press was as sceptical of the stated reasons for this major change in US strategic policy as it was unconvinced of its internal coherence.

The strategic modernisation plan which Reagan announced had five different elements to it, forces for the three legs of the triad, measures in command and control, and in strategic defences. The proposed expansion in strategic offensive forces meant a much greater emphasis on the sea- and air-based elements of the US strategic arsenal and a comparative reduction of the role of ICBMs.[25] This was in part due to the revival of the B-1 bomber, an expansion in the production of Air Launched Cruise Missiles and the acceleration of the Trident D5 and Stealth bomber programmes. It was also due, however, to a reduction in the number of MX missiles included in the defence budget. While this reduction from the 200 which Carter planned for the MPS to the 100 which Weinberger initially requested may have been 'evidence of a certain reduction of the relative importance of land based missiles in the US strategic triad', as Arbatov suggests, the main considerations were political.[26] The change in the number of missiles to be procured was not intended to be permanent, representing only the production number of missiles needed for the interim silo deployment. The final number of missiles was to be decided along with the decision for a permanent basing mode by 1984. As Edwards notes, 'one hundred deployable missiles was just the number picked for the defence budget. Whether fifty or one, two or three hundred would actually be deployed had not actually been decided at all.'[27] Ikle also indicated this in his testimony on the total cost of the MX programme, stating 'of course, the numbers that will be deployed in the 1990's and in the next century are not yet determined. Much would depend upon the arms reduction talks and other programmes, and also the exact lifetime of these systems.'[28] This fact was not immediately picked up upon, however, and the figure of one hundred MX became the bench-mark figure for subsequent deployment plans for the MX, such as the Scowcroft Commission.

Announcing the Strategic Modernisation package, Reagan claimed that it was made 'after one of the most complex, thorough, and carefully conducted processes in memory'.[29] Senator Tower did not agree with this analysis, however, stating, that the 'decision was made within a small circle, without the coordination of the best military expertise'.[30] Tower, like much of the defence establishment both inside and outside Congress, was still committed to MX in MPS and was not impressed by the administration's plans to deploy the missile in silos which were widely considered to be vulnerable. While the abandonment of the MPS system had the support of the liberal arms control community who rejected the existence and the importance of Minuteman vulnerability, the administration was not in a position to use this argument. Having made much of the vulnerability of the ICBM force, Weinberger found it difficult to sell the MX in hardened silos on Capitol Hill. In a sense the administration was a victim of its own arguments and rhetoric. This was evident in the unease expressed by normally sympathetic congressman such as Senator Exon who asked,

> I came here two and half years ago and I was not convinced at that time that we needed or could afford an MX system. Since that time I have been barraged as a member of this Committee with testimony from previous administrations, with testimony from the highest officials of our Defense Establishment, from innumerable closed door sessions with the CIA, that led me to believe that indeed there was a window of vulnerability that likely we could not have a chance of closing unless we went to the MPS-based MX. Do you believe I was misled by all these gentlemen?

It is interesting to compare how similar these concerns are to those expressed by Senator Jackson in the ABM debate. Both senators were concerned that Congress had been manipulated by individuals using arguments over ICBM vulnerability for different purposes whenever it suited them. Senator Humphrey's questioning also conveyed how 'unsettling' it was for him 'in the space of 10 months to hear completely contradictory testimony from the most respected and expert defence officials on the basing mode'.[31] Continuity was provided for Senator Humphrey, however, by the chairman of the Joint Chiefs of Staff, General David Jones, who testified, 'In my view I considered the MX in a very survivable mode to be extremely important to the security of the nation. I remain to be convinced that there is a survivable mode other than MPS.' Jones also made it clear that were the MX to go ahead in a different basing mode to the MPS, the military would afford it much less priority than it had previously.[32]

The Senate Armed Services Committee, the Air Force and the administration, it seemed, shared a common view that ICBM vulnerability was a problem and that the deployment of the MX in some form could go some way to alleviate that problem. What they could not agree on was the nature of the problem and therefore the nature of the solution. For Congress the predominant view was that Minuteman vulnerability was a technical problem with potential political costs which needed to be redressed by deploying the new generation of ICBMs in an invulnerable way, hence their support for the MPS and their scepticism about hardened silo deployment. For the Air Force, Minuteman vulnerability was primarily important due to the impact that this would have in a counterforce exchange. They were therefore eager to have the additional warheads that the MX would give, but they were also keen that the new missile should be deployed survivably, particularly in the MPS scheme. These points were made by the Air Force hierarchy both to the Defense Department transition team and in testimony before Congress in January 1981. As General Allen states,

> They [the transition team] understood my views and the Air Force's views ... that an essential feature of the MX deployment is that the basing mode be survivable. One does not obtain that through placing it in the Minuteman silos. Therefore I do not favour such a deployment.

Similar sentiments were expressed by the Commander in Chief of the Strategic Air Command, General Ellis,

> We must correct our vulnerability by deploying the MX in a mobile configuration. The Multiple Protective Shelter basing will guarantee future adaptability to unpredictable threats and, as a complement, the ability to rapidly reconfigure or reposition the entire force if an attack is imminent – a capability not achievable with silo based missiles. It is a matter of national urgency that MX in the MPS basing mode be kept on schedule ... if we had the mobility in the Minuteman force that we are building into the MX force we wouldn't need the MX.[33]

For the Air Force then, as Paine observes 'It was the 4600 aimpoint "sponge" of the MPS basing mode, more than the counterforce capabilities of the missile itself, which was the major factor in overcoming the Pentagon's projected imbalance in nuclear destructive potential after a counterforce exchange.'[34] It is not at all clear that Weinberger understood this, however, or if he did understand it whether he credited it with any weight. For the Defense Secretary the ICBM vulnerability issue was a political problem. He saw the MX as necessary as a hard-target killer not because he had much understanding of strategic theory but because he saw this as an index of strength. The deployment of MX would, he believed, also help the administration's arms control position as this would allow America to 'bargain from strength'. For Weinberger the window of vulnerability idea was a symbolic weakness which, despite the technical vulnerability, could be ameliorated by the symbolic strength which the deployment of MX would bring. To him, therefore, the deployment of the MX was more important than the invulnerable deployment of the missile. Having made much of the specific vulnerability, however, Weinberger was unable to present the silo deployment proposal as anything other than survivable. This was something which the Congress found difficult to accept.

Congress was sceptical of the long-term deployment plans which the administration was proposing for further investigation, particularly Weinberger's pet scheme, continuous airborne patrol. Doubts about the safety, environmental danger and the cost, which some estimates suggested would be greater than the MPS, were expressed about this basing mode.

Most stridently attacked, however, was the planned short-term silo deployment of the MX. During testimony, Weinberger admitted that hardening silos to 5000 psi would at best protect the missiles for a three- or four-year period and at worst for only one year.[35] General Jones also let it be known that he had reservations about the cost effectiveness of such an endeavour. General Ellis was more forthright in expressing his opinions, stating 'Rather than hardening I would use that money in some other aspect' because the experts 'never knew how to harden them strong enough in order to protect them against a CEP which was believed to be the capability of the Soviets ... I would have preferred a decision employing a deceptive basing mode such as MPS.'[36]

Weinberger's testimony before the Senate Armed Services Committee was a fascinating example of a man being hoist by his own petard. Not only were the arguments of the window of vulnerability from the 1970s and the election campaign being used against him, but the Pentagon's latest publication *Soviet Military Power* was cited as evidence of silo vulnerability. The position which the administration had adopted flew directly in the face of its own assumptions about ICBM vulnerability and attracted the wrath of defence establishment hawks as a consequence. Van Cleave criticised the President, stating that 'the candidate who campaigned on the window of vulnerability not only did not proceed to close that window of vulnerability, but opened it wider'.[37] Senator Jackson was equally precise in pinpointing the curious dilemma in which the administration found itself. Echoing the testimony which he delivered in 1972 on precisely this subject, he stated:

> I am only using the Administration's position, which I share, about the vulnerability of our land based system. Once you agree with that assumption, which I do, then the only response that you can give is that you have hardened it against everything but a direct hit. But their ability to make direct hits, based on the Administration's own assumptions as to accuracy on a saturation basis, means to me, at least, that this system is not survivable as proposed.[38]

Faced with this direct and penetrating question, Weinberger gave a forthright and revealing reply, stating,

> Senator, I don't think at this point that there is anything that one can guarantee in the future. What we need to do is to get all the added strength that we can get as quickly as we can and, meanwhile, start the search for something that is even better. We have examined literally hundreds of possible options. We have reached the conclusion that there isn't any ground-based system that is survivable, and therefore we are studying a number of things that we hope we can add to that ... Meanwhile, we can't stand still. We can't take the MX as it comes off the production line and put it in a warehouse because we don't have an MPS system finished. Therefore, we do the very best we can to get all the additional strength we can as quickly as we can get it.[39]

This frank statement by Weinberger is interesting in its mention of the notion of 'additional strength'. Clearly this does not refer to the invulnerability of the MX deployment, the rationale by which Congressional support had been secured. Nor indeed could this reference be explained as a way of providing the Air Force with a weapon system which it considered a high priority. In the absence of the MPS, the MX itself was much less of a priority. Instead the strength referred to by Weinberger is primarily political and symbolic. It is in this sense that the deployment can be seen as politically important for Weinberger in addressing the perception of weakness encapsulated in the notion of the window of vulnerability.

While Weinberger never himself elaborated on this theme, an eloquent statement of this view was given by the new Commander in Chief of SAC, General Davis, in his testimony on the strategic modernisation programme. He expressed precisely the value of the MX deployment in symbolic terms and in relation to the vulnerability question, stating,

> While the President's programme will not close the window of vulnerability overnight, it certainly will make a major contribution in reversing the adverse strategic balance ... we are likewise bolstering that less tangible element required for effective deterrence – unquestioned national resolve. By setting in motion the production lines to develop the MX missiles and the B-1 bomber while simultaneously upgrading our ... C[3]... we are sending a crucial message to friends and foes alike: America stands ready to take whatever steps are necessary to protect its vital interests at home and abroad.[40]

This, it seems, is what Secretary Weinberger meant when he talked of more 'strength' and redressing the 'strategic imbalance'. There was also another sense in which Weinberger saw the deployment of MX as politically useful, however. The deployment of the MX in a land-based form, he believed, would go some way to assuage European concern with the INF deployment, and further, it might improve the US bargaining position in START.[41]

The way the strategic modernisation programme was handled by the administration did not improve its chances of Congressional support, however. The recommendations were presented as being the product of the Townes Committee despite the fact that a major component of that panel's report had been amended without mention.[42] As the truth of the matter leaked out this caused a great deal of resentment in Washington. Similarly, the goodwill of the Air Force was lost by the administration's failure to inform it of the deployments plan before it was announced. Thus the Air Force was badly prepared and ill disposed to conduct a robust technical defence of the basing scheme in Congress. Indeed it was as much the way that this deployment plan was handled as it was the substance itself that contributed to its eventual defeat. As Holland and Hoover observe, 'The silo basing decision was a crucial error that ultimately cost the administration the confidence and support of Congress on the MX issue.'[43]

Reluctant to take responsibility for killing the MX itself, Congress gradually chipped away at the missile's deployment plans before the administration withdrew, first the silos hardening plan in February 1982 and then the entire interim basing plan in anticipation of legislative defeat on the fiscal 1983 defence authorisation bill. Furthermore, the Senate refused, as it did in 1974 and 1976, to provide funding for the deployment of the MX in an air mobile mode, eliminating this option from the Pentagon's long-term solutions. Indeed, there were some attempts to kill the MX in the Senate altogether. Once again Senator Glenn put forward his idea of abandoning the MX in favour of the development of a small mobile ICBM, while others questioned the need for a land-based missile given the prompt hard-target kill capabilities which the Trident D5 would soon provide. These moves were narrowly defeated only after an amendment was passed suspending all expenditure on the production of the missile until 30 days after Congress had been notified of a permanent basing decision. This the administration now agreed to provide by December 1982.[44] As Weinberger's deputy at the Pentagon, Frank Carlucci, said of this episode 'Congress didn't just say "no". They said, "Hell, no!"'[45]

The Dense Pack Deployment Plan

Jolted by their combined failure to achieve a solution to the MX deployment problem, the Air Force and the administration began, in early 1982, to work together in an attempt to achieve a common position. Continuing to draw on the work of the Townes Committee, they tentatively decided to proceed with the Closely Spaced Deployment Plan or Dense Pack, and to deploy the MX in this single basing mode. While not actually one of the three alternative long-term basing modes for the new ICBM which the Townes Committee had recommended for technical investigation, Dense Pack was associated with the deep underground basing scheme which was. As such, some preliminary research had been done. In order to assess the technical feasibility of Dense Pack basing mode for the MX deployment, however, a second study was commissioned in 1982. This was still to be chaired by Townes but with a somewhat different composition. Thus, as Woolsey observes, 'the second Townes Committee's character was even more limited than that of the first'.[46]

Towards the end of 1982 the committee reported its findings to the Pentagon giving the concept cautious technical approval. However, as Talbott observes, this 'lukewarm blessing, ... did neither the panel nor the basing plan much good in the eyes of Congress.'[47] True to form, Weinberger's decision to proceed with Dense Pack was based on political rather than technical criteria. As Frye observes, 'If confidence in the scheme's technical merit was tentative, confidence in its political appeal was high. It would take little land, create no distinctive environmental problems, and confine the missile to an existing military base.'[48] Abandoning the plans to deploy the MX in the Western deserts, Weinberger believed, would rid him of much of the opposition to the MX, most notably that of the Western Senators with their slim Republican majorities. The invulnerability of the MX deployment to political attack was more important to Weinberger than its strategic vulnerability. As one senior Air Force officer observed, 'The main reason for Dense Pack was to be able to put it on military land, less than to stop Soviets attacking it.'[49] Although political in nature, this decision, like so many decisions taken on this issue by Weinberger and Reagan, was focused on the political constituencies outside Washington rather than those on Capitol Hill. Unattuned to the sensitivities of the Congressional process and uninterested in Congressional strategic reservations, Weinberger moved to placate popular opposition to the original MX deployment plan. The decision to site the Dense Pack deployment at Warren Air Force Base, Wyoming, was one that was reached as much in consultation with that state's Republican Senators and Congressmen as it was with Congress or the Air Force. Indeed the services, including the Air Force, remained deeply sceptical of the strategic wisdom of the Dense Pack deployment.

Of the five Joint Chiefs of Staff, three, (Army, Navy and Marines), were opposed to Dense Pack while the Air Force and the chairman gave support.[50] JCS chairman, Army General John Vessey (a former infantryman) commented at the time 'The first time I heard of it, I thought the thing was crazy. For guys like me who'd been telling troops, spread out, don't bunch up, the idea of everyone bunching on the bull's eye seemed crazy.'[51] The form in which the Air Force presented Dense Pack to the President reflected its reservations. Option one involved 100 MX in 100 superhardened silos closely spaced. Options two and three however, while both involving 100 MX, proposed fielding 300 and 500 superhardened silos respectively, deployed in a closely spaced basing scheme with an MPS configuration included.[52] In essence the Air Force, or more specifically SAC, was trying once more to include some element of deceptive mobile basing in the MX deployment plan. A further precaution against the uncertainties of Dense Pack was suggested in the form of both active and passive defence of the closely spaced MX deployment. Applicable to any of the three options, but tailored mainly to the first, the Air Force suggested either the deep basing of the MX or the provision of a ballistic missile defence overlay for the entire deployment site.

Of these options the administration decided once more against any mobility/deception scheme and backed the plan for 100 missiles in 100 silos with an investigation into an active defence of the site. The other measures were rejected on the grounds of the cost of the redundant superhardened silos and the potential political and environmental opposition to the procurement of the additional land required for an MPS scheme.[53]

The administration's announcement of its plan for the deployment of MX in this form was made on 22 November 1982. It was very soon to run into trouble, however. As a White House source later admitted, 'We knew within five days of the President's speech that it wouldn't float. We tried to round up five eminent scientists who would testify to Congress that fratricide would work. We couldn't find one.'[54] The variety and scale of the criticism which Dense Pack attracted was unprecedented. The scheme seemed so counter-intuitive that attempts to explain the system ended up creating more opposition. As Representative Jack Edwards explained to the Defense Appropriations Subcommittee, 'I am supposed to be one of the hawks on the committee I guess, but I swear the more I sit here and listen to this, the more I wonder what in the world we are up to.' Similar sentiments about the political incredibility of the scheme were expressed by Representative Norman Dicks in reply to Defense Department witness General McCarthy,

You are never going to be able to sell this to the American people. If you think you had problems with multiple protective shelters, this is going to be much more difficult, because it sounds stupid ... this is going to be five times as hard to sell to the Congress.[55]

Indeed, supporters of Dense Pack argued that the technical feasibility of the system was not given the chance to be tested on its merits. According to one USAF general, 'Dense Pack never got a trial – it was lynched.'[56] Others, however, disagree with this analysis. One Senate staffer, for example, observed that, 'No one knew if it would work. It was seriously critiqued ... We wouldn't know in the absence of above ground testing. It wasn't just a popular rejection of a sound system.'[57]

Opposition to Dense Pack was not only based on its political saleability, however. The strategic community latched onto every aspect of this deployment plan in attacking the scheme. The reliance of Dense Pack on the theoretical feasibility of fratricide was a feature which alarmed many critics. The inability of the Air Force to test this concept in any operational sense did nothing to improve its confidence in the scheme. Not only did Dense Pack rely on the fratricide effect, it was also dependent on the silos being sufficiently 'superhardened' to withstand a series of nuclear strikes and then the missiles being able to burrow out through the rubble in order to be launched. Critics also pointed to the lack of consideration given to Soviet countermeasures such as a 'spike' attack in which the incoming warheads were timed to avoid the fratricide effect by detonating simultaneously after arrival, or deep earth penetrating warheads designed to explode after first burrowing some way towards their target, or the pin-down effect where the continuous explosion of warheads overhead would prevent the MX being launched.[58] Harold Brown was concerned about this, stating that 'Incoming re-entry vehicles are more vulnerable than hardened silos. Unfortunately the MX missiles are themselves still more vulnerable during the several minutes of their launch and powered flight and could be forced to remain in their silos, "pinned down" by the incoming Soviet attack.'[59] Brown also suggested that Dense Pack could be overcome if the Soviets employed much larger warheads of 25 megatons or more in order to destroy several silos at once. He concluded that

> there is no high confidence that a Closely Spaced Basing deployment of MX missiles would be able to survive a well-planned attack by a force of only a small fraction of the size of the present Soviet ICBM force but with appropriately rearranged payloads ... [indeed] it is likely to be vulnerable to destruction by a properly executed attack of only a few 1-megaton Soviet warheads, or even fewer larger ones: thus it is not a good military or technical solution.[60]

The provision of an ABM defensive overlay of the Dense Pack deployment was also severely criticised. Not only would such a deployment violate the ABM Treaty, but it would do so without offering any meaningful protection to the MX. The idea of active defences being used to limit attacks on a basing mode which relied on fratricide for its effectiveness was a contradiction which seems to have been overlooked by the Reagan administration.

The Political Environment

In addition to the many specific criticisms levelled at the Dense Pack basing scheme, the political environment in which the administration sought approval for its deployment plan was particularly inauspicious. Away from Washington other events of that year had overtaken the significance of the Townes Committee's technical study in the debate over the basing of the MX. The American Freeze Movement grew rapidly in 1982, strengthened by President Reagan's alarmist rhetoric detailing 'Soviet superiority' and the vulnerability of the American homeland. Opposition to Reagan's nuclear policies was also forthcoming from the seemingly unlikely quarter of the American Roman Catholic Bishops. In their pastoral letter, discussed at their Washington Conference of November 1982, the Bishops rejected the quest for superiority and expressed moral disquiet over the perpetual reliance of the US on nuclear deterrence. This statement epitomised the growing concern of a large section of American society with the nuclear policies of the Reagan presidency. The publication of Cardinal Bernadin's Pastoral letter and the activities of the Freeze Movement were widely reported by the media and became an important issue in the November 1982 mid-term elections.

The question of a nuclear freeze, in some form or another, formed part of the ballot in eleven states in the election, allowing a quarter of the US electorate to vote on the issue.[61] Only one state failed to carry the Freeze vote, with Reagan's home state of California, the most populous state in the Union, supporting the Freeze.[62] While the administration held its majority in the Senate, it lost a net 26 seats in the House. The increased importance of defence issues in the election, together with the heightened sense of alarm within the electorate on the nuclear question, resulted in the newcomers to the House of Representatives being much less conservative on defence issues than their predecessors.[63] It was against this background that the administration approached Congress for funding for the MX in the Dense Pack basing mode.

In an attempt to elicit support for the administration's proposals, America's Chief START Negotiator, Edward Rowney, warned the Senate that 'A decision not to deploy the MX/CSB [Closely Spaced Basing] would not only undercut my negotiating leverage, but would require a reassessment of our START proposal.'[64] As Talbott notes, this did nothing to win new friends for the administration on Capitol Hill. Nor did the administration's START position move toward de-MIRVing in an attempt to create greater stability, as most of Congress favoured. Instead, at the insistence of the Joint Chiefs of Staff working under the Pentagon's Defense Guidance plans, the US START position reinforced the rationale for the MX by pushing for a low launcher ceiling.[65] Thus Rowney's threat to move towards a tougher negotiating position in a START policy which was based on the MX was seen as empty by a Congress considering the abandonment of that multi-warhead missile in favour of de-MIRVing and a small ICBM. The Congress and the administration were completely out of harmony in what they saw as the best strategic nuclear policies for the United States. This disharmony was to be reflected in the decision reached by Congress on the MX missile and the Closely Spaced Basing mode.

The Dense Pack Rejection Decision

The presentation of the Dense Pack deployment plan to Congress in December 1982 was indicative of the political constituencies and issues which the Reagan White House understood and considered important. For Weinberger the deployment plan silenced the political opposition from the Western states and had the regional political backing of the new host state of Wyoming. It also proposed the most speedy deployment of the MX missile with all the 'added strength' that this would provide. This, together with the traditional reluctance of Congress to vote against the President's major procurement plans, was what the Pentagon relied on to secure legislative support for Dense Pack. Weinberger's belief that the issues which he found persuasive, and the deployment plan which caused least concern in the country, would be acceptable to Congress, was misplaced. Indeed Weinberger's approach to Congress itself also worsened the prospect for MX.[66]

The Secretary of Defense had fundamentally misjudged both the complexity of the legislative process and the strategic competence of the US Congress. Both the timing of the administration's proposal and the complexity of the basing mode itself contributed heavily to the failure of this attempt to gain support for the MX. Although presented to the lame duck Congress, the Pentagon assumed that consideration of the issue would be deferred until the next legislative session. The defence officials were therefore caught completely off guard when the House moved quickly and without prior warning to tie the appropriations vote on acquisition of the MX to Dense Pack.[67] The Air Force and Weinberger's defence team thus found themselves with no pre-planned strategy for selling the arcane basing scheme and only a week in which to do it. The problem was compounded by the fact that Congress was keen to cut some item of Pentagon expenditure in order to give the appearance of 'fairness' amid the cuts in social programmes which the legislature was also administering.[68] Dense Pack was an obvious candidate for such a cut.

The Pentagon's presentation of the Dense Pack fratricide argument proved unconvincing on Capitol Hill and accounted for some votes against the MX from Congressmen not normally noted for their opposition in defence votes. Dense Pack was not taken seriously as a credible option in the search to find an invulnerable basing mode for the MX by the members of Congress who had studied the problem intensively for many years. Instead, the term 'Dense Pack' was used in despair to describe those who continually devised such ridiculous basing modes for the MX. Clearly, as Getler observed at the time, in presenting his case for MX, Reagan had 'failed thus far to convince Congress that his plans for basing the MX will keep it safe from attack by Soviet missiles, as he once claimed was essential'.[69] Despite the considerable opposition which the Dense Pack proposal generated, Congress was still reluctant to kill the MX missile system outright. Instead, two votes were taken to reimpose a strategic mandate on the administration to proceed with the MX specifically in a way which would result in its invulnerable deployment. In essence it was a restatement of the principles imposed by the McIntyre Sub-Committee in 1976. On 7 December, by 245–176, the House rejected the $988 million in testing and production funds needed for the MX but retained funding for R&D. The following day the House further restricted the use of appropriations for procurement and even flight testing until a permanent basing mode for the missile had been approved by Congress. Furthermore, as part of the package worked out between the House and Reagan administration officials to save the missile from complete rejection, the administration was directed to re-evaluate its strategic and arms control policies, including all the possible basing modes for the MX, and to report back to Congress when an 'acceptable basing plan' had been decided on.[70] A deadline for this was set for 1 July 1983.

The rejection of funding for the MX in the Closely Spaced Basing mode represented much more than the considerable scepticism surrounding Dense Pack itself. For many it was a rejection of the multi-warhead MX missile, the White House's START proposal and the strategic thinking which they embodied. After all, President Reagan had set out in 1980 to repudiate the strategic and arms control policies of his predecessors, yet at the end of his second year in office his own policies in this area were moribund in the shattered consensus that his administration had brought about in America's national security policy.[71] Clearly the rejection by Congress of the Dense Pack scheme was a severe blow to the Reagan White House.

The large majority which defeated Dense Pack encompassed a wide variety of rationales from budgetary tactical voting to deep-seated strategic concerns and cannot be wholly explained as a vote against MX. The fact that Congress had linked a re-examination of the basing mode to the production of the MX demonstrated both that opposition to the MX was not implacable and that Congress still believed that a survivable MX deployment solution was possible.

The rejection of Dense Pack and the 'fencing' of acquisitions for MX production was the closest that Congress had come to killing the MX outright. It was in part a product of extreme frustration with the administration and the inability of the Pentagon to come up with a credible deployment plan. It demonstrated the willingness of Republicans and conservative Democrats in Congress to break with a tradition of deference to the Pentagon and to act on their own strategic judgement. The conditions laid down for the funding of MX production also made it clear that this was the last chance which they were willing to give to this troublesome missile.

The lessons of this legislative defeat were not lost on the administration. The rejection of the MX in Dense Pack created the fear within the administration that the missile would not be accepted by the Congress in any form.[72] At best, the administration realised, this was their last chance to come up with a solution which was acceptable to Congress. In order to achieve its objectives in this area the administration concluded that a bipartisan consensus was now needed in order to re-establish a coherent policy. All too aware of the divisions and inadequacy of its own policy-making apparatus, however, the administration decided to use the requirement for a report to Congress on the MX basing plan as an opportunity to set up a presidential commission on the subject. Accordingly, on 3 January 1983, the President's Commission on Strategic Forces was initiated under the chairmanship of General Brent Scowcroft.

9   The President's Commission on Strategic Forces

Introduction

By the end of 1982 the Reagan administration was approaching its third year in office without having resolved the problems which had dogged its strategic nuclear policy. The delay in formulating a position for START, it was argued, was due to a desire more fully to integrate arms control policy with strategy.[1] Yet the process by which these policies were to be formulated was unstructured and ill-disciplined.[2] Indeed, rather than producing a unified national security policy as intended, these discussions fuelled public and private disquiet about the seriousness and competence of those charged with formulating strategic policy. By early 1983 the Reagan administration seemed particularly ill-suited to resolve this impasse, having lost in quick succession its first National Security Advisor, its first Secretary of State and its first Director of the Arms Control and Disarmament Agency (ACDA).[3] Furthermore, the administration was under assault on Capitol Hill over the acrimonious confirmation hearings of the new ACDA Director, Kenneth Adelman, and the strong backing in the House for a resolution calling for a 'mutual, verifiable freeze'. As one senator observed, 'Half the guys up here don't trust the Russians – and the other half don't trust Reagan to negotiate seriously.'[4] Despite the best efforts of the White House, the central strategic problem that the administration faced at the end of 1982 was the very same issue that had bedeviled the Reagan Presidency from the outset, namely, finding an acceptable basing mode for the MX missile and the formulation of an arms control policy in harmony with such a deployment.

Following the failure of two studies commissioned by the Pentagon to produce a solution to the MX basing problem which was acceptable to all the parties concerned, the President's Commission on Strategic Forces was initiated. This 'blue ribbon' panel, under the chairmanship of Lt. Gen. Brent Scowcroft, was asked to determine a strategic modernisation programme for land-based forces which could command a higher degree of support than previous efforts had mustered. The resulting document was what has become known as the Scowcroft Commission Report.

The Formation of the Scowcroft Commission

The creation of a Presidential Commission as a way to resolve an impasse in policy was not without precedent. Indeed, Reagan had used such a device to create a consensus behind his reform of the Social Security system (the Greenspan Commission) earlier in his presidency and was to go on to use this mechanism several times during his tenure in the White House.[5] As John Isaacs observed, 'Panels are a staple of US politics to give credibility to proposals. They are stacked ... in any given vote 20 Senators and 40 House members could go either way but can be prevailed upon with a set of classy names.'[6] The way in which this device was used by the Reagan administration, however, differed substantially from the use of Presidential Commissions in the past. While traditionally Commissions were merely asked to report on technical questions by drawing on specialised expertise in a specific area, the Greenspan and Scowcroft Commissions were much more political in nature. Indeed, the two Committees chaired by Townes were, despite their political guidance, closer in character to the traditional Presidential Commission than that chaired by Scowcroft. The Townes' studies had been narrow and technical in focus, whereas the mandate of the new bipartisan commission was broad (ostensibly at least) and very political. As Greenberg and Flick explain,

> Where the old style commissions were convened to consider social and governmental questions, the new commissions were convened in effect to legislate partisan questions ... where the commissions of the past merely issued reports, the new commissions are surrogates for the political process. While once the commissions usurped at best the bureaucrats' privilege, they now usurp the statesman's privilege. In short, the statesmen have abdicated their responsibility.[7]

While not seeing it as an abdication of responsibility, the administration was explicit in its recognition of the Commission's role in the political process. The White House saw the Commission as a means of drawing on the experience and expertise of distinguished figures in order to rebuild a bipartisan consensus on national security. They did not see this as achievable through the presentation of a purely technical solution. In practice the approach which the administration had in mind was one where, 'The White House would publicly ask advice from a council of wise men, whisper in their ear what sort of advice would be helpful, then use their response to ram new policies through an impacted, fractious bureaucracy.'[8]

The idea for a Presidential Commission on the troubled question of strategic modernisation had been much mooted throughout this period.[9] It was not until Congress deleted all MX procurement money in its December 1982 continuing resolution, however, that the Reagan administration seriously addressed this option. In a meeting in the Vice President's office on the night after the vote, Senators William Cohen and Warren Rudman met White House aide Kenneth Duberstein and proposed the Commission as a way to save the MX.[10] Deputy National Security Advisor Robert McFarlane persuaded the administration of the merits of this approach and was instrumental in its composition and mandate.[11]

Ostensibly the Commission was given a broad mandate, being tasked 'to review the purpose, character, and composition of the strategic forces of the United States', with a particular emphasis on the future of land-based ICBMs, and to review basing alternatives.[12] In practice its concerns were much narrower, being focused primarily on the future of the MX. As Herbert E. Hetu, Counsellor for Public Affairs to the Commission, observed, 'It sounds broader than it was in the title; in reality – the MX was about to go down the tubes, or not to be more precise! – and the Commission's job was to try to save it.'[13] This did not mean that the Commission's recommendation of the MX was inevitable, however. As Scowcroft himself later observed, 'My notion was that the task was to find a decent burial for the MX because I was dubious that a solution to the problem could be found. But then gradually as we got into it, it didn't look quite so hopeless.'[14] Indeed, according to Hetu, 'Cancelling the MX was looked at in some detail, but they came to the conclusion that it was not a good idea strategically and they were not keen to kill it unilaterally' for a variety of political reasons.[15] It is clear that while it was potentially within the scope of the Commission to recommend the cancellation of the MX, this would only have been contemplated had the members decided that Congress was unwilling to proceed with the missile under any circumstances. Even before the inception of the Commission, however, there was some confidence in the administration that a way to save the MX could be found. As McFarlane observed at the time 'I believed there was a bipartisan consensus within the community – the family – that we had to have the MX or it would demonstrate an inability on the part of the United States to solve problems.'[16] In practice it seems that the Commission's mission was to solve the MX debacle while saving the missile if it was possible, and to do so in a way which restored the national security policy consensus.

Despite its officially broad mandate the Commission was not intended to be a major review of this entire issue area. The time given to the Commission, a mere one and a half months, reflects this fact. Furthermore, and in contrast to the Townes Committees, a separate study was commissioned by the Pentagon to prepare the detailed technical assessments of all the basing mode options and alternatives demanded by Congress in its continuing resolution. This classified report, 'Strategic Forces Technical Review', was forwarded to the Armed Services and Appropriations Committees of both Houses along with the recommendations of the Scowcroft Commission by the President on 19 April.[17] While obviously the drafters of this study liaised closely with the Commission so that in the end its 'conclusions were consistent with and supportive of the findings of the President's Commission', the fact that the more technical aspects of the study were dealt with separately is illustrative of the centrality of politics to the Scowcroft Commission.

The Commission's Composition

The Commission's composition also provides an insight into the rather limited scope of the study's mandate. While every effort was made to make the Commission's members and its Senior Counsellors as distinguished and as bipartisan as possible, it was equally clear that no opponents of MX had been chosen. As Drew observes, 'The members of the commission were people who either had supported the MX or who could be counted on to give it their support ... Not a boat rocker or, of course, an MX opponent in the group.'[18] The lack of MX sceptics on the panel was not due to a lack of senior figures worthy of consideration; rather it reflected the political outcome which the administration wished the Commission to recommend.[19] This is not how the Commission was presented by an administration keen to portray its panel as neutral and even-handed as well as bipartisan. Thus Senator Percy introduced the hearings on the President's Commission before the Senate Foreign Relations Committee by stating that 'the report can be said to represent the best thinking of the main architects of the last two decades of US national security policy'.[20]

Scowcroft, who was given the task of heading the panel, was a close associate of Kissinger, serving as his deputy under President Ford and eventually replacing him as National Security Advisor. He had also been a member of President Carter's General Advisory Committee on Arms Control. Scowcroft was qualified for this position by virtue of his experience as a Lieutenant General in the USAF, where he was a strong advocate of the development and deployment of the MX.[21] He also served as a member on the Townes Committees. It was mainly due to the broad bipartisan respect which Scowcroft had earned at the NSC, however, that Robert McFarlane and William P. Clark recommended him to head the Commission. Despite being widely viewed as an honourable public servant his appointment was not without its critics. For many arch conservatives, Scowcroft was too closely linked to Kissinger, SALT II and detente to avoid their suspicion.[22]

The other key appointment to the Commission was that of James Woolsey, who was to have a very influential role on the panel and was responsible for drafting much of the Report itself. He had served on the Townes Committee with Scowcroft and had learned from that experience the futility of thinking about the vulnerability question and MX as a purely military problem.[23] Woolsey, a Washington attorney who had been a member of the NSC and an advisor to the US SALT delegation under Nixon, and then Under-Secretary of the Navy during the Carter administration, was responsible for selecting the remainder of the Commission along with Scowcroft and McFarlane. In addition to the 11 members of the Commission, seven Senior Counsellors were appointed, who, because of their links with defence contractors and other professional associations, were non-voting members and did not sign the final report. Those selected for both roles were individuals with considerable expertise which for the most part the administration had chosen to ignore for its first two years in office. They included four former Defense Secretaries – Harold Brown, Melvin Laird, Donald Rumsfeld and James Schlesinger, former Secretaries of State Alexander Haig and Henry Kissinger and former directors of the CIA Richard Helms and John McCone.[24] Unlike the previous two panels the Commission was not full of technical specialists; rather its members were ex-military and policy specialists. Some members like Brown, Haig, Reed, Scowcroft and Schlesinger had all been very explicit in their support for the MX at various times but Scowcroft and Brown were sceptical of Dense Pack.[25]

Townes was noticeably absent from the Commission, his value to the previous studies having been as a technical, academic expert. This Commission, however, was a political rather than a technical exercise, 'It was a textbook example of ticket balancing, with something for almost every constituency – except for the anti-MX forces.'[26] At its launch, Scowcroft cautioned that the panel might not produce a workable solution, and responded to suggestions that the Commission was a safe bipartisan vehicle to revive the MX by saying 'Whatever we come up with is unlikely to meet the unanimous approval of everyone in the country, or everyone in the Congress.'[27]

The Commission was 'instructed to submit a report to the President within 60 days on how and where it recommends the MX missile ... should be based' but found that it could not meet its initial deadline of 17 Feb.[28] The time pressure was to enable Reagan to meet his 1 March deadline by which he was expected to make a proposal to Congress on the basing of the MX. The Commission was granted an extension of at 'least another month' after it acknowledged difficulties in reaching a decision and requested the need to further evaluate a number of technical issues.

The difficulty that the Commission faced in reaching a bipartisan consensus was recognised by the White House from the start. In launching the study, Reagan said that the 'Commission's task was complex and important and success hinges on cooperation with experts in Congress, the Pentagon and outside the Government.'[29] In order to insulate the administration from the possibility of the Commission's findings being unpalatable, Reagan added that he would not be bound by the report and that any plan must have the backing of the military.

The Modus Operandi

A crucial element of the administration's approach in using the Commission was that it should work closely with Congress. Unlike the traditional model of a Presidential Commission, where expert findings were delivered in a report followed by an intensive effort to sell those findings to Congress, on this occasion the deal was to be 'precooked'. That is, the report would contain a deal on the issue worked out between the various constituencies in the executive and Congress with the Commission acting as the brokers. To this end Woolsey, Scowcroft and McFarlane adopted three approaches.

First, great care was taken in the composition of the Commission itself to ensure that high-ranking Democrats who would be influential with Congress were included. Harold Brown and William Perry's role in this regard was central, as were the support and persuasive powers of Lloyd Cutler who had played a leading role lobbying for SALT II.[30] 'A top administration official' observed at the time that 'the administration was hopeful that Democrat members of the commission or consultants to it would carry the brunt of the selling job on behalf of the new MX plan'.[31]

Second, to sound Congress out on what proposals would be acceptable on the Hill, the White House recalled the veteran lobbyist Max Friedersdorf and appointed him to the post of Legislative Liaison. He had been instrumental in pushing the administration's controversial economic package through Congress in 1981 and securing the passage of Reagan's highly contentious decision to supply AWACS aircraft to Saudi Arabia.[32]

Third, and most important, the Commission decided to work directly with key members of the Congress in establishing a policy framework which would ensure political support. Central to the Commission's efforts was the participation of leading democratic figures in the Senate, such as Sam Nunn, and in the House of Representatives, such as Al Gore, Norman Dicks, Thomas Foley and especially Les Aspin.[33]

Aspin's role as a long-standing member of the Armed Services Committee made him a respected figure on defence matters in the Democratic Party. His opposition to the Dense Pack basing scheme in the 'lame duck' session of Congress in December 1982 had been instrumental in the vote defeating the missile's funding. This stance in opposition to the MX, however, had more to do with the basing mode than the missile itself. His approach to the strategic modernisation problem was a pragmatic one, adopting 'the middle position that ICBM vulnerability matters, but it's not cause for panic; we need the MX to threaten Soviet ICBMs just enough so that they'll have an incentive to cut back on their biggest ones'.[34] Holding such a moderate view and, crucially, displaying a willingness to support the MX, Aspin was a perfect Congressional ally to work with the panel and was to prove an invaluable help to the Commission on Capitol Hill. His willingness to work with the Commission in support of the MX, however, caused surprise and anger on Capitol Hill amongst the anti-MX community who had counted him as one of them.[35] Indeed, the motivation for his apparent betrayal of their cause was the source of some speculation in Congress and in the press. Drew reports that he had become more cautious after 'he had a fright in the 1980 election as his district grew more hawkish' while others suggested that he was 'positioning' himself in order to be Secretary of Defense in a future Democratic Administration. His long-standing friendship with both Scowcroft and Woolsey was also cited as a factor behind his apparent change of tack.

Frustration at the inability of Congress and the administration to resolve this issue, however, seems most likely for Aspin's, and indeed the House's, willingness to work towards a compromise solution. As Aspin himself explained

> My thinking was that this issue had been around a long time and it wasn't going to get settled – it wouldn't really be defeated and it wouldn't really be fully deployed – and my feeling was that when both sides have gone at each other for a long time it gets time to cut a deal. And even if you had the votes to defeat the MX, a year later something happens – the Soviets invade Afghanistan – and they'd say 'you see, we don't have a land based missile,' and the MX would come back, and would cost more. That's what happened with the B-1 bomber – it just kept coming back.[36]

Having established its key instruments of persuasion, the Commission conducted an extensive analysis of the political, strategic and technical questions which it faced. It had been charged with building a bipartisan consensus on national security policy on the ruins of the ICBM vulnerability controversy in which the administration was committed to the MX while the House of Representatives was firmly opposed to a vulnerable deployment. Indeed, the House was thought to be between 50 and 100 votes more opposed to the continuation of the MX programme than the 'lame duck' House which had denied the MX funding by 69 votes the previous December.[37] In order to identify policies which would be suitable to all its constituents, the panel conducted interviews with 203 experts and convened numerous meetings and small conferences on the subject.

The Commission concluded that its task had essentially two elements; to prepare an acceptable strategic modernisation plan, and to sell this to the Congress and the administration. For this purpose the Commission split into two groups, a technical and an information committee where

> the objectives of the technical committee were to outline the strategic problem facing the United States, to develop an appropriate strategic response, and to choose a basing mode for the MX that would be invulnerable, politically acceptable and square with the strategic rationale. The objective of the information committee was to keep all interests and important groups in both the executive branch and Congress abreast of the direction of the technical committee's work, and to provide input into the choices for those outside government.[38]

This description, however, gives a more orderly and deliberative impression of the Commission than was actually the case. In practice the framework of the solution was worked out before the Commission was formally established and political rather than physical survivability of the MX was the prime consideration of the proceedings. As Aspin explains,

> We started to talk even before the Commission was announced. Every other panel or commission that had looked at this thing was just looking at the narrow military-basing question, and then would try to sell it to the public, with disastrous results. So Woolsey and I thought of two things; one was you ought to start with the politics – what's possible to pass – and then, two, among the possible things to pass, what makes sense militarily.[39]

Defining the Problem: What Did the Commission Say?

As the Commission's deliberations got underway the panel set about identifying what it considered to be the central area of controversy. At an early stage the members agreed that it was the politicisation of the strategic modernisation programme, particularly the land-based component, together with the administration's arms control policies which were at the root of the problem. In short it was the political consequences of the vulnerability issue. As the Report states,

> To many the problem has become: 'How can a force consisting of relatively large, accurate land based ICBMs be deployed quickly and be made survivable, even when it is viewed in isolation from the rest of our strategic forces, in the face of increasingly accurate threatened attacks by large

numbers of warheads – and how can this be done under arms control agreements that limit or reduce launcher numbers?[40]

Once the problem faced had been identified, the Commission was able to address the components of a solution directly.

The panel's first conclusion, not surprisingly, was that the modernisation of the ICBM force was important in the long term, not least to ensure the survival of the land-based deterrent as a hedge against the development of any threats to the other legs of the Triad. The Commission, however, was not convinced of the significance of the short-term vulnerability of the Minuteman force, as expressed in its politicised form in the window of vulnerability. Accordingly, the first part of the Commission's Report is devoted to a reconceptualisation of the prevailing notion of vulnerability in an explicit attempt to change the context of this aspect of the strategic debate. The Report argues that the window of vulnerability concept had exaggerated and 'miscast' the nature of the US's strategic vulnerability.[41] The Commission's acceptance of this analysis, however, was not predicated on the belief that US ICBMs were not vulnerable. The report states that the Soviet Union 'now probably possess the necessary combination of ICBM numbers, reliability, accuracy and warhead yield to destroy almost all of the 1047 US ICBM silos, using only a portion of their own ICBM force'.[42] Rather, the Commission did not consider this vulnerability to be a particularly pressing problem. Instead, the Commission argued that while the land-based ICBM force might be vulnerable to attack, the remaining legs of the Triad, the strategic bombers with cruise missiles and the submarine launched ballistic missiles (SLBMs) were not vulnerable to the same sort of simultaneous pre-emption. In essence, the Commission's report argued, it would be impossible to attack all three legs of the Triad at the same time because of the different characteristics of both the attacking systems and the systems being attacked. The Report states, 'The different components of our strategic forces would force the Soviets, if they were to contemplate an all out attack, to make choices which would lead them to reduce significantly their effectiveness against one component in order to attack another.'[43] It was on this basis that the Commission concluded that the vulnerability of 'the different components of our strategic forces should be addressed collectively and not in isolation'.[44]

In reaching this conclusion the Commission both accepted the arguments for the vulnerability of the ICBM force and turned them on their head by showing that this was not a pressing cause for serious concern. (It accepted the existence of the elephant but refused to see it as a problem.) This conclusion was skilful both in political and strategic terms. Politically, it

managed to avoid embarrassing those who had championed the concept of
the window of vulnerability while at the same time allowing the issue to
develop in a different way from that implied by the logic of this slogan. This
was particularly important in securing the support of those in Congress and
the administration who had accepted and championed the window of
vulnerability idea, including Weinberger and Reagan. In the strategic realm,
Cimbala argues, the Commission broke new ground by

> restructuring and reconceptualize[ing] the problem of vulnerability
> compared with its formulation in prior public and strategic debates. The
> new concept was one of *strategic, complex* vulnerability, as opposed to
> *technical, simple* vulnerability. No longer would force exchange models
> of US-Soviet ICBM duels suffice to demonstrate the inferiority of US
> military power. Now, US pessimists would have to show that the entire
> Triad of strategic forces could be attacked successfully. And this few
> pessimists were willing to attempt.[45]

Cimbala goes on to state that 'what really deterred the Soviet Union from
striking first, according to the commission, was not the comparative retaliatory
power of US strategic forces. Rather the redundancy of US forces based on
land, at sea, and aloft would preclude their destruction in a pre-emptive
strike.'[46] In other words the Report restated the importance of strategic
stability, i.e., that provided by the assured destruction capability facilitated
by a redundant force posture; over the more exacting criteria of crisis stability
i.e., where an arsenal is so configured that no strategic advantage can be gained
by attacking part of that arsenal and thus benefiting from exploiting a crisis
by a pre-emptive strike.

While the Report made much of the redundancy argument in implicitly
championing strategic stability as the main criterion of a prudent force
posture against the foreboding of the window of vulnerability, it did not reject
the crisis stability component of that scenario out of hand. It did not argue
that the comparative retaliatory power of US strategic forces was unimportant.
Rather, what the Commission did was to supplement the strategic stability
through redundancy rationale with the argument that crisis stability could
also be a serious strategic problem through ICBM vulnerability. The
Commission dismissed the urgency of this problem by insisting that the
Soviets did not yet possess the terminal guidance technology to make this a
pressing problem and, in addition, argued for a strategic posture which
would create a reciprocal threat. In doing this the Commission was able to
endorse its support for ICBMs not only as a component of the Triad and
contribution to strategic stability, but also for their hard-target kill capability
as a requirement for a countervailing posture. The Report explicitly states

that the US requires the 'ability to respond promptly and controllably against hardened military targets' in the event of 'massive conventional or limited nuclear attacks'.[47] The Report goes further, contending that, 'we must be able to put at risk those types of Soviet targets – including hardened ones such as military command bunkers and facilities, missile silos, nuclear weapons and other storage, and the rest – which the Soviet leaders have given every indication by their actions they value most, and which constitute their tools of control and power'.[48] The Commission's use of this argument was politically astute, for it drew upon the concerns which generated the fear of a window of vulnerability to prepare the way for its endorsement of MX.

The Policy Recommendations

Having identified the problem and gone some way to both dispel and redirect the political force of the vulnerability scenario, the Commission set out the case for its strategic modernisation proposals. It considered three ICBM deployment options seriously before deciding on its recommendations.[49] The proposals were presented as a package with three components. One hundred MX missiles were to be deployed in existing Minuteman silos while research continued for a more satisfactory permanent basing mode; a new single warhead ICBM was to be developed as a shift away from MIRVed ICBMs and for ease of basing; and a new approach to strategic arms control was to be adopted which focused primarily on warheads rather than launchers in the interests of strategic stability.

The Commission's decision to recommend the deployment of two ICBMs was a shrewd move politically. In essence what the Commission said was that the problem as stated was impossible to solve and therefore another approach was necessary. The Report states, 'by trying to solve all ICBM tasks with a single weapon and a single basing mode in the face of the trends in technology, we have made the problem of modernising the ICBM force so complex as to be virtually insoluble'.[50] The Report did not spell out, however, that the reason for this complexity was that two of the central 'ICBM tasks' which the new missile deployment was meant to accomplish were incompatible, thus making their separation necessary. While the MX satisfied the political demands of the arms control process for a missile as large as the SS-19 with as many warheads as the SS-18, and thus SAC's requirement for additional counterforce capability, its very size prevented it from being easily deployed in a survivable manner. The nearest that the Report comes to such an admission that there was a tension between different ICBM tasks is the statement that 'The Commission would not insist on seeking a single solution to all the problems – near-term and long-term – with which the ICBM force must cope.'[51] The Commission used the notion of near- and long-term goals as a way to mask the different tasks and problems which the two ICBMs were designed to deal with. Arbatov is more explicit in his assertion that the Report

> rejected the idea of combining by technical means two features in one missile: increased survivability, and enormous destructive power directed primarily at striking a large number of hard targets on Soviet territory. The essence of the Commission's recommendations was to divide these two nearly incompatible qualities between two different weapons systems.[52]

These two features were the qualities demanded of the new ICBM in order to meet different tasks. The survivability of the ICBM force was demanded as a requirement of strategic stability to ensure the contribution of the land-based leg to the redundancy of the Triad, while the hard-target kill capability of the new missile was considered essential for the countervailing strategy and in support of extended deterrence. These two qualities, however, had proved impossible to combine in the MX, as no survivable basing mode could be agreed politically for such a large missile. As a consequence, the different ICBM tasks were to be split between two different missiles. The SICBM would provide for the long-term survivability of the land-based component of the Triad, as well as some limited counterforce capability, while the MX would provide for the immediate near-term need for a large increase in hard-target kill capability.

The division of labour between weapon systems was ingenious for several reasons. First of all it overcame the immediate impasse by removing the need to base the MX survivably. Secondly, it divided the defence community between different weapons systems. The development of these different systems, however, was dependent on support for the package as a whole. Finally, it provided the basis on which to construct an arms control and strategic modernisation programme which the Commission could claim was both philosophically coherent and politically viable.

The long-term strategic objective which the Commission set for its package of proposals was the achievement of 'stability'. The Report's Glossary defines stability as 'The condition which exists when no strategic power believes it can significantly improve its situation by attacking first in a crisis or when it does not feel compelled to launch its strategic weapons in order to avoid losing them.' It is also clear throughout that what the Report had in mind went beyond the criteria of an assured second strike encapsulated in the notion of 'strategic stability', towards the more exacting requirements of 'crisis' or 'first-strike stability'. This can be gleaned from the Commission's statement of aims set out in the concluding paragraph of the first section of the Report, which states:

> whether the Soviets prove willing or not [for arms control], stability should be the primary objective both of the modernisation of our strategic forces and of our arms control proposal ...They should work together to permit us, and encourage the Soviets, to move in directions that reduce or eliminate the advantage of aggression and also reduce the risk of war by accident or miscalculation. As we try to enhance stability in this sense, the Commission believes that other objectives should be subordinated to the overall goal of permitting the United States to move – over time – toward more stable strategic deployments, and giving the Soviets the strong incentive to do the same. Consequently it believes ... that it is important to move toward reducing the value and importance of individual strategic targets.[53]

Other statements which even more strongly imply crisis stability as the Commission's goal can be found in two single sentences on p. 15 and p. 24 of the Report which state, respectively, 'The objective of the United States should be to have an overall programme that will so confound, complicate, and frustrate the efforts of Soviet strategic war planners that, even in moments of stress, they could not believe that they could attack our ICBM forces effectively' and 'In time we should try to promote an evolution toward forces in which – with an equal number of warheads – each side is encouraged to see the survivability of its own forces in a way that does not threaten the other.' It was to serve this purpose that the Commission's recommendations were presented as a package and that the SICBM and arms control components were presented at all.

The Small, Single-Warhead ICBM

The Commission's recommendation of the small, single-warhead ICBM was designed to fulfil a number of requirements. Primarily the missile was devised as a means of securing the long-term future of the US ICBM force by being deployed survivably. The small size of the missile was a key element in its ability to be based flexibly. The SICBM was planned to weigh about 15 tons compared to the 100 tons of the MX, a feature which was to earn it the nickname 'Midgetman'. Although the Commission left open the possibility of various deployment options, including fixed silo deployment, unhardened mobile launchers or a combination of different basing modes, it was the deployment of the small missile in hardened mobile launchers which was most widely talked about. Under this deployment plan the Midgetman would be carried around military reservations on a mobile launch vehicle specially hardened to withstand nuclear attack; a combination of hardening and mobility which was designed to make the system as invulnerable as possible. The basing of a small ICBM in this deployment mode was pushed by Scowcroft and Woolsey in the Townes Committee in 1981 but was rejected by that panel then on technical grounds.[54] The Scowcroft Commission was able to recommend deployment of this missile system, however, because of certain technical advances which had been made to the design since the earlier study.[55]

Of equal significance to the small ICBM's contribution to crisis stability through being based invulnerably, however, was the new direction in strategic posture which Midgetman's single warhead was intended to signal. Although envisaged as a highly accurate missile with a hard-target kill capability, the planned deployment of a force of single warhead missiles presented the opportunity, by example, for a cooperative transition to a world in which individual strategic targets would be of lower value. The logic behind the recommendation of such a force was that single-warhead missiles would be both unattractive targets and non-threatening instruments against similar systems in any counterforce calculation provided that launcher, and therefore warhead numbers were symmetrically limited by arms control. In such a strategic regime the deployment of Midgetman would neither present nor create any vulnerability to a counterforce strike against launchers and would therefore avoid all the instabilities and insecurities attendant on such a situation. By making such a deployment, the Commission argued, the Soviets could be persuaded to field similar systems, thus moving away from a strategic force posture reliant on heavily MIRVed warheads. Such a development would have improved the crisis stability of both arsenals.

The idea of reducing the value of individual strategic targets by the deployment of a single-warhead ICBM was also a shrewd political move which drew upon the anxieties created in the protracted and controversial debate surrounding the basing plan for the ten-warhead MX. The panel's decision to proceed with the prompt development of Midgetman was a reflection of the support for the missile, and the philosophy which it represented, that was given in evidence to the Commission.[56] A wide and varied body of support had developed behind the Midgetman which ranged from liberal Democrats, such as Congressmen Gore and Aspin, to members of the conservative establishment, such as Nitze and Kissinger.[57]

The transition to Superpower force postures with improved crisis stability through lower value strategic targets could not, the Commission realised, be achieved by the deployment of the small ICBM alone. For such an evolution in force posture to come about would require a cooperative transition through arms control. It was for this reason that the Scowcroft Commission insisted that a change in arms control policy was an essential element of its proposals.

Arms Control

The Commission was very keen to stress that without a shift in the administration's arms control policies and the creation of an integrated strategic modernisation approach, its other recommendations made little sense. The recommendation to develop and deploy the Midgetman and to move in the direction of inducements towards reciprocal de-MIRVing, the Commission reasoned, could not be successfully implemented in conjunction with a START policy which advocated the limitation of launchers rather than warheads as the primary unit of account. Accordingly, the Commission recommended a 'reassessment' of the administration's proposed limit on launchers, arguing that such a policy was not compatible with an evolution toward small, single-warhead ICBMs.[58]

The Commission was critical of the arms control approach of the SALT process for encouraging the building of large missiles with many warheads, which had the unintentional effect of directly contributing to a destabilising ratio of launchers to warheads, thus threatening the ICBM force. No indication is given in the Report, however, that MIRVing of the US ICBM force was a deliberate act of policy pursued in accordance with strategic criteria very different from those being set up as an ideal by the Commission. Indeed, in one sense it would be possible to see the Commission's desire to move toward a mutual force posture of small, single-warhead ICBMs as serving one of the same policy goals as the US MIRVing programme: removing the threat of the Soviet heavy missiles. Although they differed in the details of the methods used and the ultimate goal espoused, the Commission's aims were very similar to the Reagan administration's START proposals outlined at Eureka College in May 1982. In both cases the arms control approach adopted 'essentially calls for the Soviets to restructure their strategic missile forces along lines much closer to our own'.[59]

Although widely seen as championing the cause of de-MIRVing, the Commission did not necessarily envisage this process as being as complete as the general tone of some parts of the text would imply. It states for example that, 'The recommended strategic programme thus proposes an evolution for the US ICBM force in which *a given number* of ballistic missile warheads would, over time, be spread over a larger number of launchers than would otherwise be the case.'[60]

The Commission's insistence that its recommendations on arms control be accepted as part of a complete package was illustrative of the importance it attached to this element of security policy. In its analysis of the vulnerability problem the Commission recognised the political dimension of the arms control process in reducing perceived as well as actual vulnerabilities.[61] The lack of any serious progress in strategic arms control during the first few years of the Reagan administration lay behind some of the hostility felt towards the MX in Congress, and the Commission realised that it needed to placate this in some way or other if it was to secure Congressional backing for its plans. Accordingly, the Commission lent a sympathetic ear to what Congress had to say on arms control, which was by no means inconsiderable.

Frustrated with the Executive's efforts on arms control, several key members of Congress had actually developed and promoted their own approach to the subject on Capitol Hill where support was growing for their idea of 'modernisation through reduction'. 'Build-down', as the idea was nicknamed, was initiated by Senator William Cohen and quickly gained the support of Senators Nunn and Percy and Congressmen Les Aspin, Albert Gore, and Norman Dicks. It proposed, through negotiation, that for every new warhead deployed two old ones would have to be retired. This, together with yearly mandatory reductions of a certain percentage, it was argued, would reduce the size and increase the stability of the superpower arsenals.[62]

While not embracing build-down directly, the Report was careful not to dismiss this approach to arms control in the way that the administration did, and instead offered encouragement to its supporters in an effort to gain their support. On two occasions in the Report indications were given that the build-down approach might contribute something to a new strategic arms control regime.[63] While build-down shared the Commission's concern with the need to focus on warheads, such statements of support were included more in an effort to secure the endorsement of the Panel's proposals than to be part of a coherent package. They were politically opportune rather than strategically coherent statements. While the retirement of older ICBMs on a two-for-one basis in exchange for SICBM deployments might have been considered, the idea of 2000 existing warheads being retired as a prerequisite for the immediate deployment of the MX was not seriously contemplated by the Commission. Woolsey made this point in testimony stating,

> I think we need to be careful as we assess the build-down proposal that we use counting rules in such a way that we increase stability rather than decreasing it. The Commission report, on p. 25, endorses the concept of a build-down. But the 2 for 1 numbers in the build-down could potentially raise some problems if modernisation required, for example, that two warheads be destroyed for every new one that was deployed.[64]

Other sentences appealing to other constituencies can be found in the arms control section of the Report and elsewhere, whose contribution is entirely political. On one occasion, for example, where the case is being made that 'arms control limitations and reductions be couched, not in terms of launchers, but in terms of equal levels of warheads' a new criterion is added to the statement, 'of roughly equivalent yield' (p. 23). This statement, unexplained and unmentioned elsewhere in the Report, one must surmise was included as a gesture of support to those such as Jackson and Perle, who were advocating equivalent megatonnage as an important criterion in START. The inclusion of such gestures is illustrative of the degree to which the Report was primarily a political document.

The arms control component, like the entire package of policy recommendations, was very creative politically. However, the case which the Commission made for arms control and the small ICBM had created an unintended problem for its recommendation of the MX. By divorcing the MX from its contribution to strategic stability through being based survivably, a major constituency for the MX as a contribution to closing the window of vulnerability was removed. The MX had been supported as a long-term improvement on Minuteman on the basis that it could be based more securely. With the suggestion that another, smaller missile could better accomplish this task, one of the main arguments in favour of MX was demolished. Indeed, the recommendation to deploy the MX in Minuteman silos would not only do nothing to relieve the vulnerability of the ICBM leg (thus contributing to strategic instability) it would accentuate the problem by presenting the Soviets with a more attractive target – thus contributing to crisis instability. This reasoning, which had accompanied every other attempt to deploy the MX in Minuteman silos, was bound to greet the Commission's proposals. If the MX could not be based survivably, it would inevitably be asked, then why not move on to the SICBM straight away and do away with the need for the larger missile? After all, it could be reasoned, the SICBM, like the Minuteman, would also have a hard-target kill capability, yet would lack the negative contribution to crisis stability which would attend the MX deployment. Anticipating such arguments, the Commission realised that the MX would need to be justified on other grounds in order to compensate for the lost support from its 'survivability' constituency.

The MX

In setting forth the case for the MX the Report presented various 'important needs on several grounds for ICBM modernisation that cannot be met by the small, single-warhead ICBM'.[65] Amongst these were the unlikely arguments that the US needed a large 100-ton booster in production both to place strategically important satellites in orbit should the need arise, and to be able to deploy an ICBM with a large number of decoys and penetration aids should the Soviets abrogate the ABM Treaty. In addition the Report cites the age profile of the existing ICBM force, the imminent retirement of the Titan II and the need to carry out 'rehabilitation programmes' on the Minuteman force. Much more interesting, however, were the other reasons presented in support of the MX. Of these the political reasons for the MX were more numerous than the strategic. Woolsey identifies three aspects of this political dimension – the politics of the Superpower relationship, both in deterring and negotiating with the Soviet Union; the politics of the United States dealing with its allies; and the politics of the internal American debate and the need to establish a domestic consensus. For all of these reasons, Woolsey notes, 'The importance of putting together a solution that the administration and other MX supporters could endorse, the importance of not asking our allies to deploy intermediate-range land-based systems while we would be cancelling our own analogous strategic system on land, and the importance of having some bargaining leverage with the Soviets in the ongoing START talks, all militated against unilateral cancellation' of the MX.[66]

The willingness of the Soviets to enter into negotiations which would enhance stability, the Report argues, was heavily influenced by the 'bargaining leverage' of ongoing programmes. Referring to the ABM Treaty as an arms control agreement made possible by the on-going US BMD programme, the Commission suggested that the existence of the MX would provide an important contribution to future START negotiations.[67] This was a 'major modification' to US policy which previously insisted MX deployment essential and non-negotiable.[68] While this interpretation of the Report was clearly intended to be possible in order to increase the attractiveness of the Commission's recommendations to certain constituencies, it was also left rather ambiguous. As a consequence, the bargaining chip role of the MX in the Commission's strategic regime was to cause much heated debate in the Congressional efforts to secure passage of the missile.

The Report's second argument for MX concerned deterrence and the importance of 'Soviet perceptions of our national will and cohesion'. Here the Report asserts that the cancellation of the MX at this late stage would send a signal to the Soviets that the US lacked 'the will essential to effective deterrence'.[69] This argument, following a passage which stated that coercion 'would be possible if the public or decision makers believed that the Soviets might be able to launch a successful attack', was only possible to make in the context of the concern over the window of vulnerability. In no other circumstances could the prospect of Congress deciding against the acquisition of a weapon system which could not achieve one of the primary roles for which it was intended be portrayed in this way. The Report therefore, as in its treatment of the question of ICBM vulnerability itself, was exploiting the fears of the window of vulnerability argument as part of the process of exorcising this politico-strategic ghost.

The Report's third reason for MX was the need to redress the 'serious imbalance between the Soviets' massive ability to destroy hardened land-based military targets with their ballistic missile force and our lack of such a capability'.[70] The need for this countervailing capability for 'controlled, prompt limited attack on hard targets', the Report makes clear, was to reassure US allies of the credibility of extended deterrence. In its clearest statement that the MX deployment was designed to serve purposes beyond the central deterrent relationship, the Report states that 'This capability casts a shadow over the calculus of Soviet risk taking at any level of confrontation with the West.'[71] Schlesinger was even more explicit in his testimony to this effect, stating

> We are engaged in deterrence on a worldwide basis, and the purpose of this missile is to augment our extended deterrent capability to deal with the problems of Western Europe. The Soviets have a much higher probability of moving against Western Europe ... than the hypothetical bolt from the blue ... the development of this missile continues to couple American strategic forces with deterrence in Europe that will preserve Western Europe from an attack ...[72]

The MX was necessary for this purpose, the Commission insisted, because it presented the earliest ability to put at risk Soviet hardened targets, thereby matching the capability of the Soviet SS-18 and SS-19 ICBM force.

While this argument was certainly valid with regard to the Trident D-5 missile or indeed the SICBM, it is not clear why, as the Report states, MX deployment would have necessarily been any quicker than the deployment of Minuteman III missiles with MX guidance systems, a missile which would also have had a hard-target kill capability.[73] The main reason why the MX was preferred to an improved version of the Minuteman III probably had little to do with the speed with which it could be brought into service. Rather, the eagerness of the administration and the Air Force to deploy MX was due to the number and, more importantly, the size of the warheads which the new missile could contribute to the arsenal and thus the type of hardened targets in the Soviet Union which the US could threaten.[74] The counter-leadership targeting strategy initiated by Brzezinski had commissioned several targeting studies which stressed the need for the MX. One Defense

Intelligence Agency study of the Odessa Military District in early 1982 'identified so many targets that it provided justification for a threefold increase in US missile warheads', while other studies discovered underground facilities which were so deep and superhardened that, 'few of the known bunkers were targeted because they were too well fortified for [existing] US weapons'.[75] Toth cites a frustrated former US targeteer, stating that 'We probably could not have dug them out, but I was surprised that even a few years ago, we were not trying to lay down a few [weapons] on them just to ring their bells.'[76] That this reasoning was behind the Commission's desire for an early deployment of MX missiles was confirmed by a senior Congressional aide, who stated that

> He [Scowcroft] shared the basic Air Force view that there was a number of Soviet targets which appeared to be getting harder and harder as the evidence was being presented to him at that time about which we had declining confidence we could attack with the Minuteman force even as modernised. He shared the tendency too, in my view, to underestimate the capability of the Minuteman III. He did not feel confident that it [Minuteman III] could do the job required up against the perceived superhardening taking place on the Soviet side.[77]

Furthermore, General Vessey, the Chairman of the Joint Chiefs of Staff, commenting on the need for the large missile, seemed to confirm this capability, stating that 'the accurate MX warheads will let the Soviets know that their missile silos, their leadership, and associated command and control are placed at risk'.[78]

The Commission's decision not to emulate the recommendation of the first Townes Report in proposing the deployment of the MX in 'superhardened' Minuteman silos may also have been a consequence of a desire to make the new missile available to the targeteers as soon as possible. Certainly it was not due to any technical difficulties associated with superhardening. Indeed, support for such a recommendation would have been made easier by the presentation of new evidence on the hardening of missile silos since the Townes Committee.[79] Instead, the Commission mentions the improvements in superhardening only to dismiss it, stating that such an innovation would still not offer any long-term survivability to the Minuteman silos. The added cost of superhardening the existing silos may have been a consideration but given the opportunity of making the MX appear more survivable it seems unlikely that such an option would have been rejected on cost grounds alone. Clearly concern for the survivability of the MX force in Minuteman silos was a lower priority for the Commission than its immediate contribution to the US strategic arsenal.

Despite its efforts to make a separate case for the MX, the Commission still considered it necessary to promote the heavy missile by stressing its part in a coherent package. The Report sought to link the two missiles together by demonstrating that they were instruments of the same strategy, and, furthermore, that the deployment of the MX would improve the prospects and ultimately serve the goals of the small ICBM's deployment. In doing this the Commission was attempting to demonstrate that the two purposes for which the new ICBMs were being deployed, the SICBM for the long-term goal of redundancy and crisis stability, and the MX for the near-term goal of countervailance and damage limitation in support of extended deterrence, could ultimately serve the same ends; that is, the crisis stability of both superpower arsenals.

The way that the Report did this was to restate the long-term goal and then to introduce the MX countervailing role as an instrument of persuasion towards that goal while at the same time stressing the integrity of its policy recommendations as a whole. The Commission's preferred approach to ICBM modernisation, the Report states, had three components,

> a single warhead small ICBM, to reduce target value and permit flexibility in basing for better long-term survivability; seeking arms control agreements designed to enhance strategic stability; and deploying MX missiles in existing silos now to satisfy the immediate needs of our ICBM force and to aid the transition.[80]

While the justification for the MX as a means of persuading the Soviets to move towards a de-MIRVed force posture was a politically skilful attempt to give the package a degree of coherence, the inclusion of the need 'to satisfy the immediate needs of the ICBM force' was seriously to mar the integrity of the proposals. The Report's explanations of the need for the different components of the package sit uneasily together as the next two paragraphs show.

> A more stable structure of ICBM deployments would exist if both sides moved toward more survivable methods of basing than is possible when there is a primary dependence on large launchers and missiles. Thus from the point of view of enhancing such stability, the Commission believes that there is considerable merit in moving toward an ICBM force structure in which potential targets are of comparatively low value – missiles containing only one warhead. A single warhead ICBM, suitably based, inherently denies an attacker the opportunity to destroy more than one warhead ... If force survivability can be additionally increased by arms control agreements which lead both sides towards more survivable modes

of basing than is possible with large launchers and missiles, the increase in stability would be enhanced.

In the meantime, however, deployment of MX is essential in order to remove the Soviet advantage in ICBM capability and to help deter the threat of conventional or limited nuclear attacks on the alliance. Such deployment is also necessary to encourage the Soviets to move toward the more stable regime of deployments and arms control outlined above.

Gone from the former paragraph is the enthusiastic endorsement found earlier in the Report of the need to move towards a regime in which target value was reduced and crisis stability enhanced. Instead the endorsement of the supposed overall long-term rationale is portrayed in language which is descriptive and circumspect. It states that strategic stability 'would exist', that 'the Commission believes that there is considerable merit in moving toward [such] an ICBM force', and 'If force survivability can be additionally increased by arms control ... stability would be enhanced.' It does not state this as a clear policy objective. This is very different language from the extremely positive and actionful endorsement of the MX above which states that 'deployment of the MX is essential' and 'necessary'.

This lukewarm endorsement of the long-term goal, compared to the much stronger recommendation of forces justified as part of a coherent package as an instrument to aid that transition, can be explained, however, by an analysis of the contradictory position of the MX missile in the Commission's recommendation. Although portrayed as part of the package and necessary to persuade the Soviets to move towards de-MIRVing, the Report never fully reconciles its stated long-term goal of crisis stability through reduced target value and SAC's need for the MX in its countervailing role in support of damage limitation and extended deterrence. This ambiguity with regard to the purpose of the MX is very evident from this section of text. What the language of the two paragraphs above indicates is that while there was a long-term goal which the MX deployment was in part meant to serve, this was a different and less urgent requirement for the MX than the 'immediate needs of our ICBM force'. What the Report does here is describe the ideal and then advocate the MX for a purpose which was different from and at odds with that stated goal. Or in one Congressional Staffer's words, 'So this is heaven, the way we get to heaven is to go to hell first.'[81] That the Report fails to reconcile these differences in purpose for the MX and the other two elements of the package within its pages, however, is less a manifestation of strategic ineptitude than it is a triumph of political obfuscation. Indeed the extent to which the Report succeeds in intertwining these two strategic rationales into one proposal is testimony to the political craft of its authors. This is especially true when the contradictory strategic goals behind the endorsement of the MX and the SICBM are considered.

The goal of crisis stability, so clearly exalted by the Commission's Report, makes its contribution to security by reducing the risk that a deep crisis would lead to war by configuring the superpower force postures in such a way as to reduce the incentive to use nuclear weapons. The countervailing, damage limiting approach to deterrence, however, makes a virtue of those incentives to use nuclear weapons in a crisis in order to deter Moscow from initiating such a conflagration in the first instance, such as by an attack on Western Europe. Such a damage limiting, countervailing posture was considered essential if extended deterrence was to have any credibility.[82] As Gray and Payne explain,

> American strategic forces do not exist solely for the purpose of deterring a Soviet nuclear threat or attack against the United States itself. Instead, they are intended to support US foreign policy, as reflected, for example, in the commitment to preserve Western Europe against aggression. Such a function requires American strategic forces that would enable a President to initiate strategic nuclear use for coercive, though politically defensive, purposes.[83]

As can be seen, a contradiction clearly exists between the Commission's stated aim of 'stability' and its decision to deploy the MX in support of extended deterrence. It is a conflict, however, which lay unresolved at the heart of the US strategic debate and which the Commission was not alone in seeking to avoid confronting head on. As Kent and Thaler observe,

> The United States has key national security objectives other than first-strike [crisis] stability and the objectives of first strike stability conflict with the objectives of limiting damage and extended deterrence ... Enhancing first strike stability relieves pressure on both super-power leaders – based on the posture of forces – to strike first in a deep crisis. Conversely, extended deterrence implies that the Soviets are deterred from taking actions severely detrimental to US interests because they perceive a grave danger of unwanted and uncontrollable escalation in a crisis. Thus as they modernise US forces and formulate arms control proposals, US policy makers must consider the trade-offs between these competing national security objectives[84]

Reconciling those trade-offs in the US strategic modernisation process, however, was not something which the administration was keen to address directly. Indeed, the debate over the deployment of the MX, which in part had been a substitute for the debate over objectives, had been so acrimonious and unproductive as to generate the need for the President's Commission on Strategic Forces. Accordingly, the Commission was eager not to point out any contradictions in its policy recommendations which were designed first and foremost to appear both coherent and consistent, while at the same time giving every constituency something they wanted in return for their support.

Interpreting the Scowcroft Commission Report

It is perhaps unsurprising that the relationship between the countervailing role of the MX and the aim of crisis stability in the Report is characterised by a studied ambiguity. Indeed this ambiguity permeates the Report to such an extent that it is possible to identify three different interpretations of what precisely the Commission's long-term strategic goals were based on. At one extreme, it is possible to see the Report as advocating the unconditional transition to a force posture embracing crisis stability as the highest priority. Secondly, it is possible to identify a position where the goal of crisis stability is conditional on Soviet reciprocity; and thirdly, certain sections of the Report indicate that the MX in a countervailing role would be necessary come what may but that some improvements in the crisis stability of both arsenals would be desirable.

Different parts of the text emphasise different aspects of the Commission's pronouncements, allowing conflicting interpretations. Part One of the Report, for example, includes the first and most categoric statement that,

> whether the Soviets prove willing or not, stability should be the primary objective both of the modernisation of our strategic forces and of our arms control proposal ...They should work together to permit us, and encourage the Soviets, to move in directions that reduce or eliminate the advantage of aggression and also reduce the risk of war by accident or miscalculation. As we try to enhance stability in this sense, the Commission believes that other objectives should be subordinated to the overall goal of permitting the United States to move – over time – toward more stable strategic deployments, and giving the Soviets the strong incentive to do the same.[85]

The language and substance of this statement is clearly intended to be interpreted as representing a goal of crisis stability in which the notion of countervailing targeting would have been 'subordinated' as an 'other objective' towards the 'overall goal' of 'strategic stability'. Indeed, reading these parts of the Report it is not even clear that the MX could be justified in aiding the transition to this new regime.

In the second possible interpretation, the MX has a central role as instrument of Soviet persuasion. Under this version of the Commission's goal the transition to a crisis stability regime, while still the stated aim, is conditional on Soviet reciprocity. This statement from Part VI, for example, follows a sentence espousing the criteria of crisis stability with a statement which seems to deny the wisdom of its own counsel by insisting that US acceptance of such a change in policy is entirely conditional on Soviet reciprocity.

> In time we should try to promote an evolution toward forces in which – with an equal number of warheads – each side is encouraged to see the survivability of its own forces in a way that does not threaten the other. But if the Soviet Union chooses to retain a large force of large missiles, each with many warheads, the US must be free to match this by the sort of deployment it chooses.[86]

Here MX deployment is linked to the continued existence of Moscow's heavy missiles. The justification is that if the Soviets have a large force of heavy MIRVed missiles then the US would be justified in matching that capability. No mention is made here that the MX would be necessary anyway for the purposes of extended deterrence. This argument mirrors quite closely the justification of the US INF deployment in Europe which were also justified by reference to their 'equivalent' systems, the SS-20s, rather than as a necessary element of extended deterrence.[87]

The third possible interpretation of the role of the MX is that while it would be beneficial to move some way towards crisis stability, this in no way should be done at the expense of maintaining the capability for countervailing. Part Three of the Report *Preventing Soviet Exploitation of their Military Programs* provides the most explicit statements to this effect.

> The Soviets must continue to believe what has been NATO's doctrine for three decades: that if we or our allies should be attacked – by massive conventional means or otherwise – the United States has the will and the means to defend with the full range of American power ... Soviet leaders must understand that they risk an American nuclear response.[88]

From this statement it is evident that the Commission believed that the regional imbalance of conventional forces in Europe was likely to persist and would thus have to be offset by the provision of extended deterrence. As Kent and Thaler observe 'US – Soviet cooperation to enhance first-strike stability with respect to strategic nuclear forces mandates the creation of a stable environment in central Europe.'[89] Clearly this was not an aspect of the Commission's mandate nor could it be covered by its recommendations. The provision of the MX for extended deterrence, however, could.

The Need for Consensus

That the Commission's Report straddles contradictions and can be interpreted in different ways by focusing on different sections of its 29 pages demonstrates that it is primarily a political document. In presenting its proposals the Commission was attempting to provide in one package a comprehensive answer to the problems it was devised to address. Consequently, strategic coherence was less important than satisfying enough constituencies to re-establish the consensus necessary to overcome the impasse in strategic procurement policy. America's failure to achieve this in the past, the Commission noted, had been the cause of much of the 'now-chronic pattern of perpetual strife and resulting stalemate on these questions'.[90]

The ending of this perpetual strife and the creation of a defence consensus was seen by the Commission as an essential element of its task in solving the strategic vulnerability and modernisation problem. Implicit in the Commission's statement to this effect was the realisation that much of the perception of vulnerability which permeated the debate was itself the product of that constant acrimony and criticism. The policy process, as much as the missiles, was a source of weakness and vulnerability for it was in an attempt to manipulate that process that the vulnerability issue had been generated and sustained.

The Commission's call to rise above the conflicts of the previous decade was an attempt to gain as many supporters for the package as possible. The Report's carefully balanced recommendations were also designed for this purpose, to offer something to everybody in order that the Commission could command at least the initial support of all those concerned, and enough support beyond that to sustain a majority in Congress over the longer term. Thus the last paragraph of the Report stresses the need for a

> broad approach to strategic force modernisation and arms control that can set a general direction for a number of years. Clearly there will be, and should be many different views about specific elements in that approach. But the Commission unanimously believes that such a new consensus – requiring a spirit of compromise by all of us – is essential if we are to move toward greater stability and toward reducing the risk of war.

Although mentioned, the strategic goals of the Commission's package of policy recommendations are not the focus of this concluding piece of text. Indeed the stability uppermost in the minds of the authors of this section of the Report seems to be the political stability of the US national security policy process. Here the emphasis is less on a balanced package of proposals than on a 'broad approach' in which 'many views about specific elements' need to be yielded in a 'spirit of compromise'. Reconciling contradictions in order to establish a clear direction in strategic policy, this last section seems to imply, is less vital than the need to reach an acceptable agreement and to move forward. In short, the Report's concluding paragraph is making the political point that consensus and compromise are more important than consistency and coherence. The political test of this, however, would be whether the Commission could get the Congressional support wanted. That test would in large part depend on whether all the parties involved were willing to see these proposals as the basis of a new consensus, or at least the minimal elements of a temporary and specific bargain.

10   Reactions to the Commission's Recommendations

Introduction

Reaction to the Report's recommendations was mixed, with considerable opposition from some quarters, especially on those provisions relating to the MX. Within both branches of Government there was a reluctance to give up the previously favoured basing schemes for the MX and to embrace the Commission's new plans. This was due to a desire to see the MX based survivably and the belief that it could still be done. As late as 12 March 1983, for example, Presidential Science Advisor George Keyworth and SAC Commander General Davis were still publicly promoting Dense Pack as the executive branch's favoured solution, while Assistant Secretary of Defense Richard Perle and START negotiator Edward Rowney also let their opposition to the new plans be known.[1] This opposition was effectively quelled by the White House, however, which was all too aware of the importance of the Commission politically for the survival of MX.

In Congress, on the other hand, there was still residual support for the only basing scheme which had won the confidence of both Houses, the MPS plan. The testimony before Congress of several Commission members, most notably Brown and Scowcroft, also fuelled the desire to stick with the MPS, especially when these experts conceded 'that political and environmental pressures, rather than purely military factors, figured most prominently in the unanimous recommendation' on MX basing, and that without such constraints they would have 'favoured an elaborate "shell game" of the sort advocated by Carter' of 200 missiles in thousands of shelters.[2] Brown's subsequent endorsement of the Commission's proposals that, 'we have to proceed from where we are now ... there is no way to go back', was not helped by this earlier frankness.[3] Brown's testimony, together with the Report's admission of the importance of local political opposition to the MPS, brought angry reaction from some members who still demanded an ideal rather than a politically acceptable solution.[4]

Many Congressmen expressed concern at the abandonment of a secure basing mode for the MX and rejected the Commission's proposals as a shallow political compromise that did not provide the invulnerability originally planned.[5] Rep. Joseph P. Addabbo, Chairman of the House Defense Appropriations Subcommittee and leader of the fight against MX funding in 1982, expressed fears that 'Putting a $20 billion program in vulnerable

Minuteman II silos makes no sense unless you are looking forward to a first strike capability, and it could easily be envisioned by the Russians as that.'[6]

The Commission's argument that the MX was necessary to persuade the Soviets to move in the direction of a more stable force posture was questioned from a number of quarters. Tom Wicker, for example, was typical in his support for part of the package while being critical of specific elements. He said that the recommendations on arms control and Midgetman made much sense but that 'the commission is not so persuasive in linking these proposals to its plans to deploy 100 MX missiles in existing Minuteman silos'.[7] The idea that the B1, the Stealth bomber, the Minuteman III, the Trident D5 and cruise missiles all provided incentives enough without MX to persuade the Soviets to move away from fixed-based heavy missiles made vulnerable by these American systems was commonly expressed.

By making a strong political case for the MX the Commission hoped to discredit the argument that ICBM vulnerability was a problem that mattered. Without there being any attempt to link these events in logic, Scowcroft, for example, argued that, 'Four American Presidents have said that the MX is important, if not essential, to our national security. If we back away from it now, it will underscore our paralysis for both our opponents and for our friends and allies.' If the MX were rejected, he argued, the INF deployment 'will be in deep trouble, that's the first thing. Arms control talks would be in jeopardy, and the Soviets could begin behaving with greater impunity.'[8] This was a new twist to the use of threats for political purposes. While previously it was suggested that ICBM vulnerability would result in Soviet adventurism, now not deploying a vulnerable MX was used to argue the same point. Senator Glenn was not convinced, pointing out that,

> we have had four Presidents ... who have favoured 200 MXs in hardened
> sites and various modes proposed. This did not move the Soviets to
> negotiate apparently. Why do we think that now putting half that force in
> soft sites is going to induce the Soviets to negotiate?[9]

Others, such as Jeff McMahan, argued that to justify MX as a way of influencing Soviet 'perceptions of our national will and cohesion' was ironic since 'The MX has not been notable for its beneficial effects on national cohesion, and this is unlikely to change in the future.'[10]

Reactions to the Strategic Implications

Concern over Launch on Warning
Of more concern than the credibility of the Commission's arguments, however, was the anxiety felt in many quarters about what the deployment

of vulnerable MX missiles meant for American strategy. It seemed absurd to many that the missile justified for so long as a solution to ICBM vulnerability was now to be based in vulnerable silos. Senator Biden, for example, asked how the MX could deter an attack on the ICBM force while it was itself vulnerable unless the missile was designed to be either launched on warning or used in a first strike capacity. Biden questioned the expenditure of $15 billion for a period of 2.5–3 years on a capability only 3 per cent of which was likely to survive a Soviet attack, 'unless you are talking about launching on warning?'[11] Weinberger and General Vessey heightened this speculation by testifing before Congress that the MX would only be vulnerable 'if we ride out an attack'.[12] The basic concern with the countervailing role of the MX was not without foundation. The new Air Force leadership which took office in 1982 was less concerned with survivability precisely because it was more willing to contemplate what it termed 'prompt retaliatory launch'.[13] Indeed, Robert Toth reports one four star General as stating that he wanted the MX even if it had to be 'put in the Pentagon parking lot', that is, above ground and extremely vulnerable.[14] Toth goes on to explain that as well as the obvious disadvantages that vulnerable deployments have for crisis stability, that same vulnerability increases the probability that these systems would actually be used in countervailing roles, thereby increasing the credibility of their deterrent effect. Toth explains that,

> The less survivable the weapons, the faster the United States must respond in a crisis. And a strategy of faster US reaction means more certain and more punishing retaliation against the Soviets, while a policy of riding out a surprise attack before retaliating opens the way to all kinds of problems and potential failure.[15]

Although such a posture has obvious dangers, the absence of such elements from a force posture could cause the opposite problem. As Kent and Thaler explain,

> the more robust the Soviets believe first strike stability to be in a crisis, the less they might hesitate to precipitate a deep crisis by engaging in serious aggression, for example, in Western Europe ... one might argue that an optimal amount of first-strike instability is possible: that is, enough to deter the Soviets from generating a major crisis (say, by invading Western Europe), but not enough to allow a major crisis to spiral out of control.[16]

A 'limited' deployment of 100 MX missiles may well have constituted such an optimum in the opinion of some strategists.[17]

This view, however, was not widely shared, especially in Congress. The prospect of the MX being launched on warning or even on 'certain' knowledge of an attack created concerns that America's strategy, and indeed America's survival, would be put on a hair trigger. Furthermore, the adoption of this posture would put a considerable amount of pressure on the Soviet Union to do something to alleviate the vulnerability of its ICBM force. As retired Air Force Lt General Kelly H. Burke, then deputy chief of staff for research and development, said in 1981,

> So long as we feel that our missiles are threatened – and we do feel this – two things happen. When we get into confrontation situations, we are going inevitably to want to inch our finger close to the trigger because under attack, we will be under a use-it-or-lose-it circumstance. The Russians will know that we feel this way and will put their finger closer to the trigger.[18]

With 75 per cent of Soviet warheads deployed on land-based system compared to 25 per cent of the US arsenal, the vulnerability of their ICBMs was much greater than that in the US and would have been accentuated by this MX deployment. Rather than forcing the Soviets to move away from high-value fixed targets, as the Report suggested as a justification of MX, it was widely believed that the deployment of the Peacekeeper would prompt the Soviets to adopt a launch on warning posture in fear of a first strike.[19] Thus, rather than bringing about the improvement in crisis stability which the Commission claimed as its ultimate aim, the reverse would be the case. Furthermore, the critics felt, rather than being presented on its own merit as an alternative strategic concept, the case for the MX was sheltering behind a rationale which was completely counter to its real purpose. 'On this crucial point', McGeorge Bundy complained, of making the adoption of 'launch on warning' necessary, 'the Commission is alarmingly silent. It would have done better to recognise more candidly its deliberate abandonment of our most important single standard for strategic force planning.'[20] This aspect of the solution to the vulnerability problem, however, was not debated candidly. This was mainly due to the fact that no political purposes could be served by such a debate and no agreement was likely since,

> the parties to the debate over basing schemes for ICBMs and over strategic policy in general held views that could not be bridged. Consensus foundered because their underlying premises did not mesh and because launch on warning was too controversial to advocate openly.[21]

Efforts were made to justify the case for the MX in ways which directly countered these allegations. Indeed Scowcroft argued that under 'a massive attack on our ICBM silos, I think the Commission would acknowledge, yes we will lose them ... that it would destroy a substantial portion of the ICBM force.' Thus Scowcroft implicitly rejected the launch on warning rationale but went on to state that 'in any other circumstances of war initiation ... arising from a substantial war in Europe, with or without the use of nuclear weapons, we believe that those weapons would be available for use'.[22] By advancing the extended deterrent rationale for the MX, Scowcroft demonstrated less concern with the consequences of ICBM vulnerability at the level of a central counterforce exchange than he did for the need for the limited options counterforce role which the MX was to provide. That there were situations in which the MX could be used defensively even if in escalation, however, was a source of alarm to those critics who feared that the MX could be used in a first strike capacity.

Concern Over MX's First Strike Potential

Allegations over the first use potential of the MX were met by the argument that the planned MX deployment was too small to constitute a destabilising first strike force. The Report makes this point in two ways. First, 'The throw-weight and megatonnage carried by the 100 MX missiles is about the same as that of the 54 large Titan missiles now being retired plus that of the 100 Minuteman III missiles that the MXs would replace.'[23] While accurate, this focus on throw-weight and megatonnage was disingenuous, as these measures of capability were far less important than the substantial increase in accuracy and warheads which the MX represented over the older systems. In warhead numbers alone, 54 Titan and 300 Minuteman III warheads were still considerably fewer than their 1000 MX replacements. Even if insufficient for all possible targets, 1000 warheads was not viewed as a 'limited' strike by its critics. Furthermore, the MX also had a longer range than the existing force, enabling it to target all of the Soviet SS-18s which were 'out of the normal range of the Minuteman ICBMs'.[24]

The second argument presented by the Commission had more credibility, 'It would provide a means of controlled, limited attack on hardened targets but not a sufficient number of warheads to be able to attack all hardened Soviet ICBMs, much less all of the many command posts and other hardened military targets in the Soviet Union.'[25] The flexibility of a missile with ten warheads for use in a 'controlled' and 'limited' way cast some doubt on this rationale, however. Moreover, the force of this argument was reduced substantially when the longer-term implications of the MX deployment were considered in conjunction with the other elements of the strategic modernisation proposals since 'a force of 10 Trident submarines armed with [D5] missiles and 100 MX ICBM would provide enough warheads to target each Soviet ICBM with two silo-busting warheads while leaving approximately 600 warheads in reserve'.[26] The deployment in Europe from

1983 of 108 Pershing II missiles, each equipped with a reloadable missile, also caused Moscow great concern about the growing counterforce capability of the US arsenal. Although the MX deployment was presented as an 'interim' measure until an unspecified number of SICBMs had been built, the Report remained silent as to the conditions under which the MX would be removed.

The Commission's arguments did not convince all the critics of the MX who asserted that once the MX production line had been opened and the principle of deployment conceded, there would be considerable pressure to augment the force. Indeed, the Report states that 'Should the Soviets refuse to engage in stabilising arms control and engage instead in major new deployments, reconsideration of this and other conclusions would be necessary.'[27] News that the Pentagon planned to buy 223 MX missiles to facilitate the deployment of 100 missiles in silos, the rest supposedly being necessary for training, testing and spares, caused further alarm as they could also be used for reloading the silos.[28]

MX Missile Numbers

Whether the proposed deployment of 100 MX represented all the missiles that the Air Force and the administration wanted or just the first tranche was a subject of some speculation at the time, as was the reason that the Commission had settled on the figure of 100. Several Congressional staffers who had pressed for a figure of 50 MXs were under the impression that the Commission 'were about to recommend 50, that was their instinct, but they were told by DOD that if they wanted administration support they needed 100'.[29] Other evidence, however, suggests that this story was merely a way of pacifying this constituency. Indeed, what debate there was within the Commission on numbers was mainly concerned with whether there ought to be 200 or 100 MXs. The idea of a deployment of 50 was discussed and rejected as not being sufficiently worthwhile. Schlesinger, Brown, Reed and Haig all pressed hard for a recommendation of 200 missiles, arguing the need to get a good return on the investment on research and development already spent on the missile and a desire to give the President maximum bargaining power with Moscow. There was also a feeling that Congress might want to cut this figure and that it would be better for them to do this rather than the Commission. Therefore it was better to start high in order to have a decent number left in the end.[30]

The main discussion on numbers concerned capability but for political reasons the Commission decided to recommend what it regarded as the minimum necessary for targeting purposes. As Scowcroft explains, actually the Commission basically thought that there should be 200, but since the administration had already said 100 we didn't feel we could go back on to 200 ... the MX was designed to give us additional, quick hard target kill capability and for the additional [capability] 100 was a minimum [and as such] it was OK, we wouldn't have proposed it, but too we would have been comfortable with 200 for the longer run, see we never did come up with a specific number of the single warhead ICBM ... it was, you know a question of what the traffic would bear, and the Government of the time were prepared to make concessions on the numbers in order to get the programme, so that's basically it.[31]

Scowcroft's admission that the Commission was influenced by the precedent set by the adoption of 100 MX missiles for Dense Pack deployment is ironic as this figure was purely provisional. It is a further indication of the less than ideal way in which the US decision-making process operated in relation to this issue. The decision to recommend 100 missiles also shows how sensitive the panel was to political pressures. It also shows that the limitation to 100 missiles was not arrived at in order to avoid a larger deployment which might have appeared destabilising in Moscow. Indeed, 'had the traffic been able to bear it' a deployment of twice the size may well have been proposed. The critics' fears, it seems, that 100 missiles could represent the thin end of the wedge, were not without foundation.

The MX as Bargaining Chip

Concern about the prospect of greater numbers of MX missiles being deployed once the principle of building the missile had been conceded was furthered by the discussion which surrounded one of the Commission's other rationales for the missile, that it would be useful in arms control negotiations with the Soviets. As Schlesinger explained, 'The original motive for the MX as we emerged from the SALT I discussions was to persuade the Soviet Union to move down in throw-weight and we would then be prepared to abandon the MX.'[32] Scowcroft, asked if the MX was on the negotiating table replied,

I do not think we ought to build systems solely to negotiate them away. But just as we build military systems for our security, we ought to be prepared to get rid of them if that security can be obtained in any other way. And as Mr Schlesinger said, I think everything is on the table in that sense.[33]

This position was not universally shared. Just before the Commission's initiation Reagan distanced himself from this position stating that

> This [MX] is not in the sense of a bargaining chip ... No. We need modernisation. Even if we get the reduction of arms ... this would not be the missile that would be taken out of circulation.[34]

Nor did the delivery and endorsement of the Commission's Report seem to change the administration's line on this subject.[35] Leon Sigal cites Commission member John Deutch as indicating the line that 'only the second tranche of 100 MX is to be available ... to be swapped for cuts in Soviet SS-18s and SS-19s'.[36] Clearly it was not agreed what was meant by the argument that the MX could be used to persuade the Soviets to negotiate. The prospect that a larger deployment of MX missiles could be threatened as an inducement to Soviet concessions only redoubled the efforts of its critics.

Opposition to the Small ICBM

The Midgetman was envisaged by the Commission as having something to offer every constituency. It was supposed to be attractive to the hard liners in Congress who were eager to see new weapons built to offset what they perceived to be a Soviet advantage in land-based missiles. It also had something to offer those whose main concern was arms control and stability because it would be less threatening to Soviet land-based forces than the MX. The small missile, however, attracted criticism from all sides. Most significant of this was the hostility displayed towards it by the Air Force.

USAF's main concern was its cost implications. Already forced to contemplate cuts in the defence budget, USAF saw the SICBM with its 1:1 ratio of warheads to missiles as an extravagance compared to the 10:1 provided by the MX. While it was ready to go along with the Midgetman if that was the price of securing the deployment of the MX, it made sure that its concerns received full press coverage.[37] Reports appeared that there would need to be between 3000 and 5000 SICBMs, that they would be vulnerable to barrage attacks by large Soviet missiles with multiple warheads, and that in any case the Midgetman would not be ready until the 1990s. It was also inaccurately alleged that Midgetman's deployment would violate SALT II because of the limitation on mobile missiles and only testing one new ICBM. The latter contradicted the argument on the missiles' in service date as the unratified SALT II treaty's duration was only planned to extend to 1985. There was also much concern expressed that Midgetman, by virtue of its mobility, would not be secure from accident, sabotage, terrorist hijacking, or protesters. Thus the old arguments against mobile missiles were used because at this time and to this constituency this form of ICBM vulnerability was politically useful.

So widely reported was the Air Force's disquiet with the small missile that Woolsey addressed the subject directly in testimony, stating that

> within the Air Force, just speaking frankly, there are a number of people who would strongly prefer continuing to move forward with the MX as the long run basis of the US ICBM force, but I believe that the political problems that the missile has had in Congress, the importance of having an ICBM force in the long run ... would lead a number of civilian and military leaders in the Department of Defense to look favourably ... upon an evolution toward a small single warhead ICBM.[38]

While Midgetman offered the best technical solution to the long-term threat to the ICBM force its progress was not supported by the administration and Air Force. This was because the wider issue of ICBM vulnerability no longer served their political purposes and its technical solution in the form of Midgetman threatened to take resources from other cherished programmes. The idea of Midgetman had solved the political problem of ICBM vulnerability, therefore the reality of the missile was not considered necessary. Thus new arguments were now found to support this changed political agenda and reports abounded about the prohibitive cost of the small missile.[39] 'Military concerns' were also reported over whether it would have 'enough power to carry a big enough warhead to knock out Soviet missile silos and command bunkers if the Soviets increase the strength of such underground installations' and about accuracy concerns resulting from its mobility. 'Technical questions' were also raised over 'developing vehicles able to carry the missile around at 40 to 50 mph and still protect itself, its crew and its missile cargo from atomic attack'.[40]

The case for Midgetman was not advanced by the actions of Harold Brown despite the much vaunted unanimity of the panel. Brown 'issued a separate statement of caution' on the small ICBM after the publication of the Report, which said,

> This new system still has many uncertainties, particularly in terms of cost and of the feasibility of hardening truck mobile missiles or super hardening of fixed shelters ... [and] unless the US can negotiate severe limits on a level of ICBM warheads, the number of single warheads needed for a force of reasonable capability could make the system costs prohibitively great.[41]

Weinberger was also hostile to Midgetman. Speaking shortly after leaving office in 1987, Weinberger spoke frankly about what he thought of both the Commission's package generally and the small missile specifically.

I wasn't happy with some of the recommendations. I was happy with the fact that they endorsed completely the entire modernisation plan of the President ... That's the part I liked. But then they said, the political realities are that in order to do this you have to satisfy the small missile people. So after you do all of these things that the President recommended, then in order to get some votes, you've got to give the small missile people what they wanted. And I thought that was pretty silly.[42]

The Secretary of Defense was no less reticent about expressing this hostility at the time. Indeed Weinberger demanded that the Commission's endorsement of the programme be highly conditional.[43] Thus the Report states,

Decisions about such a small missile and its basing will be influenced by several potential developments: the evolution of Soviet strategic programmes, the path of arms control negotiations and agreements, general trends in technology, the cost of the programme, operational considerations, and the results of our own research on specific basing modes. Although the small missile programme should be pursued vigorously, the way these uncertainties are resolved will inevitably influence the size and nature of the programme.[44]

This was in marked contrast to the much more categoric language used with regard to the MX.

The lukewarm support for the Midgetman emanating from the Air Force and the Pentagon generated concern amongst the proponents of the SICBM and an uncertainty over future commitment to the concept. It was pointed out that the only vote in the Congress on the Scowcroft Commission's rec-ommendations would be for or against production money for the MX missile and that no one in Congress could guarantee that a vote for the MX was also a vote for Midgetman.[45] The White House could simply use the Commission's recommendation to gain support for a compromise over the MX and go on to expand the MX force while not really putting its weight behind Midgetman.

This was not a groundless concern. There were those in the executive branch who were quite candid in their reference to the Report's equivocal language, on which they had advised, to question the nature of the commitment which the White House had undertaken.[46] It is also interesting to note the impression which the arms control component of the Report made on the Secretary of Defense. Recalling the Commission in both his memoirs and in a 1988 TV interview, Weinberger talked only of a deal involving the two ICBMs. At no point did he recall a commitment to radical change in the administration's approach to the START negotiations championing the cause of crisis stability.[47]

Reaction to the Arms Control Component

Despite the fact that the Commission's arms control proposals offered the means to ameliorate the threat to the ICBM force, reaction to them was mixed. The Joint Chiefs of Staff and the State Department were concerned about changing the unit of account in START from launchers to warheads because of the problem of verification.[48] This difficulty was even more daunting when considered alongside the implications of mobile missiles. There was a feeling even amongst those in the arms control community who favoured the proposals on strategic grounds that there might come a day when the deployment of mobile systems might be regretted as heralding the end of negotiated, verifiable agreements. As one analyst pessimistically observed,

> Wait till the hard-liners get started. They'll say the Soviets have a missile in every garage; they'll say prove they don't have that. We've been through that before. That's what the missile gap was about.[49]

Positive reaction to the Commission's proposals in this area came from the many Congressmen who saw the Report as a vehicle for moving the administration towards a more constructive and reasonable position on arms control.[50] Support for the MX, it was felt, would be a price worth paying if it provided enough leverage to persuade the administration to adopt a negotiable and stabilising approach to START in Geneva. Nor did this approach to the executive branch seem unreasonable or unobtainable. The President seemed genuinely keen to emphasise the arms control implications of the plan in his meetings with Congressional leaders on the Commission's recommendations. The reason for this, however, was less to do with Reagan's support for the package than that the administration was facing an uphill battle to defeat a resolution on a nuclear freeze in the House and was in need of Congressional support and a new initiative in this area.[51] In this instance, as in so many others, the short-term agenda dictated Presidential action at the expense of long-term policy or strategic coherence.

Selling It: Forging a Coalition for the Commission

A hard-sell campaign was organised by the panel to present their case to Congress before, during and after the deliberations of the Commission. In January informal meetings took place at the houses of Aspin and Woolsey, attended by these two key players together with Scowcroft, where the likely Congressional support of various proposals was discussed. More formally, between January and April, the Commission heard evidence from 203 witnesses in 31 sessions.[52] Not all the lobbying on strategic modernisation at this time was being carried out by the Commission itself, however. When the study was commissioned there was a great deal of speculation in the press about the conclusions that it would reach, with many reports which, though purporting to be descriptive, were in effect more prescriptive. Supporters and lobbyists for a whole variety of schemes were keen to have their idea paraded in the press and associated with the distinguished panel of experts, even if erroneously.[53] Press speculation on the prospects for strategic defence continued throughout the Commission's deliberations but was particularly intense after the President's speech on national TV on 23 March which launched the Strategic Defence Initiative (SDI).[54] As a consequence of SDI, the Commission's comments on this subject were carefully scrutinised by the press.[55]

Efforts to promote the Commission's recommendations and thus to bury the vulnerability issue were also undertaken by the White House. On 5 April 1983, the day before the Commission was due to present its Report to the President, Reagan quoted some of the calculations from the Report and announced that if it were accepted he could cut $8 to $10 billion off the defence budget over the next five years. Most of these savings, he explained, were to come from the less costly basing plan proposed for the MX. The cost of the strategic modernisation programme was to be $19.9 billion, $14.6 billion of which was earmarked for MX. Many administration officials also went out of their way to explain the merits of the Report and to pave the way for its acceptance. In apparent anticipation of a Congressional backlash against the plan to deploy MX missiles in vulnerable Minuteman silos, Weinberger sent letters to members of Congress urging them to tone down their focus on the vulnerability of the land-based deterrent. Weinberger wrote,

> The tendency in the past, both in the Pentagon and on the Hill, has been to over-focus on the basing issue and to disregard the real question as to the need for modernizing the ICBM force. The ICBM vulnerability problem is only one of the myriad of strategic issues that requires serious examination by the Congress before casting a decisive vote this year.[56]

Aspin had also advised the Defense Secretary not to greet the Report with too much enthusiasm in order to give the impression that he had not got things entirely his own way. 'I said to Cap and others' Aspin explained, "Don't crow when this comes out; we need you to grouse. Say this isn't very good, but, etc, etc". This Weinberger duly did, testifying that 'No one is saying this is a perfect solution.'[57]

Brown's role in persuading Democrats on Capitol Hill to support the package was invaluable to the administration. His contribution was that of bipartisan support, something materially lacking from the Carter administration's approach to the vulnerability issue. Brown appeared on television to support the package and gave numerous interviews to the press.[58] Other Commission members stressed different aspects of the recommendations.[59] Woolsey, for example, emphasised that a new consensus had been achieved because agreement had been reached not to repeat the counterproductive feuds that had characterised the strategic modernisation process of the past.[60]

According to White House spokesman Larry Speakes, the President himself did 'a fair amount of personal lobbying' for the MX in the period immediately after the Commission Report was presented on 6 April. Reagan urged support for the package and 'especially MX', stating that 'If Congress rejects these proposals, it will have dealt a blow to our national security that no foreign power would ever have been able to accomplish.'[61] Reagan's personal support for the Commission was an important element in removing the concern for the vulnerability which he had helped create.[62]

The Congressional Response

Getting approval for the Commission's package from a Congress which had embraced the vulnerability issue was no easy task. It was a skilfully manipulated process in which Aspin's role was central. Ensuring at least the acquiescence of the Democratic party leadership was an early priority. Aspin approached House Majority Whip Thomas Foley first, then using his support the two men broached the idea of bipartisan support for the package with House Speaker and senior Democrat Tip O'Neill. Because the leadership of the Party in the House was split on the issue, Aspin persuaded O'Neill not to formally oppose the package.[63] Aspin's second tactic was to build a coalition of moderate Democrats and Republicans in the House which would support the proposals as they emerged. Central to this approach was the support of Representatives with a high profile in defence matters whose judgement on this subject would influence less committed and knowledgeable members. The recruitment of Gore and Dicks was an early and significant fillip to this campaign. Other recruits included Vic Fazio, Dan Glickman and Richard Gephart.

Aspin's third and most important contribution concerned the placement of the deliberations on the panel's proposals in the House legislative timetable. This political masterstroke was instrumental in extending the duration of the Commission, ensuring that the Report arrived at the White House later than planned, and that there was a delay before the President made his recommendations to Congress.[64] The thinking behind this move, as Aspin explained, was that,

Everyone was looking to cut money for defence; if the Scowcroft report was up first it would sink ... We had a vote on the budget resolution, and people could vote to cut the defence budget there, and the senate could vote on [prospective ACDA Director] Adelman and all the doves could vote against him, and the House could vote on the freeze ... people will then have voted three dove votes. The usual pattern of this place is that people begin to get a little uncomfortable if they've gone too far one way and start looking for a way to pop back the other way.[65]

It was particularly important that the Report be delayed until after the freeze resolution was considered by Congress, as this had generated considerable public interest and support and was sure to attract the votes of members not normally known for supporting such causes. Presenting the opportunity for these members to vote in a way which preserved the appearance of balance, Aspin calculated, would maximise the chances of legislative success for the first vote on the Commission's proposals. The House vote to carry an albeit ambiguous freeze resolution on 4 May strengthened the chances of success still further for Aspin's plans.

The biggest difficulty which the supporters of the Commission encountered in trying to generate support for the recommendation was convincing people that the administration was serious on arms control and that it would genuinely treat the proposals as a package. Aspin's problem was how to portray the first legislative test of the proposals as anything other than a vote for funding the MX. In order to stress the concept of the package, Aspin devised the idea of writing to Reagan to solicit a more formal and specific endorsement of support for arms control and the small missile than had been implied by the President's acceptance of the Commission's Report.[66] The House letter sent on 2 May carried the support of forty members; it read:

Statements in the press – attributed to 'high ranking officials' in the Department of Defense and others – have already raised the suspicion that there are some in the administration who embrace the Scowcroft Report, not in its entirety, but only as a means to the end of securing Congress' approval for the deployment on MX ... [it demanded that] a major effort will be promptly undertaken to bring sharper focus to the proposed single warhead ICBM, and to allay concerns that it cannot be realised in a reasonable period of time.[67]

The letter, together with a similar one from the Senate, stated that support for the MX would only be forthcoming and sustained if the President gave his assurance that he would adopt all the recommendations of the Commission and if tangible evidence to this effect was evident in a short period of time.

There was also some consideration given to attaching a provision to the MX appropriations bills to guarantee that the provisions on arms control were observed and that work on the Midgetman would proceed as quickly and as efficiently as possible.[68] This would have been added to the 1984 DOD authorisation bill limiting the number of MXs to be funded until Congress was satisfied with the administration's progress.

The administration was happy to agree to this request for an endorsement of arms control and allowed Aspin, Gore and Dicks to collaborate with the administration, including Perle, on the wording of the response. The President's reply, sent on 10 May, stated that the administration was reviewing its START position in the light of the Scowcroft Commission and that it supported the Report's endorsement of the MX and the SICBM and would not deploy systems which could give the impression of being a first strike force.

Precisely how the administration interpreted the Report was left unstated, however, as was any mention of the MX as a transitional weapon or indeed as a bargaining chip. Critics of the President's letter castigated its language as vague and insubstantial.[69] The response which the letter to the Senators received from the President was identical in all but one important respect. The Senate letter had included mention of their support for the 'build-down' proposal and the response which they received from the White House stated that this approach would be taken very seriously in the next START round. The proposal adopted by the Senate on build-down, however, did not embrace the logic of the Commission's thinking on stability and did not preclude the replacement of older systems with MIRVed warheads or other larger and potentially destabilising systems.[70] Accordingly, the promises and reassurances granted by the White House to both houses of Congress contradicted each other. 'So the President was bowing in the direction of both deploying more missiles (the Midgetman) in the name of stability and removing more warheads (the build-down) at the same time that he was seeking to deploy one thousand warheads on one hundred missiles.'[71]

The exchange of letters which Aspin orchestrated was a crucial element in securing the support of many sceptical members. Another part of his tactics was to stress continually the incremental nature of the control which Congress had over the progress of the administration's modernisation plans. Persuading members that funds for the MX could be controlled on a step-by-step basis was central to their willingness to accept the assurances of the administration that it would follow through on the other recommendations once initial authorisation of the MX had been granted. Because of the labyrinthine nature of Congressional approval, it was believed, there would be other opportunities, in Dicks' words, to 'hold the administration's feet to the fire'.[72] Critics were much less confident of this approach. Once the missile entered production, they argued, it would develop a considerably wider constituency and be much more difficult to kill.[73] 'There is no package in this resolution', Joseph Addabbo insisted in the House debate, 'Do not kid yourselves. That is what you are voting for this afternoon – the procurement of MX missiles and the deployment of MX missiles.'[74] In an attempt to win every possible vote for their campaign, however, the opponents of the resolution also used the issue of the vulnerability of the new ICBM in its fixed silo as an attempt to gain support from the right. The use of this argument was a rather ironic twist in the fortunes of the MX, which shows the essentially political nature of the vulnerability argument, which was used and abused when and where and by whomever it suited.

In practice the vote for Congressional approval of the first element of the Commission's proposals came on 25 May 1983 in the form of Concurrent Resolution 113 appropriating funds to approve both flight testing and silo basing for the MX.[75] The administration won the vote by a majority of 53 votes but with a very fragile coalition of support. The 239 to 186 vote, however, gave a majority of 20 more than the opponents in the House had hoped for.[76] In all, 44 members who voted against the MX in July 1982 voted for it on this occasion, as did 55 who had voted for the freeze resolution. Clearly Aspin's calculations on the desire of members to 'balance' their voting record and thus the timing of the vote had proved fruitful for this key MX vote.

The debate itself was extremely acrimonious, particularly in the Democratic Party whose members had led both groupings on the issue.[77] There was also considerable resentment among the rank-and-file members that the leadership of the party had nearly all supported the MX while two-thirds of the House Democrats had voted against it.[78]

From Consensus to Discord

Partly due to this internal friction in the Democratic Party but mainly as a consequence of declining confidence in the administration's willingness to make progress on arms control, the fragile coalition which Aspin had put together soon began to disintegrate. A letter to the Senate Foreign Relations Committee from Arms Control Director Adelman in June indicating that the MX would be bargained away only if the Soviets dismantled their entire force of large MIRVed ICBM convinced many that there had been no genuine 'movement' in the administration's position.[79]

The next vote in the House on 20 July, in the form of an amendment to delete the $2.6 billion for MX saw a substantially reduced majority (220 to 207) for Aspin's coalition. Two amendments were adopted by the House on voice votes, however, which showed the impatience and frustration of the House with the administration. The first of these did what had been contemplated at an earlier stage, it prohibited the procurement and development of the MX from outrunning the development of the SICBM, while the second cut the number of missiles authorised from 27 to 11.[80] The latter was submitted by Congressmen Gore and Dicks, eager to show that their promises of support really were conditional on tangible progress.

The first vote on the Commission's proposals in the Senate took place the day after the watershed division in the House on 25 May, with a majority for de-fencing funds for the MX being registered through Concurrent Resolution 26 which was passed 59 to 39. The following day 19 of those who had voted for the MX wrote to the President informing him that their continued support for the missile was contingent on significant progress in arms control. Nevertheless, even without substantial progress being made in the arms control process, these threats to withdraw support from the administration did not materialise.

This was one of the main achievements of the President's Commission. By breathing life into the MX missile it had overcome the political obstacle of the vulnerability issue. The threat to the US ICBM force had mattered most in policy terms as a constraint on MX deployment and this had now been removed. From now on MX's constituencies would grow as industrial and political interests fell in behind organised labour which had already declared itself in favour of the missile. The Reagan administration had shown itself to have learned a great deal about the political process in Washington by its third year and had traded both military and domestic porkbarrel with key legislators with considerable political skill for this crucial vote. Whether support for the MX could be sustained, however, and whether the other goals set out in the Commission could be achieved, remained to be seen.

Undaunted by their failure in the Senate, the opponents of the MX continued their campaign over the summer of 1983 by mobilising the support of anti-nuclear groups engaged in Congressional lobbying. The House Democrats succeeded in persuading the administration to make some modest changes in its START position and, more interestingly, to continue the existence of the Scowcroft Commission in an effort to advise on the implementation of the recommendations.[81] The Commission, which was drawn from both parties, was intended to provide the appearance of bipartisanship and continuity in national security policy.[82] This unprecedented development, creating in effect a new body with no constitutional authority, demonstrates the degree to which the Commission had become part of the political process necessitated by the failure of the established institutions to command the respect necessary for effective government.

The continuation of the Commission provided a bridge between legislators and the administration as the wrangles continued throughout 1983 and 1984 with regard to the future of the MX. In response to their threat to withdraw support for the MX they secured from the administration several concessions on arms control in advance of the resumption of START talks on 6 October 1983. Among these, were the inclusion of the build-down proposal in the American negotiating position, the rejection of fierce demands for Soviet reductions, the recognition of the need to trade American advantages in bombers for Soviet advantages in ICBM, and the appointment of Commission member James Woolsey to the START team in Geneva.[83] The inclusion of build-down as one of the Commission's concessions is indicative of the way in which its agenda had also changed. Having succeeded in burying the vulnerability issue, the Commission now felt free to pursue a broader arms control agenda with the administration, even though this would not necessarily have reduced ICBM vulnerability.

The confidence of the Congressional opponents of MX was shattered by events in the autumn of 1983 far from Capitol Hill which altered their calculations of victory. The Soviet destruction of the Korean airliner, together with the Kremlin's decision to end all arms control negotiations following the deployment of INF missiles in Europe, plunged East–West relations into deep crisis. It was in this climate that the House and Senate granted approval on 1 and 7 November respectively for the purchase of the first 11 MX missiles. Those legislators who had expressed such confidence in their ability to control the fortunes of the MX were learning the limits to which their control over external events extended.

The resumption of Congressional consideration of the MX question in the spring of 1984 coincided with the 'final report' of the Scowcroft Commission. Issued on 21 March 1984 this nine-page document was a didactic exposition on the merits and limitations of arms control, containing arguments explaining the need for an understanding of asymmetrical force postures, recommending 'extreme caution in proceeding to engineering development of an active strategic defence system' and containing a very forthright statement expounding the virtues of crisis stability, stating, 'The first goal of nuclear arms control efforts should be to ensure that the nature of the forces on each side does not provide a military incentive to strike first with nuclear weapons in a crisis.'[84] Reiterating its advocacy of its original proposals the Final Report points out the need for the package of the SICBM to achieve stability and arms control limitations in order to make Midgetman viable, thus providing one of the main rationales for the MX as an instrument of persuasion towards arms control.[85] In doing this, however, the Commission was highlighting the dilemma which Congress faced. With the Soviet Union absent from all arms control negotiations and refusing to set a date for their resumption, the basis for supporting MX as a means to encourage a de-MIRVed and more stable regime was removed. Yet for Congress to reject the MX now might also be seen as rewarding the Soviets for their actions and could also sink any prospect of the de-MIRVing regime outlined by the Commission.[86] The absence of any real prospect of MX exerting any leverage either on Moscow or the administration led the supporters of the package to adopt new measures in order to save the fragile coalition which they had built. Supporters in the Senate proposed to reduce by half or more the 40 MX missiles the administration had proposed to procure, while in the House Aspin and Pritchard managed to get an agreement to hold off MX procurement for six months, in which time if the Soviets resumed negotiations a further six-month delay might be contemplated.[87] This arrangement, designed as a stalling device until the presidential election result was known, broke down in less than a week. As a result the future of the MX – and indeed of US strategic nuclear modernisation – returned once more to the partisan, stop–go politics of the pre-Commission period, characterised by division within and between the legislative and executive branches of government but without the vulnerability issue at its core.

Why Was the Commission Successful?

The eventual breakdown in 1983–4 of the procurement proposals and arms control processes recommended by the Scowcroft Commission do not entirely detract from the significant role which this body played in the national security policy of the first Reagan administration. From a situation of near-total disarray in late 1982, the Commission provided a mechanism for achieving a great deal of constructive dialogue and consensus building within and between Congress and the administration. It also provided a means by which US strategic modernisation, and the vulnerability issue in particular, could be discussed and evaluated in a broader and more sophisticated context than had been the case for at least the previous seven years.[88]

The Scowcroft panel was not a Commission in the ordinary sense of a body simply involved in deliberating on a subject and then presenting its findings. Rather, the President's Commission on Strategic Forces, following the trend set by the Greenspan Commission on Social Security, was part of the political process. Not only was this Commission different from what had gone before but the contrast between it and the previous studies organised by Weinberger and the Pentagon could not have been greater. The Townes Committees conducted technical studies of a technical issue, the vulnerability of the US Minuteman force, and they produced technical answers to this problem as was their charter. Their only political involvement was the interference of Weinberger, which only hindered their mission. These reports, however, were wholly unsatisfactory in dealing with the problem because the issue had become politicised. As a consequence, the Scowcroft Commission, recognisably a political construct, was necessary to resolve the impasse which the administration found itself in. Accordingly, the White House's search changed from looking for an MX basing plan that was technically survivable to one that was politically survivable, and the Scowcroft Commission played a vital role in this. As Greenberg and Flick explain,

> The Scowcroft Commission succeeded in acting where the Department of Defense, Department of State, ACDA and NSC had failed. And it succeeded precisely because it was a commission. Any similar plan emanating from an executive agency (assuming, of course, that the president would have had the temerity to suggest it on the heels of 'Big Bird' and 'dense pack') would beyond doubt have been rejected by Congress.[89]

This analysis was shared by a Congressional aide to a Democratic member, who expressed the similar sentiment that,

> Without the Scowcroft Commission, we'd never have the MX. If Weinberger had said he wanted to put the MX in Minuteman silos, he'd have been laughed off the hill. But you have Brent Scowcroft and Harold Brown – who advise Democrats – saying it, and you had a bipartisan commission of genuine experts. It was a beautiful move.[90]

The central role played by Woolsey and Aspin was also a politically astute decision. The fact that neither of them had any position of responsibility in either the executive branch of government or the Democratic leadership in the legislature meant that they were not identified with any bureaucratic position. It was this feature of the body which Commission member Alexander Haig identified as both its strength and its weakness, stating that, 'Because the commission operated outside the framework of the executive branch, it was able to cut across the interrelated disciplines and the competing priorities of foreign, defence, domestic and arms control policy and achieve a coherent approach.'[91] Important though the process was, however, that alone was not enough to account for the willingness of both the Reagan administration and Congress to reach an agreement on a set of proposals including the MX in

Minuteman silos. More important than the instrument, was the desire to be delivered from this thorny problem. There was an enormous sense of frustration and exhaustion with the MX basing saga which had become the most tangible manifestation of the ICBM vulnerability problem. This translated into a tremendous desire to put the issue behind them and move on to other important questions. This general willingness to cut a deal resulted in most participants being willing to accept proposals which earlier did not meet the requirements which they then applied.[92] As one observer noted, 'The Scowcroft Commission was accepted with reservations but also with relief to get the problem over.' He went on to add that a 'lot of people were very sceptical with the amount of money being spent on systems for esoteric arguments at the time [MPS] – the window of vulnerability was less widely accepted than imagined'.[93]

No one got everything that they wanted from the Commission's report but most got enough to satisfy them sufficiently to support the package as a whole.[94] This was the basis of the bargain at which Scowcroft aimed, explaining,

> We got, in a political sense, people who supported the MX, would accept the small missile as a way to get the MX. People who didn't like the MX but liked the small missile, but would accept the MX because of the small missile. And people who perhaps didn't feel any modernisation was necessary, but in order to get the Reagan administration active in arms control, would support a strategic modernisation.[95]

The Report itself was skilfully written and did a competent job in presenting competing rationales in a single package. As a key Commission member remarked, the reaction to the two missiles was different, there was 'a different kind of embrace, as, the one for the MX comparatively speaking was a short term embrace, not quite a one night stand, but the small missile was something special that there was a pretty long term commitment to'.[96] For this reason consistency was seen as less important. It was a short-term infidelity to crisis stability for the sake of invulnerability. One witness to the Commission, General Kent, was equally philosophical about the contradictory elements of the Commission's proposals, stating, 'I testified and kept quiet about the illogic 'cos it was a good thing. It looks bad to the world that we don't have direction ...[and anyways] Why not overlook logic, we overlooked logic getting into the thing.'[97] A similar, though less eloquent, explanation was offered by a Congressional staffer to explain the willingness of Congress to accept the proposals, stating 'The Scowcroft Commission came up with non solutions to non problems that were acceptable because they were not really seen as major problems any more.'[98] While the Commission is given credit for closing the window of vulnerability, however, it is important to note that it did not do this in a way which would have discredited those who had championed this notion. Instead, what the Commission did was to redefine the problem out of existence by changing the theoretical assumptions of the analysis. As Scowcroft told the Senate Foreign Relations Committee Hearings

> We have not, as many have suggested, reversed or closed the window of vulnerability. Whatever one thinks about the vulnerability of those silos, they are likely to become more vulnerable in the future ... But we feel that survivability at the moment is not so crucial an element of our overall problem as to require further immediate steps.[99]

Not everyone was happy with the conclusions reached by the Commission, however. The Committee on the Present Danger and the other right-wing groups who had been so instrumental in promoting the notion of the window of vulnerability were not convinced either by the arguments of the Commission or indeed the policies of the Reagan White House. In July 1982 the Heritage Foundation produced a report which castigated the White House for 'procrastinating over solving the ICBM vulnerability problem [while] the USSR is building 200 modern high yield, highly accurate ICBMs a year'.[100] Similarly, the CPD's March 1982 paper *Is the Reagan Defence Program Adequate?* warned that 'timely program to restore the survivability of US strategic forces are not included in the administration's programs ... [and that] Regretfully, the conclusions reached by the CPD in its first statement on 11th November 1976, remain valid today: "Our country is in a period of danger, and the danger is increasing ..."'[101]

Such criticisms, however, were of little consequence for several reasons. First of all, most of the personalities of substance had left these organisations, particularly the CPD, for positions in the administration. From such a position they could not criticise the President. More importantly Reagan's reputation on defence matters was such that it would be difficult to criticise him from the right with any credibility. Furthermore, this criticism from outside the political process failed to appreciate that the debate had moved on. No longer could narrow technical issues excite the same concerns as they once did, because the more general feeling of vulnerability on which they fed had been both satisfied and exhausted by three years of the Reagan administration.

There were of course some 'true believers' in the administration itself who clung on to the notions peddled by the CPD, but on the whole they were either unaware that the concept was essentially political and that the political context had changed or else they were forced to go along with the Commission, justifying it purely as a means to get the MX. In the latter group were Weinberger and Ikle who merely paid lip service to the Commission.

Ikle, it seems, did not fully understand the necessity of the political role of the Commission, criticising it for its lack of intellectual rigour, stating,

> At the Pentagon Weinberger and me didn't think it was necessary ... They got de-railed from doing a thorough analysis into doing a patched up job with Congress. That's not the role of a bipartisan Commission. Most bipartisan Commissions try to get the facts together, like the Kissinger Commission on Central America.[102]

Others among the supporters of the window of vulnerability idea, who had not been convinced by the intellectual dexterity or the political necessity of the Commission, were provided with an alternative strategic rallying point by the President in the form of SDI. This *Washington Times* editorial demonstrated beautifully the ease with which certain constituencies could switch their attention from ICBM to societal vulnerability; 'Replacing an aging and vulnerable Minuteman system with a youthful and vulnerable Peacekeeper arsenal is like replacing rotten house timbers with balsa wood ... [a better solution would be to follow] ... the President's farsighted decision to embrace the strategy of defence.'[103] The threat and promise value of the window was exhausted so why not move onto something else – hence SDI. The old threat was the window of vulnerability and the promise of a buildup. Both of these had gone sour for Reagan. SDI played on the threat of nuclear war and the buildup, and the promise was of invulnerability. It was the case of the Great Communicator replacing the window of vulnerability – a rhetorically created problem – with SDI, a rhetorically creative answer. In a sense the Commission allowed the Reagan administration to 'escape forward' from the problems of the national security policy in the eyes of informed observers of the defence scene, while SDI allowed Reagan to 'escape forward' at a more popular level. Both SDI and the Scowcroft Commission dispelled the immediate danger of the time and made the problem seem neither immediate nor insuperable. In this sense both polices, by rhetoric, closed the window of vulnerability in a way which Carter's elaborate strategic modernisation programmes did not.

Conclusions

The aim of this study has been to examine the evolution of the debate over the pre-launch vulnerability of the US force of land-based intercontinental ballistic missiles to a Soviet pre-emptive strike within the American political and strategic debate. More specifically the study asks why the issue of Minuteman vulnerability rose to prominence in the way it did in the late 1970s during the Carter Presidency and fell away as an issue in the early 1980s under President Reagan without any apparent solution to the problem as it had come to be defined. It also seeks to determine what this episode tells us about the US strategic and political debate. Why did this rather arcane threat construction play such a prominent and enduring role in these debates?

If the problem of ICBM vulnerability had been identified and efforts taken to alleviate the threat in the form of the Trident/ULMS programme then why did the issue achieve and maintain its profile as such a central concern of strategic debate while other threats were ignored? Why was the US strategic debate dominated by the threat to ICBMs while failing to be 'disturbed by the fact that the Russians could have easily wiped out those SLBMs which were in port ... and [was] not concerned about Soviet "suitcase" bombs being brought into Washington, circumventing all radars and destroying the US leadership without any warning'?[1] Jervis concludes that part of the explanation of threat construction lies in the terrible nature of the nuclear condition. 'When one faces a set of terribly unlikely but catastrophic contingencies, it is hard to sort out which should be of concern.'[2] While this argument undoubtedly offers part of the explanation, his further assertion that 'The selection of problems is quite arbitrary' requires further elucidation.

The growing vulnerability of the ICBM force achieved a degree of legitimacy as an issue for debate because it could not be dismissed out of hand *a priori* since most experts accepted that the threat to Minuteman was a problem in some form or other. The debate was so protracted and acrimonious, however, because there was no agreement as to what the nature of that problem was, and consequently, there could be no agreement as to how it could be resolved. The repeated references to 'the threat to Minuteman', meaning different things, was possible because it was an issue which operated simultaneously on several different levels. It is possible to identify at least five of levels of meaning.

(1) As a threat to the ICBM force which did not really matter. At its most basic level was the acceptance that increases in Soviet accuracy made

the US ICBM force more vulnerable but that this could be offset by improvements in the other legs of the Triad.

(2) As a threat to the ICBM force which did matter. At this level was the view that the invulnerability of the ICBM leg had to be maintained to avoid the Soviets's ability to concentrate their efforts in overwhelming the air- and sea-based elements of the Triad.

(3) As a threat to US deterrence at the level below assured destruction. At this level it was argued that the lack of a reciprocal prompt hard-target kill capability in the form of a survivable ICBM force would have grave implications for extended deterrence in Europe and for American diplomacy in countering Soviet adventurism in the third world.

(4) As a threat to assured destruction. At its most extreme level the threat of a Soviet attack against the ICBM force was seen as sufficient to nullify America's deterrent threat since, it was argued, to respond to an attack on Minuteman would be to invite societal destruction.

(5) As a symbol of American weakness in the face of Soviet strategic and geopolitical advances. At this the most general level ICBM vulnerability was viewed as evidence of America's alleged 'decade of neglect' and of its lack of moral and political will to compete with Moscow.

With all these confused levels of meanings surrounding 'ICBM vulnerability', it is little wonder that debates about its implications proved a fertile ground in which to propagate other arguments concerning strategic innovation and the procurement of cherished projects. An amorphous subject shrouded in the mystique of arcane debate over nuclear deterrence certainly provided opportunities for exploitation for other purposes.

The fact that the debate operated at different levels, however, does not in itself explain how the issue became established in the way it did. Nor does an explanation of the issue's profile lie in the argument that ICBMs were a uniquely valuable component of the Triad, as ICBMs, as some have argued. The argument that survivable ICBMs were necessary to provide a prompt second strike counterforce threat was not demonstrated.[3] Furthermore, an analysis of the vulnerability of the ICBM force and the command, control and intelligence systems which supported it demonstrates that, while the survivability of both these systems would be necessary to ensure the integrity of the land-based leg, it was the threat to the missiles and not the C^3I which was politicised. This was the case despite the fact that throughout the entire ICBM vulnerability issue most studies of the subject, including Strat-X and Carter's Nuclear Targeting Policy Review, concluded that the threat to the ICBMs themselves was much less important than that to their supporting command and control networks. As Bruce Blair explains, 'For both sides, command and control vulnerability was the main drawback of retaliation after rideout ... [with the result that] the option of retaliation after ride-out was not technically viable.'[4] Thus the vulnerability of the C^3I network necessitated the institution of launch on warning without becoming an issue of political debate in its own right. That it should be the vulnerability of the ICBM force as opposed to that of the C^3I networks which became an issue, however, demonstrates the importance of the politicisation of this subject in establishing its place in the US strategic and political debate. It does not however explain why one issue should be politicised and the other not. Several possible explanations for this must be examined.

One explanation could be that those concerned to publicise the threat to the ICBM force viewed C^3I vulnerability as part of the same problem. If this was the case, however, then much of the highly technical debate about building a survivable replacement for Minuteman was conducted in ignorance of the real problem. If the concern was genuinely two-fold then why not say so? This explanation does not account for why one and not the other vulnerability became politicised, however. An alternative explanation, perhaps, was that the vulnerability of C^3I was ignored because it was viewed as too arcane a subject matter, so obscure and esoteric a set of technologies that it was not amenable to public debate. Did those who politicised the threat to the ICBM force feel that the threat to the command and control network would not be comprehended by Congress or the public?[5] This explanation, however, can not itself explain the differential treatment by the political process of these two vulnerabilities, both of which constituted the same strategic and political problem.

Perhaps a more plausible explanation is that Minuteman vulnerability was politicised because a technical solution to this problem was seen as being readily at hand while the threat to C^3I was seen as more intractable. Certainly the link between the repeated references to ICBM vulnerability and the procurement of a weapons system heralded as the solution to this problem was a constant feature of this strategic and political issue.

The politicisation of the ICBM vulnerability issue was not, however, exclusively linked to the acquisition of one particular weapons system or indeed to the procurement process in general. Rather, the issue was introduced into the US strategic and political debate and maintained as a source of concern for a variety of political purposes which did not always necessarily reflect a genuine concern for this development in its own right. It was a subject which was used to advance strategic and political purposes other than, and in addition to, a concern with the vulnerability of the US ICBM force. In doing so it had consequences and built a momentum unimagined by those who sought to exploit the convenience of this argument.

It was a problem which was introduced at an official level by the Nixon administration for whom the growing vulnerability of the ICBM force provided a very convenient problem for a pre-existing solution (ABM) which neatly tied together a number of domestic and strategic loose ends. As a consequence, ICBM vulnerability became established as an issue at this time because both sides in the ABM debate felt it useful to accept ICBM vulnerability and argue their case from that perspective. It was a problem which the administration introduced because it thought that it had the solution in the form of Safeguard. Once this solution was no longer available for the defence of Minuteman due to the ABM Treaty, however, the problem remained. This pattern of events was to repeat itself throughout the history of the ICBM vulnerability issue.

It is a subject replete with examples of the use and abuse of this threat construction for tactical and expedient purposes by all parties in the debate. Furthermore, where efforts were made to address the issue as a potential problem, these were invariably undermined by the temptation of one group or other to restate the threat. Having established the Minuteman vulnerability issue on the political and strategic agenda as a consequence of the ABM debate, the Nixon administration, for example, set about trying to resolve this concern through the SALT process. The weakness of the American position in these negotiations in the face of the Soviet strategic buildup, however, meant that the US was forced to compromise the objective of limiting the threat to the ICBM force in order to reach an agreement in the form of SALT I. Thus for critics of SALT, ICBM vulnerability gave them an issue around which they could criticise the agreement for its inadequacy in relation to this issue. As a consequence, the SALT I process, rather than resolving the anxieties raised by the concern over ICBM vulnerability, actually heightened the profile of the issue. Nixon's decision to play up the threat to the Minuteman force in order to ensure the passage of both SALT I and his forthcoming defence budget was a further instance of the tactical use of the issue which maintained its presence on the strategic agenda. Similarly the decision of the Carter administration to deploy the MX in the MPS deployment mode was an endorsement of the ICBM vulnerability argument in an effort to secure the passage of SALT II.

In addition to the procurement process the tactical use of the ICBM vulnerability issue was also exploited for other purposes. The strategic innovations promulgated by Secretary Schlesinger together with the modernisation of the Minuteman force's command and control system; much of the criticism of SALT; and the 'competitive intelligence exercise' carried out by Team B were all instances where recourse to the ICBM vulnerability issue was made for tactical political advantage.

This tactical and expedient use of the ICBM vulnerability issue in successive strategic and political debates goes a long way to explain how this threat construction became politicised during this period. It also demonstrates the susceptibility of the US strategic debate to the consequences of decisions taken to satisfy short-term, expedient purposes. It is an issue which demonstrates that while the construction of strategic reality may be prompted for immediate and tactical reasons, and represent only one of a series of alternative realities available at any time, once propelled with authority into the public arena, particular constructions can shape the terms of the subsequent debate, long after the particular issue which prompted it has passed.

Other aspects of this issue are also important in explaining the politicisation of this subject however. These include the role of the strategic arms control process, the prevalence of strategic reductionism in this debate and the symbolic resonance of the threat to Minuteman to the wider geopolitical mood.

Although inextricably linked to the tactical and expedient use of the ICBM vulnerability issue, SALT also contributed to its politicisation by the intrinsic nature of the arms control process itself. SALT focused attention on weapons systems, not targets (or command networks) and in so doing radically altered the way in which the superpower arsenals were measured. SALT also focused attention on ICBM numbers, as opposed to areas of US advantage such as its technological lead and bomber and MIRV superiority which were excluded from the substance or the language of the accords. The tendency to define parity as equal numbers and rough symmetry in the major measures of strategic power was also an approach which led to the view that parity could be easily and meaningfully upset by significant developments away from this symmetry by one side's unilateral action. In this way ICBM vulnerability gave SALT's critics both an issue with which they could attack the agreements and a measure of strategic inequality around which they could coalesce.

The arms control process also contributed to the politicisation of the ICBM vulnerability issue by promoting a technical, as opposed to the political, evaluation of the Soviet strategic threat. The 'bean counting' aspect of the SALT process seemed to legitimise by association a similar approach in calculations of mathematical models of strategic nuclear exchanges. The idea that numbers and weapons' characteristics mattered for SALT seemed to strengthen the argument that such factors had some meaning in threat constructions. The arms control process was instrumental in establishing and elevating the status of strategic experts in the public debate. For the first time SALT had created public discussion of the finer points of nuclear minutia and established the credentials in the public mind of those skilled in this black art. This veneration of experts also explains why much of the discussion of ICBM vulnerability was conducted by groups of insiders with the non-expert public essentially excluded from what became an arcane and technical debate. Although it became a debate dominated by 'experts' it was also one in which the strategic arguments were often used for contradictory purposes. This tactical and expedient use of the ICBM vulnerability issue by both sides in this debate contributed to a general willingness to view the subject in an abstract manner. Even when opposing experts debated the intricacies of a particular point they often did so in a way which lost sight of the more sobering political context. No one it seemed was above the fray. In consequence there was very little common ground which could be appealed to. In a debate in which academics had inflated the threat to Minuteman in order to defeat the Safeguard ABM system and then argued its irrelevance in support of SALT, and in which successive governments had used the threat to justify contradictory programmes in quick succession, what was and was not plausible had become difficult to determine for many observers.

The various levels at which this issue was debated also contributed to its impenetrability to outside observers. With all participants in the debate accepting that the issue was a problem in some sense, however, it is easy to understand how a general acceptance of ICBM vulnerability as 'a problem' developed. How much of a problem and why were the only parameters of the debate. It was in this context that the reductionist arguments of the critics were able to present the ICBM vulnerability issue in its most politicised form, the window of vulnerability scenario. The argument that the growing vulnerability of the US ICBM force substantially nullified the deterrent capability of the United States was presented as a mathematically deduced product of force comparisons between the strategic arsenals of both powers. It claimed to explain by reference to the strategic balance the reasons why the Soviet Union was engaged in 'adventurism' in the third world. In practice, however, it was a threat construct which was heavily dependent for its plausibility on the political mood of the country at that time. The CPD's scenario seemed to have a resonance in the US strategic debate because it offered a simple, technical, military, explanation for new and alarming geopolitical events. By linking US fears about the consequences of the Soviet nuclear buildup with the fear that the world was out of control, or more precisely was beyond the control of US foreign policy, the alarmists' case seemed to offer explanation. The oil shocks of 1973–4; the US defeat and expulsion from Vietnam in 1975; the loss of Iran and the subsequent hostage crisis together with Soviet activity in Africa and the invasion of Afghanistan were events which could not otherwise be explained without an acceptance of the failure of containment policy and the limitations of

American power.[6] By contrast the CPD offered a simple explanation of the prevailing situation and an apparently viable solution. It was, they argued, a technical problem requiring a technical fix, the simple matter of military procurement and increased defence spending. This explanation provided both a simple diagnosis and a simple solution for a feeling of vulnerability which was more political, complex and irresolvable than the alarmists over ICBM vulnerability were willing or able to admit. Despite its lack of sophistication, however, this explanation united technical strategic determinism (ICBM vulnerability explains Soviet adventurism) with political symbolism (Minuteman is vulnerable and is symbolic of political neglect) and thus further politicised the issue as the window of vulnerability.

Throughout its history the issue had been defined in terms that were apparently most amenable to solution with the instruments available at the time. By the time that the issue was presented in the window of vulnerability incarnation, however, the issue had achieved a momentum of its own. Although presented as a technical problem requiring a technological, military fix, by this stage the issue had become inextricably linked at a symbolic level to the prevailing political mood. As a consequence the problem was impossible to solve at the first level without a solution being found at the more substantive but intractable political level. Thus attempts by the Carter administration to recast the ICBM vulnerability problem by trying to explain the technical implausibility of the scenario failed because the symbolism of the vulnerability still resonated with the public's wider sense of anxiety. Similarly, attempts by the Carter administration to embrace the importance of ICBM vulnerability in support of the deployment of MX/MPS and SALT II also failed to quash this issue because its national security policies were judged incapable of removing that sense of strategic anxiety which the window of vulnerability issue symbolised. Carter was seen as too weak to solve the general sense of vulnerability which the ICBM issue had now come to symbolise, no matter what he actually proposed for the missiles themselves. The Carter administration was simply not strong enough to recast the issue politically.

The relationship between the technical vulnerability of the US ICBM force and the symbolism which it had come to represent was only resolved with the advent of a new administration. While Carter eventually embraced the technical vulnerability of the ICBM force while rejecting the symbolic significance of the issue, the opposite was true of Reagan. The new President's endorsement of the window of vulnerability was based not on a technical appreciation of the threat to the US ICBM force but instead on a more general feeling of inadequacy in America's military provisions. Only when the ICBM vulnerability issue was recognised for what it was, a political, symbolic issue and the Scowcroft Commission convened in 1983 to broker an acceptable way forward between the administration and the Congress, was it possible to lay the issue to rest. Though the Commission relied on many of the technical and political arguments which had been common currency for many years, by the time this panel brokered its deal there had been an important shift in the prevailing strategic climate. The sense of societal vulnerability which the threat to Minuteman had symbolised had been dispelled by the Reagan administration's arms buildup and the uncompromising rhetoric of the President himself. It was not that the new administration had altered the strategic balance in a way which reduced the vulnerability of the ICBM force. Indeed they were more technically vulnerable in the 1980s than ever before. What had altered was the perception of the symbolic importance of that vulnerability. The reversal in the public's perception of threat led to a reversal in the reductionist logic of the ICBM vulnerability problem. From the perception that since the problem was caused by a technological change there must be a technological solution, came the reversal of this logic by the Scowcroft Commission that, since there was no technological solution then there must be no technological problem. Even the limited technical solution that the Scowcroft Commission recommended, the small ICBM, did not actually need to be deployed for the vulnerability issue to disappear. It was almost as if the idea of the Midgetman alone was enough to satisfy those concerned with the threat to the ICBM force.

Only the intellectual and political dexterity of the Scowcroft Commission and its artfully crafted Report, it seems, were able to put this issue to rest. Thus the politically contrived vulnerability issue led to a politically contrived solution which put political obfuscation and consensus above the immediate security concerns of the United States. What the Scowcroft Commission did for elite opinion in defusing the salience of the ICBM vulnerability issue Reagan's Strategic Defense Initiative did at a popular level, replacing the focus on the vulnerability of the deterrent with a new agenda promising the invulnerability of the population.

The fact that the issue fell away as a concern in the US strategic and political debate following the Scowcroft Commission Report and the Strategic Defense Initiative reinforces the argument that it was the repeated politicisation of the issue rather than the technical vulnerability which created this political problem. Introduced and exploited by successive administrations and their critics the issue developed a momentum which by the late 1970s had taken on a new identity as a symbol of vulnerability well beyond the technical threat to Minuteman. As a result it was a problem which could only be solved at this political level.

The ICBM vulnerability issue also suggests some interesting conclusions about the relationship between the politicisation of this subject and the policy process itself. Not only did the weaknesses inherent in the political process allow the issue to be politicised and manipulated for tactical advantage but the process itself was also altered by that politicisation.

The vulnerability of the political process to the dangers of short-termism is clearly demonstrated by the way in which the threat to the ICBM force was continually exploited for political advantage. The spectre of the threat to Minuteman was repeatedly resurrected to justify solutions which were meant to solve this problem but ultimately left an unsatisfied sense of anxiety. This was true of the debates on Sentinel, Safeguard, SALT I and SALT II and on the MX missile. All parties in the debate used arguments concerning the threat to the ICBM force in highly tactical ways with little apparent thought to the long-term implications of their actions on the cohesion of the strategic policy of the United States. If the administration of the day did not like the results of a particular study then a new one was instituted to make sure that supporting evidence for a given position was found. If the CIA's National Intelligence Estimates did not produce the expected results then an outside group of hawks could be found to give a more supportive interpretation of the existing evidence. The damage that these actions did to the integrity and the reputation of the policy process seems to have been routinely ignored in favour of some immediate political advantage.

The development of the ICBM vulnerability issue also illustrates the vulnerability of the decision-making process to actions which were less professional than one might have expected. The resort to the rationale that Sentinel and then Safeguard were needed because of ICBM vulnerability, or that the MX deployed in Minuteman silos would be no more vulnerable than in the MPS basing scheme demonstrates a remarkable willingness to rely on flimsy intellectual arguments for major policy decisions. The history of this issue is replete with examples where key decisions were made based on incorrect or poorly understood evidence. Kissinger's belief that the American scientific community would support a point defence system even if it relied on area defence technologies, or the Scowcroft Commission's decision not to recommend 200 MX missiles in the mistaken belief that this would be an increase in the total number that the administration had planned for Dense Pack, are two examples of policy made on the basis of imperfect knowledge. The Ford administration's decision to allow Team B to conduct their influential exercise without the basic knowledge of current Soviet or indeed American strategic thinking was yet another example of lack of professionalism in the policy process.

The longevity of the ICBM vulnerability issue provides an opportunity to see how each administration drew upon the institutional knowledge on this issue that had been accrued over the years. After all many of the technical options of how to deal with the problem had been extensively set out in the Strat-X study of 1968. The result of such an analysis is very instructive in demonstrating the unwillingness of successive administrations to learn from the policy failures or even the technical evaluations conducted by preceding officials. This is no more clearly illustrated than in Weinberger's approach to the MX missile and the cancellation of the MPS basing scheme and his insistence on the re-evaluation of the air mobile concept. It was the Reagan administration's contempt for the available institutional knowledge on the issue of MX basing which was largely responsible for the failure of this element of its strategic modernisation plan. In this instance, as in so many other ways in which the ICBM vulnerability issue was mishandled and cynically manipulated, the policy process was as much a source of weakness and vulnerability as the missiles themselves. Indeed, the device which the Reagan administration used to finally dissipate the ICBM vulnerability issue further illustrates the institutional weakness of the American policy process to resolve this issue. Despite the many permanent actors and agencies provided by the highly pluralistic system of government in Washington it was an ad hoc presidential commission acting beyond the usual parameters of such a body which was used to dissipate this issue. Acting as a parallel policy-making body it was the Scowcroft Commission which was able to draw upon the institutional knowledge of the national security community and create a bi-partisan device to put this issue to rest. This use of an outside body invited in by an administration to make policy recommendations on its behalf was an interesting parallel to the introduction into government thinking of the ICBM vulnerability issue in its most politicised form by the Team B exercise in 1976. In these instances then, the politicisation of the issue was not only facilitated by the policy process but the process itself was altered by that politicisation.

The ICBM vulnerability episode provides a unique window on the relationship between the political and technical efforts of governments to secure defence postures which they believed provided for America's security, and the effect that these efforts had on the perception of the Soviet threat. It is an issue which shows the highly political nature in which one aspect of the Soviet threat could be used in American politics. Although presented as a technically deduced product of Soviet advances, the way in which the threat to the ICBM force was presented, manipulated and exploited demonstrates how politically contingent these threat constructions were on the immediate policy needs of the moment. Although the ULMS/Trident programme had been set in motion in response to the threat to Minuteman, the issue was to become inextricably linked to various other procurement processes because it served other political purposes to do so. The implications of the threat to Minuteman were also debated as part of these procurement processes as a substitute for a more candid discussion of the strategies necessary to deter the Soviet Union. That this debate was conducted in this abstracted form raises the question as to whether the United States was capable of having a more open strategic debate at this time. Was the Minuteman vulnerability issue and the debate over the role of ICBMs in American strategy which it produced the most acceptable form for a debate about strategy because it was conducted in terms of the threat to the US rather than American plans for attacking the Soviet Union? Certainly it was a debate which successfully exploited the vulnerability which the American people felt to the prospect of a Soviet nuclear threat. As such it was the issue best suited to the manipulation of the politics of threat.

Appendix A

Members of the Scowcroft Commission

Nicholas F. Brady, New Jersey businessman and investment banker.

William Clement, former Deputy Under Secretary of Defense for Nixon and Ford and former Governor of Texas.

John Deutch, Dean of Science at MIT, and former Under Secretary at the Department of Energy under Carter.

Alexander M. Haig Jr, former NATO SACEUR and Secretary of State under Reagan.

Richard Helms, CIA Director under Nixon.

John H. Lyons, a Vice President and Defense Subcommittee Chairman of the American Federation of Labour Congress of Industrial Organizations and the chairman on the committee on defence issues.

William J. Perry, former Under Secretary of Defense under Carter.

Thomas C. Reed (Vice Chairman), former Secretary of the Air Force and Special Assistant to Reagan on National Security.

Brent Scowcroft (Chairman), National Security Adviser to Ford.

Levering Smith, retired Vice Admiral and former Director of Special Projects for the Navy, coordinator of the Polaris programme.

R. James Woolsey, Secretary of the Navy under Carter.

Senior Counsellors to the Scowcroft Commission

Martin Atkins (Executive Secretary), Director of Offensive and Space Systems for the Secretary of Defense.

Harold Brown, Secretary of Defense under Carter.

Lloyd N. Cutler, Washington lawyer who worked for Carter over SALT II ratification.

Henry A. Kissinger, Secretary of State to Ford and National Security Adviser to Presidents Nixon and Ford.

Melvin R. Laird, former Secretary of Defense.

John McCone, former Director of the CIA.

Donald H. Rumsfeld, former Secretary of Defense.

James R. Schlesinger, former Secretary of Defense under Nixon and Ford.

Appendix B

Non Confidential Interviewees

Kenneth Adelman
Nicole Ball
Richard Betts
Bruce Blair
General Kelly Burke
Al Carnesale
Richard Clark
Beth Cohen-DeGrasse
John Collins
Robert De Grasse
Ralph Earle
Robert Ellsworth
Terry Frieze
Joseph Fromm
Frank Gaffney
Andrew Goldberg
General Daniel Graham
Colin S. Gray
Morton Halperin
Herb Hetu

Fred Ikle
John Isaacs
Robert H. Johnson
Spurgeon Keeny
General Glenn Kent
Michael Krepon
Jonathon Medelia
Mike Mawby
Ken Mayers
Paul Nitze
General William Odom
George Quester
General Brent Scowcroft
Larry Smith
Paul Stares
Strobe Talbott
David J. Tracktenberg
Paul Warnke
Larry Weilder

Bibliography

United States Government Documents

Statements by Secretaries of Defense
Statement of Secretary of Defense Robert S. McNamara before the House Armed Services Committee on the *Fiscal Year 1964–68 Defense Program and 1964 Defense Budget*, (Washington DC: US Government Printing Office, 30 January 1963).
Statement of Secretary of Defense Robert S. McNamara before the House Armed Services Committee on the *Fiscal Year 1966–70 Defense Program and 1966 Defense Budget*, (Washington DC: US Government Printing Office, 18 February 1965).
Statement of Secretary of Defense Clark M. Clifford on the *1970 Defense Budget and Defense Program For Fiscal Year 1970–74*, (Washington DC: US Government Printing Office, 15 January 1969).
Statement of Secretary of Defense Melvin R. Laird before a Joint Session of the Senate Armed Services and Appropriations Committee on the *Fiscal Year 1971 Defense Program and Budget*, (Washington DC: US Government Printing Office, 20 February 1970).
Statement of Secretary of Defense James R. Schlesinger to the Congress on the *Fiscal Year 1975 Defense Budget and Fiscal Year 1975-79 Defense Program*, (Washington DC: US Government Printing Office, 4 March 1974).
Statement of Secretary of Defense James R. Schlesinger, to the Congress on the *Fiscal Year 1976 and Transition Budgets, Fiscal Year 1977 Authorization Request and Fiscal Year 1976–80 Defense Program*, (Washington DC: US Government Printing Office, 5 February 1975).
Report of Secretary of Defense Donald H. Rumsfeld to the Congress on the *Fiscal Year 1977 Budget and Its Implications for the Fiscal Year 1978 Authorization Request and the Fiscal Year 1977–81 Defense Program*, (Washington DC: US Government Printing Office, 27 January 1976).
Statement of Secretary of Defense Harold Brown, *Department of Defense Annual Report, Fiscal Year 1979*, (Washington DC: US Government Printing Office, 1978).
Statement of Secretary of Defense Harold Brown, *Department of Defense Annual Report, Fiscal Year 1980*, (Washington DC: US Government Printing Office, 1979).
Statement of Secretary of Defense Harold Brown, *Department of Defense Annual Report, Fiscal Year 1981*, (Washington DC: US Government Printing Office, 1980).

Presidential Statements
R.M.Nixon, 'A Report to the Congress: US Foreign Policy for the 1970s, A New Strategy for Peace', *Public Papers of the Presidents of the United States, Richard M. Nixon*, (Washington DC: US Government Printing Office, 18 February 1970).
R.M.Nixon, 'Second Annual Report to the Congress on United States Foreign policy,' *Public Papers of the Presidents of the United States, Richard M. Nixon*, (Washington DC: US Government Printing Office, 1971).
Inaugural address of President Jimmy Carter, 20 January 1977, *Presidential Documents: Jimmy Carter*, 1977, Vol. 13, No. 4: 89.

President Ford, 'State of the Union', The President's Address Delivered before a Joint Session of the Congress, 12 January, Presidential Documents, Vol. 13 (Washington DC: US Government Printing Office, 1977).

'Announcement by President Reagan: Strategic Arms Program, 2 October 1981.' *Weekly Compilation of Presidential Documents*, 5 October 1981. *Documents on Disarmament in 1981*, United States Arms Control and Disarmament Agency, (Washington DC: US Government Printing Office, 1981).

President Reagan, 'America's Foreign Policy Challenges for the 1980s', Address before the Center For Strategic and International Studies, Washington DC, 6 April 1984. in *Realism, Strength, Negotiation: Key Foreign Policy Statements of the Reagan Administration*, (Washington: United States Department of State, Bureau of Public Affairs, 1984).

Congressional Hearings and Reports

United States House of Representatives, Armed Services Committee, *Hearings: US Strategic National Security Programs*, 96th Congress, 2nd Session, (Washington DC: US Government Printing Office, 1978).

United States House of Representatives, Subcommittee of the House Committee on Appropriations, *Department of Defense Appropriations for 1986*, 99th Congress, 1st Session, (Washington DC: US Government Printing Office, 1985), Part 2.

United States House of Representatives, Subcommittee of the House Appropriations Committee, *Safeguard Anti Ballistic Missile System*, 91st Congress, 1st Session, (Washington DC: US Government Printing Office, 22 May 1969).

United States House of Representatives, Subcommittee on International Political And Military Affairs of the Committee On International Relations, *US–USSR Relations and Strategic Balance*, 94th Congress, 2nd Session, (Washington DC: US Government Printing Office, September 1976).

United States House of Representatives/United States Senate, Joint Committee on Defense Production, *Defense Industrial Base: Industrial Preparedness and War Survival*, (Washington DC: US Government Printing Office, 17 November 1976).

United States Senate, Appropriations Committee, *Department of Defense Appropriations, Fiscal Year 1973*, Part 1, 92nd Congress, 2nd Session, (Washington DC: US Government Printing Office, 17 November 1972).

United States Senate, Armed Services Committee, *Authorising Appropriations for Fiscal Year 1971 for Military Procurement*, 91st Congress, 2nd Session, (Washington DC: US Government Printing Office, 14 July 1970). Report No. 91–1016.

United States Senate, Armed Services Committee, *Military Authorization of Defense Appropriations for Fiscal Year 1971*, 91st Congress, 2nd Session, (Washington DC: US Government Printing Office, 20 February 1970), Part I.

United States Senate, Armed Services Committee, *Military Implications of the Treaty on the Limitations of Anti Ballistic Missile Systems and the Interim Agreement on Limitations of Strategic Offensive Arms*, 92nd Congress, 2nd Session, (Washington DC: US Government Printing Office, 25 July 1972).

United States Senate, Armed Services Committee, *Military Implications of the Treaty on the Limitations of Strategic Offensive Arms and Protocol Thereto (SALT II Treaty)*, 96th Congress, 1st Session, (Washington DC: US Government Printing Office, 1979), Part 1.

United States Senate, Armed Services Committee, *Modernisation of the US Strategic Deterrent*, 97th Congress, 1st Session, 1981 (Washington DC: US Government Printing Office, 1982).

United States Senate, Armed Services Committee, *Strategic Force Modernisation Programs*, 97th Congress, 1st Session, (Washington, DC: US Government Printing Office, October 1981).

United States Senate, Armed Services Committee, Preparedness Investigating Subcommittee, *Status of US Strategic Power*, 90th Congress, 2nd Session, (Washington DC: US Government Printing Office, 1968).

United States Senate, Armed Services Committee, Subcommittee on Research and Development, *Department of Defense Authorization for Appropriations for Fiscal Year 1979*, 95th Congress, 2nd Session, Part 8. (Washington DC: US Government Printing Office, February 1978).

United States Senate, Foreign Relations Committee, *The Arms Control and Foreign Policy Implications of the Scowcroft Commission Report*, 98th Congress, 1st Session, (Washington DC: US Government Printing Office, 11 May 1983).

United States Senate, Foreign Relations Committee, *Military Implications of the Treaty on the Limitations of Anti Ballistic Missile Systems and the Interim Agreement on Limitations of Strategic Offensive Arms*, 92nd Congress, 2nd Session, (Washington DC: US Government Printing Office, June 1972).

United States Senate, Foreign Relations Committee, *Nuclear Test Ban Treaty*, 88th Congress, 1st Session, (Washington DC: US Government Printing Office, August 1963).

United States Senate, Foreign Relations Committee, *Nuclear Weapons and Foreign Policy in Europe*, 93rd Congress, 2nd Session, (Washington DC: US Government Printing Office, 20 February, 4 April 1974).

United States Senate, Foreign Relations Committee, *The SALT II Treaty*, 96th Congress, 1st Session, Parts 1–5. (Washington DC: US Government Printing Office, 1979).

United States Senate, Foreign Relations Committee, *US–USSR Strategic Policies*, Subcommittee on Arms Control, International Law and Organization, 93rd Congress, 2nd Session, (Washington DC: US Government Printing Office, 4 March 1975).

United States Senate, Foreign Relations Committee, *Warnke Nomination*, 95th Congress, 1st Session, 8 and 9 February 1977. (Washington DC: US Government Printing Office, 1977).

United States Senate, Foreign Relations Committee, Subcommittee on Arms Control, International Law, and Organisation, *Briefing on Counterforce Attacks*, 93rd Congress, 2nd Session, (Washington DC: US Government Printing Office, 11 September 1974).

United States Senate, Foreign Relations Committee, Subcommittee on International Law and Disarmament Affairs, *Strategic and Foreign Policy Implications of ABM Systems*, 91st Congress, 1st Session, (Washington DC: US Government Printing Office, 27 March 1969).

United States Senate, Foreign Relations Committee, Subcommittee on Arms Control, International Law and Organisation, *US and Soviet Strategic Doctrine and Military Policies*, 4 March 1974. (Secret hearing held on 4 March, sanitised and made public on 4 April 1974). (Washington DC: US Government Printing Office, September 1974).

Report of the President's Commission on Strategic Forces, (Washington DC: US Government Printing Office, April 1983).
Final Report of the President's Commission on Strategic Forces, (Washington DC: US Government Printing Office, 21 March 1984).
Jonathan Medalia, *Domestic Considerations Affecting the Deployment of a Multiple Protective Structure Basing Scheme for the MX Missile*, Congressional Record Office, (Washington DC: US Government Printing Office, 1980).
'The SALT Syndrome: Charges and Facts: Analysis of an Anti-SALT "Documentary"', *Congressional Record-Senate*, (Washington DC: US Government Printing Office, 30 July 1980), S 10366-71.

Jimmy Carter Library Archive Material

Letter from Douglas J. Bennet, Jr, Assistant Secretary for Congressional Relations, to Congressman Jack Kemp, Carter Presidential Library, White House Central File, Box FO 40, File No. FO 6-1 11/21/78-2/10/79.
Letter from Professor Waldo Chamberlain, Dartmouth College, New Hampshire, to President Carter, 1 June 1979. Carter Presidential Library, White House Central File, Box FO 43, File No. FO 6-1 7/1/79-10/24/79.
Letter from Samuel P. Huntington, Director, Harvard University Center for International Affairs, to Hon. Zbigniew Brzezinski, 9 August 1979. Document No. FO 61, 7/1/79-10/34/79. White House Central File, Box FO 43. Jimmy Carter Presidential Library, Atlanta, Georgia.
Letter from Rostow to Carter and associated White House documentation, 10 August 1977. Carter Presidential Library, White House Central File, Box FO 40, File No. FO 6-1 7/1/77-12/19/77.
Brice Clemow, 'This "Travelling Show" Debates SALT II,' *West Hartfield News*, 17 July 1978. Article sent by Peter B. Johnson of the SALT working group to Tim Kraft at the White House. Carter Presidential Library, White House Central File, Box FO 40, File No. FO 6-1 7/1/78-9/30/78.
Memorandum, Carter Presidential Library, White House Central File, Box FO 40, File No. FO 6-1 7/1/77-12/19/77.

Books

Alexei G. Arbatov, *Lethal Frontiers: A Soviet View of Nuclear Strategy/ Weapons and Negotiations*, (New York: Praeger, 1988).
John C. Baker, and Robert P. Berman, *Soviet Strategic Forces*, (Washington: Brookings Institution, 1982).
Desmond Ball, 'Targeting for Strategic Deterrence', *Adelphi Paper No. 185*, (London: International Institute for Strategic Studies, Summer 1983).
Desmond Ball and Jeffrey Richelson, eds, *Strategic Nuclear Targeting*, (Ithaca: Cornell University Press, 1986).
William H. Baugh, *The Politics of Nuclear Balance: Ambiguity and Continuity in Strategic Policies*, (New York: Longman, 1984).
John Baylis and John Garnett, *Makers of Nuclear Strategy*, (London: Pinter, 1991).
Coral Bell, *The Reagan Paradox: US Foreign and Defense Policy in the 1980s*, (New Brunswick: Rutgers University Press, 1989).

Bruce W. Bennett, *How To Assess the Survivability of US ICBMs*, Rand Corporation, R-2577-FF, (June 1980).

Richard K. Betts, *Surprise Attack: Lessons for Defense Planning*, (Washington DC: The Brookings Institute, 1982).

Richard K. Betts, *Nuclear Blackmail and Nuclear Balance.*, (Washington DC: The Brookings Institute, 1987).

Bruce G. Blair, *The Logic of Accidental Nuclear War*, (Washington DC: Brookings Institution, 1993).

Barry Blechman and Stephen S. Kaplan, *Force Without War: US Armed Forces as a Political Instrument*, (Washington DC: The Brookings Institution, 1978).

Christoph Bluth, *Soviet Strategic Arms Policy Before SALT*, (Cambridge: Cambridge University Press, 1992).

Philip Bobbitt, *Democracy and Deterrence: The History and Future of Nuclear Strategy*, (London: Macmillan, 1988).

Philip Bobbitt, Lawrence Freedman, and Gregory Treverton, *US Nuclear Strategy: A Reader*, (London: Macmillan, 1989).

Mike Bowker and Phil Williams, *Superpower Detente: A Reappraisal*, (London, Royal Institute For International Affairs/Sage, 1988).

Bernard Brodie, *The Absolute Weapon*, (New York: Harcourt, Bruce and Co., 1946).

Harold Brown, *Thinking About National Security: Defense and Foreign Policy in a Dangerous World*, (Boulder: Westview, 1983).

Zbigniew Brzezinski, *Power and Principle: Memoirs of the National Security Advisor 1977–81*, (London: Weidenfeld and Nicolson, 1983).

McGeorge Bundy *Danger and Survival: Choices About the Bomb in the First Fifty Years*, (New York: Random House, 1988).

Richard Burt, (ed.), *Arms Control and Defense Postures in the 1980s*, (London: Croom Helm, 1982).

R.B. Byers, (ed.), *Deterrence In The 1980s: Crisis and Dilemma*, (London: Croom Helm, 1985).

Dan Caldwell, *The Dynamics of Domestic Politics and Arms Control: The SALT II Ratification Debate*, (Columbia South Carolina: University of Carolina Press, 1991).

Lou Cannon, *President Reagan: The Role of a Lifetime*, (New York: Touchstone/Simon and Schuster, 1991).

Michael Charlton, *From Deterrence to Defense: The Inside Story of Strategic Policy*, (Cambridge: Harvard University Press, 1987).

James Chase and Caleb Carr, *America The Invulnerable: The Quest for Absolute Security from 1812 to Star Wars*, (New York: Summit Books, 1988).

Andrew Cockburn, *The Threat: Inside the Soviet Military Machine*, (New York: Vintage Books, 1984).

Paul M. Cole, and William J. Taylor, *The Nuclear Freeze Debate: Arms Control Issues for the 1980s*, (Boulder: Westview, 1983).

Robert Dallek, *The American Style of Foreign Policy: Cultural Politics and Foreign Affairs*, (New York: Knopf, 1983).

Donald C. Daniel (ed.), *International Perceptions of the Superpower Military Balance*, (New York: Praeger, 1978).

Lynn E. Davis, 'Limited Nuclear Options: Deterrence and the New American Doctrine'. *Adelphi Paper* No. 121, (London: International Institute for Strategic Studies, Winter 1975/6).

John Edwards, *Super Weapon: The Making of the MX*, (London: Norton, 1982).

Randall Forsberg, Richard Garwin, Paul Warnke, and Robert Dean, *Seeds of Promise: The First Real Hearings on the Nuclear Arms Freeze*, (Andover, Massachusetts: Brick House Publishing Company, 1983).

Lawrence D. Freedman, *US Intelligence and the Soviet Strategic Threat*, (London: Macmillan, 1986).

Lawrence D. Freedman, *The Evolution of Nuclear Strategy*, (London: Macmillan, 1989).

Alton Frye, *A Responsible Congress: The Politics of National Security*, (New York: McGraw-Hill, 1975).

Raymond L. Garthoff, *Detente and Confrontation*, (Washington DC: Brookings Institute, 1985).

David Gold, Christopher Paine and Gail Shields, *Misguided EXpenditure: An Analysis of the Proposed MX Missile System*, (New York: Council on Economic Priorities, 1981).

Leon Goure, *War Survival in Soviet Strategy*, (Advanced International Studies Institute, University of Miami, 1976).

Erik K. Graben, *What Don't We Need Anymore?: US Land-Based Strategic Weapons Modernization and the End of the Cold War*, (Lanham; University Press of America, 1992).

Colin S. Gray, 'The Future Of Land Based Forces', *Adelphi Paper*, No. 197, (London: International Institute for Strategic Studies, 1976).

Jonathan Green, *The A–Z of Nuclear Jargon*, (London: Routledge, 1986).

Alexander Haig Jr, *Caveat: Realism, Reagan and Foreign Policy*, (London: Weidenfeld and Nicolson, 1984).

Fred Halliday, *The Making of the Second Cold War*, (London: Verso, 1983).

Gregg Herken, *Counsels of War*, (New York: Knopf, 1985)

Seymour M. Hersh, *The Price of Power: Kissinger in the Nixon White House*, (New York: Summit Books, 1983).

Louise Hodgden, *The MX Missile System: The Decision Making Process and Implications for Arms Control*, (Santa Monica, California: The California Seminar on International Security and Foreign Policy, 1981).

Lauren H. Holland and Robert A. Hoover, *The MX Decision: A New Direction in US Weapons Procurement Policy*, (Boulder: Westview, 1985).

David Holloway, *The Soviet Union and the Arms Race*, (London: Yale University Press, 1983).

William G. Hyland, *Mortal Rivals: Superpower Relations from Nixon to Reagan*, (New York: Random House, 1987).

Carl G. Jacobsen, *Strategic Power USA/USSR*, (London: Macmillan, 1990).

Robert Jervis, *The Illogic of American Nuclear Strategy*, (Ithaca: Cornell University Press, 1984).

Michio Kaku and Donald Axelrod, *To Win a Nuclear War: The Pentagon's Secret War Plans*, (London: Zed Books, 1987).

Fred M. Kaplan, *Dubious Specter: A Sceptical Look at the Soviet Nuclear Threat*, (Washington DC: The Institute for Policy Studies, 1980).

Fred M. Kaplan, *The Wizards of Armageddon*, (New York: Simon and Schuster, 1983).

Edward Kennedy, and Mark Hatfield, *Freeze!*, (New York; Bantam Books, 1982).

Henry Kissinger, *White House Years*, (Boston: Little, Brown and Company, 1979).

Barbara G. Levi, Mark Sakitt, and Art Hobson, (eds) *The Future of Land-Based Strategic Missiles*, (New York: American Institute of Physics, 1989).

William P. Lineberry, *The United States in World Affairs 1970*, (New York: A Council on Foreign Relations Publication/ Simon Schuster, 1972).

Michael McGwire, *Perestroika and Soviet National Security*, (Washington: Brookings, 1991).

Jeff McMahan, *Reagan and the World: Imperial Policy and the New Cold War*, (London: Pluto Press, 1984).

John Newhouse, *Cold Dawn: The Story of SALT*, (New York: Holt, Rinehart and Winston, 1973).

John Newhouse, *The Nuclear Age: From Hiroshima to Star Wars*, (London: Michael Joseph, 1989).

Paul H. Nitze, *From Hiroshima to Glasnost: At the Centre of Decision – A Memoir*, (London: Weidenfeld and Nicolson, 1989).

Janne E. Nolan, *Guardians of the Arsenal*, (New York: Basic Books, 1989).

Robert L. Pfaltzgraff, Jr and Jacqueln K. Davis, *SALT II: Promise or Precipice?*, (Miami: Current Affairs Press/ Center For Advanced International Studies University of Miami, 1976).

Alan Platt, *The US Senate and Strategic Arms Policy*, (Boulder: Westview Press, 1978).

John Prados, *The Soviet Estimate: US Intelligence Analysis and Russian Military Strength*, (New York: Dial Press, 1982).

Gwyn Prins, ed., *The Nuclear Crisis Reader*, (New York: Vintage, 1984).

Steven L. Reardon, *The Evolution of American Strategic Doctrine: Paul H. Nitze and the Soviet Challenge*, (Boulder: Westview, 1984).

Jerry W. Sanders, *Peddlers of Crisis: The Committee on the Present Danger and the Politics of Containment*, (Boston: South End Press, 1983).

Robert Scheer, *With Enough Shovels: Reagan Bush and Nuclear War*, (New York: Vantage, 1983).

Herbert Scoville, *MX: Prescription for Disaster*, (Cambridge MA: MIT Press, 1981).

Paul Seabury, ed., *The Balance of Power*, (San Francisco: Chandler, 1965).

John Sharnik, *Inside the Cold War: An Oral History*, (New York: Arbor House, 1987).

Christopher Simpson, *National Security Directives of the Reagan and Bush Administration: The Declassified History of US Political History 1981–1991*. (Boulder: Westview Press, 1995).

Gaddis Smith, *Morality, Reason and Power*, (New York: Hill and Wang, 1986).

Gerard Smith, *Doubletalk: The Story of SALT I*, (Lanham: University Press of America, 1985).

Roger D. Speed, *Strategic Deterrence in the 1980s* (Stanford: Hoover Institution Press, 1979).

Strobe Talbott, *Endgame: The Inside Story of SALT II*, (London: Harper and Bow, 1979).

Strobe Talbott, *Deadly Gambits*, (Picador: London, 1984).

Strobe Talbott, *The Master of the Game: Paul Nitze and the Nuclear Peace*, (New York: Knopf, 1988).

W. Scott Thompson, ed., *National Security in the 1980s: From Weakness to Strength*, (San Fransico: Institute for Contemporary Studies, 1980).

E. P. Thompson, and Ben Thompson, *Star Wars: Self Destruct Incorporated*, (Merlin Press: Manchester, 1985).

W. Scott Thompson and William Van Cleave, eds, *Strategic Options for the Early Eighties: What Can be Done?*, (White Plains MD: Automated Graphic Systems, 1980).

Richard C. Thornton, *The Carter Years: Towards a New Global Order*, (New York: Washington Institute Press, 1991).

Gregory Treverton, 'Nuclear Weapons In Europe', *Adelphi Paper*, No. 168, (London: International Institute for Strategic Studies, 1981).

Charles Tyroler, (ed.), *Alerting America: The Papers of the Committee on the Present Danger*, (Washington: Pergamon-Brassey's, 1984).

Cyrus Vance, *Hard Choices: Critical Years in America's Foreign Policy*, (New York: Simon and Schuster, 1983).

Karl Von Clausewitz, *On War*, edited and translated by Michael Howard and Peter Paret, (Princeton: Princeton University Press, 1976).

Casper Weinberger, *Fighting for Peace: Seven Critical Years at the Pentagon*, (London: Michael Joseph, 1990).

A.J. Wohlstetter, F.S. Hoffman, R.J. Lutz and H.S. Rowen, *Selection and Use of Strategic Air Bases*, (Rand Corporation, R-266, April 1954).

A.J. Wohlstetter, F.S. Hoffman, H.S. Rowen, *Protecting US Power to Strike Back in the 1950's and 1960's*, (RAND Corporation, R-290, September 1956).

Roberta Wohlstetter, *Pearl Harbor: Warning and Decision*, (Stanford: Stanford University Press, 1962).

Thomas Wolf, *The SALT Experience*, (Cambridge, Mass: Ballinger, 1979).

Alan Wolfe, *The Rise and Fall of the Soviet Threat: Domestic Sources of the Cold War Consensus*, (Boston: South End Press, 1984).

Articles and Book Chapters

Edward Anderson, 'First Strike: Myth or Reality', *Bulletin of the Atomic Scientists*, (November 1981).

Les Aspin, 'How To Look at the Soviet–American Balance', *Foreign Policy*, No. 22 (Spring 1976).

Les Aspin, 'The MX Bargain', *Arms Control Today*, (November 1983).

Brig. Gen. Atkenson, (ed.), 'Hemispheric Denial: Geopolitical Imperatives and Soviet Strategy', *Strategic Review*, Vol. IV, No. 2 (Spring 1976).

Desmond Ball and Edwin Coleman, 'The Land-Mobile ICBM System: A Proposal', *Survival*, Vol. XIX, No. 4 (July/August 1977).

Desmond Ball and Robert Toth, 'Revising the SIOP: Taking Warfighting to Dangerous Extremes', *International Security*, Vol. 14, No. 4 (Spring 1990).

Peter Berger, 'The Greening of American Foreign Policy', *Commentary*, (March 1976).

Ken Booth, 'US Perceptions of Soviet Threat: Prudence and Paranoia', in Carl G. Jacobsen, *Strategic Power USA/USSR* (London: Macmillan, 1990).

Ken Booth and Phil Williams, 'Fact and Fiction in US Foreign Policy: Reagan's Myths About Detente', *World Policy Journal*, (Summer 1985).

Harold Brown, 'American Defense Policy', Statement by US Secretary of Defense, 25 January 1979. *Survival*, Vol. XXI, No. 3 (May/June 1979)

Thomas A. Brown, 'Number Mysticism, rationality and the strategic balance', *Orbis*, 21 (Fall 1977).

Arthur Broyles, Eugene Wigner, and Sidney Drell, 'Civil Defence: The New Debate', *Survival*, Vol. XVIII, No. 5 (September/October 1978).

Carl H. Builder, 'Why Not First-Strike Counterforce Capabilities?', *Strategic Review*, Vol. VII, No. 2 (Spring 1979).

232 *The Politics of Threat*

McGeorge Bundy, 'To Cap the Volcano,' *Foreign Affairs*, Vol. 48, No. 1 (October 1969).

McGeorge Bundy, 'The MX: Not Buried Yet', *The Bulletin of the Atomic Scientists*, (June/July 1983).

Matthew Bunn, 'What Is Throw-Weight?', *Arms Control Today*, (November 1986).

Matthew Bunn, 'Does Throw-Weight Really Matter?', *Arms Control Today*, (November 1986).

Albert Carnesale and Charles Glaser, 'ICBM Vulnerability: The Cures Are Worse Than the Disease', *International Security*, Vol. No. 7, Issue. No. 1 (Summer 1982).

Stephen J. Cimbala, 'Strategic Vulnerability: A Conceptual Reassessment', *Armed Forces and Society*, Vol. 14, No. 2 (Winter 1988).

Committee on the Present Danger, *What is the Soviet Union Up To?*, Washington DC (4 April 1977).

Committee on the Present Danger, *Is America Becoming Number Two?*, Washington DC (5 October 1978).

Committee on the Present Danger, *Has America Become Number Two?*, Washington DC (June 1982).

Lynn E. Davis and Warner R. Schilling, 'All You Ever Wanted to Know about MIRV and ICBM Calculations But Were Not Cleared to Ask', *Journal of Conflict Resolution*, 17, No. 2 (June 1973).

Theodore Draper, 'Detente', *Commentary*, (June 1974).

Hon. Robert Ellsworth, 'Military Force and Political Influence in an Age of Peace', *Strategic Review*, Vol. IV, No. 2 (Spring 1976).

John Erickson, 'The Soviet Military, Soviet policy, and Soviet Politics', *Strategic Review*, Vol. 1, No. 4 (Fall 1973).

John Erickson, 'Detente: Soviet Policy and Purpose', *Strategic Review*, Vol. IV, No. 2 (Spring 1976).

John Erickson, 'The Chimera of Mutual Deterrence', *Strategic Review*, Vol. VI. No. 2 (Spring 1978).

John Erickson, 'The Soviet View of Deterrence: a General Survey', *Survival*, 24 (November–December 1982).

Colonel Thomas A. Fabyanic, 'Strategic Analysis and MX Threat Deployment', *Strategic Review*, Vol. X, No. 4 (Fall 1982).

Robert Foelber, *The Reagan Administration: Failing to Meet the Threat*, Heritage Foundation 'Backgrounder' No. 196 (14 July 1982).

Randall Forsberg, 'A Bilateral Nuclear-Weapon Freeze', *Scientific American*, (November 1982).

Alton Frye and William D. Rogers, 'Linkage Begins at Home', *Foreign Policy*, No. 35 (June 1979).

Alton Frye, 'Congress: Defense and the Foreign Policy Process', in Hunter, Berman, and Kennedy, (eds) *Making Government Work* (Boulder: Westview Press, 1986).

The Gallup Poll, 30 January–2 February 1976, *Current Opinion*, Vol. 4, No. 4 (April 1976).

Raymond Garthoff and Richard Pipes, 'A Garthoff-Pipes Debate on Soviet Strategic Doctrine', *Strategic Review*, Vol. X, No. 4 (Fall 1982).

Leon Goure, and Michael J. Deane, 'The Soviet Strategic View', *Strategic Review*, Vol. VIII, No. 1 (Winter 1980).

Colin S. Gray, 'Foreign Policy and the Strategic Balance', *Orbis*, (Fall 1974).

Colin S. Gray, 'SALT II and the Strategic Balance', *British Journal of International Studies*, (July 1975).

Colin S. Gray, 'SALT and the American Mood', *Strategic Review*, (Summer 1975).

Colin S. Gray, 'A Problem Guide to SALT', *Survival*, Vol. XVII, No. 5 (September/October 1975).

Colin S. Gray, 'Detente, Arms Control and Strategy', *American Political Science Review*, (1976), Vol. 70.

Colin S. Gray, 'The Future Of Land Based Forces', *Adelphi Papers*, No. 197 (1976).

Colin S. Gray, 'The Strategic Forces Triad: End of the Road?', *Foreign Affairs*, Vol. 57, Iss. 2 (July 1978).

Colin S. Gray, 'The MX Debate', *Survival*, Vol. XX, No. 3 (May/June 1978).

Colin S. Gray, 'Nuclear Strategy: A Case for a Theory of Victory', *International Security*, Vol. 3 (Summer 1979).

Colin S. Gray, 'The SALT II Debate in Context', *Survival*, Vol. XXI, No. 5 (September/October 1979).

Colin S. Gray, 'Understanding Soviet Military Power', *Problems of Communism*, (March–April 1981).

Colin S. Gray, 'The Most Dangerous Decade: Historic Mission, Legitimacy, and the Dynamics of the Soviet Empire in the 1980s', *Orbis*, (Spring 1981).

Colin S. Gray, and Keith Payne, 'Victory is Possible', *Foreign Policy*, Vol. 39. (Summer 1980).

Mark Greenberg and Rachael Flick, 'The New Bipartisan Commissions', *Journal of Contemporary Studies*, Vol. VI, No. 4 (Fall 1983).

Morton Halperin, 'The Decision to Deploy the ABM', *World Politics*, XXV (October 1972).

Bruce D. Hamlett, 'SALT: The Illusion and the Reality', *Strategic Review*, Vol. III, No. 3 (Summer 1975).

Heritage Foundation, 'Technology Transfer and Export Controls,' *National Security Record*, Washington, DC (September 1979).

Brig. General John Hopfer, 'M-X and the Land Based ICBM', *Astronautics and Aeronautics*, (February 1975).

Fred Charles Ikle, 'Can Deterrence Last Out the Century?' *Foreign Affairs*, (January 1973).

Robert Jastrow, 'Why Strategic Superiority Matters', *Commentary*, (March 1983).

Robert Jervis, 'Why Strategic Superiority Doesn't Matter,' *Political Science Quarterly*, Vol. 94, No. 4 (Winter 1979–80).

Robert H. Johnson, 'Periods of Peril: The Window of Vulnerability and Other Myths', *Foreign Affairs*. Vol. 61, No. 1 (Spring 1983).

T.K. Jones in *Strategic Options for the Early Eighties: What Can Be Done?*, edited by W. Scott Thompson and William Van Cleave, (White Plains MD: Automated Graphic Systems).

T.K. Jones, and Scott Thomson, 'Central War and Civil Defense', *Orbis*, (Fall 1978).

Fred Kaplan, 'Soviet Civil Defence: Some Myths in the Western Debate', *Survival*, Vol. XX, No. 3 (May/June 1978).

Jack F. Kemp, 'Congressional Expectations of SALT II', *Strategic Review*, Vol. VII, No. 1 (Winter 1979).

Jack F. Kemp, 'US Strategic Force Modernisation: A New Role for Missile Defense?', *Strategic Review*, Vol. VIII, No. 3 (Summer 1980).

William Kincade, 'Missile Vulnerability Reconsidered', *Arms Control Today*, Vol. 11, No. 5 (May 1981).

Henry Kissinger, 'Foreign Policy and National Security' delivered in Texas, 22 March 1976 and reprinted in *International Security*, 1976, Vol. 1.

Leopold Labedz, The Illusions of SALT', *Commentary*, (September 1979).

Walter Laqueur, 'Containment for the 1980s', *Commentary*, (October 1980).

Richard Ned Lebow, 'Windows of Vulnerability: Do States Jump Through Them?', *International Security*, Vol. 9, No. 1 (Summer 1984).

Richard Ned Lebow, 'Malign Analysts or Evil Empire?: Western Images of Soviet Nuclear Strategy', *International Journal*, XLIV, (Winter 1988–9).

Jan M. Lodal, 'Assuring Strategic Stability: An Alternative View', *Foreign Affairs*, Vol. 54 (April 1976).

Hon Clare Boothe Luce, 'What Ever Happened to the American Century?', *Strategic Review*, Vol. III, No. 3 (Summer 1975).

Edward Luttwak, 'Nuclear Strategy: The New Debate', *Commentary* (April 1974).

Edward Luttwak, 'America and the World: the Next Four Years: Defense Reconsidered', *Commentary*, (March 1977).

Edward Luttwak, 'Ten Questions About SALT II', *Commentary*, (August 1979).

Lt Col Joseph J. McGlinchey and Jacob W. Seelig, 'Why ICBMs Can Survive a Nuclear Attack', *Air Force Magazine*, (September 1974).

David C. Morrison, 'ICBM Vulnerability', *Bulletin of the Atomic Scientists*, Vol. 40, No. 9 (November 1984).

Michael Nacht, 'A Strategic Symposium: SALT and US Defense Policy.' *Washington Quarterly*, Vol. No. 2, Iss. No. 1 (Winter 1979).

Paul H. Nitze, 'Atoms Strategy and Policy', *Foreign Affairs*, Vol. 34, (January 1956).

Paul H. Nitze, 'The Strategic Balance Between Hope and Skeptisism,' *Foreign Policy*, (Winter 1974–5).

Paul H. Nitze 'The Vladivostok Accord and SALT II', *The Review of Politics*, (University of Notre Dame), (April 1975).

Paul H. Nitze, 'Assuring Strategic Stability in the Era of Detente', *Foreign Affairs*, Vol. 54, No. 2 (January 1976).

Paul H. Nitze, 'Deterring Our Deterrent', *Foreign Policy*, No. 25, (Winter 1976–7).

Christopher Paine, 'Running in circles with the MX', *Bulletin of the Atomic Scientists*, (December 1981).

Christopher Paine, 'MX: too dense for Congress', *The Bulletin of the Atomic Scientists*, (February 1983).

Richard Perle, 'Echoes Of The 1930s', *Strategic Review* Vol. VII, No. 1 (Winter 1979).

Richard Pipes, 'Why the Soviet Union Thinks it could Fight and Win a Nuclear War', *Commentary*, (July 1977).

Norman Podhoretz, 'Making the World Safe for Communism', *Commentary*, (April 1976).

Norman Podhoretz, 'The Culture Of Appeasement', *Harper's*, (25–30 October 1977).

Norman Podhoretz, 'The Present Danger', *Commentary*, (April 1980).

Norman Podhoretz, 'The Future Danger', *Commentary*, (April 1980).

Thomas Powers, 'Choosing a Strategy for World War III', *The Atlantic Monthly*, Vol. 250, No. 5 (November 1982).

George H. Quester, 'Through the Nuclear Strategic Looking Glass, or Reflections off the Window of Vulnerability', *Journal of Conflict Resolution*, Vol. 31, No. 4 (December 1987).

Eugene V. Rostow, 'The Safety of the Republic', *Strategic Review*, Vol. IV, No. 2 (Spring 1976).

Eugene V. Rostow, 'The Case Against SALT II', *Commentary*, (February 1979).

Myron Rush, 'Guns Over Growth in Soviet Policy', *International Security*, (Winter 1982–83).

Warner R. Schilling, 'US Strategic Nuclear Concepts in the 1970s: The Search for Sufficiently Equivalent Countervailing Parity,' *International Security*, Vol. 6 (Fall 1981).

James Schlesinger, *Flexible Strategic Options and Deterrence*, Excerpts from the Press Conference of US Secretary of Defense, 10 January 1974, at the National Press Club, Washington, DC, reprinted in *Survival*, (March/April 1974).

William Schneider Jr, 'Survivable ICBMs', *Strategic Review*, Vol. VI, No. 4 (Fall 1978)

Robert Schrum, 'The Shell Game Strategy,' reprinted from *Politics Today*, (undated) in the Congressional Record, 9 July 1979, S.8944.

William F. Scott, 'Soviet Military Doctrine and Strategy: Realities and Misunderstanding', *Strategic Review*, Vol. III, No. 3 (Summer 1975).

Leon Sigal, 'Tilting Toward War Fighting', *Arms Control Today*, (September 1983).

Leon V. Sigal, 'Warming to the Nuclear Freeze', *Foreign Policy*, (Fall 1982).

Lt General Alton D. Slay, 'MX: A New Dimension in Strategic Deterrence', *Air Force Magazine*, (September 1976).

Leon Sloss and Marc Dean Millet, 'US Nuclear Strategy in Evolution,' *Strategic Review*, Vol. 12. No. 1 (Winter 1984).

R. Jeffrey Smith, 'An Upheaval in US Strategic Thought', *Science*, 6/4/82.

John D. Steinbruner, 'Nuclear Decapitation', *Foreign Policy*, No. 45 (Winter 1981).

John D. Steinbruner and Thomas M. Garwin, 'Strategic Vulnerability: The Balance Between Prudence and Paranoia' *International Security*, Vol. No. 1, Issue. No. 1 (Summer 1976).

Paul N. Stockton, 'Arms Development and Arms Control: The Strange Case of the MX Missile', in Allan P. Sindler (eds) *American Politics and Public Policy* (Washington, DC: Congressional Quarterly Press, 1982).

David S. Sullivan, 'A SALT Debate: Continued Soviet Deception', *Strategic Review*, Vol. VII, No. 4 (Fall 1979).

Strobe Talbott, 'Buildup and Breakdown', *Foreign Affairs*, Vol. No. 62, Iss. No. 3 (Summer 1983).

Alan Tonelson, 'Nitze's World', *Foreign Policy*, No. 35 (Summer 1979).

Kosta Tsipis, 'Precision and Accuracy', *Arms Control Today*, (May 1981).

Kosta Tsipis, 'Not Such a Bargain After All', *Arms Control Today*, (November 1983).

Edgar Ulsamer, 'MX: The Missile System for the Year 2000', *Air Force Magazine*, (March 1973).

William Van Cleave, 'SALT on the Eagle's Tail', *Strategic Review*, Vol. IV, No. 2 (Spring 1976).

John M. Weinstein, 'Soviet Civil Defence: The Mine Shaft Gap Revisited', *Arms Control Today*, Vol. 12. No. 7 (July/August 1982).

Peter Wiles, 'Declining Self Confidence', *Survival*, Vol. XII, No. 8 (August 1971).

236 *The Politics of Threat*

Albert Wohlstetter, 'The Delicate Balance of Terror', *Foreign Affairs,* No. 37 (January 1959).
Albert Wohlstetter, 'Is There a Strategic Arms Race?', *Foreign Policy,* 15 (Summer 1974).
Albert Wohlstetter, 'Rivals but no "Race"', *Foreign Policy,* 16 (Fall 1974).
Albert Wohlstetter, 'Optimal Ways to Confuse Ourselves', *Foreign Policy,* 20 (Fall 1975).
R. James Woolsey, 'The Politics of Vulnerability 1980–83', *Foreign Affairs,* Vol. 62, No. 4 (Fall 1984).

Unpublished Material

Desmond Ball, 'The Strategic Missile Programme of the Kennedy Administration, 1961–63', (unpublished PhD Thesis, ANU, 1972).
Peacekeeper (M-X) History and Current Status, General Kelly Burke USAF (Retired). Private papers of Kelly Burke given to the author.
General Glenn A. Kent and David E. Thaler, *First-Strike Stability: A Methodology for Evaluating Strategic Forces,* (June 1989). Unpublished paper given to this author from the private papers of General Kent.
The Nuclear Age, Central Television Transcript No. 10, Liddell Hart Centre and Military Archive.
Terry Terriff, *The Innovation of US Strategic Nuclear Policy in the Nixon Administration 1969–1974,* unpublished PhD, Kings College, London University, 1991.
Terry Terriff, 'The Shifting Strategic Balance: From Superiority to Parity', unpublished paper, 1991.

Newspapers and Magazines

In addition, articles have been cited from the following newspapers and periodicals: *Aviation Week and Space Technology; Baltimore Sun; Boston Globe; Christian Science Monitor; Guardian; Los Angeles Times; National Journal; New York Times; New York Times Magazine; New Yorker; Newsday; Newsweek; Philadelphia Inquirer; Space/Aeronautics; Time; Washington Post; Washington Times; West Hartfield News* and *US News and World Report.*

Notes

INTRODUCTION

1. Colin S. Gray, 'The Most Dangerous Decade: Historic Mission, Legitimacy, and the Dynamics of the Soviet Empire in the 1980s', *Orbis*, (Spring 1981) p. 13.
2. Colin S. Gray, 'The Future Of Land Based Forces', *Adelphi Papers*, No. 197, 1976 p. 1 and Daniel Seligman, 'Our ICBMs are in Danger', *Fortune*, 2 July 1979, p. 50.
3. Hearings before the Senate Foreign Relations Committee, 96th Congress, 1st Session, *The SALT II Treaty*. Kissinger, Part 3, p. 154 and p. 206.
4. Thornton argues that ICBM vulnerability was the issue around which the foreign policy tensions of the Carter White House's security policy turned. Richard C. Thornton, *The Carter Years: Towards A New Global Order*, (New York: Washington Institute Press, 1991) p. 8.
5. T.K. Jones in *Strategic Options for the Early Eighties: What Can Be Done?* Edited by W. Scott Thompson and William Van Cleave, (White Plains MD: Automated Graphic Systems, 1979) pp. 119–120.
6. Harold Brown, *DOD Annual Defense Posture*, Fiscal Year 1979, p. 62.
7. The multiple shelter basing plan was originally put forward by Schlesinger in 1975. See Secretary Schlesinger, *Annual Defense Department Report FY 1976*, (5 February 1975), pp. II–27, 28. See also Desmond Ball and Edwin Coleman, 'The Land-Mobile ICBM System: A Proposal', *Survival*, Vol. XIX, No. 4. (July/August 1977).
8. Colin S. Gray, 'The Strategic Forces Triad: End of the Road?', *Foreign Affairs*, Vol. No. 56, Issue 4, (July 1978) p. 771.

CHAPTER 1

1. John Edwards, *Super Weapon: The Making of the MX*, (London: Norton, 1982) p. 39.
2. See Bernard Brodie, *The Absolute Weapon*, (New York: Harcourt, Brace and Co. 1946). For a detailed analysis of the contributions to nuclear strategy of thinkers such as Brodie and Wohlstetter, see Baylis and Garnett, *Makers of Nuclear Strategy*, (London: Pinter, 1991).
3. Wohlstetter, 'The Delicate Balance'. See also Stephen J. Cimbala, 'Strategic Vulnerability: A Conceptual Reassessment', *Armed Forces and Society*, Vol. 14, No. 2, (Winter 1988) p. 144.
4. See Fred M. Kaplan, *The Wizards of Armageddon*, (New York: Simon and Schuster, 1983) Chapter 8.
5. Roberta Wohlstetter, *Pearl Harbor: Warning and Decision*, (Stanford: Stanford University Press, 1962) p. 400.
6. As Kaplan observes (with some exaggeration), Wohlstetter '...would impose the concept on nearly everything he analyzed... the concern about vulnerability

grew into an infatuation, then an obsession and finally a fetish of sorts.'
Wizards, p. 110.

7. Thomas C. Schelling, in R. Wohlstetter, *Pearl Harbor,* p. vii.
8. Lawrence D. Freedman, *US Intelligence and the Soviet Strategic Threat,* (London: Macmillan, 1986) p. 97.
9. See David C. Morrison. 'ICBM Vulnerability', *Bulletin of the Atomic Scientists.* Vol. 40, No. 9. (November 1984). The first major study was conducted by A.J. Wohlstetter, F.S. Hoffman, R.J. Lutz and H.S. Rowen, *Selection and Use of Strategic Air Bases,* (The Rand Corporation, R-266, April 1954).
10. A.J. Wohlstetter, F.S. Hoffman, H.S. Rowen *Protecting US Power to Strike Back in the 1950's and 1960's,* (RAND Corporation, R-290, Sept. 1956) pp. 2–3.
11. On the psychological affect of Sputnik see James Chase and Caleb Carr, *America the Invulnerable: The Quest for Absolute Security from 1812 to Star Wars,* (New York: Summit Books, 1988) p. 306.
12. Bruce W. Bennett, *How to Assess the Survivability of US ICBMs,* Rand Corporation, R-2577-FF (June 1980) p. v.
13. Edwards, pp. 56–7.
14. David C. Morrison, 'ICBM Vulnerability', *Bulletin of the Atomic Scientists,* Vol. 40, No. 9. (November 1984) p. 22. Gold et al., suggest that the total number of missiles planned was 300, see David Gold, Christopher Paine and Gail Shields, *Misguided EXpenditure: An Analysis of the Proposed MX Missile System,* (New York: Council On Economic Priorities, 1981) p. 39.
15. *Missile and Rockets Magazine,* 1959, cited by Edwards, p. 56.
16. Robert Schrum, 'The Shell Game Strategy', reprinted from *Politics Today,* (undated) in the *Congressional Record,* 9 July 1979, S.8944. Cited by Gold et al., p. 39.
17. Morrison, p. 22.
18. William H. Baugh, *The Politics of Nuclear Balance: Ambiguity and Continuity in Strategic Policies,* (New York: Longman, 1984) p. 161. During the trial exercises along western rail routes the union crews insisted on changing at each division point, a practice considered unacceptable by the Kennedy administration. Edwards, p. 56.
19. See Desmond Ball and Edwin Coleman, 'The Land-Mobile ICBM System: A Proposal', *Survival,* Vol. XIX, No. 4. (July/August 1977) p. 155. and Desmond Ball, 'The Strategic Missile Programme of the Kennedy Administration, 1961–63', (unpublished PhD Thesis, ANU, 1972).
20. Gold et al., pp. 39–40.
21. John Newhouse, *Cold Dawn: The Story of SALT,* (New York: Holt, Rinehart and Winston, 1973) p. 26.
22. Earl Voss in *Washington Star,* cited by Freedman p. 100.
23. See John Prados, *The Soviet Estimate: U.S. Intelligence Analysis and Russian Military Strength,* (New York: Dial Press, 1982) p. 189 and Freedman, *US* p. 100.
24. Statement of Secretary of Defense Robert S. McNamara before the House Armed Services Committee on the *Fiscal Year 1966–70 Defense Program and 1966 Defense Budget,* (Washington DC: US Government Printing Office, 18 Feb. 1965) Feb. 1965, p. 50.

25. Freedman, *US*, p. 100 who cites A.E. Fitzgerald, *The High Priests of Waste*, (New York: Norton, 1972) p. 111.
26. Testimony of Secretary McNamara to Senate Foreign Relations Committee, *Hearings on the Nuclear Test Ban Treaty*, 88th Congress, 1st Session, (Washington DC: US Government Printing Office, August 1963) p. 102–3.
27. Freedman, *US*, p. 104.
28. The view which prevailed at the Pentagon at the time was that Soviet production levels were perfectly rational, assuming that the aim was the construction of a secure second strike capability. To attempt to go beyond such plans, McNamara believed, would have been a pointless diversion of Soviet military expenditure. See Prados, p. 186.
29. See Prados pp. 190–1 and Freedman, *US*, p. 108.
30. *McNamara Posture Statement for FY 1964*, (Classified) (Washington DC: US Government Printing Office, 1963) p. 29.
31. See Prados, p. 190.
32. As Freedman observes 'The bulk of the US force was composed of the 1 MT Minuteman and so its total megatonnage could not be much more than 1250 MT [the 250 was 50 Titans each with 5 MT]. It needed no more than 50 SS-9s to reach this total', *US*, p. 109.
33. Circular Error Probable (CEP) is the unit of missile accuracy defined as the radius of a circle centred on the target within which 50% of the re-entry vehicles would land in repeated tests, assuming no bias. Thus the re-entry vehicles of the SS-9 with a 1.0 n.m. CEP would have a 50% probability of landing within a circle of one nautical mile radius of the target.
34. Freedman, *US*, p. 109.
35. Christoph Bluth, *Soviet Strategic Arms Policy Before SALT*, (Cambridge: Cambridge University Press, 1992). See especially chapters 3 and 7.
36. Bluth, p. 188, Raymond L. Garthoff, *Detente and Confrontation*, (Washington D.C.: Brookings Institute, 1985) p. 55, David Holloway, *The Soviet Union and the Arms Race*, (London: Yale University Press, 1983) p. 44 and Prados p. 184.
37. Lawrence D. Freedman, *The Evolution of Nuclear Strategy*, (London: Macmillan, 1989) pp. 366–9.
38. Freedman, *Evolution*, p. 230 and Michael Charlton, *From Deterrence to Defense: The Inside Story of Strategic Policy*, (Harvard University Press: 1987) p. 8.
39. See Fred Halliday, *The Making of The Second Cold War*, (London: Verso, 1983) pp. 46–54, and Barry Blechman and Stephen S. Kaplan, *Force Without War: US Armed Forces as a Political Instrument*, (Washington DC: The Brookings Institution, 1978).
40. As its name suggests the main focus of this study was on the various implications of MIRVing missile warheads. See Michio Kaku and Donald Axelrod *To Win a Nuclear War: The Pentagon's Secret War Plans*, (London: Zed Books, 1987) p. 147.
41. Freedman, *US*, p. 120.
42. Louise Hodgden, *The MX Missile System: The Decision Making Process and Implications for Arms Control*, (Santa Monica, California: The California Seminar on International Security and Foreign Policy, 1981) p. 31. Cited by

Lauren H. Holland and Robert A. Hoover, *The MX Decision: A New Direction in US Weapons Procurement Policy*, (Boulder: Westview, 1985) p. 66.

43. 'Strat-X was conducted by Fred Payne in the Institute for Defense Analysis for the Director of Defence Research and Engineering (DDR&E) using the resources of the whole Pentagon.' Freedman, *US*, p. 121 see also Edwards p. 59 and Herbert Scoville, *MX: Prescription for Disaster*, (Cambridge MA: MIT Press, 1981) p. 98. All twenty volumes of The Strat-X Report, (Report R -122) have now been declassified.

44. The Navy later decided to pursue the ULMS in preference to SLMS when it was forced to make a choice between the two for funding reasons. Gold, et al. p. 40–1.

45. Edwards, p. 59.

46. Gold, et al. p. 40.

47. Edwards, p. 59.

48. United States Senate, Preparedness Investigating Subcommittee of the Armed Services Committee, *Status of US Strategic Power*, 90th Congress, 2nd Session. (Washington DC: US Government Printing Office, 1968) pp. 52–7.

49. Ibid.

50. Ibid.

51. Nor did USAF like the idea of Army interceptors protecting their missiles. See Morton Halperin, 'The Decision to Deploy the ABM', *World Politics*, XXV (October 1972) p. 69, and Newhouse, *Cold Dawn*, p. 80. Hard Rock missile basing as a means of increasing Minuteman survivability was allocated $25 million in FY 1970. Hearings, Senate Armed Services Committee, *Military Authorization of Defense Appropriations for FY 71*, 20 February 1970, Part I, p. 325.

52. Janne E. Nolan, *Guardians of the Arsenal*, (New York: Basic Books, 1989) p. 92–3.

53. See Newhouse, *Cold Dawn*, p. 96.

54. See ibid, p. 99.

55. John Foster, (DDR&E), testified to this effect stating 'The deployment of the Sentinel system permits us any time within a year to make a decision on whether or not we want to defend Minuteman silos.' Subcommittee on the Military Applications of the Joint Committee on Atomic Energy, p. 37. See also Freedman, *US*, p. 126.

56. As Newhouse explains 'Hard site, unlike the other option, never in those days had a major bureaucratic constituency', Newhouse, *Cold Dawn*, p. 93.

57. Indeed, as Freedman notes, at this stage the Minuteman vulnerability issue was 'peripheral to everything and central to nothing', *US*, p. 128.

58. Ibid.

59. Wohlstetter begrudgingly acknowledged that this concern had been 'the most effective but probably the weakest argument against the ABM'. Gregg Herken, *Counsels of War*, (New York: Knopf, 1985) p. 236.

60. Henry Kissinger, *White House Years*, (Boston: Little, Brown and Company, 1979) p. 208.

61. This study, plan 1-69, was conducted by Deputy Secretary of Defense David Packard, and Laurence Lynn of the NSC staff.

62. Kaplan, *Wizards*, p. 350.

63. Freedman, *US*, p. 131. Kissinger illustrated this point, demonstrating his frustration, 'Thinning out the defense of the population was a purely political decision ... Our dilemma was that we could sell an ABM programme to the Congress apparently only by depriving it of any military effectiveness against our principal adversary.' Kissinger, ibid., p. 208.
64. Herken, p. 233.
65. See Alton Frye, *A Responsible Congress: The Politics of National Security*, (New York: McGraw-Hill, 1975) pp. 15–46.
66. *Clark M. Clifford Posture Statement for FY 1970*, (Washington DC: United States Government Printing Office; Jan. 1969) p. 46.
67. International Law and Disarmament Affairs Subcommittee of the Senate Foreign Relations Committee, *Strategic and Foreign Policy Implications of ABM Systems*, 91st Congress, 1st Session. 27 March 1969, p. 239.
68. Ibid.
69. He continues 'Aside from the objective qualities of the SS-9, the supermissile acquired in the minds of many planners and commentators an almost mystical ominousness. A glowering, lumbering bully, redolent of barbarism, scornful of the refined, essentially defensive concepts that held sway in the West ... the SS-9 came to symbolize Russian brutishness.' Strobe Talbott, *Endgame: The Inside Story of SALT II*, (London: Harper and Row; 1979) pp. 27–8. See also Jan M. Lodal, 'Assuring Strategic Stability: An Alternative View', *Foreign Affairs*, Vol. 54. (April, 1976), pp. 467–9.
70. See Prados, p. 204. ACDA Director Gerard Smith made the similar point that the Russians, 'perhaps because they like the Tsar Cannon, which was the biggest cannon in the world, and the Tsar Bell, which was the biggest bell that ever was built – have gone in for very large yield weapons'. Hearings before the Committee on Foreign Relations United States Senate, 92nd Congress, Second Session *Military Implications of the Treaty on the Limitations of Anti Ballistic Missile Systems and the Interim Agreement on Limitations of Strategic Offensive Arms,* June 1972, p. 46.
71. Laird was not alone in his ideological approach to this subject as Newhouse's description of the Congressional evidence on ABM illustrates. 'Neither the debate nor the expert testimony was always logical, objective, or even relevant. Extravagant claims and assertions were made by people on both sides of the issue. Administration witnesses exaggerated the imminence of the SS-9 threat to Minuteman, while some scientists and academics who should have known better tended to write off the threat and to load the case against Safeguard.' Newhouse, *Cold Dawn*, p. 155.
72. Quoted in 'Reflections on the Quarter', *Orbis,* XIII (Summer 1969), p. 401.
73. Freedman, *US*, p. 133.
74. Letter dated 1 July 1969. Published in the preface to *Intelligence and the ABM*, p. x. United States Senate, Foreign Relations Committee, 91st Congress, 1st Session (1969).
75. United States House of Representatives, Subcommittee of the House Appropriations Committee, *Safeguard Anti Ballistic Missile System*, 91st Congress, 1st Session. (Washington DC: US Government Printing Office, 22 May 1969) p. 8.
76. Indeed at one stage Wohlstetter involved the Operational Research Society of America (ORSA) in order to dispute Rathjens's methodology. The report

which the ORSA eventually produced, like a microcosm of the larger debate, concentrated on very narrow technical questions accessible only to 'experts' and ostensibly soluble by 'scientific' method. In doing this the terms of the debate were set in such a narrow way as to be beyond the scope of the larger, essentially political dimensions of the issue. See Kaplan, *Wizards*, pp. 351–5 and Herken pp. 239–41.

77. See *Clifford Posture Statement for FY 1970*, Jan. 1969, pp. 79–90. See also Prados, p. 208.

78. Prados, p. 208.

79. See Prados, pp. 208–9, Kaplan *Wizards*, pp. 351–3 and Freedman, *US*, pp. 140–3.

80. See the prepared statement of Herbert Scoville Jr, *Congressional Record*, 20 April 1970 p. S-5986-87. Cited in SIPRI Yearbook 1969/70 p. 366.

81. See Prados, p. 212, and Freedman, *US*, p. 142.

82. Prados, p. 218.

83. United States Senate, Committee on Appropriations, Hearings, *Department of Defense Appropriations, Fiscal Year 1973*, Part 1, 92nd Congress 2nd Session. (Washington: Government Printing Office, 1972), p. 86. See also Prados, p. 222.

84. Freedman, *US*, p. 145.

85. He continues, 'Using other figures one could show that the danger was minimal or alternatively that it would be of such dimensions that Safeguard would be unable to handle it successfully.' Ibid., pp. 146–7.

86. As Freedman observes, 'The technical analysis made during the Administration's review of the ABM programme during February/March 1969 does not appear to have been thorough. Kissinger asked for some technical advice from a group of his former colleagues at Cambridge, Massachusetts, and was told that a hardpoint defence would win 'at least 50–50 acquiesence of the scientific community' [no doubt because of its ability to protect ICBMs]. But this was assuming that this would be a purpose-built defence – a point which Kissinger apparently missed.' Ibid., p. 148.

87. Not consulting thoroughly with the experts concerned was a feature of the Nixon–Kissinger approach to government. Richard Garwin, one of Nixon's science advisors, complained that the Administration ignored a special NSC committee report on the technical problems of Safeguard, stating that 'All of this would have been prevented if they had just talked to the committee.' Herken, p. 237.

88. See Herken pp. 234–6, Kaplan, *Wizards*, p. 351 and Freedman, *US*, p. 149.

89. See Freedman, *US*, pp. 149–50 and *Laird Posture Statement for FY 1971*, Feb 1970, p. 48.

90. Hearings, Senate Armed Services Committee, *Military Authorization of Defense Appropriations for FY 71* 20 February 1970, Part I, p. 36.

91. Kaplan, *Wizards*, p. 351. Rathjens also co-authored with Jerome Wiesner and Steven Weinberg a paper circulated among Congressmen which presented this and other anti-ABM arguments. *A Commentary on Secretary Melvin Laird's May 22nd Defence of Safeguard*, (unpublished paper, 1969).

92. Frye, *Responsible Congress*, p. 43.

93. Freedman, *US*, p. 150.

94. Committee on Armed Services, U.S. Senate, *Authorising Appropriations for Fiscal Year 1971 for Military Procurement, etc.*, 91st Congress, 2nd Session, Report No. 91–1016, July 14, 1970, pp.18–23, 105. See also Frye, p. 42.
95. Ibid.
96. Freedman, *US*, p. 152.
97. Ibid.

CHAPTER 2

1. Lawrence D. Freedman, *US Intelligence and the Soviet Strategic Threat*, (London: Macmillan, 1986) p. 159.
2. William P. Lineberry, *The United States In World Affairs 1970*, (New York: A Council on Foreign Relations Publication/ Simon Schuster, 1972) p. 77.
3. *Air Force Magazine*, March 1971.
4. Gerard Smith, *Doubletalk: The Story of SALT I*, (Lanham: University Press of America, 1985), Smith also notes 'it was doubtful that Congress would fund a mobile ICBM force even if permitted under a SALT agreement'. p. 209. The NSC also had concerns about hijack by criminal or radical groups. 'Kissinger used this horrific prospect along with the misuse of parkland, to squash the case for putting Minuteman on wheels.' John Newhouse, *Cold Dawn: The Story of SALT*, (New York: Holt, Rinehart and Winston, 1973) p. 27.
5. The JCS were firmly opposed to an ABM ban arguing that ABM might be needed in the future. Smith, p. 205.
6. Freedman, *US*, p. 161. See also Newhouse, *Cold Dawn*, Chapter 5.
7. Newhouse, *Cold Dawn*, p. 177.
8. Ibid., pp. 177–8.
9. See Newhouse, *Cold Dawn*, Smith, *Doubletalk*, and Raymond L. Garthoff, *Detente and Confrontation*, (Washington DC: Brookings Institute, 1985) Chapter 5.
10. According to Newhouse, 'Whereas the other options had been methodically shaped and honed by the entire SALT apparatus, Option E was strictly a White House affair', *Cold Dawn*, p. 186. Herken, however, claims that 'its earliest origins had included an eighty-five-page memorandum written by Albert Wohlstetter and others for Kissinger's consideration'. p. 246.
11. Newhouse, *Cold Dawn*, p.197.
12. Freedman, *US*, p. 162. See also Newhouse, *Cold Dawn*, p. 201.
13. Freedman, *US*, p. 163.
14. Ibid., p. 164.
15. Newhouse, Ibid., p. 240.
16. Transcript of the 'Face The Nation' television show, 7 March 1972. Cited by Newhouse, ibid., p. 201.
17. Newhouse, ibid., p. 218.
18. Ibid., p. 245.
19. According to Hersh, Kissinger reached an agreement by linking SALT to a lifting of restrictions on US grain sales to the USSR. Seymour M. Hersh, *The*

Price of Power: Kissinger in the Nixon White House, (New York: Summit Books, 1983) pp. 343–4. See also Smith, p. 225.

20. Smith, p. 225.
21. These is considerable evidence to suggest that Kissinger, in his eagerness to conclude limitations on ICBMs in the Interim Agreement, was out-negotiated by the Soviets in this important area of strategic offensive forces. See Garthoff, *Detente*, pp. 157–68, Smith, pp. 226–44, and Newhouse, *Cold Dawn*, Chapter 5.
22. Hersh, p. 155.
23. Had the efforts of Senator Brooke in Congress been listened to at an early stage and a ban on the testing of MIRVs been implemented a cap on this technology would have been more feasible. See Frye, *Responsible Congress*, Chapter 5.
24. William G. Hyland, *Mortal Rivals: Superpower Relations from Nixon to Reagan*, (New York: Random House, 1987) p. 43; Garthoff, *Detente*, p. 135; and Hersh, pp. 155–6.
25. Terry Terriff, 'The Shifting Strategic Balance: From Superiority to Parity', unpublished paper, 1991, p.108. Kissinger's frustration with the unwillingness of Congress to support what he considered to be necessary defence modernisation programmes and his belief that this affected SALT is evident throughout his memoirs. See for instance Henry Kissinger, *White House Years*, (Boston: Little, Brown and Company, 1979) pp. 810–17.
26. Freedman, *US*, p. 167.
27. Terriff, 'Shifting Balance', p. 119.
28. Lawrence D. Freedman, *The Evolution of Nuclear Strategy*, (London: Macmillan, 1989), p. 356.
29. Richard Betts, *Nuclear Blackmail and Nuclear Balance*, (Washington, DC: The Brookings Institution, 1987), p. 185. See also Warner R. Schilling, 'US Strategic Nuclear Concepts in the 1970s: The Search for Sufficiently Equivalent Countervailing Parity', *International Security*, Vol. 6 (Fall 1981), p. 57.
30. Betts, *Nuclear Blackmail*, see Chapter 5 especially pp. 186–9. See also Mike Bowker and Phil Williams, *Superpower Detente: A Reappraisal*, (London, Royal Institute For International Affairs/Sage, 1988) pp. 213–15.
31. Betts notes, 'The administration could not claim that any American superiority remained under the SALT I treaty without undercutting its bargaining position with the Soviets. The agreement, however, encompassed only ballistic missiles and submarines, while the United States held a huge advantage in the excluded categories of intercontinental bomber numbers and payload, not to mention so-called forward-based systems, which Moscow considered strategic since they could strike Soviet territory.' p. 187.
32. Bowker and Williams, p. 215.
33. Hearings before the Committee on Armed Services United States Senate, 92nd Congress, 2nd Session *Military Implications of the Treaty on the Limitations of Anti Ballistic Missile Systems and The Interim Agreement on Limitations of Strategic Offensive Arms,* (Washington DC: United States Government Printing Office; 25 July 1972) p. 414.
34. 'Second Annual Report to the Congress on United States Foreign policy', *Public Papers of the Presidents of the United States, Richard M. Nixon*, (Washington, DC: Government Printing Office, 1971) p. 311.

Notes   245

35. Freedman, *Evolution*, p. 356. See also Edward Luttwak, 'The Missing Dimension of US Policy: Force, Perception, Power', in Donald C. Daniel (ed.), *International Perceptions of Superpower Military Balance*, (New York: Praeger, 1978) pp. 21–3.
36. Schilling, p. 50. See also Betts, p. 185.
37. United States Senate, Armed Services Committee, *Military Implications of the Treaty on the Limitations of Anti Ballistic Missile Systems and the Interim Agreement on Limitations of Strategic Offensive Arms*, 92nd Congress, 2nd Session, (Washington DC: US Government Printing Office, 25 July 1972) p. 585.
38. Ibid., p. 231.
39. Ibid., p. 233. emphasis added.
40. Ibid., p. 5. and p. 549.
41. In the hearings, Richard L. Garwin was at pains to differentiate the potential vulnerability of the prelaunch ICBM force and the vulnerability of all American offensive forces, explaining that this confusion was being 'exploited by various individuals and groups for their own reasons'. Ibid., p. 351.
42. Ibid., p. 169.
43. Ibid., p. 47.
44. Ibid., p. 565. (Quotation from President Nixon's remarks, 29 June 1972) When asked by Senator Jackson in which National Intelligence Estimate this ICBM growth was forecast, the DOD answer very illuminatingly stated, that 'A growth of 1000 in the Soviet ICBM force over the period 1972–77 is not projected in any NIE. The President was alluding to Soviet capabilities. The Soviets have demonstrated a capability to deploy some 200 ICBMs per year.' p. 565.
45. Ibid., pp. 524, 564. Laird also detailed what this added expenditure could be used for, including 'ICBMs with a larger throw weight and a larger carrying capability ... an advanced tanker ... additional SRAMS ... the deployment of a modified Spartan ... [and] the accelerated construction of submarines and aircraft'. p. 541.
46. Ibid., pp. 470–3. See also Freedman, *US*, p. 168.
47. Hearings, *Military Implications of the Treaty on the Limitations of Anti Ballistic Missiles*, p. 367. Furthermore, commenting directly on Laird's 1969 testimony in which the Secretary predicted the destruction of 95 per cent of the Minuteman force, General Allison observed that this calculation was based on 'a 20 per cent failure rate and a retargeting capability' but 'if you did not have a very sophisticated retargeting capability, the results of the study would change dramatically'. p. 368.
48. Ibid., p. 469. See also pp. 467–74 and pp. 401–15.
49. Ibid., p. 470.
50. Ibid., p. 472.
51. Ibid., p. 467. 'Hardening', General Ryan explained was 'our main hedge for survivability'. See pp. 471–3.
52. The amendment's language was imprecise in its definition of equality, merely requesting the President to 'seek a future treaty that, *inter alia*, would not limit the United States to levels of intercontinental strategic forces inferior to the limits provided for the Soviet Union'. *Military Implications of the Treaty on the Limitations of Strategic Offensive Arms and Protocol Thereto (SALT II Treaty)*, Hearings before the Senate Committee on Armed Forces, 96th Congress, 1st Session (GPO, 1979). Part 1, p. 30. See also Betts, p. 187–8.

CHAPTER 3

1. See Lawrence D. Freedman, *US Intelligence and the Soviet Strategic Threat*, (London: Macmillan, 1986), chapter 10 and John Prados, *The Soviet Estimate: U.S. Intelligence Analysis and Russian Military Strength*, (New York: Dial Press, 1982) Chapter 15.
2. Freedman, *US*, p. 170.
3. For their part the Soviets had not disguised their intention to deploy new systems of this size, hence their refusal to accept these restrictions as part of the main text of the treaty. See Jack F. Kemp, 'Congressional Expectations of SALT II', *Strategic Review*, Vol. VII, No. 1. (Winter 1979) p. 18.
4. See Prados, pp. 233–6.
5. *Schlesinger Posture Statement for FY 1976*, pp. 11–12, See also Freedman, *US* p. 173.
6. Subcommittee on Arms Control, International Law and Organisation, of the Senate Foreign Relations Committee, *Briefing on Counterforce Attacks*, 93rd Congress, 2nd Session, (Washington DC: United States Government Printing Office, 11 September 1974) p. 10.
7. Freedman, *US*, p. 175.
8. Newsweek reported that the slower than expected deployment of Soviet MIRVs may have been due to difficulties with the miniaturisation necessary for the warhead computers and engines required for MIRVs and a shortage of highly refined nuclear material. *Newsweek*, 7 June 1976.
9. Freedman, *US*, p. 176.
10. For a full discussion of Congressional efforts to prevent the development of MIRV and accuracy improvements, see Alton Frye, *A Responsible Congress: The Politics of National Security*, (New York: McGraw-Hill, 1975) Chapters 3 and 4.
11. Letter to Senator Edward W. Brooke from the Secretary of Defense Melvin Laird, 5 November 1970; reprinted in *Public Statements by the Secretaries of Defense*, Part 4, Vol. V, p. 2057.
12. *Air Force Magazine*, March, 1971. Cited by Freedman, *US*, p. 178. Kaplan describes these 'bomb-damage calculators' of kill-probability as simple to operate 'circular slide-rules that do neat little tricks without which the doomsayers would be nowhere', Fred M. Kaplan, *Dubious Spectre: A Sceptical Look at the Soviet Nuclear Threat*, (Washington DC: The Institute For Policy Studies, 1980) p. 41.
13. Lt. Col. Joseph J. McGlinchey USAF and Jacob W. Seelig, 'Why ICBMs Can Survive a Nuclear Attack', *Air Force Magazine*, September, 1974 pp. 82–5. Cited by Freedman, *US*, p. 217. See also Kaplan, *Dubious*, p. 82, and John D. Steinbruner and Thomas M. Garwin, 'Strategic Vulnerability: The Balance Between Prudence and Paranoia', *International Security*, Vol. No. 1, Issue No. 1 (Summer 1976). The latter article was part of the sceptical analysis of ICBM vulnerability which was conducted at this time, as was Lynn E. Davis and Warner Schilling's, 'All You Ever Wanted to Know about MIRV and ICBM Calculations but Were Not Cleared to Ask.' *Journal of Conflict Resolution*, 17, No. 2, June 1973.
14. Freedman, *US*, p. 178.

15. Fred M. Kaplan, *The Wizards of Armageddon*, (New York: Simon and Schuster, 1983) pp. 374–7.
16. James R. Schlesinger, Testimony before the Subcommittee on Arms Control, International Law and Organisation of the Senate Committee on Foreign Relations, Hearings on *US and Soviet Strategic Doctrine and Military Policies*, 4 March 1974. (Secret hearing held on 4 March; sanitised and made public on 4 April 1974) pp. 17, 37.
17. Ibid., p. 36.
18. Gregg Herken, *Counsels of War*, (New York: Knopf, 1985) p. 248. See also Lynn E. Davis, 'Limited Nuclear Options: Deterrence and the New American Doctrine', *Adelphi Paper* No. 121, (London: International Institute for Strategic Studies, Winter 1975/6) p. 9.
19. Fred Charles Ikle, 'Can Deterrence Last Out The Century?' *Foreign Affairs*, (January, 1973). Reprinted in Philip Bobbitt, Lawrence Freedman, and Gregory Treverton (eds), *US Nuclear Strategy: A Reader*, (London: Macmillan, 1989) p. 352 and p. 349.
20. Kissinger observes in his memoirs that assured destruction 'implied the most inhumane strategy for conducting a war ... the mass extermination of civilians', Henry Kissinger, *White House Years*, (Boston: Little, Brown and Company, 1979) p. 216.
21. Richard K. Betts, *Nuclear Blackmail and Nuclear Balance*, (Washington DC: The Brookings Institute, 1987) pp. 185–91.
22. Philip Bobbitt, *Democracy and Deterrence: The History and Future of Nuclear Strategy*, (London: Macmillan, 1988) p. 79.
23. Evidence of William Van Cleave, University of Southern California. Hearings, Senate Foreign Relations Committee, *Military Implications of the Treaty on the Limitations of Anti Ballistic Missile Systems and the Interim Agreement on Limitations of Strategic Offensive Arms*, 92nd Congress, 2nd Session, (Washington DC: US Government Printing Office, June 1972) p. 587.
24. Bobbitt, p. 83.
25. Gregory Treverton,'Nuclear Weapons In Europe' *Adelphi Paper No. 168*, (London: International Institute for Strategic Studies, 1981) p. 3. See Bobbitt, p. 82.
26. As Davis explains, 'a variety of different concerns combined to produce the new doctrine. The new Administration was uneasy about relying on Assured Destruction, given the build-up of Soviet strategic forces, and also wondered whether the large number of warheads entering the American inventory might have more utility than earlier Administrations had predicted. Systems analysts in the Defense Department worried about the rigidity of existing nuclear plans. Some military and civilian officials undoubtedly saw the new doctrine as a way to justify new weapons they wanted for other reasons. Finally, officials in the State Department hoped that the new doctrine would allay European anxieties about the credibility of the American strategic deterrent.' Lynn E. Davis, 'Limited Nuclear Options: Deterrence and the New American Doctrine'. *Adelphi Paper* No. 121, (London: International Institute for Strategic Studies, Winter 1975/6) p. 4.
27. R.M. Nixon, *A Report to the Congress: US Foreign Policy for the 1970s, A New Strategy for Peace*, 18 February 1970, in Bobbitt, et al. *US Nuclear*, p. 387.
28. Bobbitt, p. 77.

248   *The Politics of Threat*

29. Nixon, *US Foreign Policy for the 1970s*, pp. 54–5. See also Desmond Ball, 'Targeting for Strategic Deterrence', *Adelphi Paper* No. 185, (London: International Institute for Strategic Studies. Summer 1983) pp. 17–20.
30. Kaplan, *Wizards*, p. 366.
31. Kissinger, *White House Years*, pp. 216–17.
32. NSSM-3, revised version, 8 May 1969; cited by Kaplan, *Wizards*, p. 366.
33. Ibid.
34. Kaplan, ibid., p. 366.
35. Nixon's NSC had actually conducted a number of staff analyses on questions of strategic vulnerability in the first year of the new administration's term, and as William Hyland – an NSC staffer at the time-observes, 'the vulnerability of American ICBMs was thoroughly examined in 1969 including the countermeasures that would later evolve ... Of special concern was the impact of a new vulnerability on the behaviour of both sides during a crisis. If one side could in fact launch an effective attack against the other side's missile silos, would the temptation prove irresistible?' As Hyland notes 'all of this was a heretical challenge to the prevailing doctrine of deterrence'. William G. Hyland, *Mortal Rivals: Superpower Relations From Nixon To Reagan*, (New York: Random House, 1987) p. 42.
36. See Freedman, *Evolution*, pp. 376–7; Davis, p. 4. and Kaplan, *Wizards*, pp. 367–70.
37. See Desmond Ball and Jeffrey Richelson, (eds), *Strategic Nuclear Targeting*, (Ithaca: Cornell University Press, 1986), p. 18. and Kaplan, *Wizards*, p. 369. In addition, for a full discussion of the politics of this process see Terry Terriff, *The Innovation of US Strategic Nuclear Policy in the Nixon Administration 1969–1974*, unpublished PhD, Kings College, London University, 1991 Chapter 6.
38. Terriff also suggests that several unauthorised alterations were made to the memorandum while at the NSC in an attempt to tone down some of its recommendations. Ibid. pp. 395–6. Kaplan makes a similar point but makes less of it, stating 'Aaron sat on it, fidgeted with a few words here or there, raised doubts, tried to study it into oblivion.' Op. cit., p. 372.
39. At RAND Schlesinger's research included work on the intellectual origins of the concepts now being discussed by the administration. Janne E. Nolan, *Guardians of the Arsenal*, (New York: Basic Books, 1989) p. 118.
40. *Flexible Strategic Options and Deterrence*, Excerpts from the Press Conference of US Secretary of Defense, James R. Schlesinger, 10 January, 1974, at the National Press Club, Washington, D.C., *Survival*, March/April, 1974 p. 86. Interestingly, his remarks were made as a reply to a reporter's question rather than as part of the speech. See Terriff, op. cit., for the politics of the promulgation, pp. 399–410.
41. James R. Schlesinger, *Annual Defence Department Report 1975*, 4 March 1974. reprinted in Bobbitt et al., p. 378.
42. Ibid.
43. Schlesinger, testimony, US Senate, Committee on Foreign Relations, *Nuclear Weapons and Foreign Policy in Europe*, hearings, 93rd Congress, 2nd Session., 4 April 1974 p. 196.
44. Kaplan, *Wizards*, p. 374. see also Terriff, *Innovation*, pp. 415–20.
45. *DoD Report, FY 1975*, p. 379.

46. Ibid., p. 383.
47. Ibid., p. 379.
48. Ibid., p. 381.
49. Much time in the Hearings was spent discussing various ways of calculating the collateral damage resulting from a counterforce attack on US ICBM fields and SAC bomber bases. Hearings, *Briefing on Counterforce Attacks*, p. 24.
50. Secretary of Defense James Schlesinger, *Annual Defense Report FY 1976*, 5 February 1975, pp. I–13, I–14. emphasis added.
51. *DoD Report, FY 1975*, p. 385.
52. Ibid., p. 384.
53. *Defense Department Report of FY 1976*, p. I–16.
54. Freedman, *Evolution*, p. 391.
55. Ibid., p. 369.
56. Terriff, *Innovations*, pp. 420–1.
57. Herken, p. 268.
58. *Aviation Week And Space Technology*, 22 June 1970, p. 22. Cited by David Gold, Christopher Paine and Gail Shields, *Misguided EXpenditure: An Analysis of the Proposed MX Missile System*, (New York: Council On Economic Priorities, 1981) p. 41. Previously it took between 16 and 24 hours to change a target tape on an individual missile, which involved entering the silo. Under this new system all 550 Minuteman IIIs could be centrally controlled and reprogrammed post-attack from SAC headquarters by an electronic system that was secure, hardened against EMP, blast and shock. See *Briefing On Counterforce Attacks*, pp. 21–2. See also Davis, p. 19 and Edgar Ulsamer, 'MX: The Missile System for the Year 2000', *Air Force Magazine*, March 1973, and Hearings, Senate Armed Services Committee, *Military Authorization Of Defense Appropriations for FY 71* 20 February 1970, Part 2, p. 1082. and pp. 1116–7. The system permitted 'retargeting of the force in response to known missile losses, failures or other situations. It permits rapid revisions and updating of the SIOP targeting', p. 1184.
59. Gold et al. p. 41.
60. *Space/Aeronautics*, June 1968. cited by Gold et al. p. 41.
61. James W. Canan, *The Superwarriors* (New York: 1975) p. 175; *Space/Aeronautics*, January 1970, p. 69. Both cited by Gold et al. p. 43.
62. Gold et al. p. 40 and Lauren H. Holland and Robert A. Hoover, *The MX Decision: A New Direction in US Weapons Procurement Policy*, (Boulder: Westview, 1985) p. 125.
63. Holland and Hoover, pp. 125–7; John Edwards, *Super Weapon: The Making of the MX*, (London: Norton, 1982) pp. 100–2; and Gold, et al. p. 40.
64. Paul N. Stockton, 'Arms Development and Arms Control: The Strange Case of the MX Missile', in Allan P. Sindler (eds) *American Politics and Public Policy* (Washington, DC: Congressional Quarterly Press, 1982) p. 227. Cited by Holland and Hoover, p. 125.
65. Gold, et al., p. 41.
66. Maj. Gen. Richard D. Cross was Director of Operational Requirements and Development Plans in USAF's Office of the Deputy Chief of Staff for Research and Development. Edwards, pp. 100–2.

67. Accordingly in June 1973 an office for the programme was established at Norton Air Force Base, California. Holland and Hoover, p. 124.

68. Edgar Ulsamer, 'M-X: The Missile System For the Year 2000', *Air Force Magazine*, March 1973; Lt. Gen. Alton D. Slay, 'MX: A New Dimension in Strategic Deterrence', Ibid., September 1976; Brig. Gen. John Hopfer, 'M-X and the Land Based ICBM', *Astronautics and Aeronautics*, Feb. 1975. Cited by Freedman, *US*, p. 180.

69. Holland and Hoover, p. 127. The idea of using Utah as a mobile ICBM basing area was suggested by Senator Symmington in 1970 in Hearings. Underestimating the opposition, Symmington stated, 'When you consider that 75 percent of Utah and 65 percent of California are owned by the Federal Government, you have a lot of wasteland where you could put a movable MINUTEMAN and end a lot of these arguments about such things as ABMs and SS-9s.' Hearings, Senate Armed Services Committee, *Military Authorization of Defense Appropriations for FY 71,* 20 February 1970, Part 2, p. 932.

70. The trench idea was finally rejected when technical investigations indicated that the blast effect of a Soviet warhead on any part of the trench 'would send shock waves through the tunnel, collapsing the roof, buckling the track and wrecking the missile'. Strobe Talbott, *Endgame: The Inside Story of SALT II*, (London: Harper and Bow, 1979) p. 167.

71. Edwards, p. 110.

72. Edwards, p. 111.

73. Ibid.

74. Ibid.

CHAPTER 4

1. Cited by Strobe Talbott, *The Master of the Game: Paul Nitze and the Nuclear Peace*, (New York: Knopf, 1988) p. 134. See also Alexei G. Arbatov, *Lethal Frontiers: A Soviet View of Nuclear Strategy, Weapons and Negotiations*, (New York: Praeger, 1988) p. 31.

2. Talbott, ibid. As a consequence of the very different force structures possessed by the superpowers this requirement would have necessitated deep and asymmetrical reductions by the Soviet Union in its ICBM throw-weight.

3. Hyland criticised the Jackson Amendment arguing that it meant that 'one of two things would have to occur: the Soviets would have to permit the United States a substantial increase in categories of weapons, which we could not develop in any case for several years, or we would have to persuade the Soviets to reduce their weapons, presumably to earn our good will'. William G. Hyland, *Mortal Rivals: Superpower Relations from Nixon to Reagan*, (New York: Random House, 1987) p. 79–80.

4. See Strobe Talbott, *Endgame: The Inside Story of SALT II*, (London: Harper and Bow, 1979) p. 31–2, and *Master*, p. 137.

5. The utility of arms control began to be questioned as an 'American reaction to the adverse shift in the East–West military balance and to the expanding reach of Soviet power and influence in vulnerable areas of the Third World'.

Robert Osgood, in Richard Burt, (ed.), *Arms Control And Defense Postures in the 1980s*, (London: Croom Helm, 1982) p. ix.

6. Burt, p. 2.

7. Eugene V. Rostow, 'The Case Against SALT II', *Commentary*, (February 1979) p. 24.

8. Rostow, Senate Foreign Relations Committee, *The SALT II Treaty*, 96th Congress, 1st Session, (Washington DC: US Government Printing Office, 1979), Part 4, pp. 4–5. See also Kissinger's testimony, Part 3, p. 202 in which he extols the necessity of linking SALT to the geostrategic balance.

9. Nitze initially tried to return to the Pentagon as Assistant Secretary for International Security Affairs at Schlesinger's behest but was blocked by Senators Goldwater and Tower of the Senate Armed Services Committee who, ironically, considered Nitze too liberal. See Talbott, *Master*, pp. 137–9 and Paul H. Nitze, *From Hiroshima to Glastnost: At the Centre of Decision - A Memoir*, (London: Weidenfeld and Nicolson, 1989) pp. 338–40.

10. Wolfe, *The SALT Experience*, (Cambridge, Mass: Ballinger, 1979) p. 14.

11. Nitze's speech at Los Alamos was reported in *Aviation Week and Space Technology*, 3 February 1975. Cited by Talbott, *Master*, p. 142.

12. Nitze detailed elsewhere his role and subsequent objection to the results of the SALT process. See Paul H. Nitze, 'The Vladivostok Accord and SALT II,' *The Review of Politics*, (University of Notre Dame), (April, 1975), pp. 147–60, and 'The Strategic Balance Between Hope And Skepticism', *Foreign Policy*, (Winter 1974–5), pp. 136–56.

13. Paul H. Nitze, 'Assuring Strategic Stability in the Era of Detente', *Foreign Affairs*, Vol. 54. No. 2, (January 1976) p. 207.

14. Ibid., p. 220.

15. Ibid., pp. 211–22. Nitze conceded that the 'The Soviets may well overestimate the effectiveness of their civil defence programme, but what is plain is that they have made, for 20 years or more, an approach to the problem of nuclear war that does assume ... that nuclear war could happen, and that the Soviet Union could survive.' p. 212.

16. Ibid., p. 223.

17. Ibid., p. 227.

18. Ibid., p. 223.

19. Ibid., p. 225. For alternative views on the significance of throw-weight as a strategic indicator see; Matthew Bunn, 'Does Throw-Weight Really Matter?' *Arms Control Today*, (November 1986) p. 6; Kaplan, *Dubious*, p. 29; Matthew Bunn, 'What Is Throw-Weight?' November 1986 p. 8; Strobe Talbott, *Deadly Gambits*, (London: Picador, 1987), pp. 214–15; Jan Lodal, 'Assuring Strategic', p. 466; Richard Ned Lebow, 'Malign Analysts or Evil Empire?: Western Images of Soviet Nuclear Strategy', *International Journal*, XLIV, (Winter 1988–9), p. 18; and Thomas A. Brown, 'Number Mysticism, rationality and the strategic balance', *Orbis* 21 (Fall 1977).

20. Nitze, ibid., p. 226.

21. Both articles were submitted into the Congressional Record along with Nitze's testimony in September 1976. See *US–USSR Relations and Strategic Balance*, Hearings before the Subcommittee on International Political and Military Affairs of the Committee on International Relations, House of Representatives, 94th Congress, 2nd Session, (September 1976).

22. Paul H. Nitze, 'Deterring Our Deterrent', *Foreign Policy*, No. 25, (Winter, 1976–7), p. 199.
23. Ibid., p. 201.
24. Ibid., p. 203.
25. Ibid., pp. 207–8. For alternative views on the effectiveness of civil defence see; John M. Weinstein, 'Soviet Civil Defence: The Mine Shaft Gap Revisited', *Arms Control Today*, Vol. 12, No. 7. (July/August 1982) p. 1; Fred Kaplan, 'Soviet Civil Defence: Some Myths in the Western Debate', *Survival*, Volume XX, No. 3. (May/June 1978) and Arthur Broyles, Eugene Wigner and Sidney Drell 'Civil Defence: The New Debate', *Survival*, Vol. XVIII, No. 5. (September/October 1978).
26. Ibid., p. 206.
27. Ibid., p. 208. Emphasis added.
28. Ibid., pp. 209–10.
29. Fred M. Kaplan, *The Wizards of Armageddon*, (New York: Simon and Schuster, 1983) p. 379.
30. John Newhouse, *The Nuclear Age: From Hiroshima to Star Wars*, (London: Michael Joseph, 1989) p. 295.
31. Interview with Paul Nitze, 8/9/89. Several years on Nitze remained certain of his 'calculations'.
32. Ibid., p. 297.
33. Nitze, 'Assuring Strategic Stability', p. 225.
34. Kennan, cited by Talbott, *Master*, p. 57.
35. Nitze, interviewed in Michael Charlton, *From Deterrence to Defence: The Inside Story of Strategic Policy*, (Cambridge: Harvard University Press, 1987) p. 52. Original emphasis. Other commentators have expressed similar views on Nitze. Alan Tonelson in 'Nitze's World', *Foreign Policy*, No. 35. (Summer 1979) for instance describes 'a preoccupation with data and hard statistical evidence and a corresponding tendency to down play less tangible political considerations'. p. 77. See also Steven L. Reardon, *The Evolution of American Strategic Doctrine: Paul H. Nitze and the Soviet Challenge*, (Boulder: Westview, 1984) and Nitze's memoirs *From Hiroshima*.
36. Interview, Larry Smith, 12/9/89, Washington.
37. Talbott, *Master*, p. 143.
38. Albert Wohlstetter, 'Is There a Strategic Arms Race?' *Foreign Policy*, 15 (Summer 1974), 'Rivals but no "Race"', *Foreign Policy*, 16 (Fall 1974) and 'Optimal Ways to Confuse Ourselves', *Foreign Policy*, 20 (Fall 1975).
39. See Robert Scheer, *With Enough Shovels: Reagan Bush and Nuclear War*, (New York: Vantage, 1983) p. 57 and Freedman, *US Intelligence*, p. 197, and Les Aspin, 'How To Look at the Soviet–American Balance', *Foreign Policy*, No. 22 (Spring 1976).
40. Interview, Larry Smith, 12/9/89. See also Jerry W. Sanders, *Peddlers of Crisis: The Committee on the Present Danger and the Politics of Containment*, (Boston: South End Press, 1983) p. 198.
41. Keegan cited by Freedman, *US*, p. 196. and Scheer, p. 59.
42. Scheer, p. 59.
43. See John Prados, *The Soviet Estimate: U.S. Intelligence Analysis and Russian Military Strength*, (New York: Dial Press, 1982) p. 209 and Thomas Powers,

'Choosing a Strategy for World War III', *Atlantic Monthly*, Vol. 250, No. 5, (November 1982), p. 101.

44. Interview, General Daniel Graham, Virginia, 1/9/89. Graham went on, 'It proved the estimating process was determined to put out rosy pictures. The Team A-B thing was a useful exercise, it sobered up those people, the biggest bias was the desire for consistency with their own previous record.'

45. Murry Marder, 'Carter To Inherit Intense Dispute On Soviet Intentions', *Washington Post*, 2 January 1977.

46. Ibid.

47. The panel consisted of seven members who were fully outsiders – Pipes, Nitze, Foy Kohler from the University of Miami, William Van Cleave from the University of California, retired USAF Generals Daniel Graham and John Vogt, and Thomas Wolfe of the RAND Corporation. The five 'insider' members were USAF Generals Keegan and Jasper A. Welch, Seymour Weiss from the State Department; Paul Wolfowitz of ACDA and Robert Ellsworth from CIA. Gregg Herken, *Counsels of War*, (New York: Knopf, 1985) p. 277 and Sanders, p. 199.

48. Sanders, pp. 200–1.

49. David Binder, 'New CIA Estimate Finds Soviets Seeks Superiority In Arms', *New York Times*, 26 December 1976. Reprinted in Scheer, p. 153. See also Herken p. 277 and Sanders, p. 201.

50. See Prados, pp. 251–2 and Herken, p. 277.

51. Nitze, *Hiroshima*, p. 352.

52. Hyland, p. 85.

53. Scheer, p. 54.

54. Richard Ned Lebow, 'Malign Analysts or Evil Empire?: Western Images of Soviet Nuclear Strategy', *International Journal*, XLIV, (Winter 1988–9) p. 22.

55. Stephen Rosenfeld, *Washington Post*, (31 July 1981). Reprinted in Scheer, p. 157.

56. Cited by Prados, pp. 254–5.

57. Editorial, 'Handicapping the Arms Race,' *New York Times*, 19 January 1977. Reprinted in full in Scheer, p. 152.

58. Ibid.

59. After Reagan's victory Kissinger sent a $100 donation to the Committee on the Present Danger, a symbolic act to the new administration that he now agreed with their analysis (and wanted a job?). Scheer, p. 40. It interesting to contrast the reversal of Kissinger's views in the late 1970s. See for example his speech 'Foreign Policy and National Security' delivered in Texas, 22 March 1976 and reprinted in *International Security*, 1976, Vol. I, and compare it to his remarks in the summer of 1979 both in his Congressional testimony, *SALT II*, Part 3, and his Brussels' address, 'The Future of NATO', in Kenneth Myers, (eds) *NATO The Next Thirty Years*, (London: Croom Helm, 1980).

60. 'Rumsfeld Says Russia Could Become Dominant Power', *San Francisco Chronicle*, 19 January 1977. See also Prados, p. 254 and Sanders, p. 203.

61. Sanders, p. 203.

62. Marder, *Washington Post*, 2 January 1977.

PART TWO

1. Cited by Robert H. Johnson, 'Periods of Peril: The Window of Vulnerability
    and Other Myths', *Foreign Affairs*, Vol. 61, No. 1 (Spring 1983) p. 950.
2. Michael Charlton, *From Deterrence To Defence: The Inside Story of Strategic
    Policy*, (Cambridge: Harvard University Press, 1987) p. 78.
3. McGeorge Bundy, 'To Cap the Volcano', *Foreign Affairs*, Vol. 48, No. 1
    (October 1969) pp. 1–20.

CHAPTER 5

1. Dan Caldwell, *The Dynamics of Domestic Politics and Arms Control: The
    SALT II Ratification Debate*, (Columbia South Carolina: University of Carolina
    Press, 1991) p. 101.
2. Michael Charlton, *From Deterrence to Defense: The Inside Story of Strategic
    Policy*, (Cambridge: Harvard University Press, 1987) p. 52. That committee
    was the Coalition for a Democratic Majority (CDM) set up as part of the
    ideological split following McGovern's nomination for the party ticket in 1972.
    Thirteen of its eighteen members were to join the CPD. Jerry W. Sanders,
    *Peddlers of Crisis: The Committee on the Present Danger and the Politics
    of Containment*, (Boston: South End Press, 1983) p. 150.
3. Charlton, p. 52. Emphasis original.
4. Max Kampelman, in Charles Tyroler, (ed.), *Alerting America: The Papers
    of the Committee on the Present Danger*, (Washington: Pergamon-Brassey's,
    1984) pp. xvii–iii.
5. Caldwell, p. 102. See also Paul H. Nitze, *From Hiroshima to Glasnost: At
    the Centre of Decision - A Memoir*, (London: Weidenfeld and Nicolson,
    1989), pp. 347–9. Strobe Talbott, *The Master of the Game: Paul Nitze and
    the Nuclear Peace*, (New York: Knopf; 1988) Chapter 7, and Fred M. Kaplan,
    The Wizards of Armageddon, (New York: Simon and Schuster, 1983) p. 380.
6. This often told story of the meeting at Carter's Pond House graphically
    illustrates the gulf in views between Nitze and the future President. See
    Talbott, *Master,* pp. 147–51, Nitze, *Hiroshima,* pp. 348–50, and Gregg
    Herken, *Counsels of War*, (New York: Knopf; 1985) pp. 280–1.
7. Herken, pp. 280–1.
8. Talbott, *Master*, p. 149.
9. Ibid.
10. The rumour that Harold Brown's appointment as Secretary of Defense was
    a compromise from Carter's original choice of Warnke further angered the
    right. Sanders, p. 180.
11. See Nitze's testimony, *Warnke Nomination*, Hearings Before the Committee
    On Foreign Relations, United States Senate, 95th Congress, 1st Session, 8
    and 9 February 1977. See also Nitze's, *Hiroshima*, pp. 354–5.
12. See for example James Robert's testimony that Warnke was in favour of
    'unilateral disarmament' and was 'not qualified' to be ACDA Director since
    he lacked 'any grasp of or desire to understand the Soviets' motives and
    strategic doctrine'. *Warnke Nomination*, p. 191.

13. Mike Bowker and Phil Williams, *Superpower Detente: A Reappraisal*, (London, Royal Institute For International Affairs/Sage, 1988) p. 169. As Nitze rather ominously remarks 'There being no opportunity to be an active participant in formulating government policy, I devoted my time and energy to special projects.' Nitze, *Hiroshima*, p. 350.

14. Williams and Bowker, p. 172.

15. Kampelman, in Tyroler, p. xv.

16. Nitze, *Hiroshima*, p. 354.

17. Tyroler, pp. 3 and 5. Emphasis added.

18. See Johnson.

19. *Commentary*, published by the American Jewish Committee and edited by CPD member Norman Podhoretz was to become the 'house magazine of neo-conservatism' producing 'the most extensive repertoire of anti-detente articles to be found in any publication', Coral Bell, *The Reagan Paradox: US Foreign and Defence Policy In the 1980s*, (New Brunswick: Rutgers University Press; 1989) p. 11.

20. See also Colin S. Gray, 'Understanding Soviet Military Power', *Problems of Communism*, (March–April, 1981) and Joseph D. Douglas Jr. and Amoretta M. Hoeber *Soviet Strategy For Nuclear War*, (Stanford: Hoover Institution Press, 1979).

21. Sanders, p. 285.

22. Richard Pipes, 'Why The Soviet Union Thinks It Could Fight And Win A Nuclear War', *Commentary*, (July 1977), pp. 32 and 21. Original emphasis.

23. See Andrew Cockburn, *The Threat: Inside The Soviet Military Machine*, (New York: Vintage Books. 1984) pp. 338–9.

24. Statement of Secretary of Defense Harold Brown, *Department of Defense Annual Report, Fiscal Year 1981*, (Washington DC: US Government Printing Office, 1980) pp. 67, 83.

25. Garwin, US Congress, House Armed Services Committee, *Hearings: US Strategic National Security Programs* 96th Congress, 2nd Session, (Washington DC: US Government Printing Office, 1978) Cited by Herken, p. 287.

26. See Fred M. Kaplan, *Dubious Specter: A Sceptical Look at the Soviet Nuclear Threat*, (Washington DC: The Institute for Policy Studies, 1980) Chapter 2.

27. Confidential interview with Soviet specialist 'A', September 1989. See also Robert H. Johnson, who explains that 'well before Pipes wrote his article, the basis of Soviet doctrine had changed and this change was beginning to be reflected in Soviet military writing ... [however] later changes in Soviet doctrine were ignored'. Robert H. Johnson, Improbable Dangers, (New York: St Martin's; 1994) p. 106 and p. 102.

28. Confidential interview with Soviet specialist 'B', 13/9/89. See also Joseph D. Douglas Jr. and Amoretta M. Hoeber *Soviet Strategy for Nuclear War*, (Stanford: Hoover Institution Press; 1979).

29. See Richard Ned Lebow, 'Malign Analysts or Evil Empire?': Western Images of Soviet Nuclear Strategy', *International Journal*, XLIV, (Winter 1988–9).

30. *Pravda* 9 May 1975. Cited by Kaplan, *Dubious*, p. 23. See also David Holloway, *The Soviet Union and the Arms Race*, (London: Yale University Press; 1983) pp. 29–64.

31. Confidential interview with Soviet specialist 'A', September 1989.

32. T.K. Jones, Hearings, Joint Committee on Defense Production, *Defense Industrial Base: Industrial Preparedness and War Survival*, (17 November 1976) p. 185.
33. Pipes, pp. 29 and 34.
34. Ibid., p. 34.
35. Robert Scheer, *With Enough Shovels: Reagan, Bush and Nuclear War*, (New York: Vantage; 1983) p. 64.
36. Colin S. Gray, 'The Most Dangerous Decade: Historic Mission, Legitimacy, and the Dynamics of the Soviet Empire in the 1980s', *Orbis*, (Spring 1981) p. 14 and p. 25. For a similar view see Myron Rush, 'Guns Over Growth in Soviet Policy', *International Security*, (Winter 1982–3) pp. 169–70.
37. John M. Weinstein, 'Soviet Civil Defense: The Mine Shaft Gap Revisited', *Arms Control Today*, Vol. 12. No. 7. (July/August 1982) p. 8.
38. Gray, *'Most Dangerous'*, p. 27.

CHAPTER 6

1. As such the CPD was both exempt from taxation and able to receive donations which were in turn tax deductible for the donor.
2. Rostow, cited by Dan Caldwell, *The Dynamics of Domestic Politics and Arms Control: The SALT II Ratification Debate*, (Columbia South Carolina: University of Carolina Press, 1991) p. 103.
3. Charles Kupperman, 'The SALT II Debate', PhD Dissertation, University of Southern California, 1980. Cited by Caldwell, p. 103.
4. Older institutions such as the National Strategy Information Center and the Georgetown Center For Strategic and International Studies also grew in prominence during this period. Mike Bowker and Phil Williams, *Superpower Detente: A Reappraisal*, (London, Royal Institute For International Affairs/Sage, 1988) p. 181. See also Jerry W. Sanders, *Peddlers of Crisis: The Committee on the Present Danger and the Politics of Containment*, (Boston: South End Press, 1983) p. 228.
5. *The Congressional Quarterly*, 23 June 1979, p. 1217.
6. Sanders, p. 224.
7. Interview, David Tracktenburg, Committee on the Present Danger. Washington, 5/9/89.
8. Sanders, p. 224.
9. Caldwell, p. 105.
10. 'The SALT Syndrome: Charges and Facts: Analysis of an Anti-SALT "Documentary,"' *Congressional Record-Senate*, 30 July 1980, S 10366-71. Cited by Caldwell, p. 105.
11. Despite a purchase price of $275 and a rental fee of $25 per day *The SALT Syndrome* was made available by being bought by conservative organisations and then distributed free of charge. *The SALT Syndrome*, American Security Council Education Foundation, leaflet, Boston, Virginia. Not dated.
12. Ibid.
13. See Sanders, p. 208–9.
14. Sanders, p. 216.

15. 'Canal Treaty Moves On', *San Francisco Examiner and Chronicle*, 23 April 1978. p. A -19. Cited by Sanders, p. 217.

16. Strobe Talbott, *The Master of the Game: Paul Nitze and the Nuclear Peace*, (New York: Knopf, 1988) p. 151.

17. Cyrus Vance, *Hard Choices: Critical Years in America's Foreign Policy*, (New York: Simon and Schuster, 1983) p. 61.

18. Talbott, *Master*, p. 155 and Rowland Evans and Robert Novack, 'A Touchy Carter: Shades of Former Presidents?' *Washington Post*, 13 August 1977. See also the letter to Carter from Rostow and associated White House documentation, 10 August 1977. Carter Presidential Library, White House Central File, Box FO 40, File No. FO 6-1 7/1/77-12/19/77.

19. See Alton Frye and William D. Rogers, 'Linkage Begins at Home', *Foreign Policy*, No. 35, (June 1979), pp. 55–6.

20. Van Cleave, in (ed.) W. Scott Thompson and William Van Cleave, *Strategic Options for the Early Eighties: What Can Be Done?* (White Plains MD: Automated Graphic Systems) p. vii.

21. Frank R. Barnett, in Thompson and Van Cleave, ibid., p. xi.

22. See also Gregg Herken, *Counsels of War*, (New York: Knopf, 1985) p. 285.

23. Thompson and Van Cleave, pp. 119–20.

24. Nitze, in Thompson and Van Cleave, pp. 119–20.

25. Ibid., p. 180.

26. John Isaacs, Interview, Washington, 15/9/89. He added, 'This problem would have been avoided had Ford's Treaty been ratified.' Mike Mawby of Common Cause made a similar point, noting that, 'Carter eventually put together a massive effort to sell SALT but it was like a weak salmon upstream – going nowhere fast. The administration's public relations office wasn't good enough against the Committee on the Present Danger.' Interview, Washington, 19/9/89.

27. According to one participant, they were to confine their discussion to a narrow brief and not to talk about anything other than the technical details of SALT, nor were they to talk about the effects of nuclear war or even to mention verification by satellite. Confidential interview with former State Department employee, Washington, 13/9/89.

28. Interview with Bob DeGrasse, Washington, 18/9/89.

29. Confidential interview with former State Department employee, Washington, 13/9/89.

30. Caldwell, p. 110.

31. See Caldwell, p. 109. Sanders, pp. 254–6, and 'Anti-SALT Lobbyists Outspend Pros 15 to 1,' *Christian Science Monitor*, 23 March 1979 p. 1.

32. Van Cleave and Thompson, p. 181.

33. Talbott, *Master*, p. 157.

34. Sanders, p. 260.

35. Memorandum from Eugene V. Rostow, Chairman, Executive Committee, to members of the Committee on the Present Danger, 1 August 1979. Cited by Sanders, p. 260.

36. Robert Scheer, *With Enough Shovels: Reagan Bush and Nuclear War*, (New York: Vantage, 1983) p. 37. See also Vance, *Hard Choices*, p. 62.

37. Supporters of SALT II from the general public wrote to Carter complaining that it was 'unfortunate that Government documents do not offer specific,

credible, readily available and easily understood evidence to support SALT II' and that supporters were therefore 'forced to rely on materials prepared by its opponents for the most detailed and readily available information'. This letter complains that the CPD present 'the best easily usable information on SALT II'. Letter of Professor Waldo Chamberlain, Dartmouth College, New Hampshire, to President Carter, 1 June 1979. Carter Presidential Library, White House Central File, Box FO 43, File No. FO 6-1 7/1/79-10/24/79.

38. Author unknown. The document also discusses the merits of a direct mail campaign 'with the "progressive" groups (New Directions, Council For A Livable World, etc.)' but concludes that 'The members of these groups, however, have the most influence where we need it least.' 9 August 1979. Carter Presidential Library, White House Central File, Box FO 40, File No. FO 6-1 7/1/77-12/19/77.

39. *Wall Street Journal*, 29 June 1979, p. 1.

40. John Isaacs agreed 'Its much easier to be against something. Some of us in the arms control community get more support when there is something clear to focus against like Reagan's anti-arms control stand or for them Carter "selling" the Panama canal.' Interview, op. cit. See also Caldwell, p. 106.

41. Interview with Bob DeGrasse, 18/9/89, Washington.

42. Brice Clemow, 'This "Travelling Show" Debates SALT II,' *West Hartfield News*, 17 July 1978. This article was sent as an example of favourable press coverage by Peter B. Johnson of the SALT working group to Tim Kraft at the White House. Carter Presidential Library, White House Central File, Box FO 40, File No. FO 6-1 7/1/78-9/30/78.

43. *What is the Soviet Union Up To?* reproduced in Charles Tyroler, (ed.), *Alerting America: The Papers of the Committee on the Present Danger*, (Washington: Pergamon-Brassey's, 1984). See also, Richard Perle, 'Echoes of the 1930s', *Strategic Review*, Vol. VII, No. 1 (Winter 1979).

44. Eugene V. Rostow, 'The Safety of the Republic', *Strategic Review*, Vol. IV, No. 2 (Spring 1976) p. 13.

45. Interview with Robert H. Johnson, September 1989, Washington.

46. Bowker and Williams, p. 174.

47. See the series of articles on the 'Decade of Neglect Controversy,' *International Security*, Fall 1985 (Vol. 10, No. 2). Booth and Williams argue that, 'for the intellectually lazy, both inside and outside the administration, simple fictitious interpretations are easier to grasp and more persuasive than complex arguments.' Ken Booth and Phil Williams, 'Fact and Fiction in US Foreign Policy: Reagan's Myths About Detente', *World Policy Journal*, (Summer 1985) p. 507.

48. President Reagan, 'America's Foreign Policy Challenges For The 1980s', Address before the Center For Strategic and International Studies, Washington DC, 6 April 1984. in *Realism, Strength, Negotiation: Key Foreign Policy Statements of the Reagan Administration*, (Washington: United States Department of State, Bureau of Public Affairs, 1984) p. 11.

49. Gaddis Smith, *Morality, Reason and Power*, (New York: Hill and Wang, 1986) p. 48. Cited by Bowker and Williams, p. 180.

50. The Gallup Poll, 30 January–2 February 1976, *Current Opinion*, Vol. 4, No. 4 April 1976. Sanders also cites other opinion poll evidence to substantiate

the point that the public mood was becoming increasingly hawkish by 1976. Ibid. p. 193.

51. Eugene V. Rostow, *Statement on Foreign and Defense Policy*, delivered before the Platform Committee of the Democratic Party National Convention, 19 May 1976. Cited by Sanders, p. 195.

52. Thomas Powers, 'Choosing A Strategy For World War III', The *Atlantic Monthly*, Vol. 250, No. 5 (November 1982) p. 84.

53. Inaugural address of President Jimmy Carter, 20 January 1977, *Presidential Documents: Jimmy Carter*, 1977, Vol. 13, No. 4: 89.

54. Vance added 'Regrettably, this correct and courageous decision became a millstone around the administration's neck and hurt us in the ratification debate.' p. 58. Perry later explained, 'My problem was that the emergence of Stealth meant we could cancel the B-1 bomber, even though I could not explain in public or to the Congress that the Stealth revolution meant that the B-1 was obsolete before it was built. I could tell a handful of security cleared senators, but Ronald Reagan hammered us for cancelling the B-1 all through the 1980 election campaign.' Martin Walker, 'US team took stealth technology from Russians', *Guardian*, 12/7/94.

55. Bowker and Williams, p. 177.

56. Fred Halliday, *The Making of the Second Cold War*, (London: Verso, 1983) p. 219.

57. William G. Hyland, *Mortal Rivals: Superpower Relations from Nixon to Reagan*, (New York: Random House, 1987) p. 208.

58. Michael Charlton, *From Deterrence to Defense: The Inside Story of Strategic Policy*, (Cambridge: Harvard University Press, 1987) p. 71. Carter wanted a 'departure from what Presidents Nixon and Ford, and others, had done. They had been very limited agreements. In fact the *words* they used were "limited agreements", with "threshold bans" and so forth. I wanted to have a comprehensive test ban – to eliminate completely the testing of all nuclear explosives ... to eliminate, totally, any use of space for the deployment of *defensive* or *offensive* weapons.' p. 72. Emphasis original.

59. Caldwell, *Dynamics*, p. 32–3.

60. Powers, p. 103. and John Edwards, *Super Weapon: The Making of the MX*, (London: Norton, 1982) p. 129.

61. Ibid., p. 103.

62. Charlton, p. 72.

63. Caldwell, p. 40.

64. The Kremlin 'especially objected to the proposition that the Soviet Union should destroy half of its land-based heavy missiles while the US would only postpone some technological innovations.' Strobe Talbott, *Endgame: The Inside Story of SALT II*, (London: Harper and Bow, 1979) p. 72.

65. Sanders, p. 242.

66. Vance, p. 55.

67. See for example Labedz, Hearings, Senate Foreign Relations Committee, *The SALT II Treaty*, 96th Congress, 1st Session, (Washington DC: US Government Printing Office, 1979) Part 3.

68. Nitze, Hearings, *The SALT II Treaty*, Part 1, pp. 527–8 and Eugene V. Rostow, 'The Case Against SALT II', *Commentary*, (February 1979) p. 29. For similar

views see Jack F. Kemp, 'Congressional Expectations of SALT II', *Strategic Record*, Vol. VII, No. 1. (Winter, 1979) p. 19.

69. Kissinger, Hearings, *The SALT II Treaty*, Part 3, p. 156. See also pp. 198–9.

70. Caldwell, p. 50.

71. See Labedz p. 61 and Robert L. Pfaltzgraff, Jr. and Jacqueln K. Davis, *SALT II: Promise or Precipice?*, (Miami: Current Affairs Press/ Center For Advanced International Studies University Of Miami, 1976) p. 4.

72. Rostow, Hearings, *The SALT II Treaty*, Part 4, p. 6.

73. Outraged, Former JCS Chairman Admiral Thomas H. Moorer asked rhetorically, 'What possible basis can there be for permitting the Soviets to demand that the United States be denied the capability which they possess?' Hearings, *The SALT II Treaty*, Part 2, p. 247. Kissinger also criticised this lack of equal entitlements on throw-weight even though he set the precedent. Ibid., Part 3, p. 159.

74. James R. Schlesinger, Senate Foreign Relations Committee, *US–USSR Strategic Policies*, Hearing Before the Subcommittee on Arms Control, International Law and Organization, 93rd Congress, 2nd Session, 4 March 1975, pp. 33–4.

75. Rostow, Hearings, *The SALT II Treaty*, Part 4, p. 28.

76. Sorrels, 'Limiting Strategic Forces', in Richard Burt, (ed.), *Arms Control And Defense Postures in the 1980s*, (London: Croom Helm, 1982) p. 168.

77. Ibid., p. 183.

78. Kissinger, Hearings, *The SALT II Treaty*, p. 170. See also Senator Percy's questioning on this, p. 185. See also Kemp, p. 21; Nitze, ibid., p. 502; and Rostow, ibid., p. 29.

79. Kissinger, ibid., p. 168. Similarly Burt warned that, 'in many instances, arms control seems increasingly to impede efforts to cope with these challenges through other means.' Ibid., p. 5.

80. Rostow, Hearings, *The SALT II Treaty*, Part 4, pp. 5–6, and pp. 9–12.

81. Burt, p. 7.

82. For advocates of ABM defence see for example Burt, p. 16; William Schneider Jr., 'Survivable ICBMs', *Strategic Review*, Vol. VI, No. 4, (Fall 1978) p. 25; and Jack F. Kemp, 'US Strategic Force Modernisation: A New Role For Missile Defense?', *Strategic Review*, Vol. VIII, No. 3 (Summer 1980).

83. See Rostow, Hearings, *The SALT II Treaty*, Part 4, p. 5; Sorrels, p. 178; Nitze, ibid., p. 498; and Labedz, p. 61.

84. See Nitze's testimony, Hearings, *The SALT II Treaty*, Part 4, p. 403 and Sorrels, pp. 178–9.

85. Moorer, Hearings, *The SALT II Treaty*, Part 4, p. 46.

86. See Vance, p. 49.

87. Edwards, p. 122.

88. R. Jeffrey Smith, 'An Upheaval in US Strategic Thought', *Science*, 6/4/82, p. 9F.

89. As Edwards notes, Perry questioned 'whether Soviet guidance accuracy on its current generation of missiles was sufficient to threaten Minuteman. He concluded that, at that time, it was not. The best estimate of the intelligence community at the beginning of the Carter administration was that it would not be until the Soviet rocket forces deployed their next generation of missiles, in the late eighties, that they would have sufficient accuracy to reliably

destroy Minuteman in its hardened silos. That seemed a reasonable estimate to him, putting the threat ten years in the future.' p. 137.

90. Ibid.
91. Ibid. See also Edwards, p. 140; Sanders, pp. 245–7; Powers, pp. 85–7; Alexei G. Arbatov, *Lethal Frontiers: A Soviet View of Nuclear Strategy/ Weapons and Negotiations*, (New York: Praeger, 1988) pp. 67–9; and Herken, pp. 295–7.
92. Desmond Ball, 'The Development of the SIOP 1960-1983', Desmond Ball and Jeffrey Richelson, (ed.), *Strategic Nuclear Targeting*, (Ithica: Cornell University Press, 1986) pp. 75–6.
93. Edwards, p. 143.
94. Edwards, p. 133 and p. 142.
95. See Talbott, *Endgame*, pp. 100–2.
96. Powers, p. 103.
97. Jim Klurfield, 'The MX Debate', *Newsday*, 3 February 1980 p. 3R.
98. Powers, p. 103.
99. Ibid.
100. According to Jonathon Green the 'window of vulnerability' was a 'term coined by General Edward Rowney, the Joint Chiefs of Staff representative at the SALT II talks in 1980 ... whose coinage was seized upon by right-wing critics of SALT II'. Jonathon Green, *The A–Z of Nuclear Jargon*, (London: Routledge, 1986) p. 190. Interestingly this language was absent from the SALT II hearings; thus Kissinger talks about 'the period of grave danger to our national security and to the global equilibrium'. See *The SALT II Treaty*, Part 3, pp. 152–4.
101. Thornton argues that ICBM vulnerability was the issue around which the foreign policy tensions of the Carter administration's security policy turned. While an interesting interpretation there is insufficient evidence to support what are exaggerated claims for the centrality of this subject. See Richard C. Thornton, *The Carter Years: Towards A New Global Order*, (New York: Washington Institute Press, 1991) p. 8.
102. It was not actually a technical breakthrough since the accuracy improvements were a result of technology transfer. 'In 1972, the United States Government permitted the export of 164 Centalign-B ball bearing grinding machines ... to the Soviet Union. In 1976, DIA Deputy Director Edwin Speaker reported to Congress that the grinders could "be used in the guidance equipment of Soviet missiles" ... It seems highly probable that the ball-bearing grinders played a critical role in enabling the Soviet Union to improve their hard target kill capability sooner than expected.' Thornton, p. 39.
103. Interview with Senior USAF officer, 15/9/89. Virginia.
104. William Perry, Hearings before Subcommittee on Research and Development of the Senate Armed Services Committee, *Department of Defense Authorization for Appropriations for Fiscal Year 1979*, 95th Congress, 2nd Session, Part 8, February 1978, see pp. 5691–733.
105. Edwards, p. 145.
106. See Edwards, pp. 146–52 and Lauren H. Holland and Robert A. Hoover, *The MX Decision: A New Direction in US Weapons Procurement Policy*, (Boulder: Westview, 1985) pp. 140–6.
107. Harold Brown, *Annual Report, Fiscal Year 1979*, pp. 63–4. Emphasis added. See also pp. 62–6 which are devoted to this question and Scoville, p. 56.

108. Carter also recognised this trait in himself. John Sharnik, *Inside the Cold War: An Oral History*, (New York: Arbour House, 1987) p. 285.
109. Powers, p. 95.
110. Powers, p. 95. Other exercises simulated Soviet attacks on command, control, communications and intelligence (C3I) nodes. In one war game based on a North Korean invasion of South Korea, Carter was reportedly unimpressed with the options available to him, desiring the ability to use an ICBM against a North Korean army division. Interview, Richard Betts, Washington, 13/9/89.
111. Powers, p. 95.
112. *Zbigniew Brzezinski, Power and Principle: Memoirs of the National Security Advisor 1977–81*, (London: Weidenfeld and Nicolson, 1983), p. 456.
113. Herken, p. 297.
114. Brzezinski, p. 457.
115. Ball and Richelson, p. 76; see also Edwards, p. 171; and Leon Sloss and Marc Dean Millet, 'US Nuclear Strategy In Evolution', *Strategic Review*, Vol. 12, No.1, (Winter 1984) p. 24.
116. Brzezinski, pp. 456–7.
117. Ibid., p. 457.
118. Bill Odom, in Charlton, p. 87. Other PDs included Presidential Directives 57 and 58 which set in motion provisions for national recovery after a nuclear war. See also Raymond L. Garthoff, *Detente and Confrontation*, (Washington DC: Brookings Institute, 1985) pp. 787–9.
119. Sloss and Millet, p. 24.
120. Powers, p. 96.
121. Ibid.
122. John D. Steinbruner and Thomas M. Garwin, 'Strategic Vulnerability: The Balance Between Prudence and Paranoia', *International Security*, Vol. No. 1, Issue. No. 1 (Summer 1976) p. 170.
123. Powers, p. 106.
124. Edwards, p. 174.
125. Edwards, p. 131.
126. Harold Brown, *Annual Report, Fiscal Year 1979*, pp. 63–4. Emphasis added. See also Edwards pp. 62–6 and Scoville, p. 56.
127. Harold Brown, *Annual Report, FY 1980*, p. 118.
128. Harold Brown, *Department of Defense Annual Report, Fiscal Year 1981*, 1980, Washington DC; US Government Printing Office, p. 69.
129. Newport Address, in Philip Bobbitt, Lawrence Freedman, and Geoffry Treverton, (ed.), *US Nuclear Strategy: A Reader*, (London: Macmillan, 1989) p. 407.
130. Newport Address, in Bobbit, et al. p. 408. Emphasis original.
131. Charlton, p. 77. Emphasis added.
132. Interview with Senior Pentagon Official 'A', Washington, 5/9/89.
133. Interview, Spurgeon Keeney, Washington DC 30/8/89.
134. Herken, p. 294.
135. See Vance, p. 357; Holland and Hoover, pp. 143–5; and Edwards, pp. 162–78.
136. See also Herbert Scoville, *MX: Prescription For Disaster*, (Cambridge MA: MIT Press, 1981) p. 104.
137. Holland and Hoover, p. 146. See also Talbott, *Endgame*, pp. 178–81.

138. David Gold, Christopher Paine and Gail Shields, *Misguided EXpenditure: An Analysis of the Proposed MX Missile System*, (New York: Council On Economic Priorities, 1981) p. 63. Perry is also reported making these claims elsewhere in support of the case for MX in 1980.

139. Edwards, ibid., p. 206. According to Congressional Staffer Larry Smith, 'In 1977 Senator Garn was white hot on the window of vulnerability, he really believed in it and wanted MX. But as the Air Force began to choose Utah and Nevada in 1978/79 Garn's position began to change as did Wallop and Domenichi and by extension Hatch.' Interview, Washington 12/9/89.

140. Herken, p. 302.

141. William H. Baugh, *The Politics of Nuclear Balance: Ambiguity and Continuity in Strategic Policies*, (New York: Longman, 1984) p. 70.

142. Newport Address, p. 411.

143. Interview with Senior Pentagon Official 'B', 14/9/89, Washington DC.

CHAPTER 7

1. Paul Warnke remains convinced that if Carter had been re-elected in 1980 he would have abandoned the MX/MPS scheme. Interview, Washington, 6/9/89. This view needs to be considered alongside Warnke's own opposition to the MX/MPS system which he considered 'an unworkable and expensive solution to a virtually non-existent threat'. See Alton Frye, 'Congress: Defence and the Foreign Policy Process', in Hunter, Berman, and Kennedy, (eds) *Making Government Work*, (Boulder: Westview Press, 1986) p. 166.

2. Lauren H. Holland and Robert A. Hoover, *The MX Decision: A New Direction in US Weapons Procurement Policy*, (Boulder: Westview, 1985) p. 171.

3. 'Quick fixes to US Strategic Forces' by William Van Cleave, in W. Scott Thompson, (eds), *National Security in the 1980s: From Weakness to Strength*, (San Francisco: Institute for Contemporary Studies, 1980) p. 96.

4. 'Reagan Trusted MX Decision to an "Inexpert" Weinberger', Lou Cannon, *Washington Post*, 16 September 1982, p. 3. See also Frye, in Hunter et al., p. 165.

5. Caspar Weinberger, *Fighting For Peace: Seven Critical Years at the Pentagon*, (London: Michael Joseph, 1990) p. 210. Under Secretary of Defense Ikle argued similarly that the MPS was planned 'against a malevolent Soviet Union, one planning a surprise attack, but at the same time depending upon a very benign Soviet Union, one that is going to abide by limitations even after the expiration of an agreement'. *Strategic Force Modernisation Programs*, Hearings, Committee on Armed Services, US Senate, 97th Congress, 1st Session, (Washington, DC: US Government Printing Office, October 1981) p. 65.

6. John Edwards, *Super Weapon: The Making of the MX*, (London: Norton, 1982) p. 213.

7. See Herbert Scoville, *MX: Prescription For Disaster*, (Cambridge MA: MIT Press, 1981) chapter 16.

8. Laxalt, a close friend of Reagan, was his national campaign manager for the 1980 presidential race while Garn had co-chaired the Congressional Task Force

which advised the Republican candidate during the election campaign. Holland and Hoover, p. 173.

9. Interview with senior USAF officer involved with MX, 15/9/89, Virginia.

10. Instead, Weinberger appointed Frank Carlucci as his deputy, losing him the support of the Republican ideological right and the votes of Senators Helms and East in his nomination hearings.

11. Lou Cannon, *President Reagan: The Role of a Lifetime*, (New York: Simon and Schuster, 1991) pp. 161–2.

12. Significantly, Van Cleave's contributions to two edited books by this group stressed the need for 'quick fixes' to be implemented on a crash basis to ensure the survivability of the Minuteman and B-52 forces from Soviet pre-emptive attack in the first half of the 1980s. 'Their purpose' he argued 'was to enable a safer pursuit of long-range solutions by helping us cross the dangerous period between now and their culmination'. p. 93. 'Quick Fixes to US Strategic Nuclear Forces' in W.S. Thompson. See also Van Cleave's chapter 'The Requirement for and Purpose of Quick Fixes to American Strategic Nuclear Forces', in Thompson and Van Cleave.

13. Interview, Colin Gray, May 1994.

14. In addition to this he called for the inland basing of the strategic bomber force; the accelerated production of the MX; a crash programme on civil defence and continental air defence; the production of a new small mobile ICBM; the retrofitting of more LaFayette submarines with Trident C4 missiles; an improved and expanded C^3 capability; the deployment of the B1 bomber and all forms of cruise missiles in order to tackle all 'areas with major vulnerabilities and deficiencies requiring immediate attention', p. 98. Van Cleave in W. S. Thompson.

15. Ibid., p. 95.

16. See Weinberger, pp. 54–5 for the full set of caustic remarks.

17. Interview, Fred Ikle, 30/8/89, Washington.

18. According to White 'Ikle concentrates on policy while Weinberger and Carlucci have concentrated on administration', Theodore White, 'Weinberger on the Ramparts', *The New York Times Magazine*, 6 February 1983, p. 20.

19. See Edwards, p. 221.

20. Edwards, pp. 226, 231–6.

21. 'Modernisation of the U.S. Strategic Deterrent,' *Hearings*, Committee on Armed Services, US Senate, 97th Congress, First Session, October 1981 (Washington, DC: US Government Printing Office, 1982) p. 21; also Edwards p. 219.

22. See Edwards, p. 219 and Weinberger p. 211.

23. Cannon, *President Reagan*, p. 165. The new administration was also briefed by the SALT delegation and showed an equally low level of understanding and interest. Interview with Ralph Earle, 6/9/89, Washington.

24. Holland and Hoover, p. 173.

25. Interview with General Kelly Burke, former USAF Deputy Chief of Staff for Research and Development, 20/9/89. Virginia.

26. Ibid.

27. Among those on the Townes Committee were General Brent Scowcroft, John Foster, Rube Butler, Simon Ramo, General Bernard Scriever, Michael

May, David Packard, General Glenn Kent and James Woolsey. Interview with Glenn Kent, 25/8/89, Washington.

28. Ibid.

29. R. James Woolsey, 'Politics of Vulnerability 1980–83', *Foreign Affairs*, Vol. 62, No. 4, (Fall 1984) p. 808.

30. Woolsey, p. 808. Even for supporters MX/MPS was 'not a pretty solution' and 'you can't come to grips with the MX/MPS problem unless you understand that you are not dealing with a beauty contest, you are not picking Miss America, its just the girl that's got the least warts is it and that's that.' Interview with Kelly Burke, 20/9/89, Virginia.

31. Holland and Hoover p. 172 and also *Desert News*, March 19, 1981.

32. Holland and Hoover, p. 172.

33. Interview with Kelly Burke, 'Well Townes was to me I think hired specifically to get a rationale for killing it [MPS]. That was his job.' Interview with Glen Kent, 'Weinberger convened the panel to endorse the Reagan position that MPS was bad. He wanted that endorsed ... Townes towed the Weinberger line. He signed a dollar contract with Weinberger.' Interview with RAND Corporation Analyst, 'It was a put up job ... Townes was used to kill MPS.' Washington, 6/9/89.

34. Cannon interview with Townes, in *President Reagan*, p. 389. On the legal obstacles which the construction of the MPS faced see Holland and Hoover, Chapters 5 and 8. Jonathan Medalia cites 35 different laws which could have been used to obstruct and delay the MPS programme, in 'Domestic Considerations Affecting the Deployment of A Multiple Protective Structure Basing Scheme for the MX Missile', (Washington, DC, Congressional Record Office, 1980) p. 47.

35. Edwards, p. 229.

36. Cannon, *President Reagan,* p. 390.

37. Edwards, p. 228.

38. 'To Townes, the vulnerability of command and control was a more important problem than the vulnerability of land missiles.' Edwards, p. 235.

39. Edwards, p. 230.

40. Cannon, *President Reagan*, p. 383.

41. Perry estimated that without SALT II limiting Soviet numbers, 400 missiles and 13 500 shelters would be needed to ensure survivability of the MX. Hearings, Senate Foreign Relations Committee, *The SALT II Treaty*, 96th Congress, 1st Session, (Washington DC: US Government Printing Office, 1979) Part 4, p. 477.

42. Woolsey cites support for a small ICBM from 'a wide range of the strategic and political spectrum, among them Herbert York, Paul Nitze, Senator John Glenn, Albert Wohlstetter, William Van Cleave, Jan Londal and Henry Kissinger', p. 809.

43. Interview with Townes and Scowcroft Commission member, 11/9/89, Washington.

44. Ibid.

45. 'Fundamental Defense Questions Likely to Arise in Missile Inquiry'. Richard Halloran, *New York Times*, 31/12/82, p. 3.

46. Committee On Armed Services, US Strategic Doctrine. Hearings, *Strategic Force Modernisation*, Hearings, 97th Congress, 1st session, James Wade, 28 October 1981, p. 88.

47. Interview with Kent.

48. Interview with Burke.

49. Interview with Townes and Scowcroft Commission member.

50. The secrecy of the Committee report became an issue in the hearings, with Senator Cohen complaining, 'I don't know what that report says but it seems to me, Mr Chairman, that we should not tolerate a situation that a military decision is based upon a report the summary of which we are getting, the conclusions of which are suggested here but we don't have an opportunity to review.' Weinberger replied 'It was a report made directly to the President and ... I don't feel I have authority to release it.' Senate Armed Services Committee, Hearings, *Modernisation of the US Strategic Deterrent*, 97th Congress, first session, 5 October–5 November 1981, p. 33 and p. 9. Ikle also refused even to summarise the report for Senator Quayle. See *Strategic Force Modernisation Programmes* p. 65. General Allen explained that 'The Air Force's access to the final report, as it was written, was very restricted ... to preserve the privacy of the President's decision process.' Ibid., p. 137.

51. Cannon, *President Reagan*, p. 390.

CHAPTER 8

1. Confidential interview with senior USAF officer.

2. Cannon, *Washington Post*, 20/4/83, p. 3.

3. 'Mormon Church Joins Opposition to MX Program', Bill Prochnau, *Washington Post*, 6 May 1981.

4. John Edwards, *Super Weapon: The Making of the MX*, (London: Norton, 1982) p. 238.

5. See Lauren H. Holland and Robert A. Hoover, *The MX Decision: A New Direction in US Weapons Procurement Policy*, (Boulder: Westview, 1985) p. 195.

6. Cannon, *Washington Post*, p. 3. MPS also had the support within the Administration of Budget Director David A. Stockman and CIA Director William J. Casey.

7. Edwards, p. 240. Continued support for the MPS within the Air Force was not limited to Chief of Staff General Lew Allen. Indeed, JCS Chairman General David Jones, Deputy Air Force Chief of Staff for R and D General Kelly Burke, SAC Commander General Richard Ellis, the Air Force Space and Missile Systems Organisation, and the Air Force Military Science Council all supported the deployment of MX in the MPS scheme. Alexei G. Arbatov, *Lethal Frontiers: A Soviet View of Nuclear Strategy/Weapons and Negotiations*, (New York: Praeger, 1988) p. 163.

8. See Holland and Hoover, p. 181, Edwards, p. 240, Alton Frye, 'Congress: Defence and the Foreign Policy Process', in Hunter, Berman, and Kennedy, (eds) *Making Government Work*, (Boulder: Westview Press, 1986) p. 167, and Cannon, *Washington Post*, p. 3.

9. John G. Tower, *Consequences: A Personal and Political Memoir*, (London: Little, Brown and Company; 1991) p. 243.

10. Cannon, *Washington Post*, p. 3. Tower conceded, 'I knew that persuasion would be difficult, not only because of the president's bias, but also because Meese had scant comprehension of the arcane theories and theology of nuclear deterrence. Nor did Meese, being new to Washington, have any experience with Congress.' Ibid., p. 242.

11. Confidential interview with senior USAF officer F. See also Edwards, chapter 9.

12. Edwards, p. 242.

13. Frye, in Hunter et al., pp. 167–8.

14. Edwards, p. 243.

15. Ibid., p. 244.

16. Cannon, *Washington Post*, p. 3.

17. See Christopher Simpson, *National Security Directives of the Reagan and Bush Administration: The Declassified History of US Political History 1981–1991.* (Boulder: Westview Press, 1995) pp. 46–8 for the declassified text of NSDD 12.

18. *The Nuclear Age* Central television transcripts, episode 10. Liddell Hart Centre and Military Archive.

19. Casper Weinberger, *Fighting For Peace: Seven Critical Years at the Pentagon*, (London: Michael Joseph, 1990) p. 210. Indeed, the administration admitted at the time that, 'While it is not the determining factor, it should be noted that the MPS basing has strong environmental opponents who would use every available tactic, and there are many, to delay MX deployment', The *New York Times*, 3 October 1981.

20. 'Announcement by President Reagan: Strategic Arms Program, 2 October 1981.' *Weekly Compilation of Presidential Documents*, 5 October 1981. pp. 1074–76. *Documents on Disarmament in 1981*, United States Arms Control and Disarmament Agency, pp. 461–4.

21. Ibid., p. 463. See also Christopher Paine, 'Running in circles with the MX', *Bulletin of the Atomic Scientists* December 1981, p. 5.

22. Robert Scheer, *With Enough Shovels: Reagan Bush and Nuclear War*, (New York: Vantage, 1983) p. 68.

23. Ibid.

24. See *Documents on Disarmament*.

25. Arbatov, p. 162.

26. Ibid.

27. Edwards, p. 244, see also Paine, p. 8.

28. Ikle, Hearings, Senate Armed Services Committee, *Strategic Force Modernisation Programs*, 97th Congress, 1st Session, (Washington, DC: US Government Printing Office, October 1981) p. 43.

29. *Documents on Disarmament*, p. 461. See also Lou Cannon, *President Reagan: The Role of a Lifetime*, (New York: Touchstone/Simon and Schuster, 1991) p. 393.

30. Frye, in Hunter et al., p. 168.

31. Ibid., p. 24.

32. Frye, in Hunter et al., p. 168 and Paine, 'Running in Circles', pp. 8–9.

33. Hearings, *Modernisation of the US Strategic Deterrent*, Senate Armed Services Committee, 97th Congress, 1st Session, 1981 (Washington DC: US

Government Printing Office, 1982), p. 28. These statements were supplied for the record as 'Previous Testimony Regarding Basing of the MX Missile'. Gen. Allen's statement was made on 29 January 1981, while Gen. Ellis's was made on 18 February 1981. Gen. Ellis's comments about briefing the transition team refer to the period before Weinberger's arrival at the Pentagon.

34. Paine, 'Running in Circles', pp. 8–9.
35. The enormous cost of this effort was a major concern in Congress, with one estimate suggesting that this use of resources would at best amount to spending $4.5 million per day for the protection of 3.5 per cent of America's strategic arsenal. Paine, 'Running', p. 9.
36. Hearings, *Strategic Force Modernisation*, p. 371 and p. 389.
37. *Nuclear Age*, TV Transcripts, Programme No. 10.
38. Senator Jackson's questioning elaborated on this dilemma with obvious irritation, stating, 'All you are talking about is hardening fixed silos?... But with their capabilities, with the SS-17's, SS-18's and SS-19's they can saturate the proposed MX sites without much trouble and, as I understand the administration's own position – and I share it – Soviet accuracy is virtually comparable to ours.' Hearings, *Modernisation of the US Strategic Deterrent*, pp. 11–12.
39. Ibid., pp. 12–13.
40. Hearings, *Strategic Force Modernisation*, p. 257.
41. Confidential interview with Townes and Scowcroft Commission member.
42. Ibid. This explains a great deal of confusion and animosity which exists among those involved with the Townes Panel who believe that Townes presented to Weinberger the ideas which he later claimed came from the panel. Some members of the committee are still under this misapprehension.
43. Holland and Hoover, p. 219.
44. See Frye, in Hunter et al., p. 169, Holland and Hoover p. 181 and p. 217, and Arbatov, p. 165.
45. Theodore White, 'Weinberger on the Ramparts', *New York Times Magazine*, 6 February 1983, p. 64.
46. R. James Woolsey, 'Politics of Vulnerability 1980–83', *Foreign Affairs*, Vol. 62, No. 4, (Fall 1984) p. 811.
47. Strobe Talbott, *Deadly Gambits*, (Picador: London, 1984) p. 302.
48. Frye, in Hunter et al., p. 170. Opposition from the ranchers in Utah and Nevada to the MPS deployment had been considerable even though they were tenants on US government land. Indeed, one Air Force officer suggested that the only way that this opposition could be got round was to give the farmers a stake in the deployment by renting the land back from them, 'Then when the liberals come out from the East coast instead of the farmer giving them coffee they'd shoot them.' Interview with Kent.
49. Interview with Kent.
50. Even in the Air Force SAC was known to be deeply unhappy with the deployment plan, and JCS chairman Vessey had to be persuaded by Weinberger to lend his support for the scheme.
51. White, p. 64.
52. Holland and Hoover, p. 223.
53. Ibid.
54. White, p. 64.

55. Frye, in Hunter et al., p. 171 and Christopher Paine, 'MX: too dense for Congress', *The Bulletin of the Atomic Scientists*, February 1983, p. 4.
56. Interview with Burke.
57. Interview with Congressional staffer 'A'.
58. Holland and Hoover, p. 222.
59. Harold Brown, *Thinking About National Security: Defense and Foreign Policy in a Dangerous World*, (Boulder: Westview, 1983) p. 68.
60. Ibid., pp. 68–9.
61. Leon V. Segal, 'Warming to the Nuclear Freeze', *Foreign Policy*, No. 4. (Fall 1982) p. 54. See also Edward Kennedy and Mark Hatfield, *Freeze!*, (New York; Bantam Books, 1982); Paul M. Cole and William J. Taylor, *The Nuclear Freeze Debate: Arms Control Issues for the 1980s*, (Boulder: Westview, 1983).
62. E.P. Thompson and Ben Thompson, *Star Wars: Self Destruct Incorporated*, (Manchester: Merlin Press, 1985) p. 14.
63. Within Congress, Freezing was popular in the House, aiming to 'end the arms race', while the Senate favoured a nuclear build down, aiming to manage the superpower competition, with Senators Nunn and Cohen strong advocates of this line. *L.A.Times*, 5/4/83.
64. Talbott, *Deadly*, p. 301.
65. Ibid.
66. McFarlane explains that 'Weinberger's contemptuous attitude toward the Congress made his dealings with that body fractious and troublesome at all times. For its part, the Congress had no confidence in Weinberger as a spokesman for defence issues; on the Hill, he was considered lacking in knowledge of the details of defence matters and incapable of explaining how the programmes he presented to the Congress for appropriation were connected to a strategy for keeping the peace.' Robert C. McFarlane, *Special Trust* (New York: Cadell and Davies; 1994) p. 223.
67. Holland and Hoover, p. 225.
68. As one White House source observed, 'You simply have to recognise the fairness issue – we can't cut benefits for poor people and increase military spending unless Cappy gives a little bit.' Theodore White, 'Weinberger on the Ramparts', *New York Times Magazine*, 6 February 1983, p. 64.
69. Michael Getler, *Washington Post*, 4/1/83.
70. Pincus, *Washington Post*, 9/2/83.
71. Indeed, Arbatov suggests that Weinberger tendered his resignation at this point but it was refused by Reagan. How reliable this source is, however, is open to question. Arbatov, p. 167.
72. White cites an unnamed Assistant Secretary of Defense observing, 'I think that there is no conceivable new plan for land-based missiles that can get any Congressional majority.' White, p. 76.

CHAPTER 9

1. R. James Woolsey, 'Politics of Vulnerability 1980–83', *Foreign Affairs*, Vol. 62, No. 4, (Fall 1984) p. 807.

2. Ibid.
3. Alton Frye, 'Congress: Defence and the Foreign Policy Process', in Hunter, Berman, and Kennedy, (eds) *Making Government Work*, (Boulder: Westview Press, 1986) p. 171.
4. Ibid.
5. See Hearings, Senate Foreign Relations Committee, *The Arms Control and Foreign Policy Implications of the Scowcroft Commission Report*, 11 May 1983, p. 34. Following the Scowcroft Commission Reagan convened the Walter Stoessel Commission on Chemical Weapons in June 1985 and the Kissinger panel on Central America.
6. Interview, Isaacs, ibid.
7. Mark Greenberg and Rachael Flick, 'The New Bipartisan Commissions', *Journal of Contemporary Studies*, Vol. VI, No. 4, Fall 1983, pp. 4–5. White wrote of the Scowcroft Commission as an abdication of responsibility, stating 'To govern is to choose: since Weinberger and Reagan could not force Congress to their choice, they have off loaded the burden to a commission whose eminence may persuade Congress to make a choice', Theodore White, 'Weinberger on the Ramparts', *New York Times Magazine*, 6 February 1983, p. 76.
8. Strobe Talbott, *Deadly Gambits*, (Picador: London, 1984) p. 302.
9. As early as 1979 Samuel Huntington wrote to National Security Advisor Brzezinski, recommending the establishment of a 'Presidential Commission on Defense Needs and Priorities' in order to develop a bipartisan consensus in this area for the period through 1985. Letter from Samuel P. Huntington, Director, Harvard University Centre For International Affairs, to Hon. Zbigniew Brzezinski, 9 August 1979. Document No. FO 61, 7/1/79 -10/34/79. White House Central File, Box FO 43. Jimmy Carter Presidential Library, Atlanta, Georgia.
10. Alexei G. Arbatov, *Lethal Frontiers: A Soviet View of Nuclear Strategy/ Weapons and Negotiations*, (New York: Praeger, 1988) p. 167 & Frye, in Hunter, p. 171.
11. See McFarlane, Ibid., p. 224.
12. 'President's Commission on Strategic Forces' (Scowcroft Commission), *Report* (Washington, DC: US Government Printing Office, April 1983), p. 1.
13. Interview, Herb Hetu, 12/9/89.
14. *Nuclear Age*, Television Transcript No. 10.
15. Interview Hetu. As one participant of both exercises conceded, cancelling the MX was considered by the Commission but was much less likely a possibility than it was during the Townes' deliberations when the political pressures to deploy the MX were much less acute. Interview with Townes and Scowcroft Commission member.
16. Elizabeth Drew, 'A Political Journal', *New Yorker*, 20/6/83, p. 47
17. *Peacekeeper (M-X) History and Current Status*, (undated). Written and given to the author by Gen. Burke.
18. Drew, p. 47.
19. Drew cites many 'members of the "community" – including a number of scientists, three former Secretaries of Defense, two former directors of the CIA, and former military officials' who were opposed to MX. p. 47.

20. *The Arms Control and Foreign Policy Implications of the Scowcroft Commission Report*, Hearings before the Senate Foreign Relations Committee, 98th Congress, 11 May 1983, p. 1.
21. Talbott, *Deadly*, p. 303.
22. One administration official complained 'I was dead against Scowcroft for the chairmanship. He was a SALT seller for Carter. I would much have preferred a hard core Reaganaut.' *Business Week,* 11/4/83.
23. Talbott, *Deadly*, p. 302.
24. For a complete list of the Commission's members and senior counsellors see Appendix A.
25. The inclusion on the Commission of Woolsey (Navy Secretary under Carter) and Vice Admiral Levering Smith (former Director of Special Projects, Navy and coordinator of the Polaris programme), was seen by some as indicating the need to base the MX at sea.
26. Talbott, *Deadly*, p. 303.
27. Francis and Clines, *New York Times,* 4/1/83
28. *Washington Post,* 1/1/84.
29. Getler, *Washington Post,* 4/1/84.
30. Lauren H. Holland and Robert A. Hoover, *The MX Decision: A New Direction in US Weapons Procurement Policy*, (Boulder: Westview, 1985) p. 230.
31. Cannon and Hoffman, 'Reagan set to propose defense cut', *Washington Post,* 5/4/83.
32. Cannon, *Washington Post,* 9/3/83. For the latter Friedersdorf was rewarded with the post of Counsel General of Bermuda. Interview 12/9/89 and also the private papers of Herbert E Hetu, Special Counsellor Public Affairs.
33. Woolsey, p. 816.
34. Talbott, *Deadly*, p. 304.
35. Drew, pp. 48–9. Interview, Beth Cohen DeGrasse, 18/9/89.
36. Drew, pp. 48–9.
37. Woolsey, p. 812.
38. Holland and Hoover, p. 231.
39. Drew, p. 49.
40. *Commission Report*, pp. 12–13.
41. Specifically it states 'The Commission believes that, because of changing technology, arms control negotiations, and our own domestic political process, this issue – the future of our ICBM force – has come to be miscast in recent years.' p. 12.
42. *Commission Report*, p. 4.
43. *Commission Report*, p. 7. See pp. 7–8.
44. Ibid., p. 8.
45. Stephen J. Cimbala, 'Strategic Vulnerability: A Conceptual Reassessment', *Armed Forces and Society*, Vol. 14, No. 2, (Winter 1988) p. 196.
46. Cimbala, p. 195.
47. *Commission Report*, p. 12.
48. Ibid., p. 6.
49. Woolsey, pp. 814–15. The other two options actively considered were, (1) the cancellation of the MX altogether and the development of a small, single warhead ICBM instead, and (2) the modification of the Dense Pack basing mode for the MX. Placing of MX in Minuteman silos was reported to be

favoured by four of the five chiefs of staff. Laird favoured water basing while Weinberger and Scowcroft were said to be more inclined towards continuous airborne patrol, the idea rejected by the Townes Committee and many other studies. Howe, *Washington Times*, 3/1/83.

50. *Commission Report*, p. 14.
51. Ibid.
52. Arbatov, p. 268.
53. *Commission Report*, p. 3.
54. Drew, p. 49.
55. The breakthrough in SICBM technology was the 'Armadillo' concept – a vehicle with a low silhouette, thick armour and the ability to 'anchor in' when under attack to reduce its profile still further and thus minimise blast damage. Gelb, *New York Times*, 8/2/83.
56. Among advocating Midgetman to the Commission were Van Cleave and Lodal. *Christian Science Monitor*, 20/4/83.
57. Kissinger, *Time* 21/3/83. See also *Christian Science Monitor*, 20/4/83.
58. *Commission Report*, p. 25.
59. These words used by Roger Molander about START could apply equally in their effect to the recommendations of the Scowcroft Commission, testimony before the Senate Foreign Relations Committee, 17 May 1982.
60. *Commission Report*, p. 22, emphasis added.
61. Cimbala, p. 196.
62. Arbatov, pp. 212–13.
63. On p. 23 it states rather obliquely that 'An agreement that permitted modernisation of forces and also provided an incentive to reduce while modernising, in ways that would enhance stability, would be highly desirable', while on p. 25 it states, 'Some current arms control proposals in Congress concentrate on warhead limitations in which reductions are forced in warhead numbers as a price of modernisation ... These general directions are also consistent with the approach suggested in this report.'
64. *The Arms Control and Foreign Policy Implications of the Scowcroft Commission Report*, Hearings before the Senate Foreign Relations Committee, 98th Congress, 11 May 1983, p. 8.
65. *Commission Report*, p. 16.
66. Woolsey, p. 815.
67. McGeorge Bundy criticised this reference to ABM arguing that this debate showed what the Soviets valued most, not their willingness to negotiate. 'The Russians' he advised, 'joined us in curbing ABM systems precisely to insure the deterrent effectiveness of their land based missiles. They are not going to be driven to sea by the MX.' Bundy, 'The MX: Not Buried Yet', *The Bulletin of the Atomic Scientists*, June/July 1983, p. 15.
68. Holland and Hoover, p. 233.
69. *Commission Report*, p. 16.
70. Ibid.
71. Ibid., p. 17.
72. *Implications of the Scowcroft Commission Report*, Hearings, p. 13.
73. The Report states that, for an improvement in the guidance system of the Minuteman III to be completed would take 'some two to three years longer than production of the MX' p. 18. Whether this estimate was for the equivalent

number of warheads or missiles to the planned MX deployment was not clear. According to one source there was a tendency on the part of the Air Force and the Administration to down-play the capability of the Minuteman III with its Mark 12A warhead and MPS 20 guidance system in order to strengthen the case for the MX. He explained that 'The guidance system and the warhead refinement gave the Minuteman III upgrade a very substantial capability against hardened targets.' Confidential interview with senior Congressional staffer 'B', 14/9/89, Washington.

74. According to one former Congressional staffer at least 50 MX missiles were needed for counter-leadership targets. Confidential interview with former Senate Armed Services Committee staffer, May 1991.

75. Robert C. Toth, 'US Shifts Nuclear Response Strategy: New Formula Designed to Eliminate Soviet Leadership Early in Conflict', *Los Angeles Times,* 23 July 1989. Reprint, p. 4. Toth also details US plans to increase its ability to destroy deep hardened bunkers by the acquisition of deep earth penetration warheads and 'Warheads with vastly higher yields and enhanced effects', p. 3. See also Des Ball and Toth, 'Revising the SIOP: Taking Warfighting to Dangerous Extremes', *International Security*, Vol. 14, No. 4 (Spring 1990).

76. Toth, p. 4.

77. Interview senior Congressional staffer 'B'.

78. Steven V. Roberts, 'Proposal to put MX in existing silos', *New York Times*, 26 April 1983.

79. Examinations of Soviet hardening in the 1970s led William Perry, then Undersecretary for Defense Research and Engineering, to conduct a study in 1978–9 which found that Soviet designs incorporated 3% steel as opposed to the US design's 1%, and were therefore 10 to 20 times as hard as American silos. At the time of this study USAF was not interested in hardening because of their involvement with MX/MPS. With the interest in Dense Pack, however, a new study was commissioned which found that silos could be improved but at four times the cost. Construction improvements could have made US silos up to 20 times harder effectively downgraded Soviet hard-target kill requiring expensive improvements to maintain their capability. *Los Angeles Times* 12/4/83.

80. *Commission Report*, p. 14.

81. He went on 'So you get to heaven by doing everything you don't want to do and which we've been talking against, and that's part of our conclusion ... If you are willing to hold your nose for the MX you get your small ICBM and survivability and stability.' Confidential interview with Congressional staffer 'C', 20/9/89.

82. *First-Strike Stability: A Methodology For Evaluating Strategic Forces*, General Glenn A. Kent and David E. Thaler, June 1989, p. 6. Unpublished paper given to this author from the private papers of General Kent.

83. Colin S. Gray, and Keith Payne, 'Victory is Possible', *Foreign Policy*, Vol. 39. (Summer 1980) p. 20.

84. Kent and Thaler, p. 61.

85. *Commission Report*, p. 3.

86. Ibid., p. 24.

87. Also similar to the INF debate was the American suggestion that the Soviet side should dispense with its existing missiles in response to the threatened deployment of their US equivalent.
88. *Commission Report*, p. 6.
89. Kent and Thaler, p. 62.
90. Woolsey, p. 813. The report states, 'For the last decade, each successive administration has made proposals for arms control of strategic offensive systems that have become embroiled in political controversy between the Executive branch and Congress and between political parties. None has produced a ratified treaty covering such systems or a politically sustainable strategic modernization program for the US ICBM force. Such a performance, as a nation, has produced neither agreement amongst ourselves, restraint by the Soviets, nor lasting mutual limitations on strategic offensive forces.' *Commission Report*, p. 25.

CHAPTER 10

1. Lauren H. Holland and Robert A. Hoover, *The MX Decision: A New Direction in US Weapons Procurement Policy*, (Boulder: Westview, 1985) p. 234.
2. *Washington Post*, 19/4/83.
3. Elizabeth Drew, 'A Political Journal', *New Yorker*, 20/6/83, p. 54.
4. Reacting to what he saw as the role of politics in the panel's decision, for example, Senator John Warner said 'What is the best system militarily for the nation?... Politics be damned ... I think we have a responsibility to go back and reexamine' the MPS scheme. *Washington Post*, 19/4/83.
5. Senator Alan Cranston, for instance, said that the decision to deploy MX was an 'act of folly' and that 'The President, with a slash of the pen, has ended the argument that there is a window of vulnerability' adding 'now we have a window of credibility'. Frances X. Clines, *New York Times*, 20/4/83. Senator James Exon stated, 'These's a considerable degree of contradiction in putting 100 MX missiles in Minuteman silos and then saying you have to build a new missile. You're really saying this missile is obsolete.' *Washington Post*, 12/4/83.
6. Clines, ibid.
7. Tom Wicker, *New York Times*, 15/4/83, p. 31.
8. *US News and World Report*, 25/4/83.
9. Hearings, Senate Foreign Relations Committee, *The Arms Control and Foreign policy Implications of the Scowcroft Commission Report*, 98th Congress, 1st Session, (Washington DC: US Government Printing Office, 11 May 1983) p. 11–12.
10. Jeff McMahan, *Reagan and the World: Imperial Policy and the New Cold War*, (London: Pluto Press, 1984) p. 36. See also McGeorge Bundy, 'The MX: Not Buried Yet', *The Bulletin of the Atomic Scientists*, (June/July 1983) p. 15.
11. Hearings, *Scowcroft Commission Implications*, p. 25.
12. Richard Halloran, 'Shift of strategy on missile attack hinted by Weinberger and Vessey', *New York Times*, 6/5/83. Similar comments were made elsewhere

by Lieutenant Colonel John Politi, Deputy Director of the Air Force MX programme, who stated that it was American strategy that the MX should be launched 'on attack'. See McMahan, p. 37 who cites Hendrick Smith, 'Colonel stirs questions on MX firing doctrine', *New York Times*, 8/4/83.

13. Interview with RAND Corporation Analyst. See also Bruce G. Blair, *The Logic of Accidental Nuclear War*, (Washington DC: Brookings Institution, 1993).

14. Robert C. Toth, 'Planners Split on How to Meet Nuclear Threat', *Los Angeles Times*, 24/7/89, p. 19 of reprint.

15. Robert Toth, 'US shifts nuclear response strategy', p. 19. Toth adds that, 'Many US weapons might never be launched, military leaders believe, because many command and control systems might not survive an initial attack. And decision making by political leaders could be paralysed.'

16. General Glenn A. Kent and David E. Thaler, *First-Strike Stability: A Methodology for Evaluating Strategic Forces*, (June 1989). Unpublished paper given to this author from the private papers of General Kent, p. 6. They go on to caution that, 'Whether or not such an optimum actually exists, the concept provides the proper intellectual framework in which to think about the trade-off between first-strike stability and extended deterrence.'

17. Kent suggested that between 50 and 100 MX was probably the ideal amount of crisis instability to add to the US arsenal. Interview ibid.

18. Gen. Burke, *National Journal*, 14/2/81, p. 260.

19. According to McGwire the Soviets had already adopted such a policy in the 1970s after technological difficulties prevented the deployment of their first generation mobile ICBMs. Michael McGwire, *Perestroika and Soviet National Security*, (Washington: Brookings, 1991) pp. 29–30. See also Blair, ibid.

20. Bundy, 'The MX', p. 14.

21. Blair, ibid., p. 178.

22. Hearings, *Scowcroft Commission*, p. 25.

23. *Commission Report*, p. 18.

24. John C. Baker and Robert P. Berman, *Soviet Strategic Forces*, Brookings Institution, 1982. Cited by Michael R. Gordon in 'The MX Again – This Time, the Issue May be Firepower v. Survivability', *National Journal*, 16/4/83, p. 802.

25. *Commission Report*, p. 18.

26. Michael Gordon, 'The MX Again: This Time, the Issue may be Firepower v. Survivability', *National Journal*, 16/4/83, citing a 1982 report for the Carnegie Endowment for International Peace, p. 802.

27. *Commission Report*, p. 18.

28. Halloran, ibid.

29. Interview Congressional staffer 'A'. This opinion was also shared by another Congressional staffer, on the House side. Interview with Congressional staffer 'C', Washington, 5/9/89. Beth Cohen-DeGrasse, an arms control lobbyist explained that a lot of things were said and promised as part of the process of selling the package on the Hill, and that the enthusiasm for the figure of 50 MXs was to resurface later in the life of the missile partly due to this supposed endorsement of this figure. Interview.

30. Interview with Herb Hetu, 12/9/89. See also Alton K. Marsh, 'New Report on MX Basing Finds Support in Congress', *Aviation Week and Space Technology*, 18/4/83. p. 28. where Commission member Levering Smith explains that 'several members, but not a majority, wanted 200 MX missiles

because 100 fails to give equivalence with the Soviet Union' and Sen. Henry Jackson comments that 'The number of 100 was a compromise reached before the commission report was released, and therefore has support of those who were consulted in Congress.'

31. Interview, General Scowcroft, 1/9/89 NSC, The White House.
32. Hearings, *Scowcroft Commission*, p. 12.
33. Ibid., p. 32.
34. The occasion was the 14 December 1982 news conference. Christopher Paine, 'MX: too dense for Congress', *The Bulletin of the Atomic Scientists*, (February 1983) p. 5. In a letter to the Federation of American Scientists on 10 December the Administration also clarified its position stating that 'We do not intend to trade MX for a new Soviet ICBM ... The MX is essential to restore a stable nuclear balance so the US can continue to deter Soviet aggression.'
35. Speaking in mid-May on ABC's 'Good Morning America', Weinberger stated that 'The question is not whether or not it's a bargaining chip. Nobody ever suggested that it was a bargaining chip. It's part of our necessary modernisation.' Drew, p. 51.
36. Leon Sigal, 'Tilting Toward War Fighting', *Arms Control Today*, (September 1983). Commission member Thomas Reed repeated this point, 'A bargaining chip is what we'll do if the Soviets don't come to the table' implying that the administration would deploy the MX and then threaten to build more. See Leslie Gelb, 'As a bargaining chip, MX may be no bargain for the Soviets', *New York Times*, 24/4/83.
37. Leslie Gelb, *New York Times*, 8/2/83.
38. Hearings, *Scowcroft Commission*, p. 27.
39. The Congressional Budget Office conducted one study which suggested the programme would cost about $106 billion dollars over 20 years, including $3 billion annual operating costs, and require 50 000 people to man and maintain. Other reports suggested that the Midgetman could cost at least twice as much as MX, and would need 47 000 people to tend a sizable missile force. 'Pentagon seeks funds for small missiles', *Washington Times*, 10/5/83.
40. Michael Getler, 'Small Missile Carries Problems of its Own', *Washington Post*, 14/4/83. See also Clarence A. Robinson, *Aviation Week and Space Technology*, 21/2/83. The Air Force Ballistic Missile Office conducted studies into the overall costs of the programme allowing Woolsey to counter negative reports by stating that 'operating costs could be considerably lower' than many of the estimates being circulated. *Report Hearings*, p. 27.
41. *Washington Post*, 14/4/83.
42. *The Nuclear Age*, TV Transcript No. 10. Liddell Hart Military Library and Archive. Weinberger continues this caustic line towards the Midgetman in his memoirs, asserting that 'The MIDGETMAN was a favourite missile of the MX opponents – primarily, I always felt, because it was easier for them to support a missile we did not, and could not, have for several years.' (Hence its derisory nickname, 'Congressman') Weinberger, p. 211.
43. Drew, p. 50.
44. *Commission Report*, p. 15.
45. *Christian Science Monitor*, 20/4/83, p. 6.

46. Perle, for example, said that it was wrong to believe that the Commission was 'calling for a fundamental change in the administration's arms-control policy – I can't find that anywhere' he also asserted that the Midgetman was not yet part of the nation's strategic policy. Drew, p. 58.

47. See Casper Weinberger, *Fighting For Peace: Seven Critical Years at the Pentagon*, (London: Michael Joseph, 1990), pp. 210–14 and *The Nuclear Age*, Central TV. Programme No. 10.

48. *New York Times*, 9/4/83.

49. Drew, p. 57.

50. Alton Frye, 'Congress: Defence and the Foreign Policy Process', in Hunter, Berman, and Kennedy, (eds) *Making Government Work*, (Boulder: Westview Press, 1986) p. 172.

51. Lou Cannon, *Washington Times*, 20/4/83.

52. This included seven breakfast meetings at Blair House where the viability of the final package was discussed with Congressional Representatives. Not all members and senior counsellors attended every meeting. On average only 9 members attended. Interview, Herbert Hetu, Washington, 12/9/89.

53. *Washington Times*, for example, carried an article which stated that the 'President's panel appears to be moving towards the most sensible MX plan advanced to date' defending MX in silos with ABMs and implementing General Graham's High Frontier. Tom Carhart, 'Amidst the Confusion on MX basing – High Frontier', 27/1/83. It is no coincidence that this article appeared the day before Lt Gen. Graham, Director of High Frontier presented his thirty-minute briefing to the Commission in the Pentagon. Personal papers of General Graham, given to author 9/12/89.

54. Most of this speech was devoted to calling for Congressional support for his defence budget in general and the MX in particular. He talked about US ICBMs becoming 'increasingly obsolete' and being 'increasingly threatened by the many huge, new Soviet ICBMs'. In a sense he was using the ICBM vulnerability argument as part of his efforts to generate support for MX. Reagan, 'Peace and National Security', Televised Address to the Nation, Washington DC, 23 March 1983. in *Realism, Strength, Negotiation: Key Foreign Policy Statements of the Reagan Administration*, (Washington: State Department, Bureau of Public Affairs, 1984) p. 38 and 41.

55. In order not to alienate supporters the Commission did not pass judgement on SDI other than to state that 'applications of current technology offer no real promise of being able to defend the United States against massive nuclear attack this century'. *Commission Report*, p. 9.

56. George C. Wilson and Margot Hornblower, 'Invulnerable MX seen as impractical', *Washington Post*, 8/4/83, p. 1.

57. Similar advice was given to McFarlane by Aspin, who complained, 'Couldn't the White House be a little less gracious about this? Couldn't it look as though you're being dragged kicking and screaming into a new START position? Otherwise, Congress isn't going to believe that you're really moving.' Strobe Talbott, *Deadly Gambits*, (Picador: London, 1984) p. 305. Brown was more convincing stating that the 'proposals deserve bipartisan support even though they are not ideal and do not provide an immediate solution to the problem of ICBM vulnerability', adding that his endorsement came 'with

an appreciation that more politically astute decisions could well have produced a better solution'. Drew, p. 55.

58. At the launch of the Report, Brown considerably overstated the case announcing that unless the deployment of the MX was passed 'It would be the first nuclear strategic defeat for any country since the second world war.' Drew, p. 55.

59. John M. Deutch, 'The MX Report: A Break with the Past', *Washington Post*, 12/4/83, p. 17.

60. 'Neither those who are most concerned about our relative decline in our strategic strength nor those most concerned about the lack of arms control want to continue the cycle we have been on since 1972 ... the price of the feuding between political parties, between the executive and Congress, between Presidential candidates has been high: no ratified treaties on offensive systems ... no agreed plan for providing a survivable American ICBM force over the long run.' R. James Woolsey, 'MX, The Deterrent', *New York Times*, 12/4/83, p. 23.

61. Robert Timberg, 'Reagan likens MX rejection to hostile act', *Baltimore Sun*, 10/5/83, p. 1. See also Mary McGrory, 'Salesman Reagan is Trying to Unload a Clunker on Congress', *Washington Post*, 12/5/83. p. 3.

62. See Ronald Reagan, 'The MX: A Key to Arms Reduction', *Washington Post*, 24/5/83 and 'Washington Roundup', *Aviation Week and Space Technology*, 11/4/83.

63. This achievement was crucial to Aspin's efforts to build a coalition. Had the Democratic leadership in the House decided to use the party machine to rally against this initiative as a symbol of Reagan's unrealistic arms control policy the chances of reversing the vote on MX and burying the vulnerability issue would have been severely damaged. See Holland and Hoover, p. 235 and Drew, pp. 49–50.

64. The Commission, initiated on 3 January was due to report on 9 February but was extended until 6 April. Not until 20 April however, did the President formally embrace the panel's recommendations and thereby set the Congressional clock running on the 45-day self-imposed limit for deciding whether to accept or reject the basing proposal.

65. Drew, p. 55.

66. Aspin, Gore and Dicks, along with six other members sent a letter from the House while Charles H. Perry (Chairman of the Senate Foreign Relations Committee), Sam Nunn and William S. Cohen sent a letter to the White House from the Senate. Alton K. Marsh, 'Congress Seeks MX Reassurance', *Aviation Week and Space Technology*, 2/5/83, p. 14.

67. See Holland and Hoover, p. 236, Drew, p. 60. and Alton K. Marsh, 'Congress Seeks MX Reassurance', *Aviation Week and Space Technology*, 2/5/83, pp. 14–15. Marsh cites White House background briefings to the press which demonstrate the conditional nature of the administration's endorsement of the small ICBM and revised arms control proposals.

68. *Christian Science Monitor*, 20/4/83, p. 6.

69. Democrat member Barney Frank's comment was that 'It's the kind of letter we send to people: "Thank you for your good suggestion. I find it very interesting, and I'll look into it."' Drew, p. 60.

70. See Talbott, *Deadly*, Chapter 16 and ibid.

71. Drew, p. 64.
72. He went on, 'We have said that if they change their minds we reserve the right to change ours. We see our responsibility as not ending with this resolution, or with the authorization bill.' Drew, p. 62.
73. Holland and Hoover, pp. 236–7 and Drew, p. 73. Rep. Les AuCoin, stressed 'There has been no strategic weapon that has passed this stage of funding that has ever been permanently cancelled. This, my friends, is the moment in which the genie leaves the bottle unless we decide to exercise our good judgement and keep it inside ... [Congress is] not strong enough to turn off the system when a massive missile like that develops an industrial and political constituency.' See also Hendrick Smith, 'US Panel May Offer MX Plan Using Silos of Minuteman Missiles', *New York Times*, 29/3/83.
74. *Congressional Record*, 1983, p. 3270.
75. Reagan even organised a dinner at the White House the night before the vote in a last attempt to convince wavering members. The event was not a conspicuous success. One Congressman commented afterwards, 'I almost wish I hadn't gone', while another stated that Reagan 'didn't betray any understanding of what the principles involved were'. Drew, p. 66.
76. R. James Woolsey, 'Politics of Vulnerability 1980–83', *Foreign Affairs*, Vol. 62, No. 4, (Fall 1984) p. 816. See also Holland and Hoover, p. 238.
77. AuCoin stated afterwards 'I'm amazed at those Democrats who have entered into this bargain with the administration ... The President gets an MX missile, and the country gets a statement of sincerity about arms control ... If that is a bargain, all I can say is, to my colleagues on this side of the aisle who have entered into it, I am pleased they are not negotiating with the Soviet Union.' More privately he exclaimed 'these clowns would give away the Mid West for a shoeshine and a smile'. Drew, p. 69, p. 73.
78. Majority Leader James C. Wright had given the Report his 'modest endorsement' saying that the plan was 'less than ideal but probably the best we can get', a decision for which he was severely criticised. Lou Cannon, *Washington Post*, 20/4/83.
79. See Frye, in Hunter et al. p. 173. Sen. Patrick Leahy's comment was that the United States was 'offering to swap a moo for a cow'.
80. *Congressional Record*, 1983, p. 5314 and pp. 5338–9.
81. Alexander Haig, Jr, *Caveat: Realism, Reagan and Foreign Policy*, (London: Weidenfeld and Nicolson, 1984) p. 223.
82. See Drew and Holland and Hoover.
83. Holland and Hoover, p. 242. and Frye, in Hunter et al. p. 174.
84. The first quotation is taken from the 'Statement by the President' issues from the White House Office of the Press Secretary, 9 April 1984 while the second comes from the *Final Report of the President's Commission on Strategic Forces*, 21 March 1984, p. 6.
85. *Final Report of the President's Commission on Strategic Forces*, 21 March 1984, p. 2.
86. See Frye, in Hunter, p. 175.
87. Ibid., p. 176.
88. Tom Wicker, *New York Times*, 15/4/83. Wicker makes the valuable point that 'the Scowcroft report makes more of a case for MX deployment, in the context of other recommendations, than anyone else has been able to do'. p. 31.

89. Mark Greenberg and Rachael Flick, 'The New Bipartisan Commissions', *Journal of Contemporary Studies*, Vol. VI, No. 4. (Fall 1983) p. 15.

90. Drew, p. 55.

91. He continued, 'But the device of the Presidential Commission ... has a subtle but debilitating effect on the effectiveness of the Cabinet members who must ensure successful implementation at home and abroad of the policies that emerge from the Commission.' Haig, p. 223.

92. Interview with Congressional staffer 'C'.

93. Interview with Joseph Fromm, 30/8/89, SAIS, Washington.

94. For example, William L. Dickinson, ranking minority member of the House Armed Services Committee, explained that he got 85% of what he wanted and therefore supported the package. *Aviation Week and Space Technology*, 18/4/83.

95. *Nuclear Age*, Television Transcript, programme 10.

96. Interview with Townes and Scowcroft Commission member, ibid.

97. Interview with Gen. Glenn Kent.

98. Interview with Congressional staffer 'C'.

99. Hearings, *Scowcroft Commission*, p. 4.

100. Robert Foelber, *The Reagan Administration: Failing to Meet the Threat*, Heritage Foundation 'Backgrounder' No. 196, 14 July 1982, p. 20.

101. Charles Tyroler, (ed.), *Alerting America: The Papers of the Committee on the Present Danger*, (Washington: Pergamon-Brassey's, 1984) p. 196.

102. Interview, Fred Ikle, 30/8/89. Washington DC.

103. *Washington Times* editorial, 12/4/89.

CONCLUSIONS

1. Robert Jervis, *The Illogic of American Nuclear Strategy*, (Ithaca: Cornell University Press, 1984) p. 54.

2. Ibid.

3. See Jervis, op. cit., p. 114–16.

4. P. 170. He goes on to explain that, 'In consequence the US system could not have expected to meet its damage expectancy requirements if it absorbed an attack before retaliation ... [and so] US military planners ... expected to protect the silo-based forces by launching them out from under an attack during the fifteen to thirty minutes interval between the lift off and arrival of Soviet missiles.' Bruce G. Blair, *The Logic of Accidental Nuclear War*, (Washington DC: Brookings Institution, 1993) p. 176.

5. Certainly, as Jonathan Medelia of the Congressional Research Service observed, 'It's much easier to envisage a missile silo being blown up rather than a bunch of wires and electronics. It doesn't play politically, you can't put C^3I on a graph. You can't say much about the connections between different bits, it's classified and so Congress and the public don't pay much attention.' Interview, Jonathan Medelia, 29/8/89, Washington.

6. Robert H. Johnson, *Improbable Dangers: US Conceptions of Threat in the Cold War and After*, (New York: St Martin's Press, 1994) p. 43.

Index

Index by Auriol Griffith-Jones